W9-AMN-494

Shojo Beat

Story & Art by
Aya Nakahara

love ★ com

contents 5

The Story So Far...

Risa and Ōtani are their class's lopsided comedy duo...except that now, Risa's fallen in love with Ōtani! With the support of all their friends, Risa screws up the courage to tell him how she feels...but Ōtani thinks she's joking! Finally, though, she manages to get the message across, only to freak out at his reaction.

Risa's solution is to avoid Ōtani at all costs! But somehow, the more she tries to do that, the more they find themselves alone, especially when they go to Hokkaido on their class trip. Things are getting really weird between them, and Risa decides that being a comedy duo is better than putting up with these uncomfortable silences. But just when she's about to tell Ōtani to forget she'd ever said anything, he tells her he can't suddenly think of her as girlfriend material... Does this mean it's all over for Risa?!

♥ To really get all the details, check out *Lovely ★ Complex* Vol. 1-4, available at bookstores everywhere!!

Shojo Beat

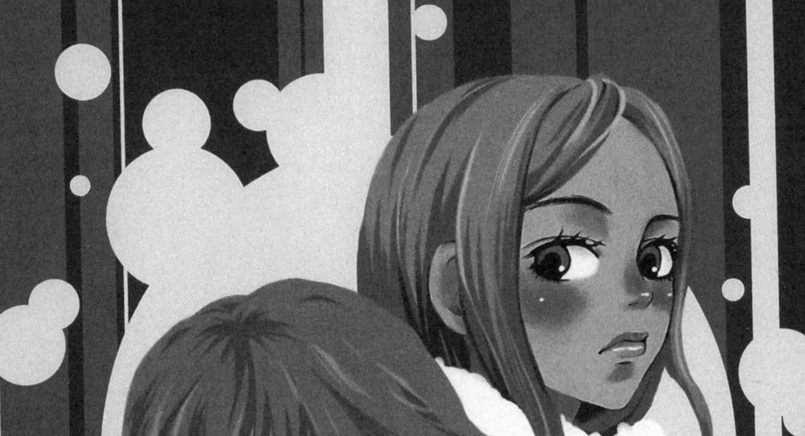

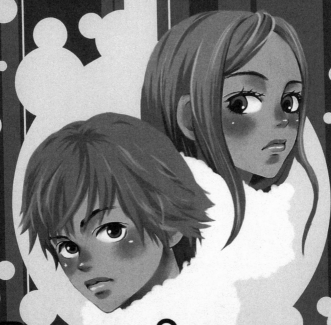

love★com

5

Story & Art by
Aya Nakahara

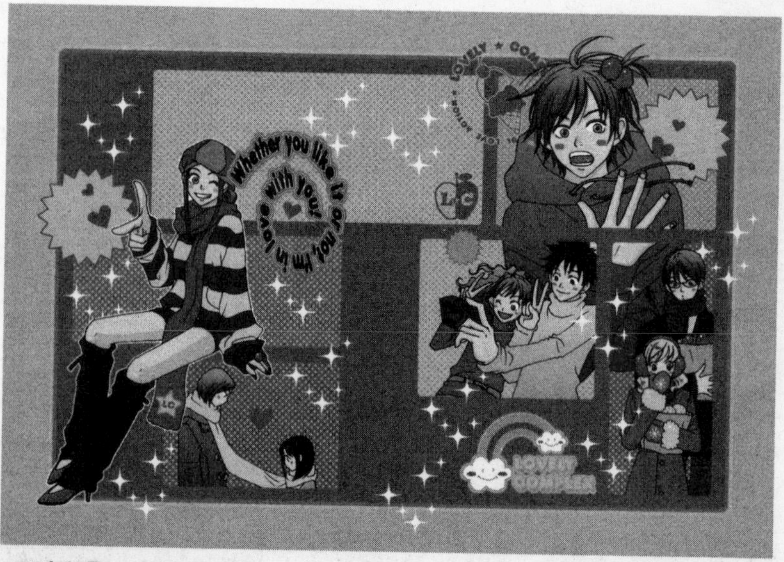
Whether you like it or not, I'm in love with you!

CHAPTER 17

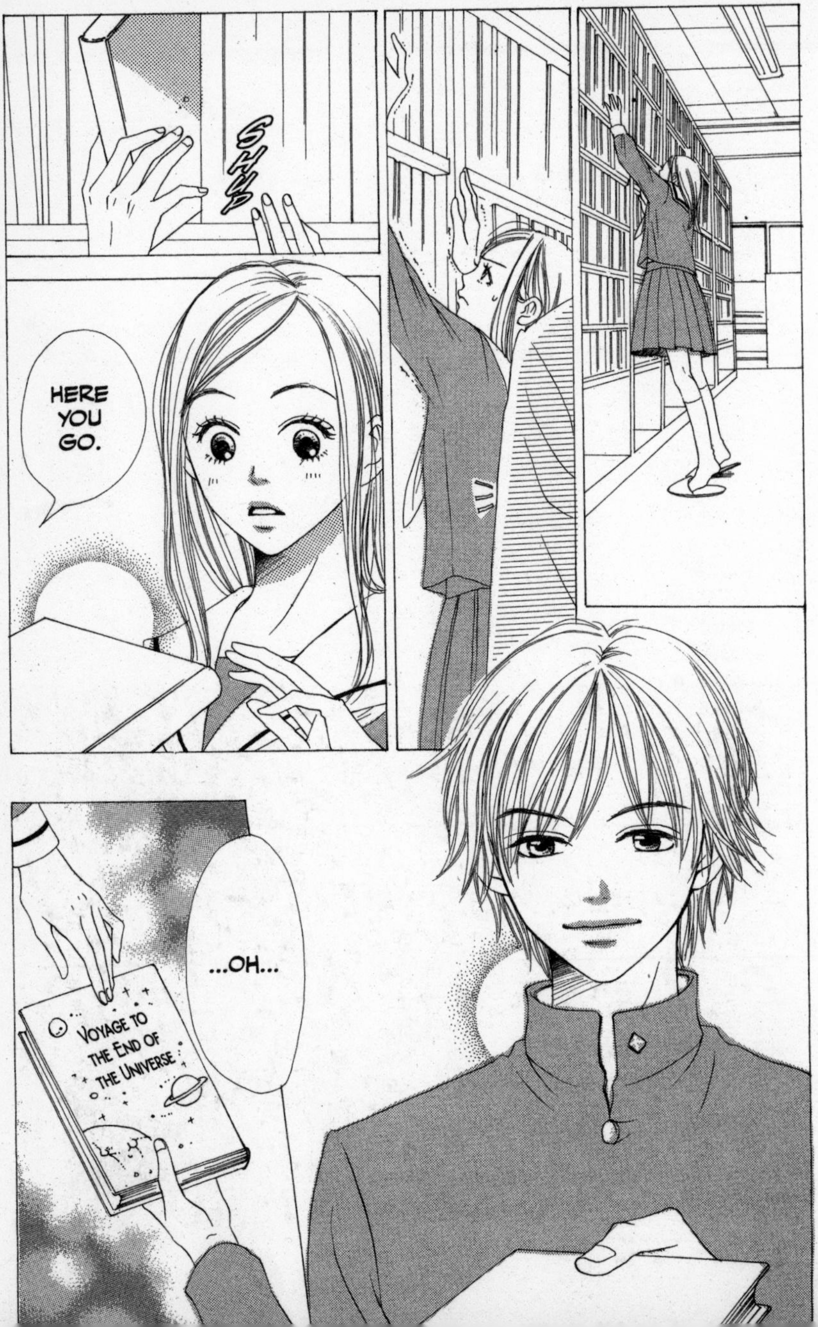
SHUP
HERE YOU GO.
...OH...
VOYAGE TO THE END OF THE UNIVERSE

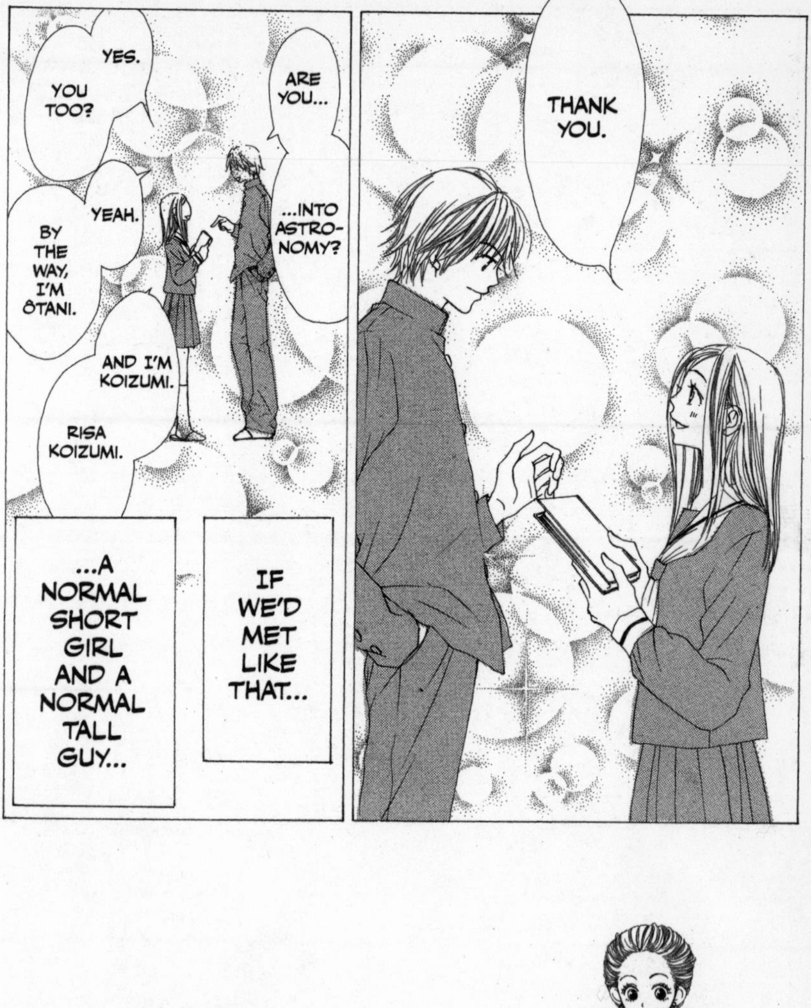
THANK YOU.
ARE YOU...
...INTO ASTRONOMY?
YES. YOU TOO?
YEAH. BY THE WAY, I'M ŌTANI.
AND I'M KOIZUMI. RISA KOIZUMI.
IF WE'D MET LIKE THAT...
...A NORMAL SHORT GIRL AND A NORMAL TALL GUY...

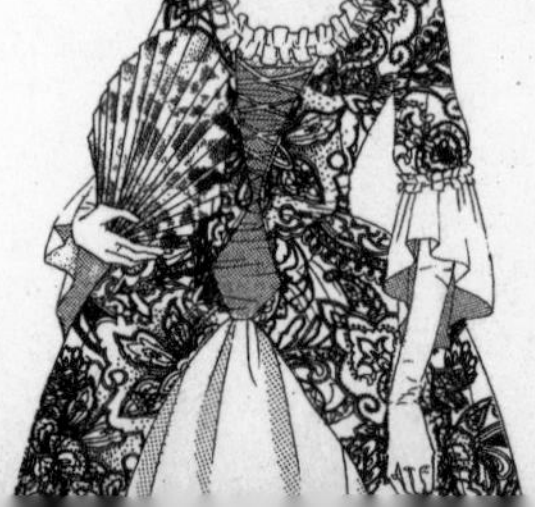

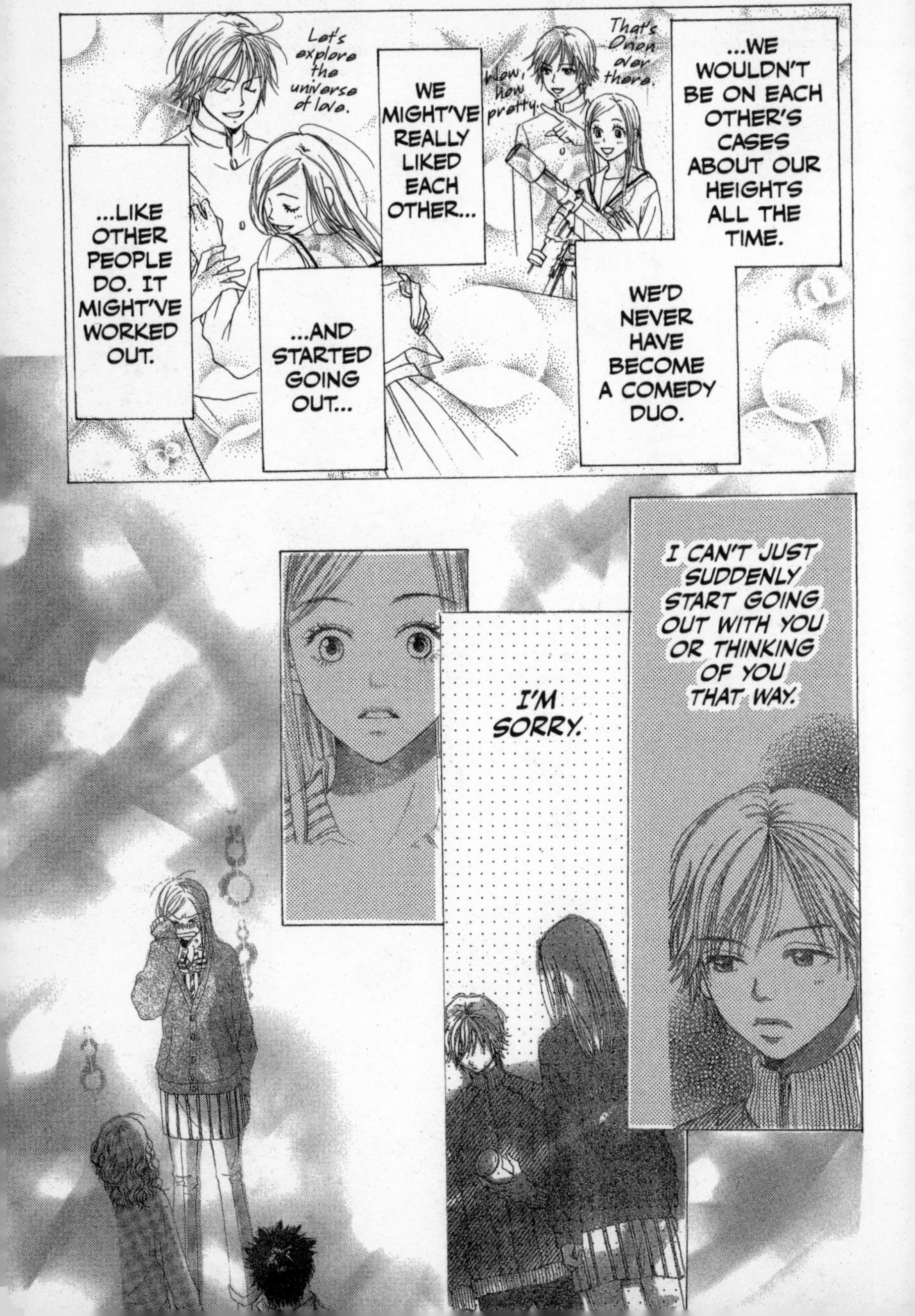
...WE WOULDN'T BE ON EACH OTHER'S CASES ABOUT OUR HEIGHTS ALL THE TIME.
WE'D NEVER HAVE BECOME A COMEDY DUO.
That's Orion over there.
Wow, how pretty.
WE MIGHT'VE REALLY LIKED EACH OTHER...
Let's explore the universe of love.
...AND STARTED GOING OUT...
...LIKE OTHER PEOPLE DO. IT MIGHT'VE WORKED OUT.
I CAN'T JUST SUDDENLY START GOING OUT WITH YOU OR THINKING OF YOU THAT WAY.
I'M SORRY.

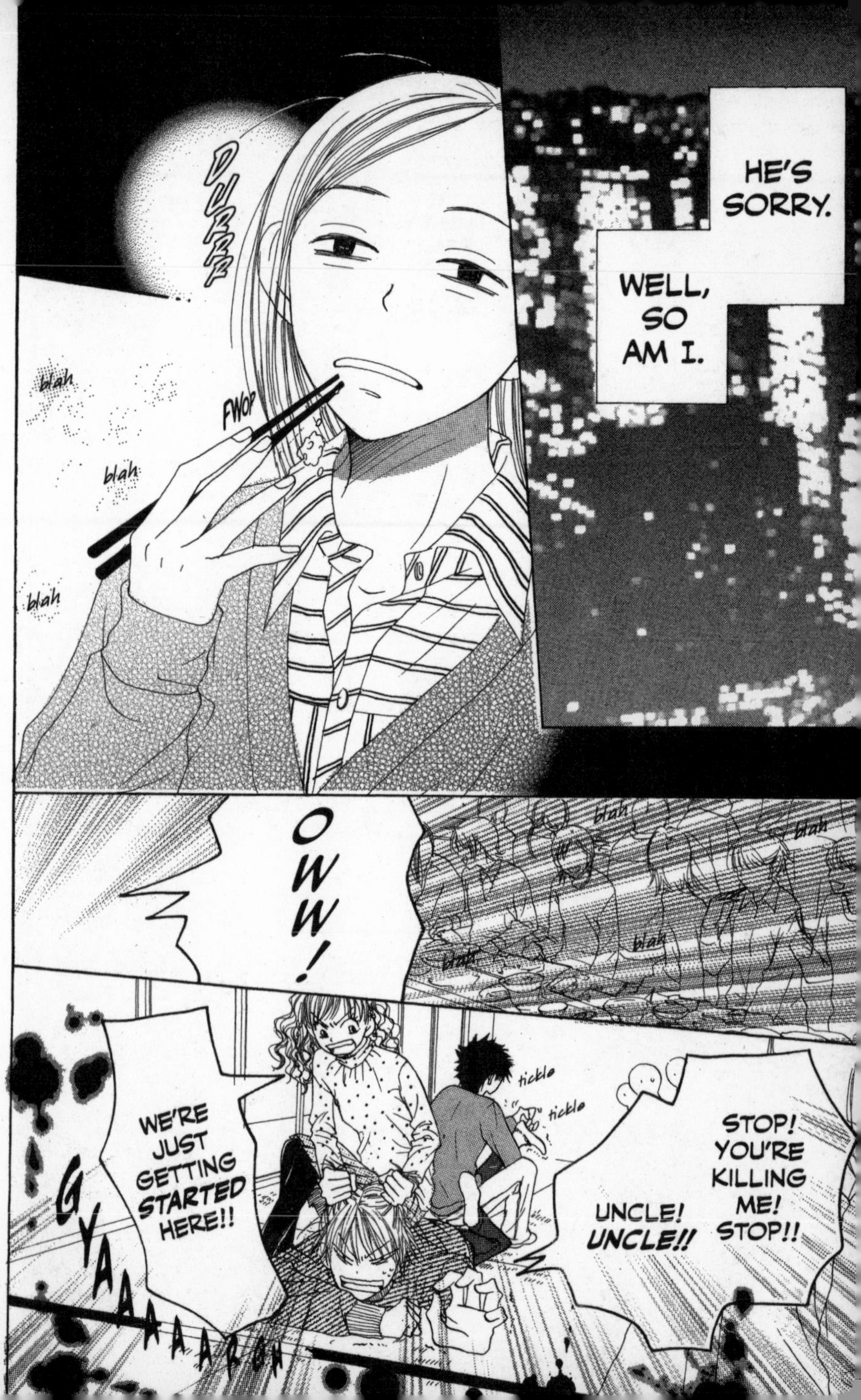
HE'S SORRY.
WELL, SO AM I.
DURRR
blah
FWOP
blah
blah
blah
blah
blah
blah
OWW!
STOP! YOU'RE KILLING ME! STOP!!
UNCLE! UNCLE!!
tickle
tickle
WE'RE JUST GETTING STARTED HERE!!
GYAAAAAARGH

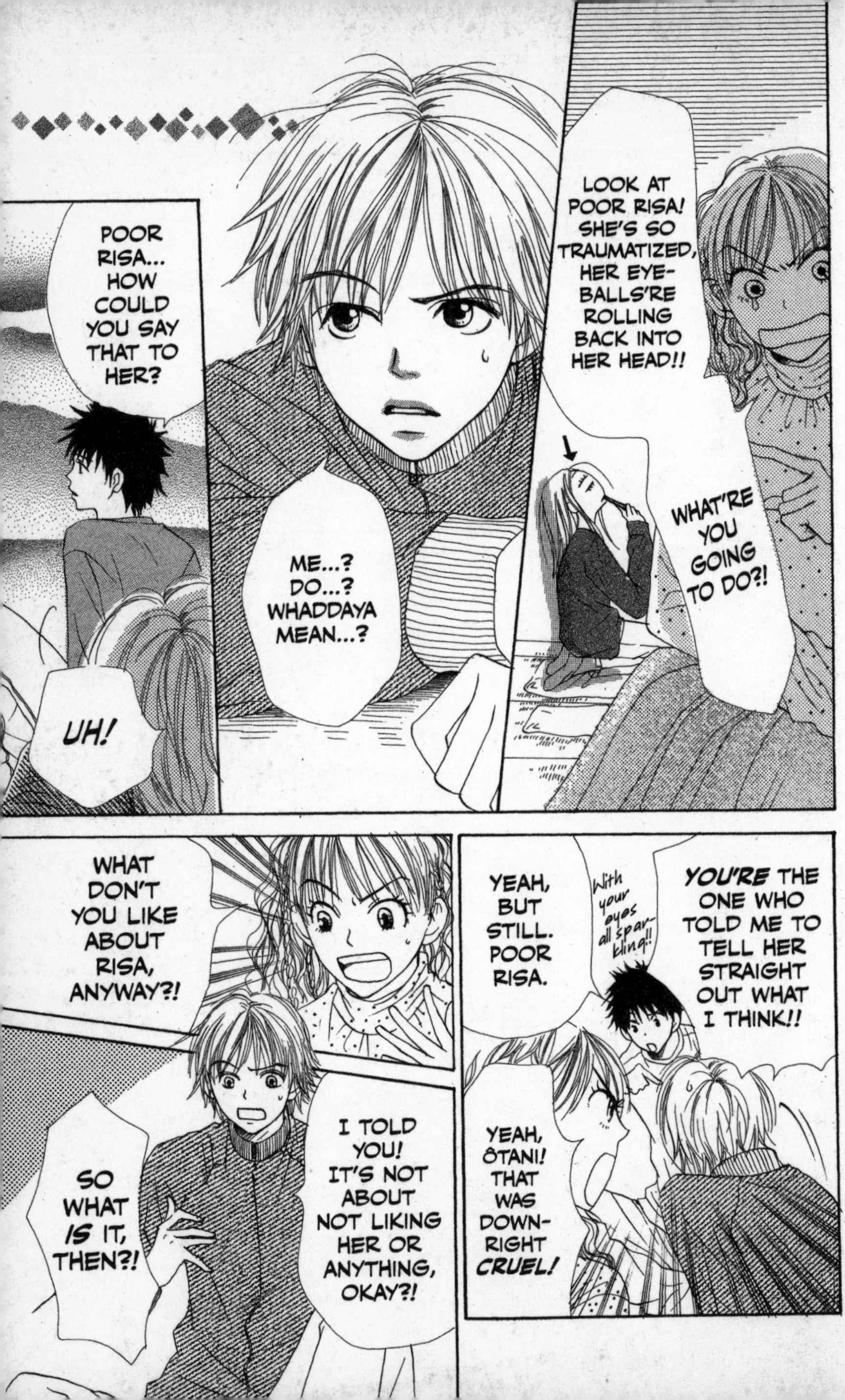
LOOK AT POOR RISA! SHE'S SO TRAUMATIZED, HER EYE-BALLS'RE ROLLING BACK INTO HER HEAD!!
WHAT'RE YOU GOING TO DO?!
ME...? DO...? WHADDAYA MEAN...?
POOR RISA... HOW COULD YOU SAY THAT TO HER?
UH!
YOU'RE THE ONE WHO TOLD ME TO TELL HER STRAIGHT OUT WHAT I THINK!!
With your eyes all sparkling!!
YEAH, BUT STILL. POOR RISA.
YEAH, OTANI! THAT WAS DOWN-RIGHT *CRUEL!*
WHAT DON'T YOU LIKE ABOUT RISA, ANYWAY?!
I TOLD YOU! IT'S NOT ABOUT NOT LIKING HER OR ANYTHING, OKAY?!
SO WHAT *IS* IT, THEN?!

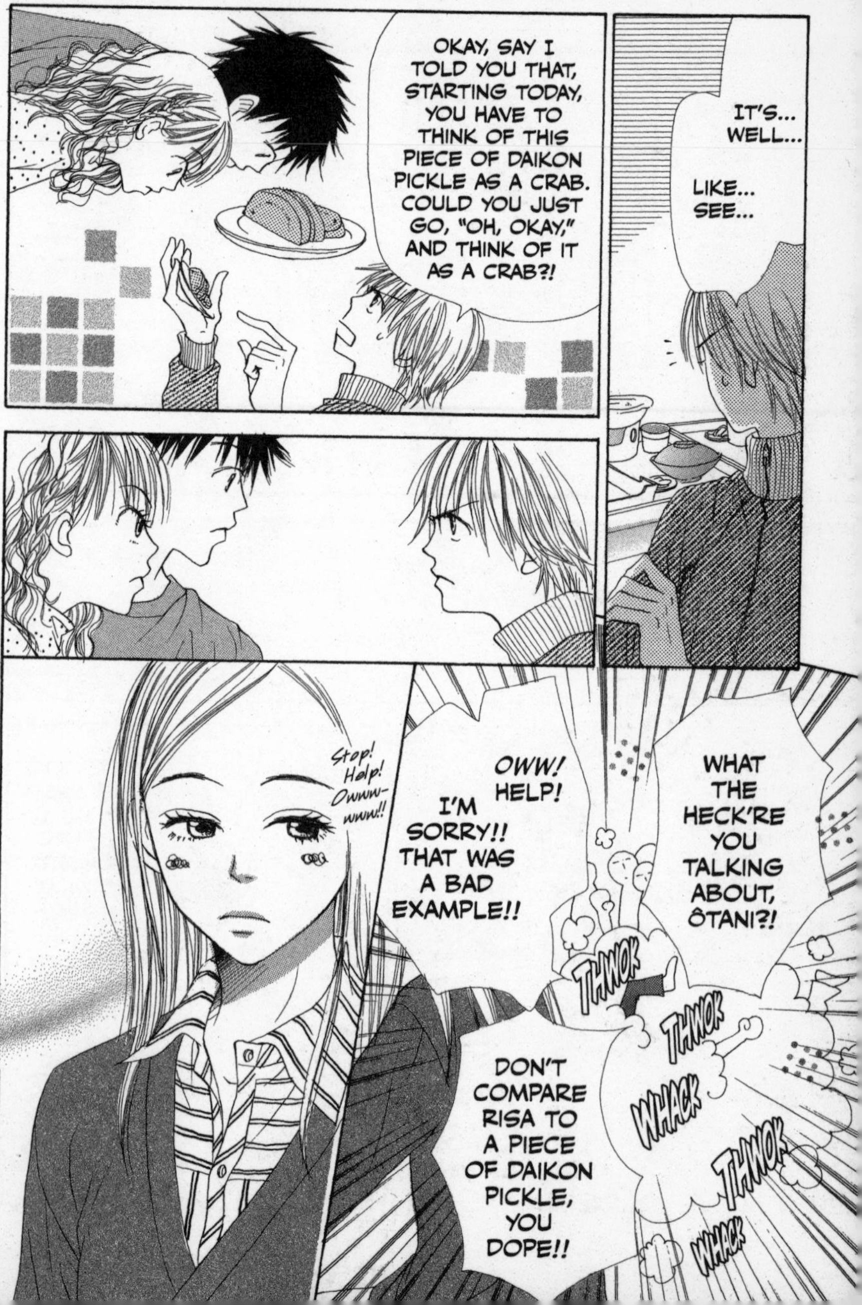
IT'S... WELL...
LIKE... SEE...
OKAY, SAY I TOLD YOU THAT, STARTING TODAY, YOU HAVE TO THINK OF THIS PIECE OF DAIKON PICKLE AS A CRAB. COULD YOU JUST GO, "OH, OKAY," AND THINK OF IT AS A CRAB?!
WHAT THE HECK'RE YOU TALKING ABOUT, ŌTANI?!
OWW! HELP!
I'M SORRY!! THAT WAS A BAD EXAMPLE!!
Stop! Help! Owwww-www!!
THWOK
THWOK
WHACK
THWOK
WHACK
DON'T COMPARE RISA TO A PIECE OF DAIKON PICKLE, YOU DOPE!!

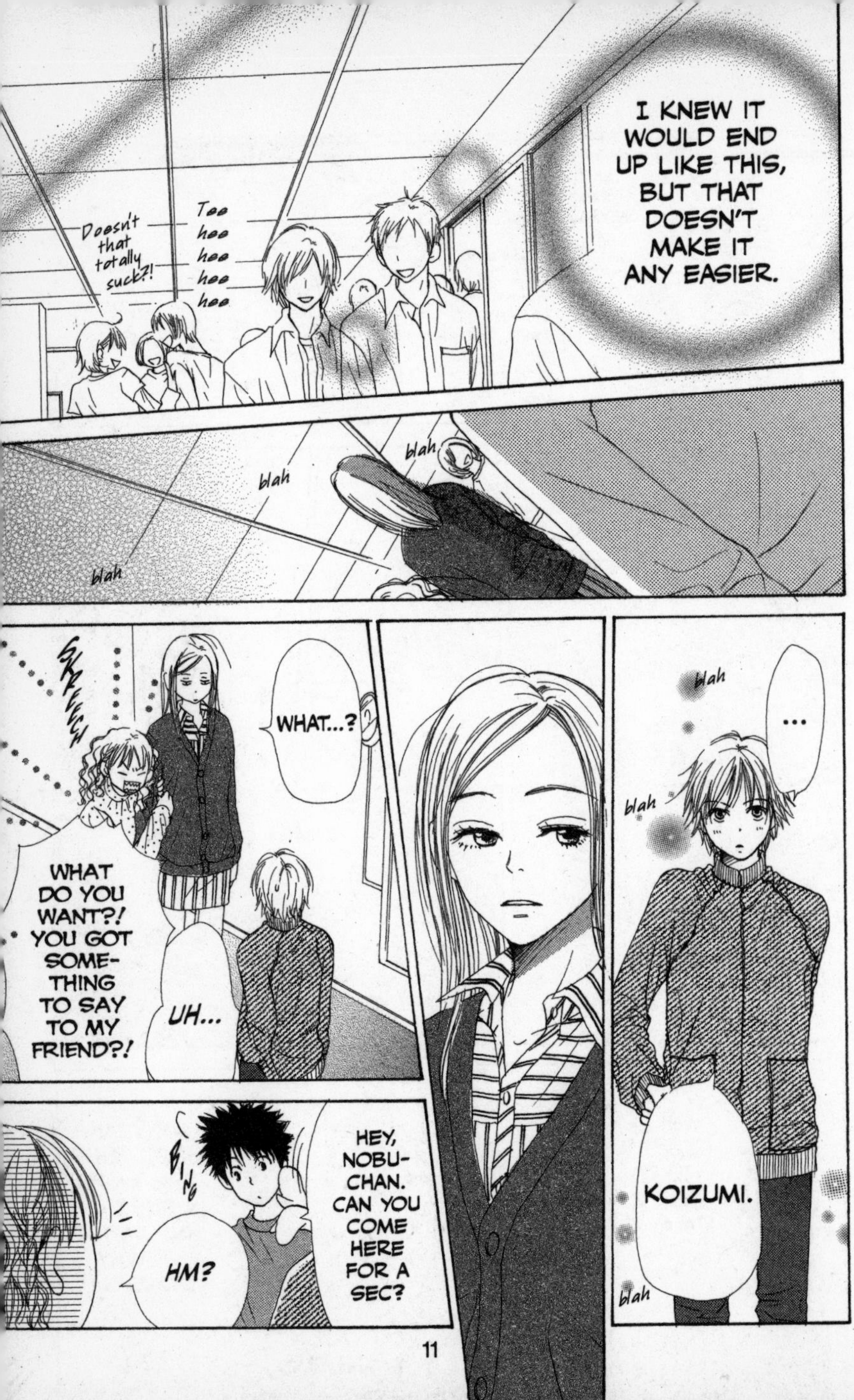
I KNEW IT WOULD END UP LIKE THIS, BUT THAT DOESN'T MAKE IT ANY EASIER.
Tee hee hee hee hee
Doesn't that totally suck?!
blah
blah
blah
blah
...
blah
KOIZUMI.
blah
WHAT...?
SKREECH
WHAT DO YOU WANT?! YOU GOT SOME-THING TO SAY TO MY FRIEND?!
UH...
HEY, NOBU-CHAN. CAN YOU COME HERE FOR A SEC?
BING
HM?

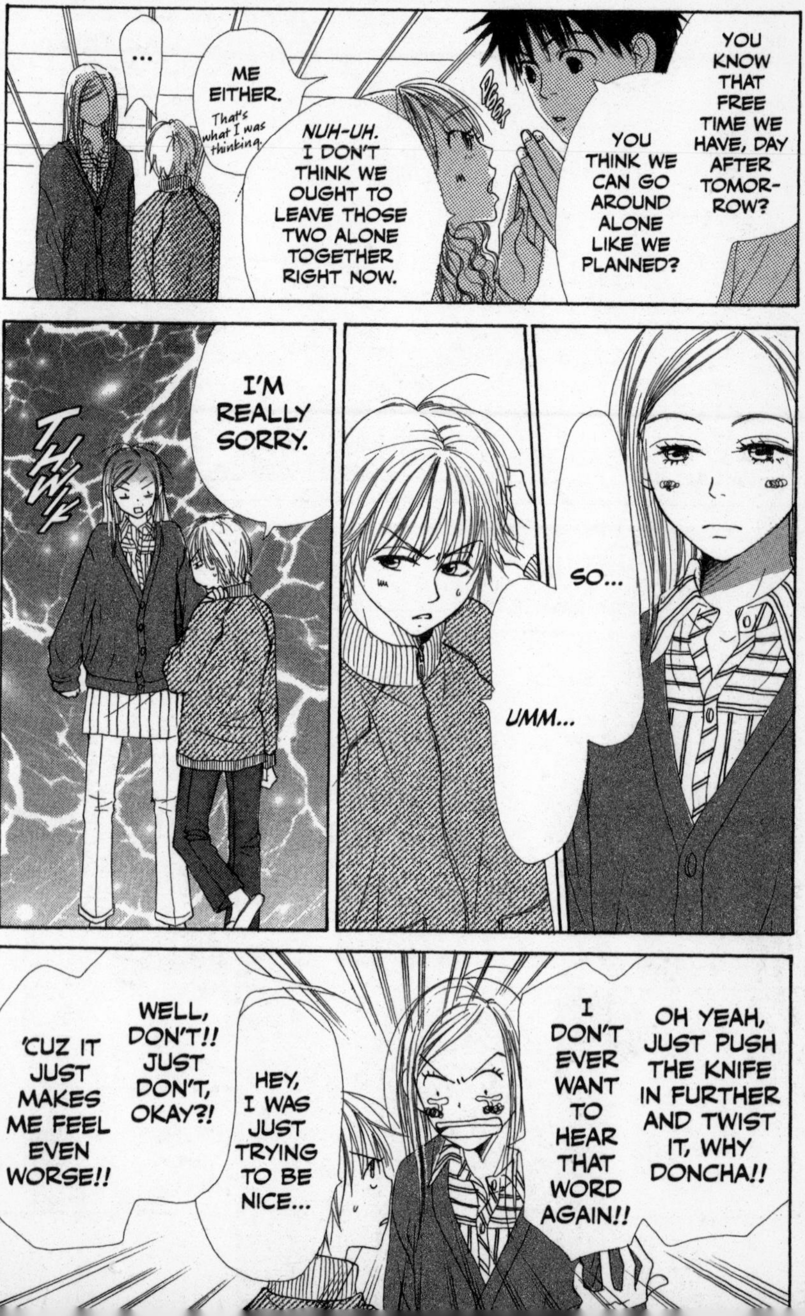
YOU KNOW THAT FREE TIME WE HAVE, DAY AFTER TOMORROW?
YOU THINK WE CAN GO AROUND ALONE LIKE WE PLANNED?
NUH-UH. I DON'T THINK WE OUGHT TO LEAVE THOSE TWO ALONE TOGETHER RIGHT NOW.
ME EITHER.
That's what I was thinking.
...
SO...
UMM...
I'M REALLY SORRY.
THWK
OH YEAH, JUST PUSH THE KNIFE IN FURTHER AND TWIST IT, WHY DONCHA!!
I DON'T EVER WANT TO HEAR THAT WORD AGAIN!!
HEY, I WAS JUST TRYING TO BE NICE...
WELL, DON'T!! JUST DON'T, OKAY?!
'CUZ IT JUST MAKES ME FEEL EVEN WORSE!!

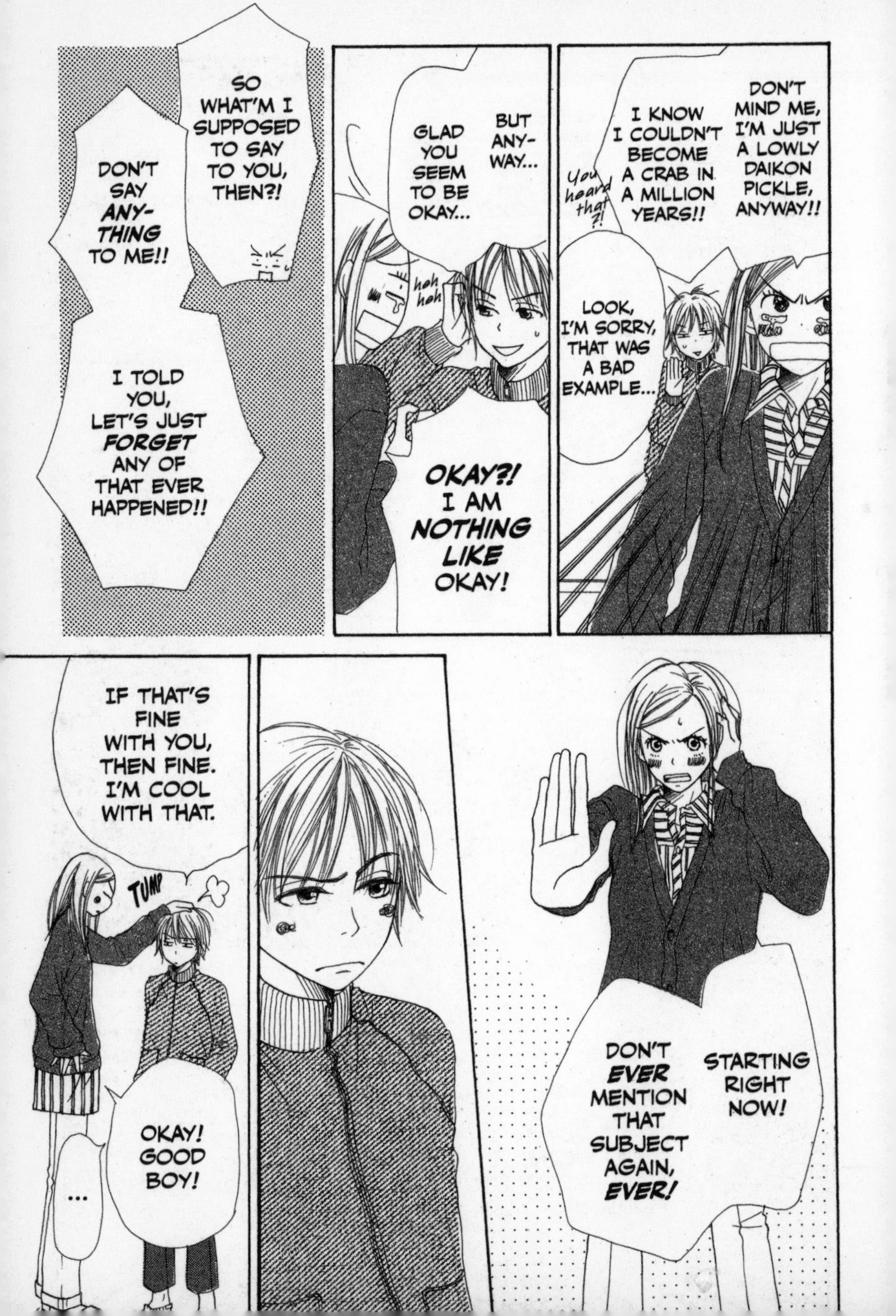
DON'T MIND ME, I'M JUST A LOWLY DAIKON PICKLE, ANYWAY!!
I KNOW I COULDN'T BECOME A CRAB IN A MILLION YEARS!!
You heard that?!
LOOK, I'M SORRY, THAT WAS A BAD EXAMPLE...
BUT ANY-WAY...
GLAD YOU SEEM TO BE OKAY...
heh heh
OKAY?! I AM *NOTHING LIKE* OKAY!
SO WHAT'M I SUPPOSED TO SAY TO YOU, THEN?!
DON'T SAY *ANY-THING* TO ME!!
I TOLD YOU, LET'S JUST *FORGET* ANY OF THAT EVER HAPPENED!!
STARTING RIGHT NOW!
DON'T *EVER* MENTION THAT SUBJECT AGAIN, *EVER!*
IF THAT'S FINE WITH YOU, THEN FINE. I'M COOL WITH THAT.
TUMP
OKAY! GOOD BOY!
...

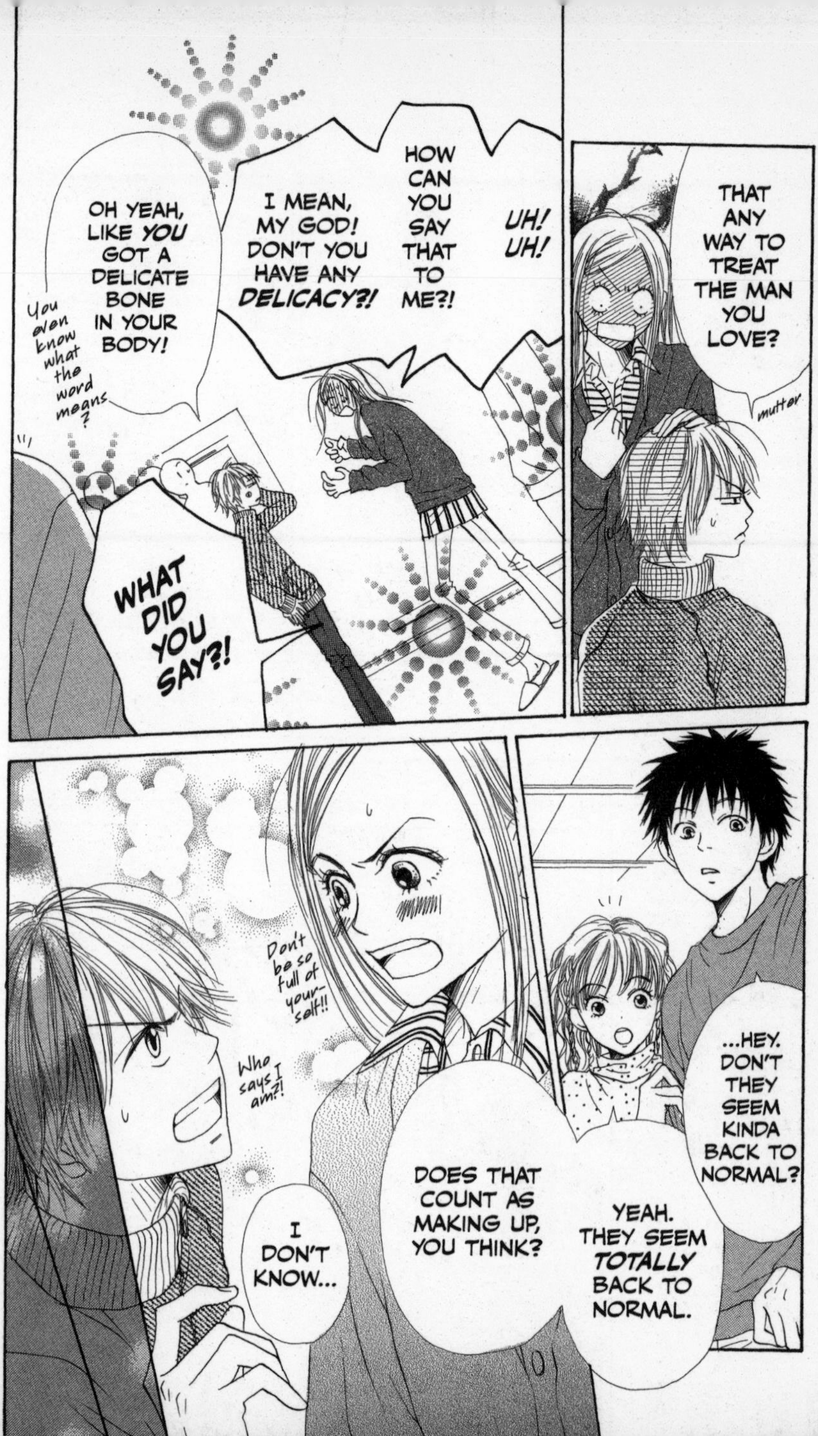
THAT ANY WAY TO TREAT THE MAN YOU LOVE?
mutter
UH! UH!
HOW CAN YOU SAY THAT TO ME?!
I MEAN, MY GOD! DON'T YOU HAVE ANY DELICACY?!
OH YEAH, LIKE YOU GOT A DELICATE BONE IN YOUR BODY!
You even know what the word means?
WHAT DID YOU SAY?!
...HEY. DON'T THEY SEEM KINDA BACK TO NORMAL?
YEAH. THEY SEEM TOTALLY BACK TO NORMAL.
Don't be so full of yourself!!
Who says I am?!
DOES THAT COUNT AS MAKING UP, YOU THINK?
I DON'T KNOW...

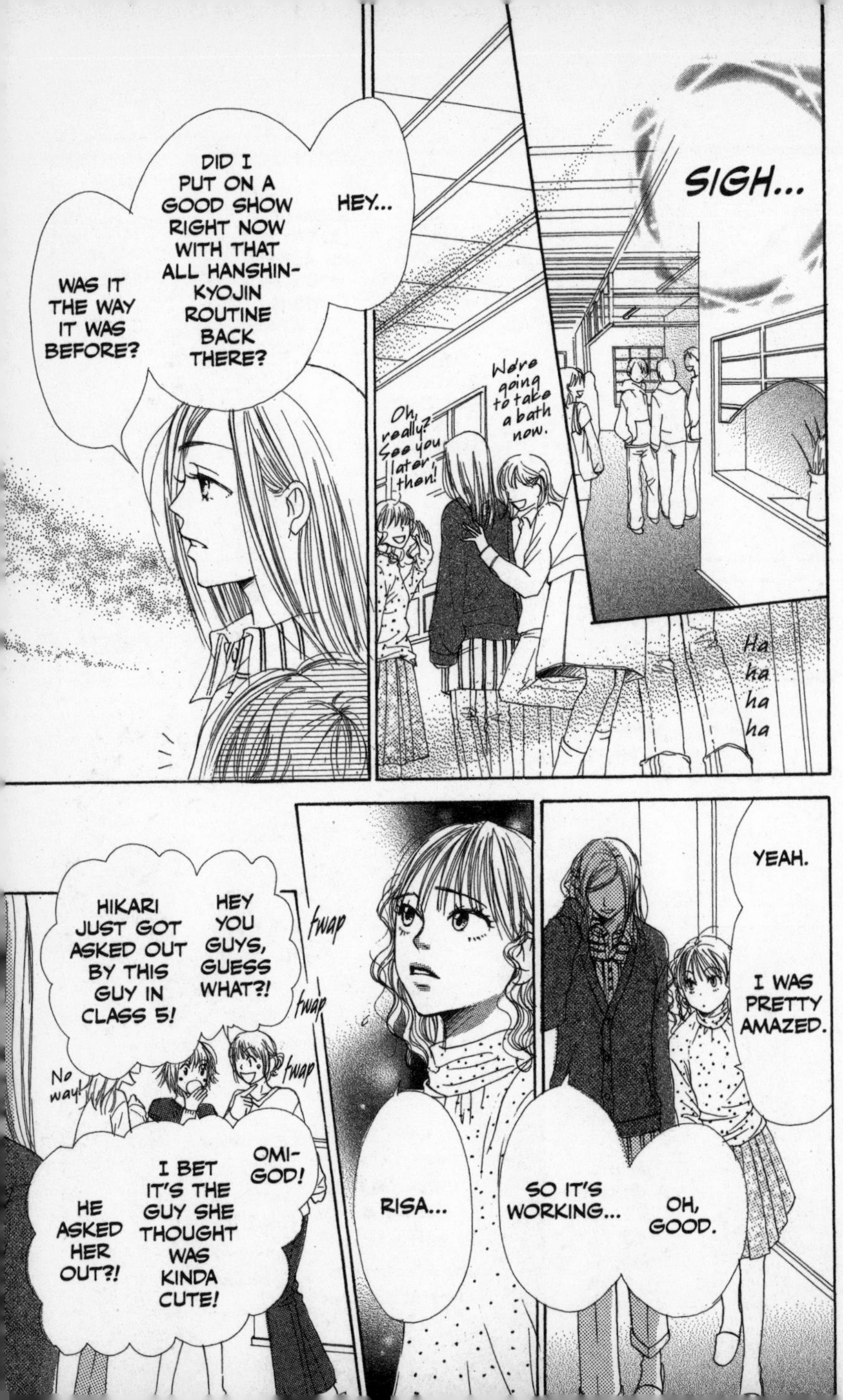
SIGH...
Ha ha ha ha
We're going to take a bath now.
Oh, really? See you later then!
HEY...
DID I PUT ON A GOOD SHOW RIGHT NOW WITH THAT ALL HANSHIN-KYOJIN ROUTINE BACK THERE?
WAS IT THE WAY IT WAS BEFORE?
YEAH.
I WAS PRETTY AMAZED.
OH, GOOD.
SO IT'S WORKING...
RISA...
twap
twap
twap
HEY YOU GUYS, GUESS WHAT?!
HIKARI JUST GOT ASKED OUT BY THIS GUY IN CLASS 5!
No way!
OMI-GOD!
I BET IT'S THE GUY SHE THOUGHT WAS KINDA CUTE!
HE ASKED HER OUT?!

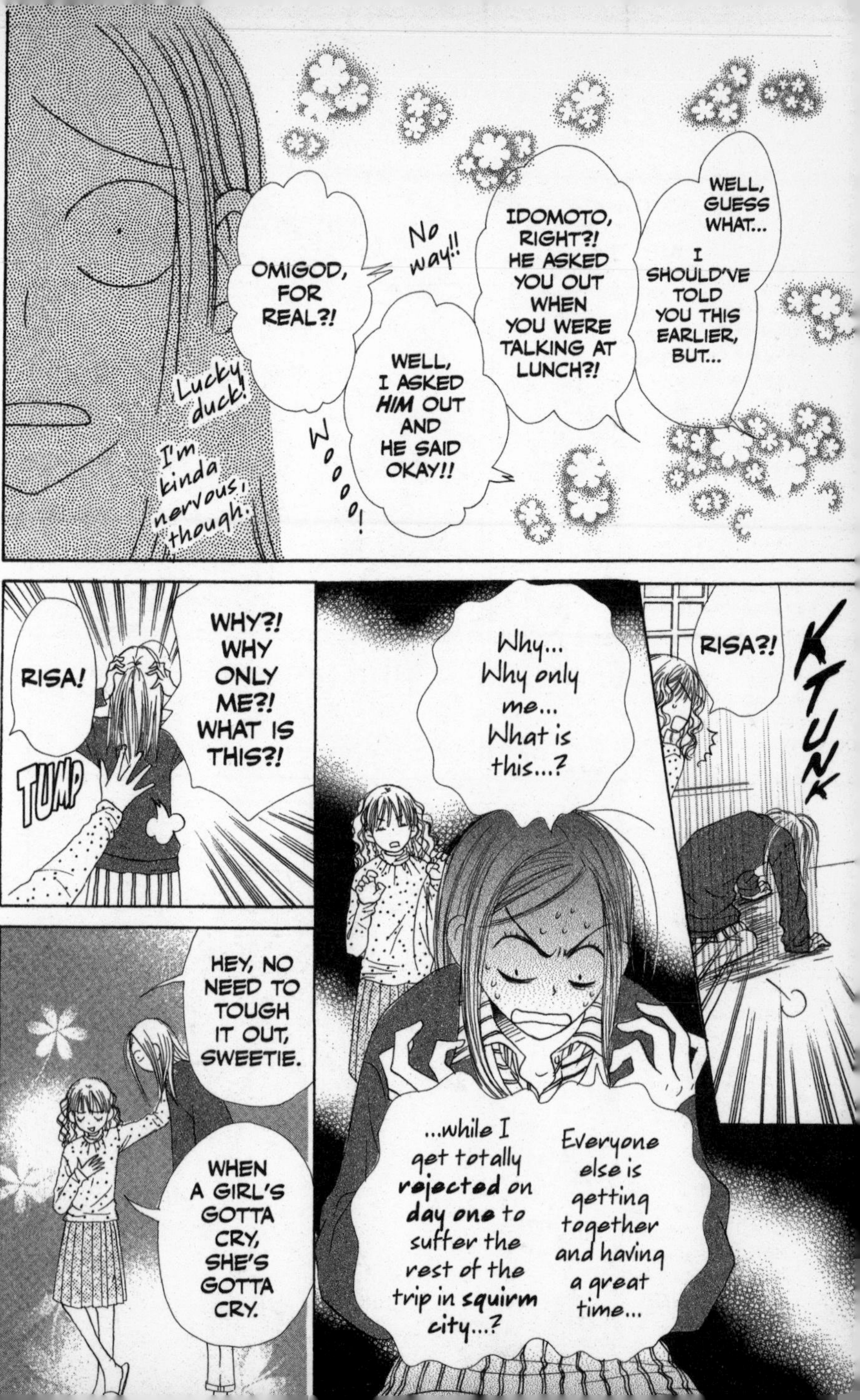
WELL, GUESS WHAT... I SHOULD'VE TOLD YOU THIS EARLIER, BUT...
IDOMOTO, RIGHT?! HE ASKED YOU OUT WHEN YOU WERE TALKING AT LUNCH?!
No way!!
OMIGOD, FOR REAL?!
WELL, I ASKED **HIM** OUT AND HE SAID OKAY!!
Wooooo!
Lucky duck!
I'm kinda nervous, though.
RISA?!
KTUNK
Why... Why only me... What is this...?
Everyone else is getting together and having a great time...
...while I get totally **rejected on day one** to suffer the rest of the trip in **squirm city**...?
WHY?! WHY ONLY ME?! WHAT IS THIS?!
RISA!
TUMP
HEY, NO NEED TO TOUGH IT OUT, SWEETIE.
WHEN A GIRL'S GOTTA CRY, SHE'S GOTTA CRY.

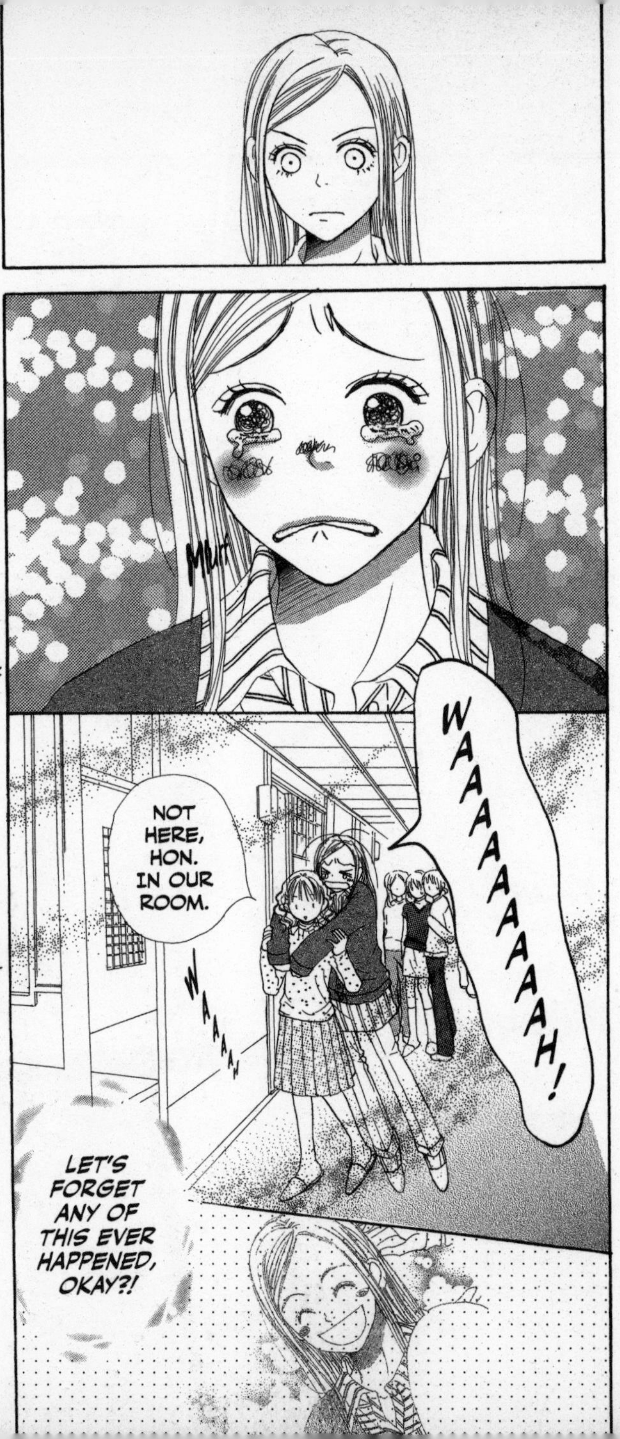
Muri
WAAAAAAAAAAH!
NOT HERE, HON. IN OUR ROOM.
WAAAAAH
LET'S FORGET ANY OF THIS EVER HAPPENED, OKAY?!

1

Hello. Nakahara here.

We're up to Volume 5. Oh dear. Almost two whole years have passed since I started this series. Oh dear. It's all thanks to your warm support. Thank you so much.

Ummm... It's really amazing how I cannot think of a single thing to write. ha ha ha ha Like, oops, two hours have passed while I was just sitting here with the pen in my hand. ha ha ha ha

Oh, yeah. While I was turning in manga installments every month these past two years, my sister got married. Her hubby's the kind of guy who gets hurt breaking up cat fights and who goes around saying "Good evening!" to stray dogs. He also helps me out with my manga. He's a great guy.

Aki & Kome, I wish you lots of happiness! ☆

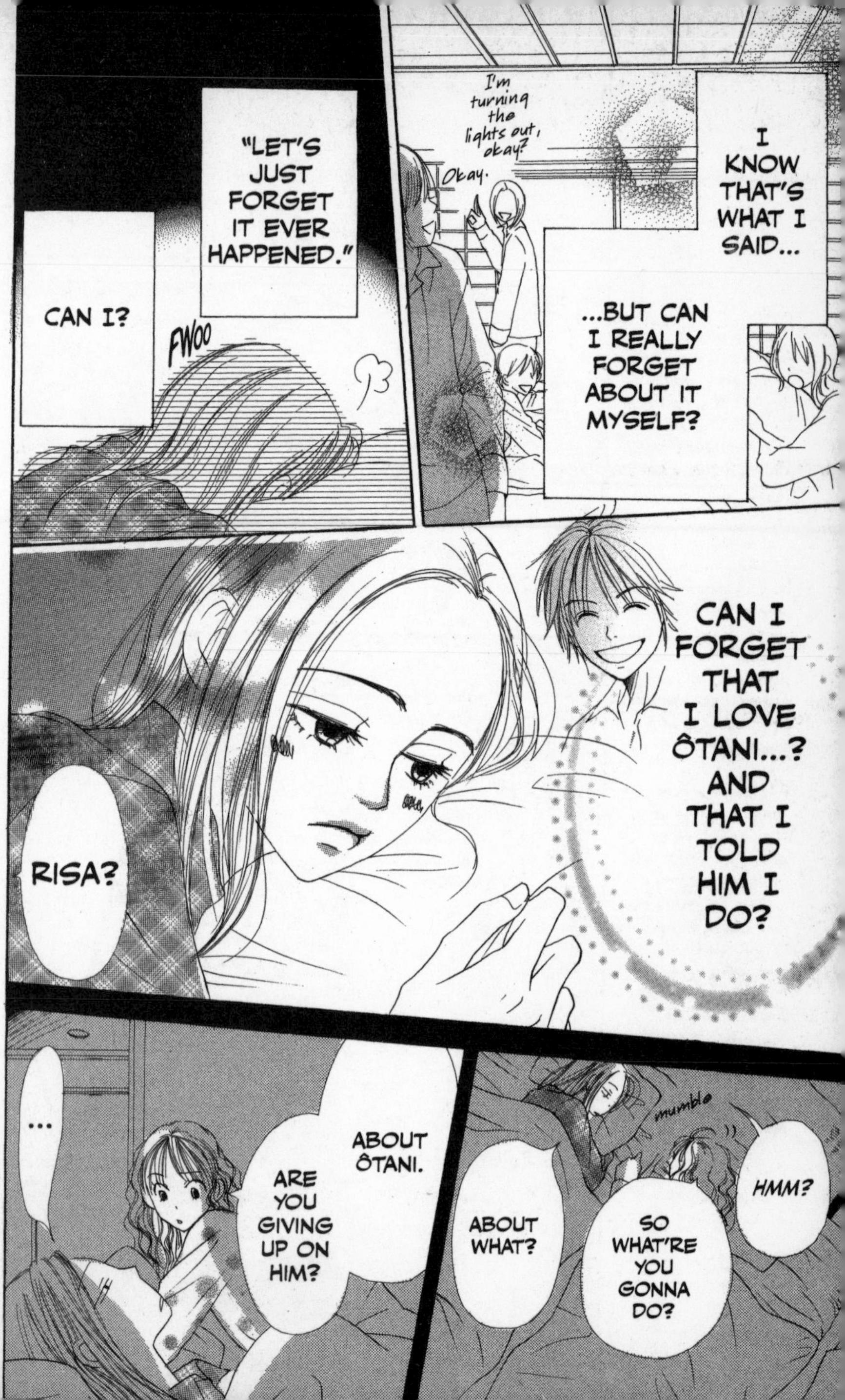
I'm turning the lights out, okay?
Okay.
I KNOW THAT'S WHAT I SAID...
...BUT CAN I REALLY FORGET ABOUT IT MYSELF?
"LET'S JUST FORGET IT EVER HAPPENED."
CAN I?
FWOO
CAN I FORGET THAT I LOVE ÔTANI...? AND THAT I TOLD HIM I DO?
RISA?
HMM?
mumble
SO WHAT'RE YOU GONNA DO?
ABOUT WHAT?
ABOUT ÔTANI.
ARE YOU GIVING UP ON HIM?
...

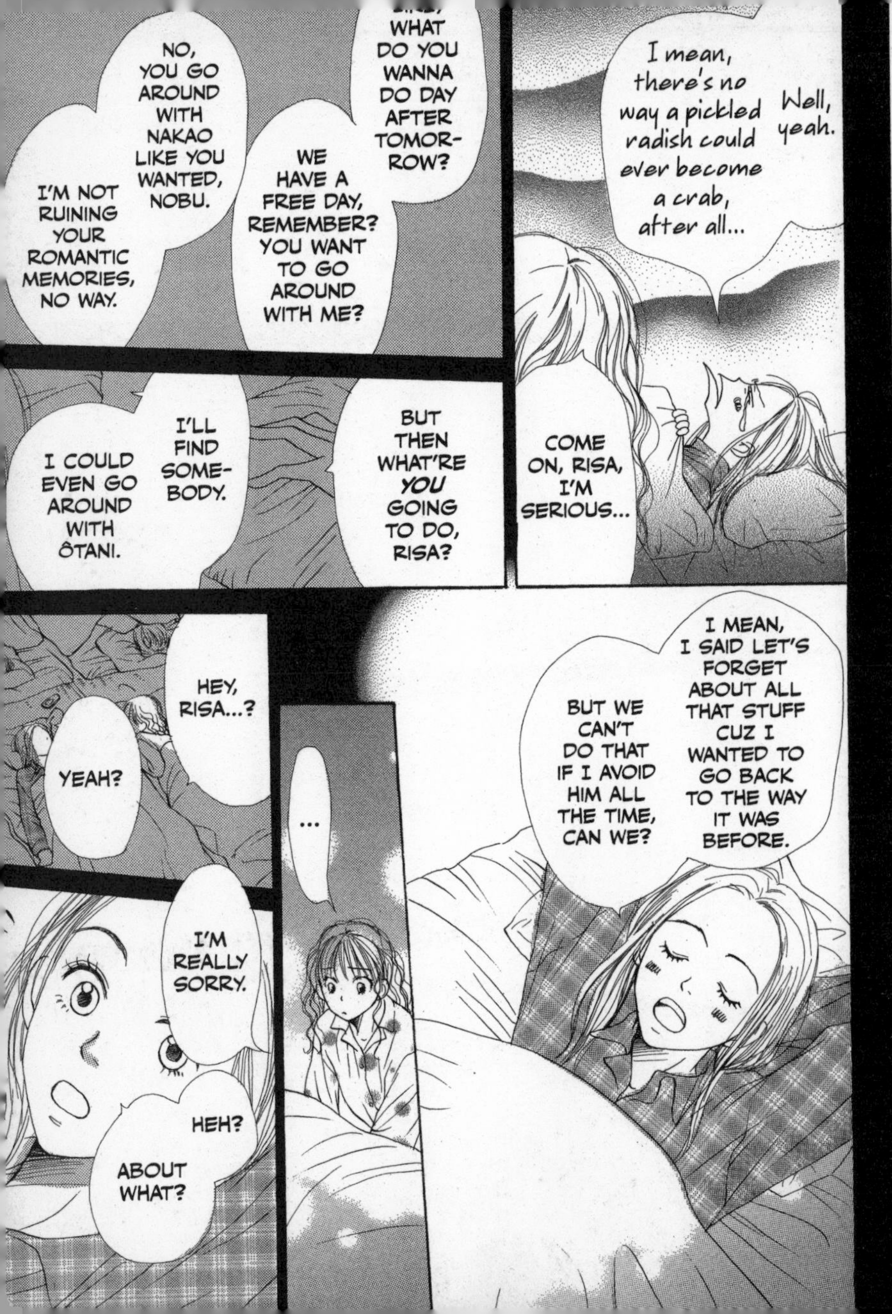
Well, yeah.
I mean, there's no way a pickled radish could ever become a crab, after all...
COME ON, RISA, I'M SERIOUS...
WHAT DO YOU WANNA DO DAY AFTER TOMORROW?
WE HAVE A FREE DAY, REMEMBER? YOU WANT TO GO AROUND WITH ME?
NO, YOU GO AROUND WITH NAKAO LIKE YOU WANTED, NOBU.
I'M NOT RUINING YOUR ROMANTIC MEMORIES, NO WAY.
BUT THEN WHAT'RE *YOU* GOING TO DO, RISA?
I'LL FIND SOMEBODY.
I COULD EVEN GO AROUND WITH ŌTANI.
I MEAN, I SAID LET'S FORGET ABOUT ALL THAT STUFF CUZ I WANTED TO GO BACK TO THE WAY IT WAS BEFORE.
BUT WE CAN'T DO THAT IF I AVOID HIM ALL THE TIME, CAN WE?
...
HEY, RISA...?
YEAH?
I'M REALLY SORRY.
HEH?
ABOUT WHAT?

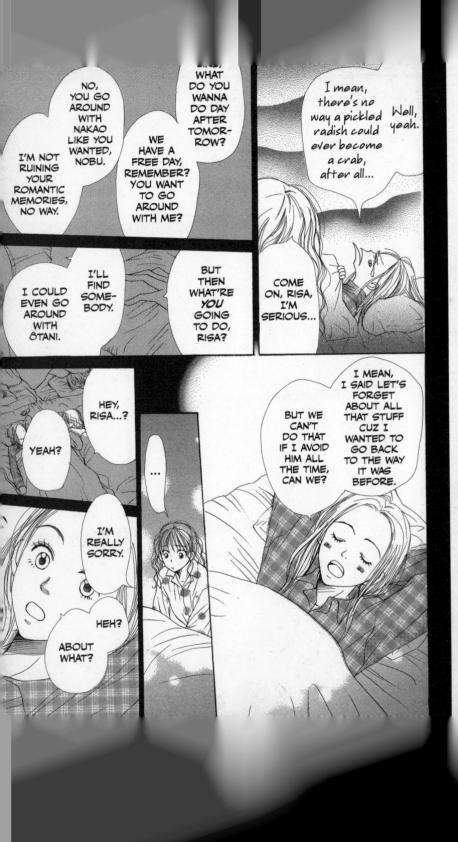

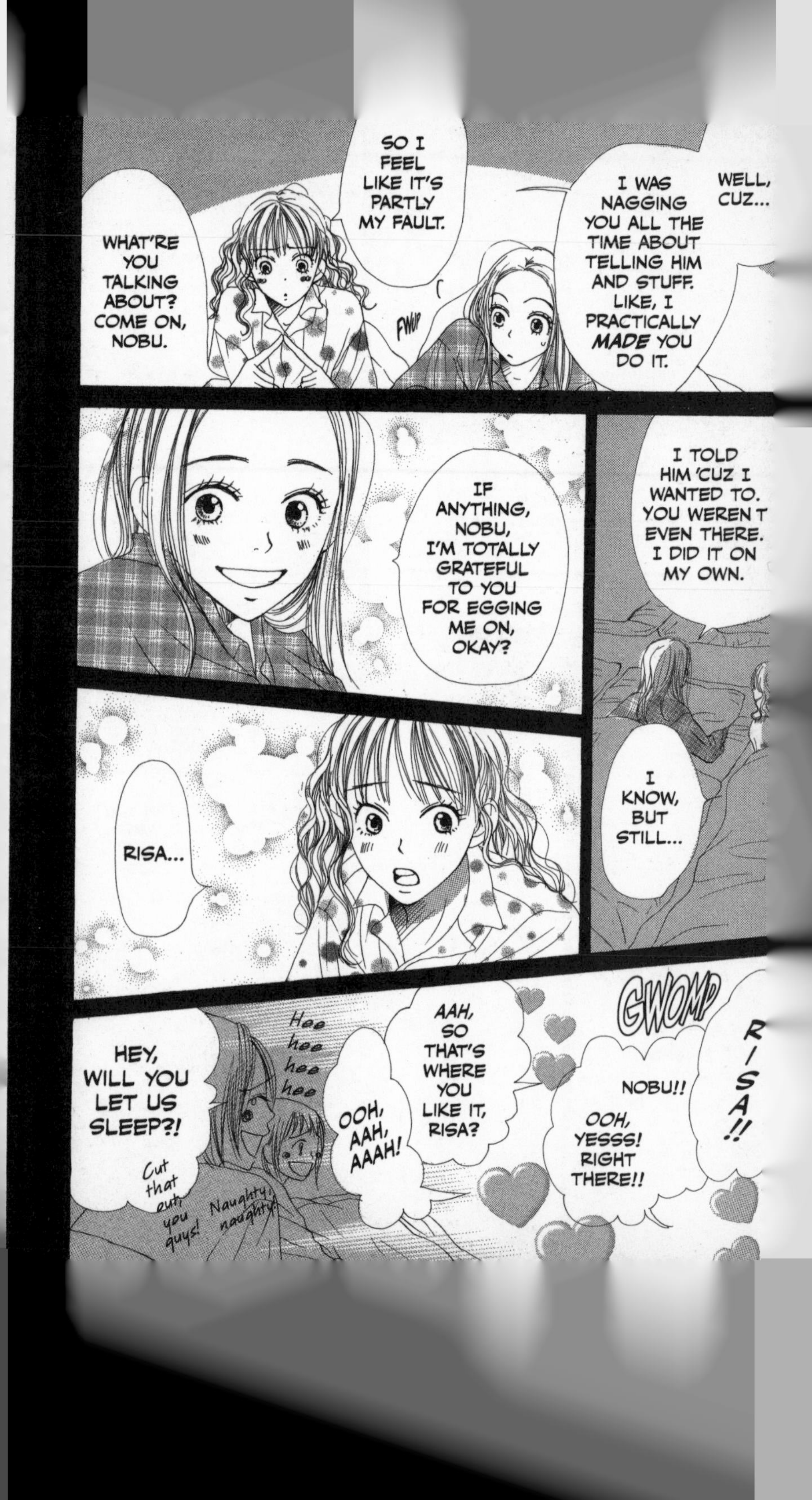
WELL, CUZ...
I WAS NAGGING YOU ALL THE TIME ABOUT TELLING HIM AND STUFF. LIKE, I PRACTICALLY *MADE* YOU DO IT.
FWUP
SO I FEEL LIKE IT'S PARTLY MY FAULT.
WHAT'RE YOU TALKING ABOUT? COME ON, NOBU.
I TOLD HIM 'CUZ I WANTED TO. YOU WEREN T EVEN THERE. I DID IT ON MY OWN.
I KNOW, BUT STILL...
IF ANYTHING, NOBU, I'M TOTALLY GRATEFUL TO YOU FOR EGGING ME ON, OKAY?
RISA...
GWOMP
RISA!!
NOBU!!
OOH, YESSS! RIGHT THERE!!
AAH, SO THAT'S WHERE YOU LIKE IT, RISA?
OOH, AAH, AAAH!
Hee hee hee hee
HEY, WILL YOU LET US SLEEP?!
Naughty, naughty!
Cut that out, you guys!

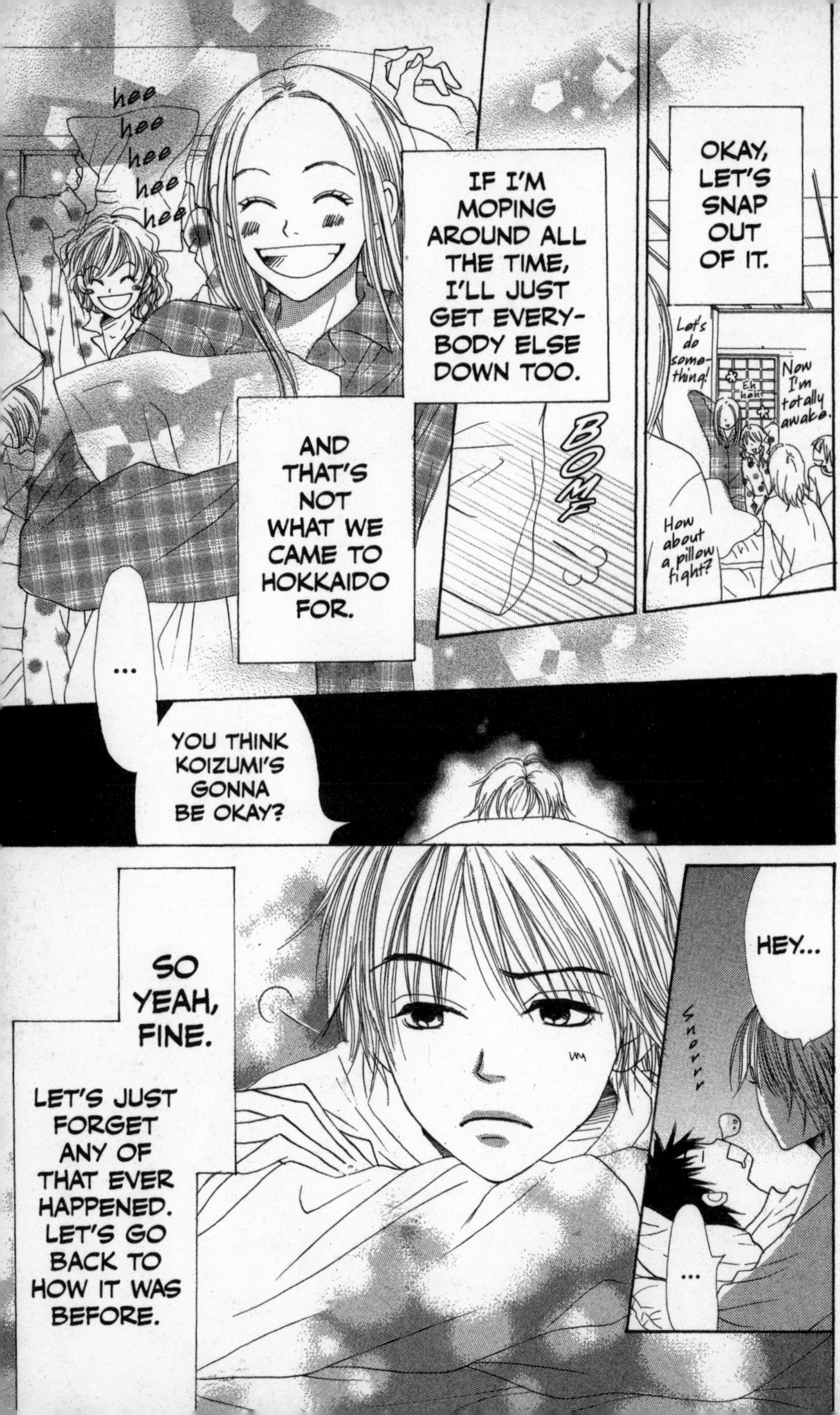
OKAY, LET'S SNAP OUT OF IT.
Let's do some-thing!
Eh heh
Now I'm totally awake.
How about a pillow fight?
BOMF
IF I'M MOPING AROUND ALL THE TIME, I'LL JUST GET EVERY-BODY ELSE DOWN TOO.
AND THAT'S NOT WHAT WE CAME TO HOKKAIDO FOR.
hee hee hee hee hee
...
YOU THINK KOIZUMI'S GONNA BE OKAY?
HEY...
Snorrr
...
SO YEAH, FINE.
LET'S JUST FORGET ANY OF THAT EVER HAPPENED. LET'S GO BACK TO HOW IT WAS BEFORE.

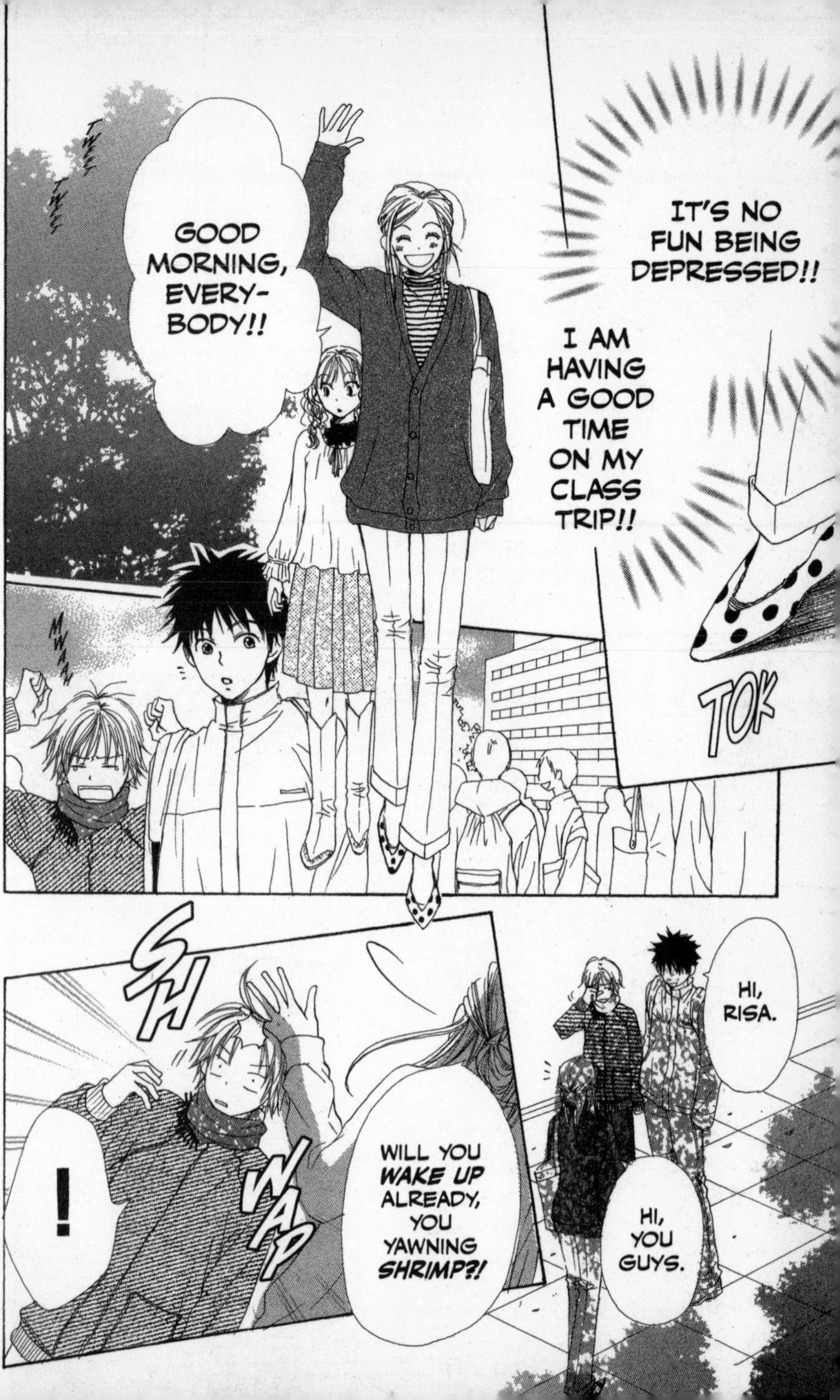
IT'S NO FUN BEING DEPRESSED!!
I AM HAVING A GOOD TIME ON MY CLASS TRIP!!
TOK
TWEE TWEE TWEE
GOOD MORNING, EVERY-BODY!!
MWAAH
HI, RISA.
HI, YOU GUYS.
SH
WILL YOU *WAKE UP* ALREADY, YOU YAWNING *SHRIMP?!*
WAP
!

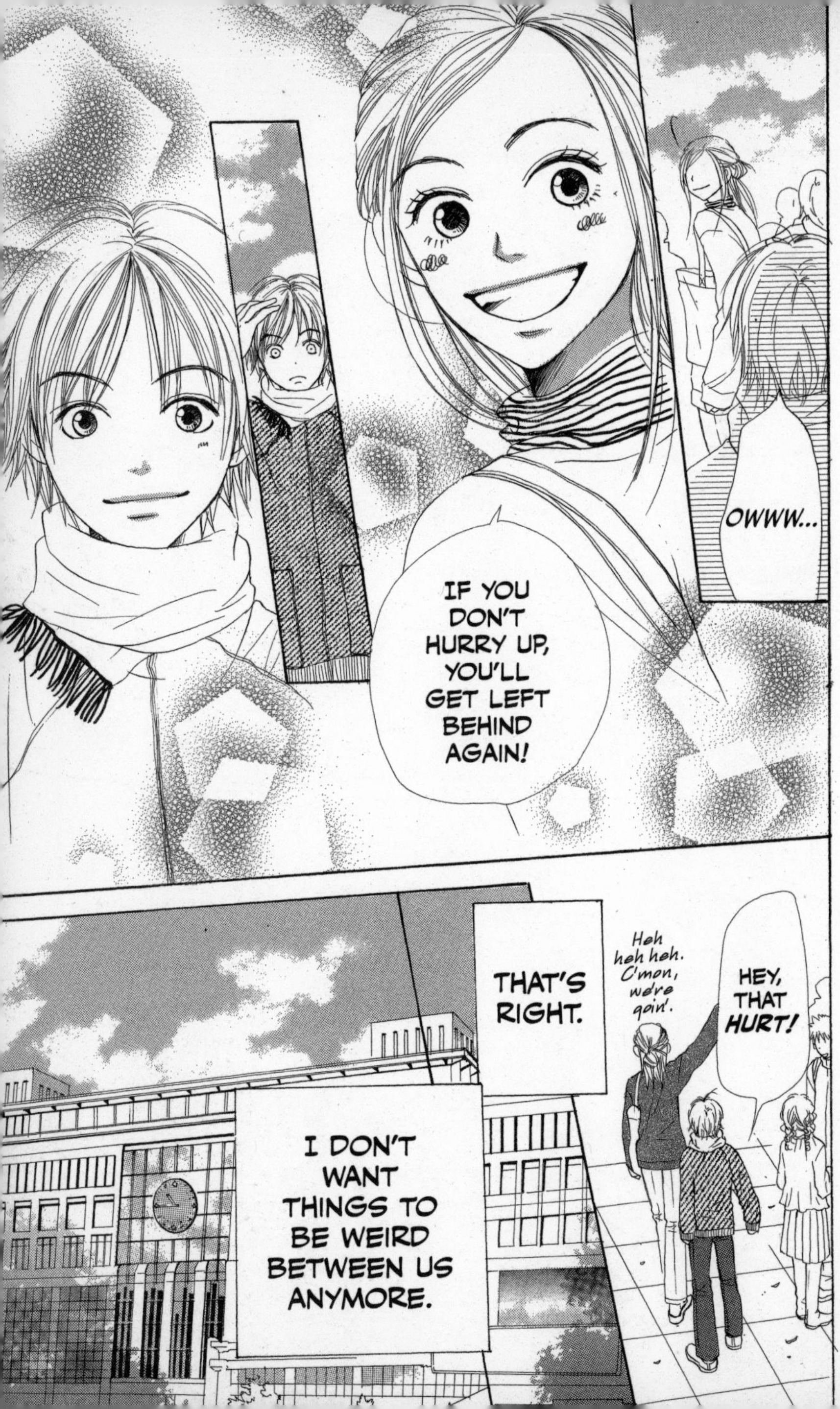
OWWW...
IF YOU DON'T HURRY UP, YOU'LL GET LEFT BEHIND AGAIN!
HEY, THAT HURT!
Heh heh heh. C'mon, we're goin'.
THAT'S RIGHT.
I DON'T WANT THINGS TO BE WEIRD BETWEEN US ANYMORE.

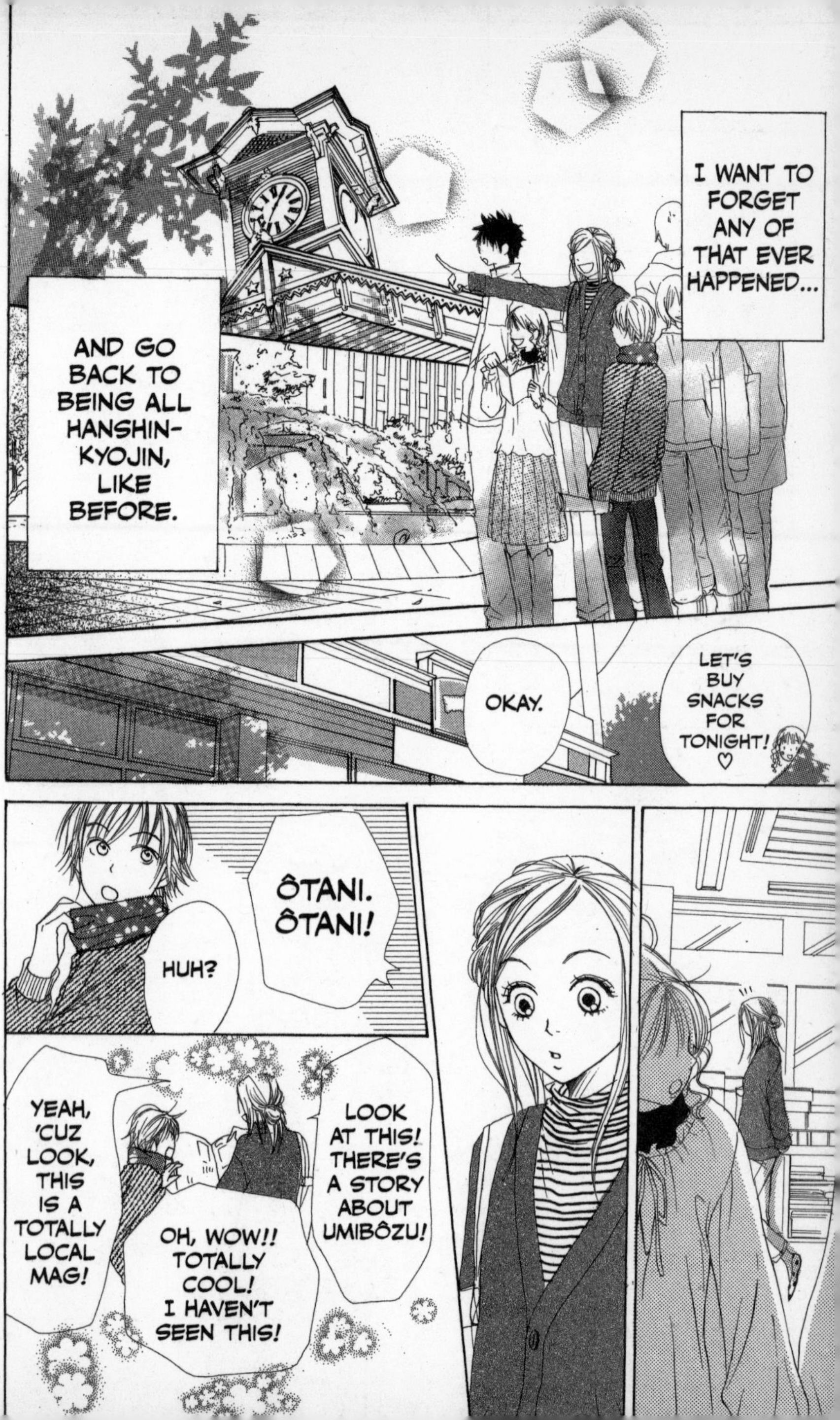
I WANT TO FORGET ANY OF THAT EVER HAPPENED...
AND GO BACK TO BEING ALL HANSHIN-KYOJIN, LIKE BEFORE.
LET'S BUY SNACKS FOR TONIGHT! ♡
OKAY.
ÔTANI. ÔTANI!
HUH?
LOOK AT THIS! THERE'S A STORY ABOUT UMIBÔZU!
YEAH, 'CUZ LOOK, THIS IS A TOTALLY LOCAL MAG!
OH, WOW!! TOTALLY COOL! I HAVEN'T SEEN THIS!

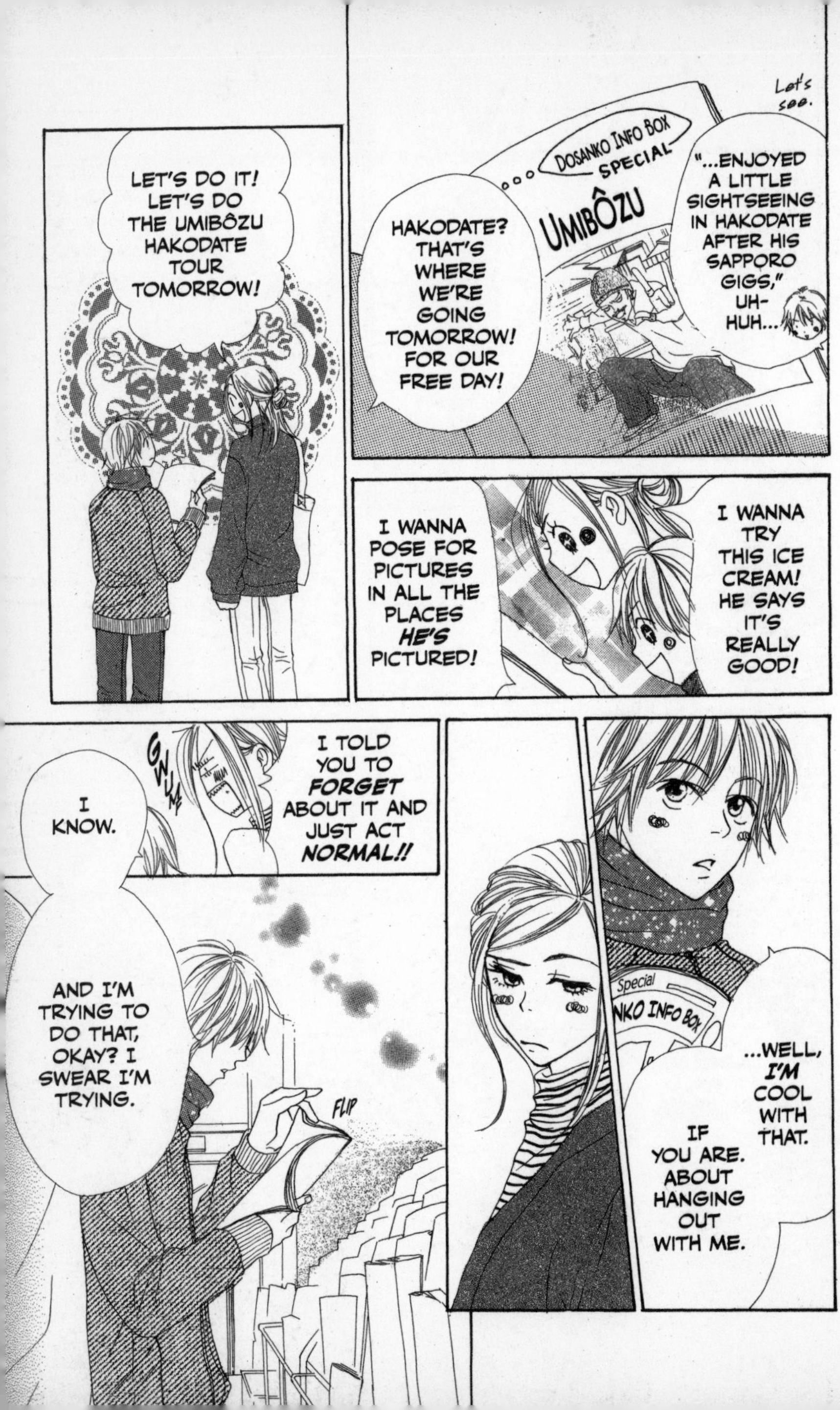
Let's see.
DOSANKO INFO BOX SPECIAL
UMIBÔZU
"...ENJOYED A LITTLE SIGHTSEEING IN HAKODATE AFTER HIS SAPPORO GIGS," UH-HUH...
HAKODATE? THAT'S WHERE WE'RE GOING TOMORROW! FOR OUR FREE DAY!
I WANNA TRY THIS ICE CREAM! HE SAYS IT'S REALLY GOOD!
I WANNA POSE FOR PICTURES IN ALL THE PLACES HE'S PICTURED!
LET'S DO IT! LET'S DO THE UMIBÔZU HAKODATE TOUR TOMORROW!
Special
NKO INFO Box
...WELL, I'M COOL WITH THAT.
IF YOU ARE. ABOUT HANGING OUT WITH ME.
I TOLD YOU TO FORGET ABOUT IT AND JUST ACT NORMAL!!
GWUM
I KNOW.
AND I'M TRYING TO DO THAT, OKAY? I SWEAR I'M TRYING.
FLIP

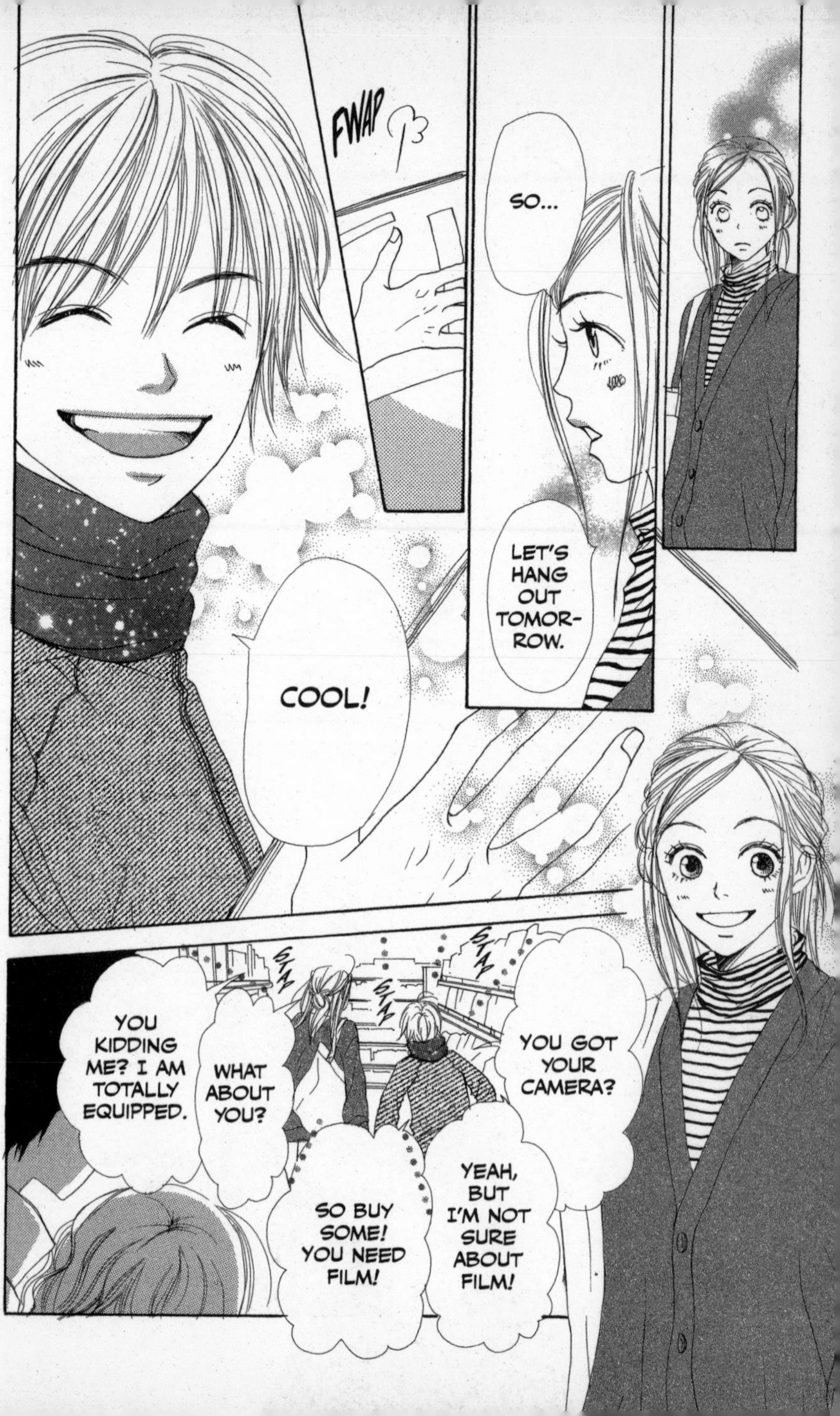
SO...
LET'S HANG OUT TOMORROW.
FWAP
COOL!
YOU GOT YOUR CAMERA?
YEAH, BUT I'M NOT SURE ABOUT FILM!
SO BUY SOME! YOU NEED FILM!
WHAT ABOUT YOU?
YOU KIDDING ME? I AM TOTALLY EQUIPPED.

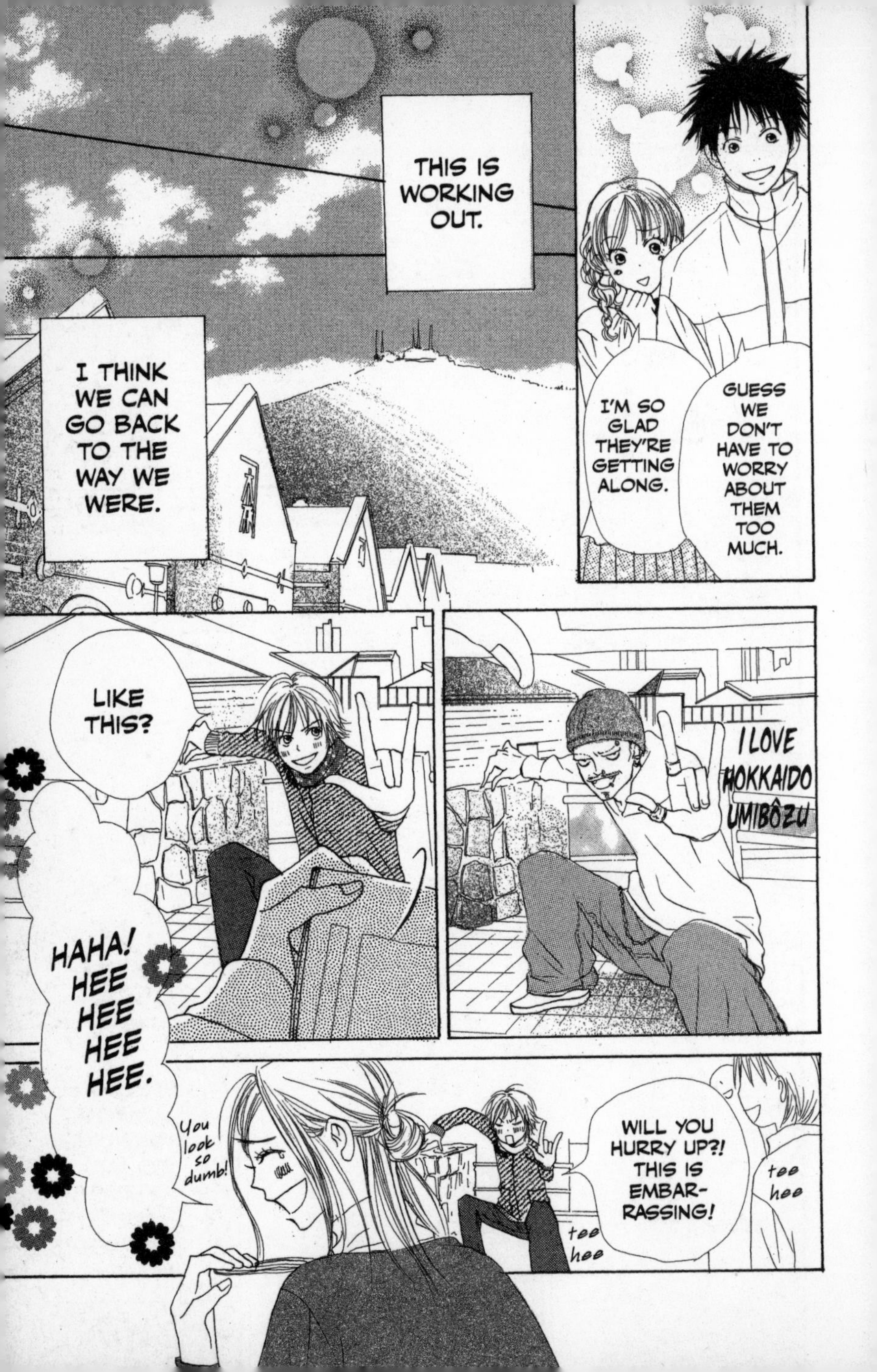
GUESS WE DON'T HAVE TO WORRY ABOUT THEM TOO MUCH.
I'M SO GLAD THEY'RE GETTING ALONG.
THIS IS WORKING OUT.
I THINK WE CAN GO BACK TO THE WAY WE WERE.
I LOVE HOKKAIDO UMIBÔZU
LIKE THIS?
HAHA! HEE HEE HEE HEE.
tee hee
WILL YOU HURRY UP?! THIS IS EMBAR-RASSING!
tee hee
You look so dumb!

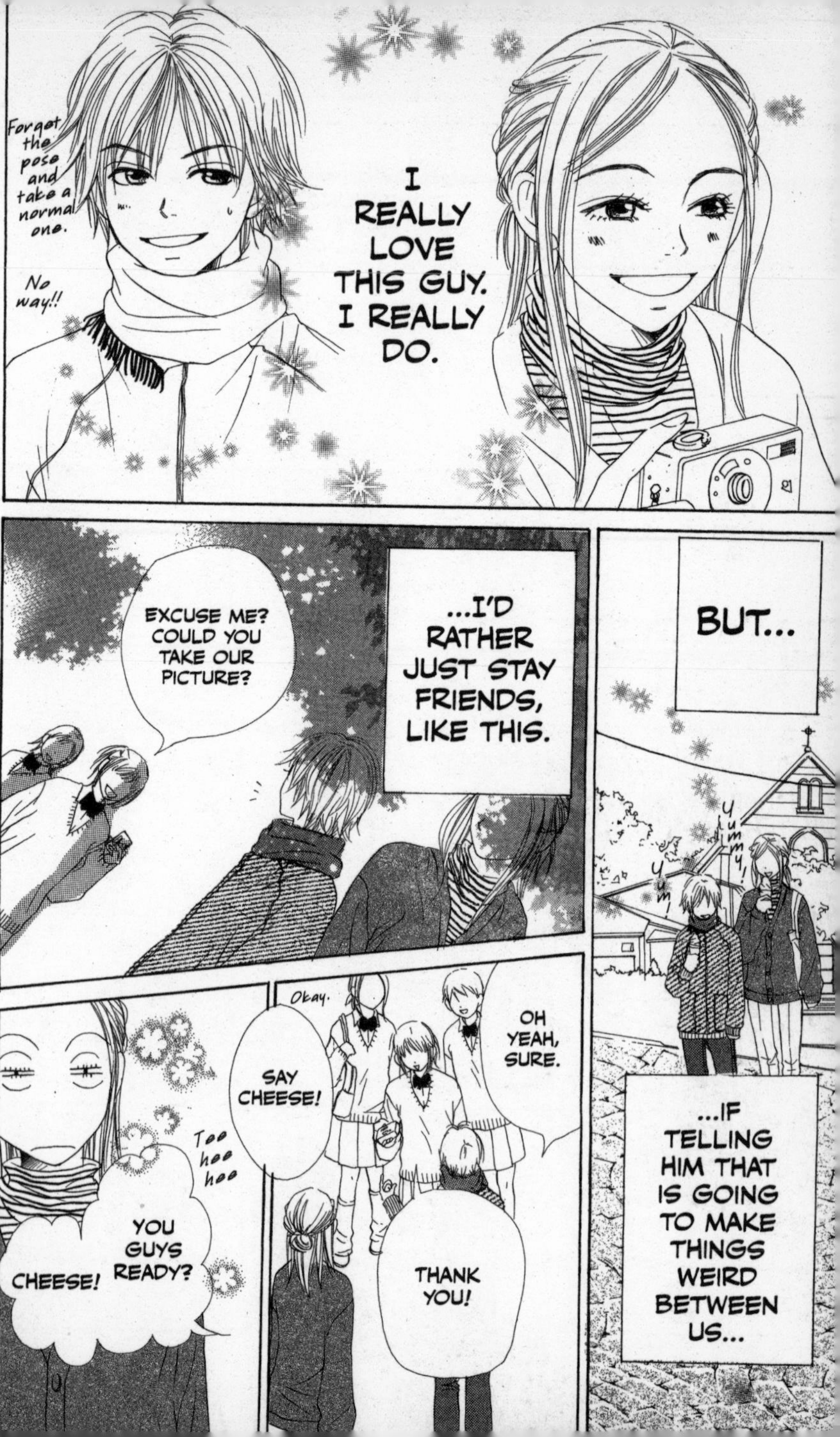
I REALLY LOVE THIS GUY. I REALLY DO.
Forget the pose and take a normal one.
No way!!
BUT...
Yummy!
Yum!
...IF TELLING HIM THAT IS GOING TO MAKE THINGS WEIRD BETWEEN US...
...I'D RATHER JUST STAY FRIENDS, LIKE THIS.
EXCUSE ME? COULD YOU TAKE OUR PICTURE?
OH YEAH, SURE.
Okay.
SAY CHEESE!
THANK YOU!
Tee hee hee
YOU GUYS READY?
CHEESE!

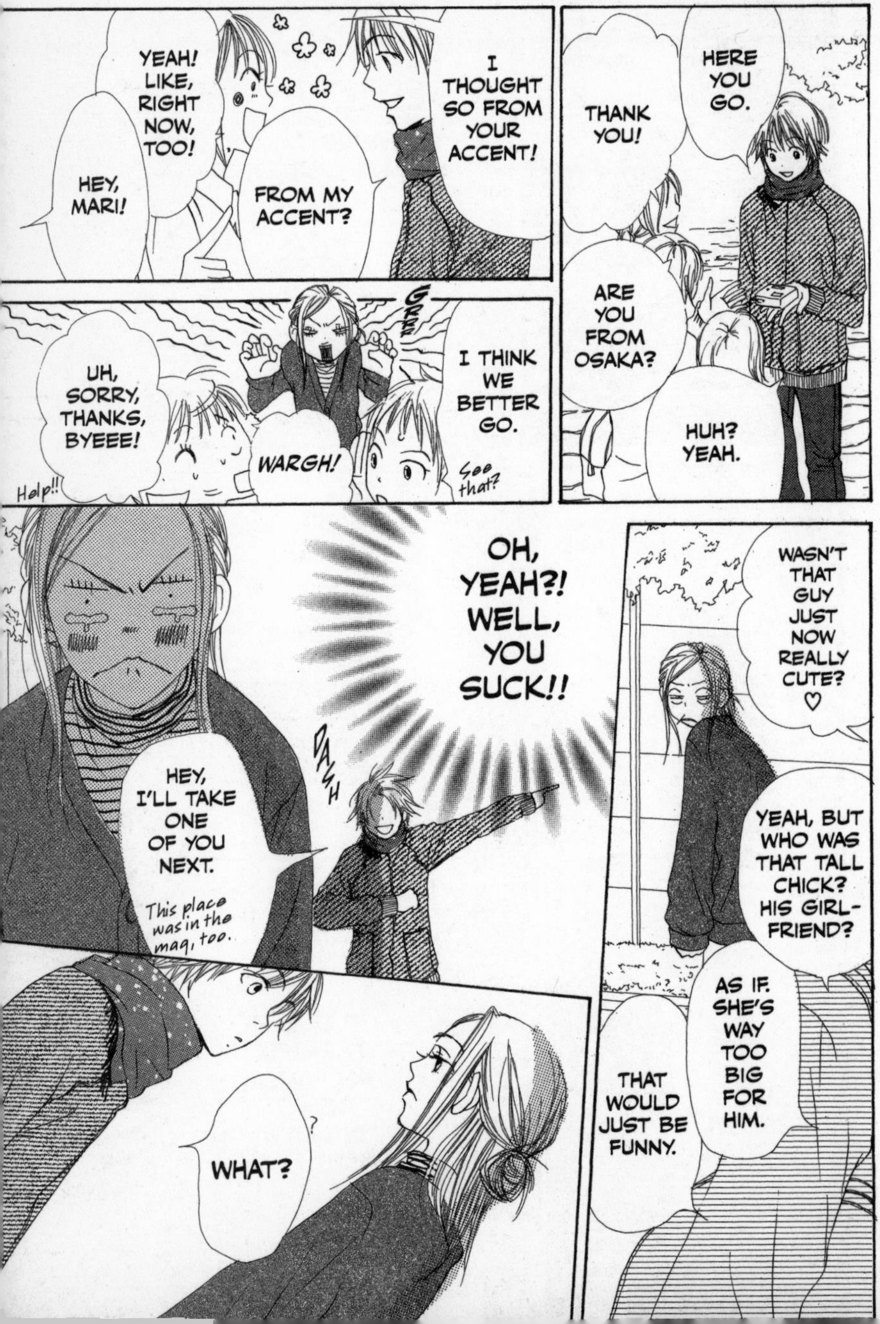
HERE YOU GO.
THANK YOU!
ARE YOU FROM OSAKA?
HUH? YEAH.
I THOUGHT SO FROM YOUR ACCENT!
FROM MY ACCENT?
YEAH! LIKE, RIGHT NOW, TOO!
HEY, MARI!
I THINK WE BETTER GO.
See that?
GRRR
WARGH!
UH, SORRY, THANKS, BYEEE!
Help!!
WASN'T THAT GUY JUST NOW REALLY CUTE? ♡
YEAH, BUT WHO WAS THAT TALL CHICK? HIS GIRL-FRIEND?
AS IF. SHE'S WAY TOO BIG FOR HIM.
THAT WOULD JUST BE FUNNY.
OH, YEAH?! WELL, YOU SUCK!!
DASH
HEY, I'LL TAKE ONE OF YOU NEXT.
This place was in the mag, too.
WHAT?

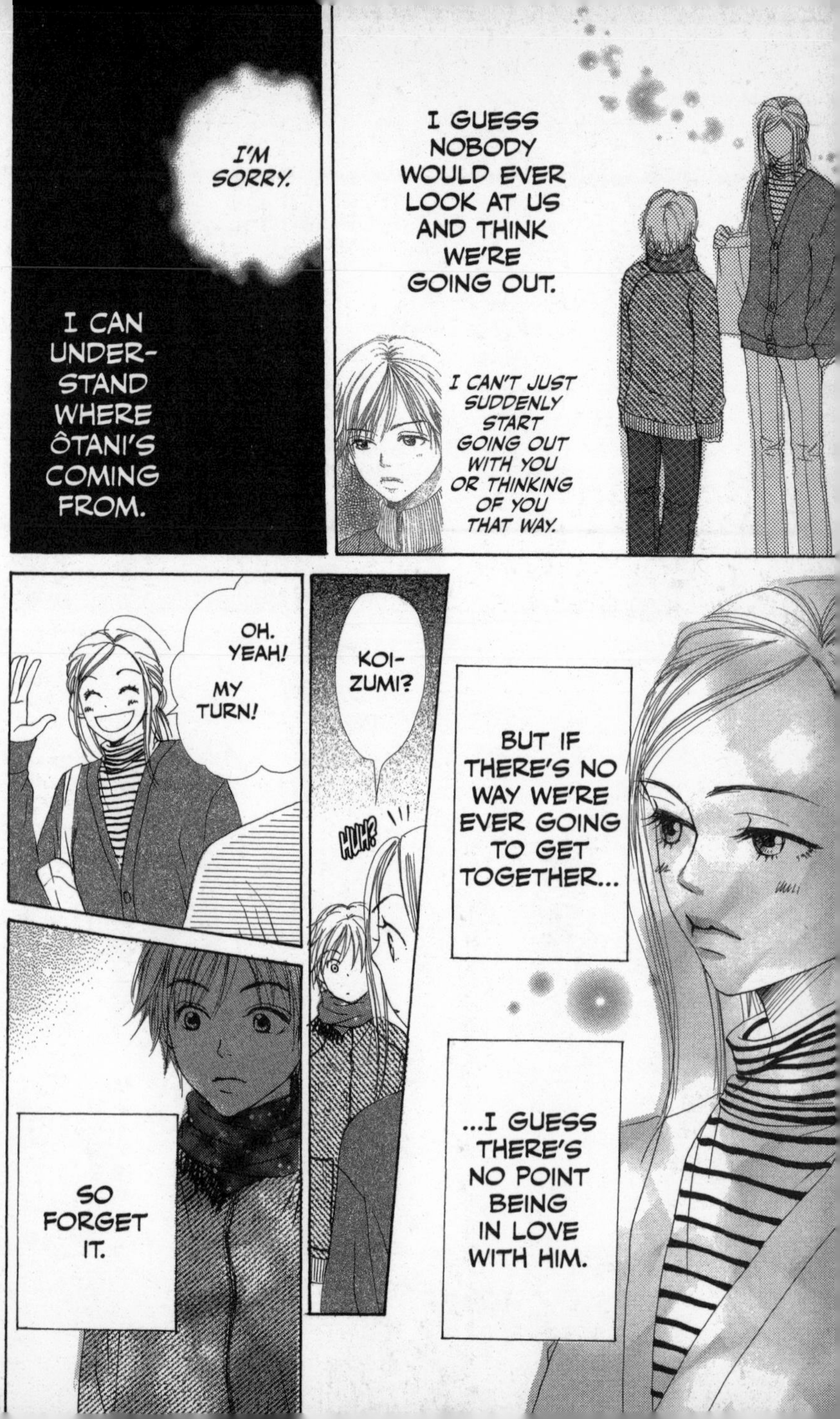
I GUESS NOBODY WOULD EVER LOOK AT US AND THINK WE'RE GOING OUT.
I CAN'T JUST SUDDENLY START GOING OUT WITH YOU OR THINKING OF YOU THAT WAY.
I'M SORRY.
I CAN UNDER-STAND WHERE ÔTANI'S COMING FROM.
BUT IF THERE'S NO WAY WE'RE EVER GOING TO GET TOGETHER...
...I GUESS THERE'S NO POINT BEING IN LOVE WITH HIM.
KOI-ZUMI?
HUH?
OH. YEAH!
MY TURN!
SO FORGET IT.

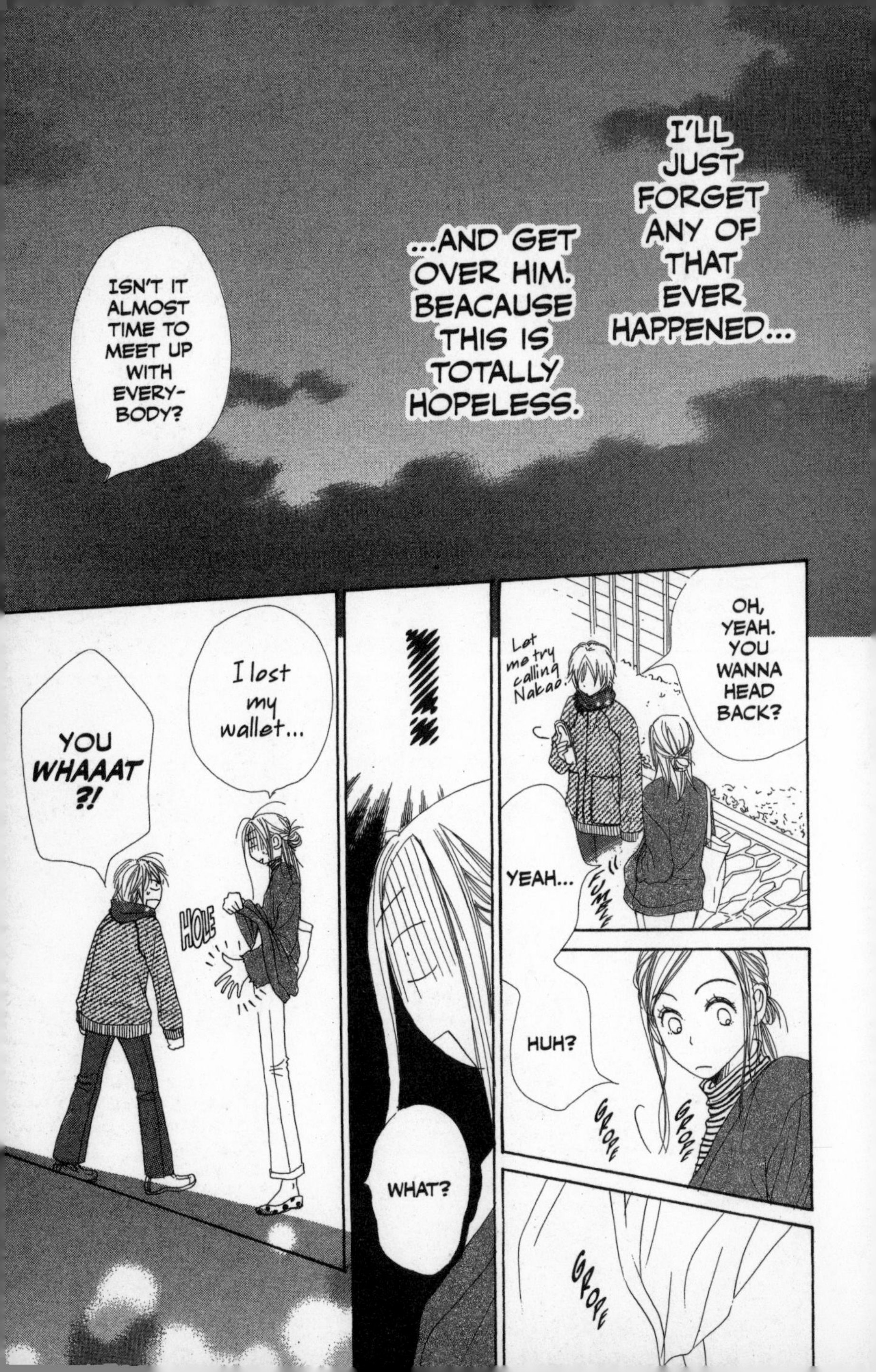
I'LL JUST FORGET ANY OF THAT EVER HAPPENED...
...AND GET OVER HIM. BEACAUSE THIS IS TOTALLY HOPELESS.
ISN'T IT ALMOST TIME TO MEET UP WITH EVERY-BODY?
OH, YEAH. YOU WANNA HEAD BACK?
Let me try calling Nakao.
YEAH...
HUH?
GROPE
GROPE
GROPE
!
WHAT?
I lost my wallet...
YOU WHAAAT?!
HOLE

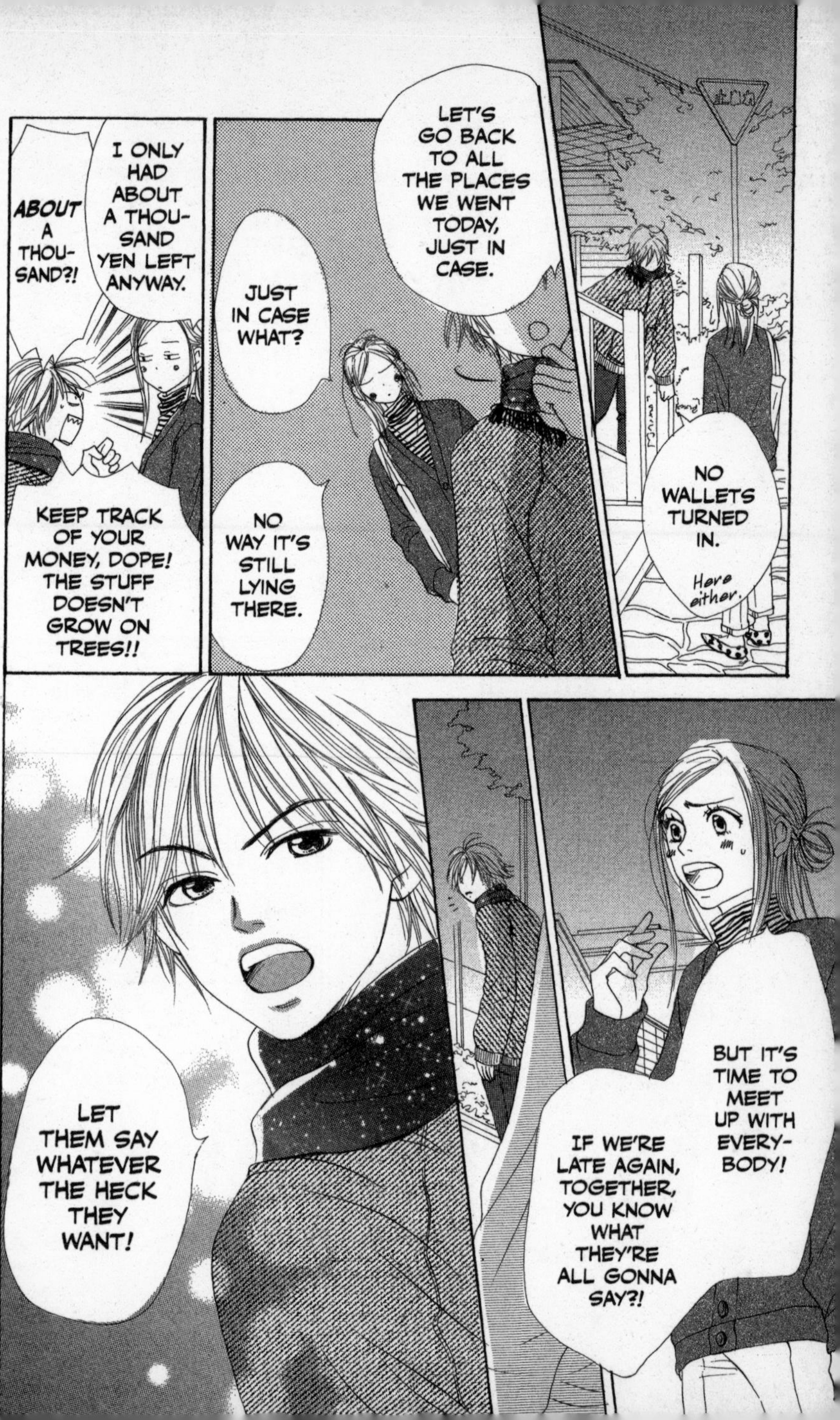
NO WALLETS TURNED IN.
Here either.
LET'S GO BACK TO ALL THE PLACES WE WENT TODAY, JUST IN CASE.
JUST IN CASE WHAT?
NO WAY IT'S STILL LYING THERE.
I ONLY HAD ABOUT A THOUSAND YEN LEFT ANYWAY.
ABOUT A THOUSAND?!
KEEP TRACK OF YOUR MONEY, DOPE! THE STUFF DOESN'T GROW ON TREES!!
BUT IT'S TIME TO MEET UP WITH EVERYBODY!
IF WE'RE LATE AGAIN, TOGETHER, YOU KNOW WHAT THEY'RE ALL GONNA SAY?!
LET THEM SAY WHATEVER THE HECK THEY WANT!

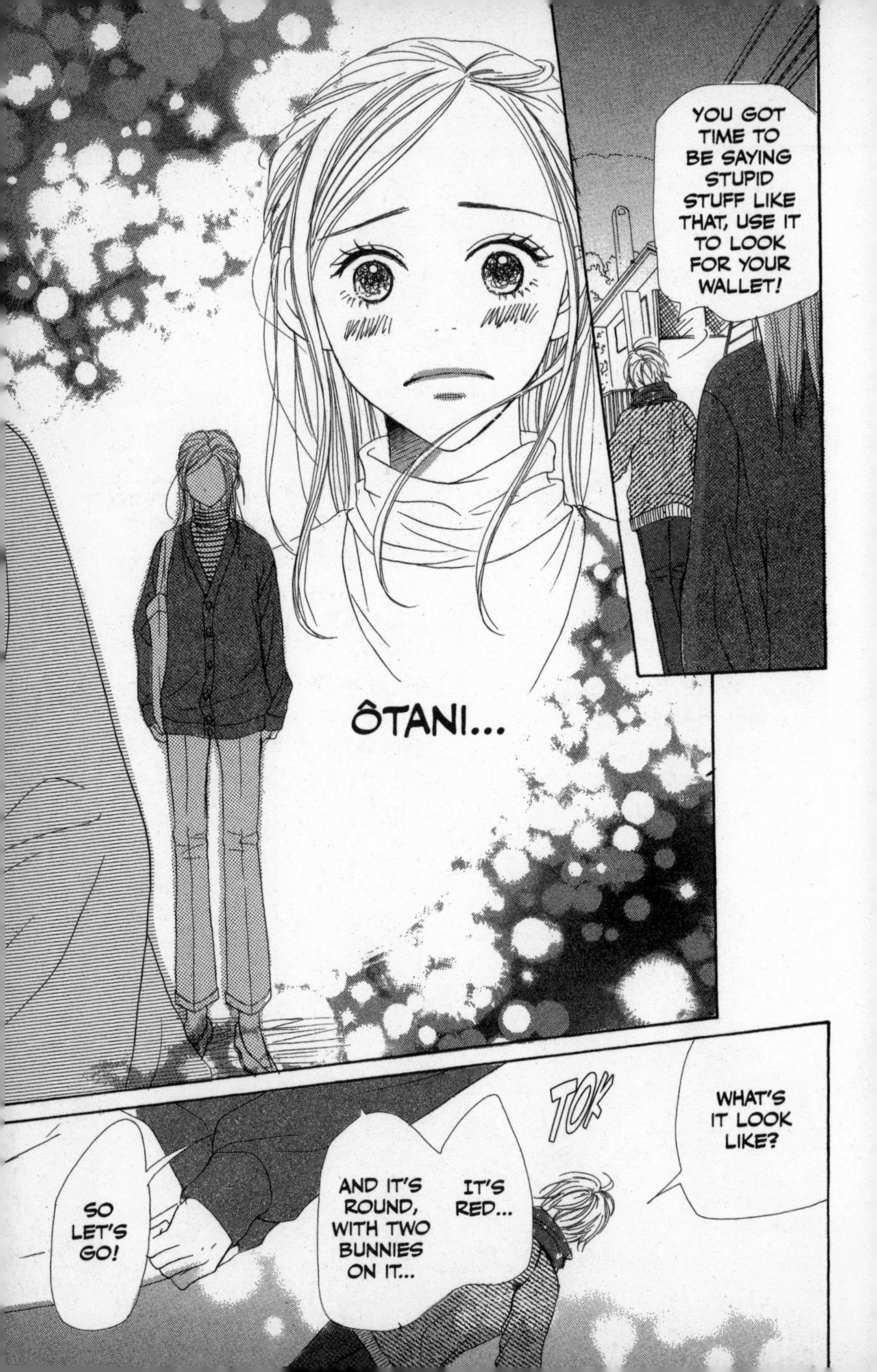
YOU GOT TIME TO BE SAYING STUPID STUFF LIKE THAT, USE IT TO LOOK FOR YOUR WALLET!
ÔTANI...
WHAT'S IT LOOK LIKE?
TOK
IT'S RED...
AND IT'S ROUND, WITH TWO BUNNIES ON IT...
SO LET'S GO!

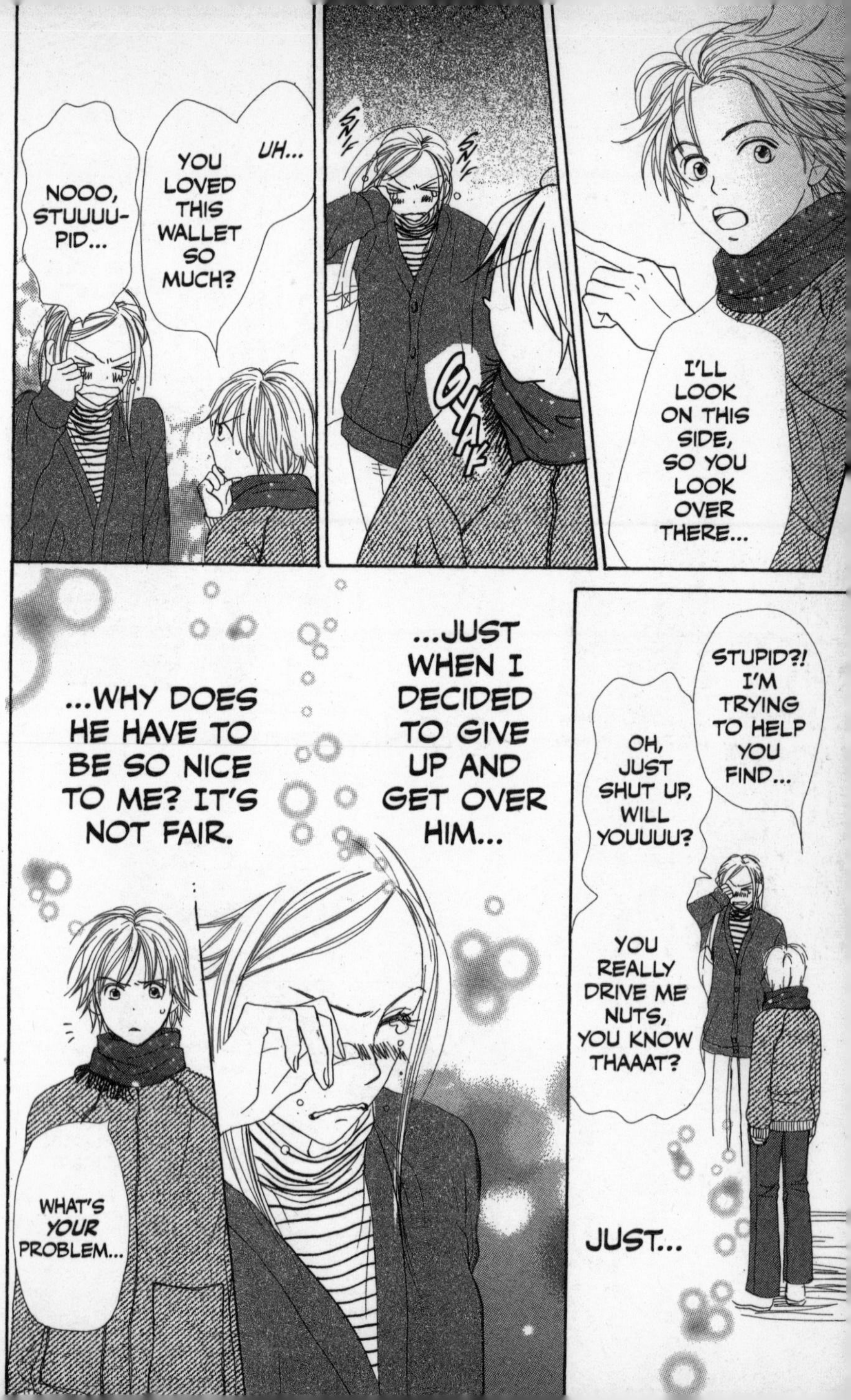
I'LL LOOK ON THIS SIDE, SO YOU LOOK OVER THERE...
SNIF
SNIF
UH...
YOU LOVED THIS WALLET SO MUCH?
NOOO, STUUUU-PID...
STUPID?! I'M TRYING TO HELP YOU FIND...
OH, JUST SHUT UP, WILL YOUUUU?
YOU REALLY DRIVE ME NUTS, YOU KNOW THAAAT?
JUST...
...JUST WHEN I DECIDED TO GIVE UP AND GET OVER HIM...
...WHY DOES HE HAVE TO BE SO NICE TO ME? IT'S NOT FAIR.
WHAT'S *YOUR* PROBLEM...

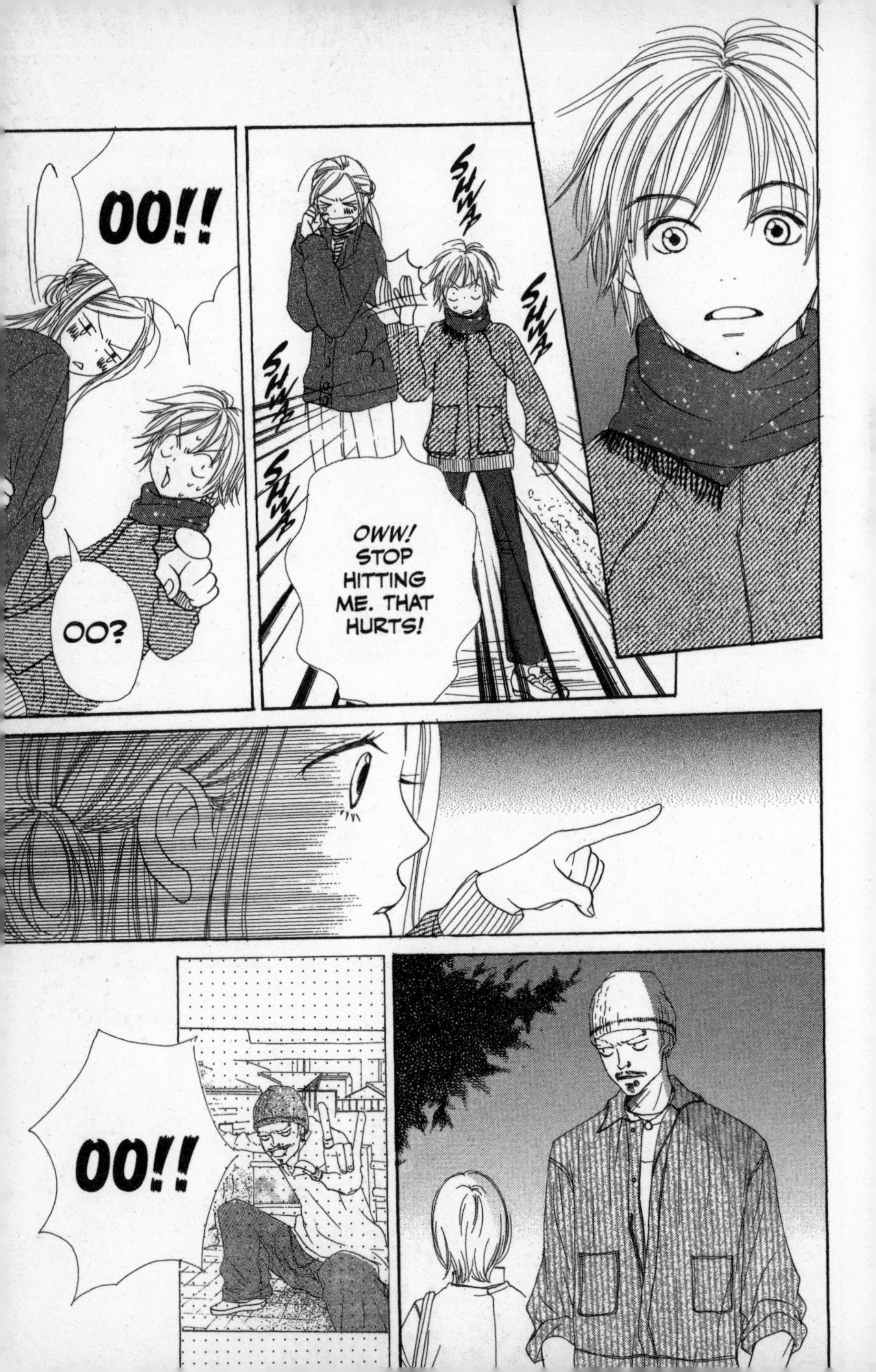
OWW! STOP HITTING ME. THAT HURTS!
OO!!
OO?
OO!!

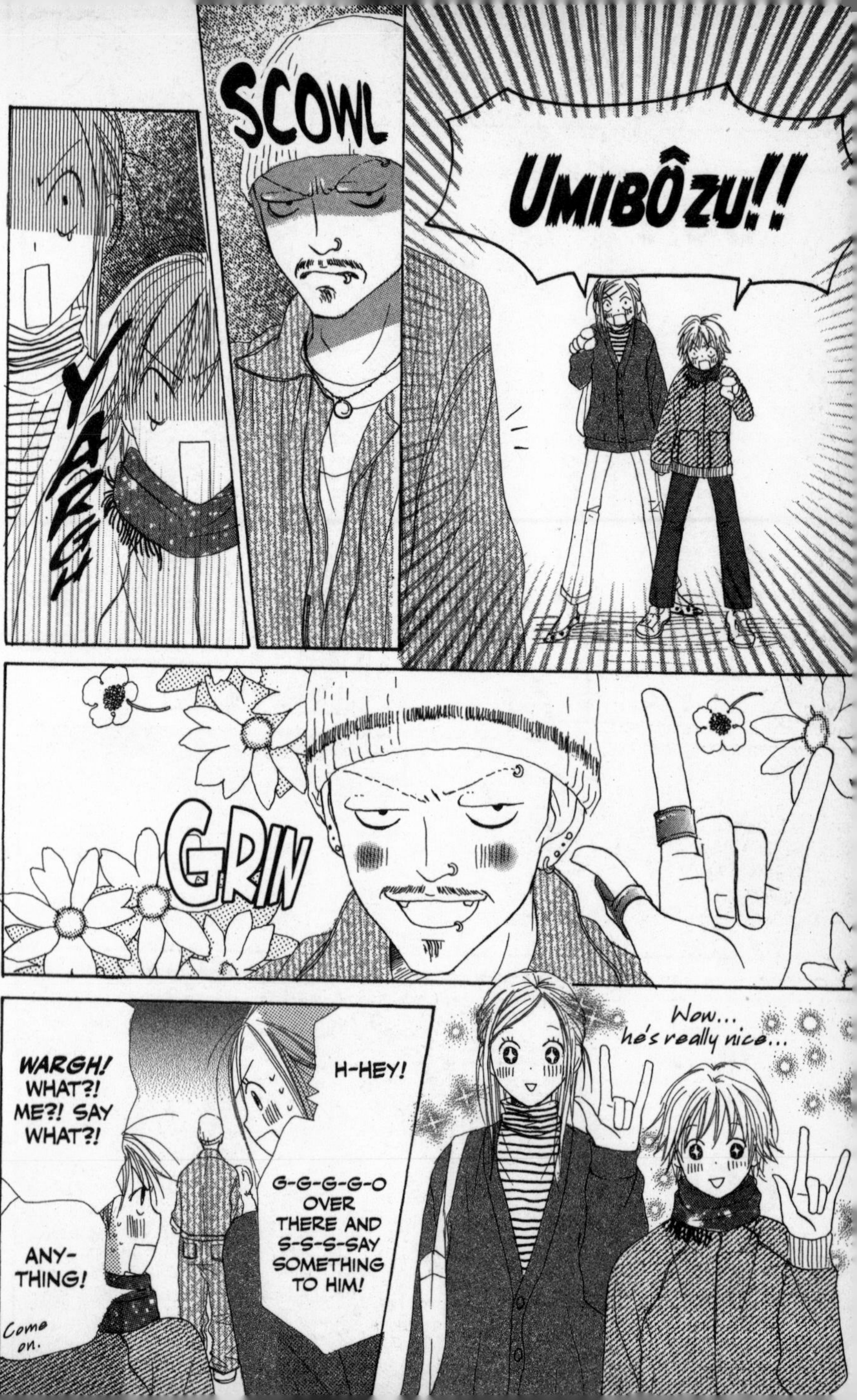
UMIBÔZU!!
SCOWL
YANK
GRIN
Wow... he's really nice...
H-HEY!
G-G-G-G-O OVER THERE AND S-S-S-SAY SOMETHING TO HIM!
WARGH! WHAT?! ME?! SAY WHAT?!
ANY-THING!
Come on.

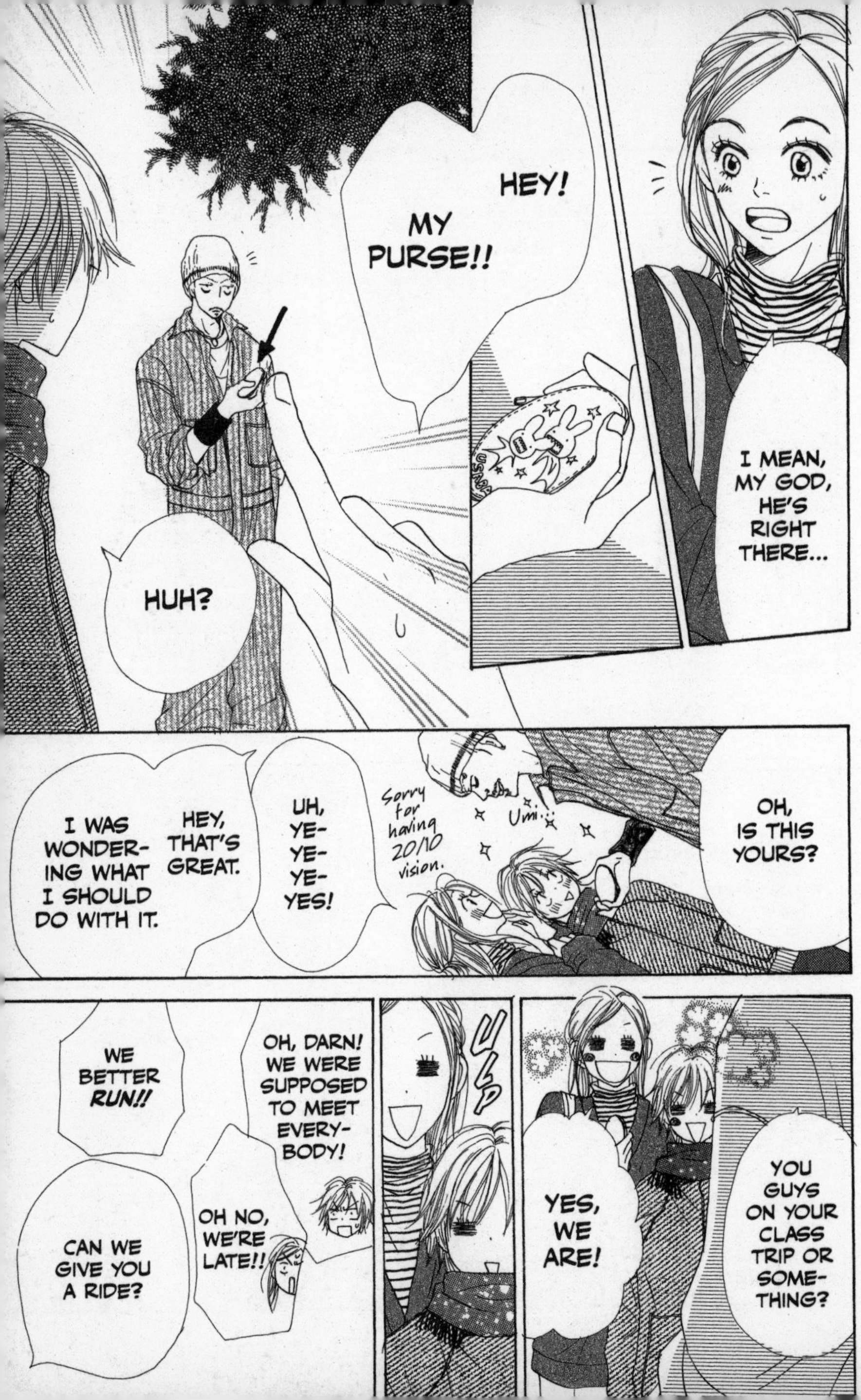
I MEAN, MY GOD, HE'S RIGHT THERE...
HEY! MY PURSE!!
HUH?
OH, IS THIS YOURS?
Umi...
Sorry for having 20/10 vision.
UH, YE-YE-YE-YES!
HEY, THAT'S GREAT.
I WAS WONDERING WHAT I SHOULD DO WITH IT.
YOU GUYS ON YOUR CLASS TRIP OR SOMETHING?
YES, WE ARE!
ULP
OH, DARN! WE WERE SUPPOSED TO MEET EVERYBODY!
WE BETTER *RUN!!*
OH NO, WE'RE LATE!!
CAN WE GIVE YOU A RIDE?

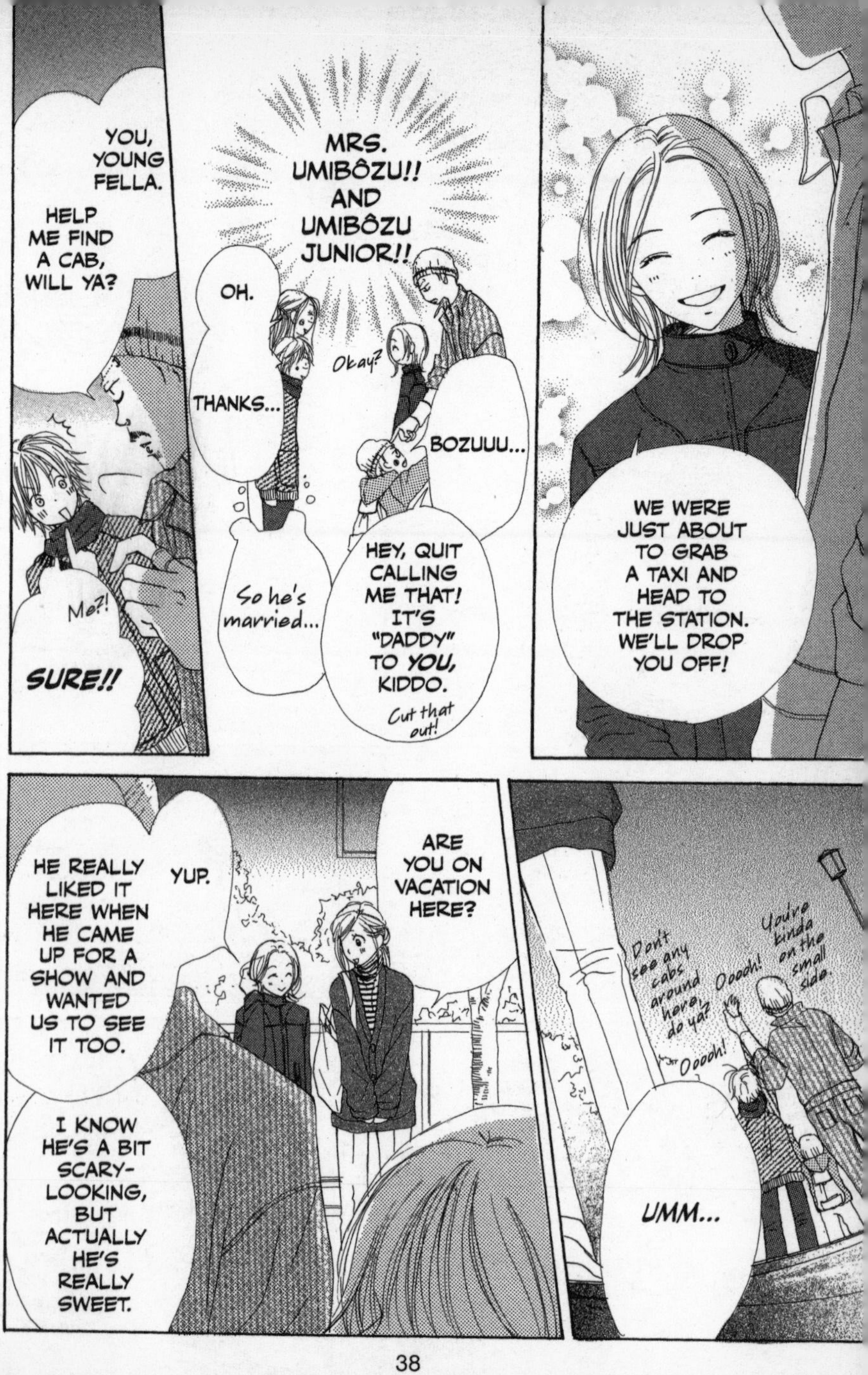
WE WERE JUST ABOUT TO GRAB A TAXI AND HEAD TO THE STATION. WE'LL DROP YOU OFF!
MRS. UMIBÔZU!! AND UMIBÔZU JUNIOR!!
BOZUUU...
Okay?
HEY, QUIT CALLING ME THAT! IT'S "DADDY" TO *YOU*, KIDDO.
Cut that out!
OH.
THANKS...
So he's married...
YOU, YOUNG FELLA.
HELP ME FIND A CAB, WILL YA?
Me?!
SURE!!
You're kinda on the small side.
Ooooh!
Don't see any cabs around here, do ya?
Ooooh!
UMM...
ARE YOU ON VACATION HERE?
YUP.
HE REALLY LIKED IT HERE WHEN HE CAME UP FOR A SHOW AND WANTED US TO SEE IT TOO.
I KNOW HE'S A BIT SCARY-LOOKING, BUT ACTUALLY HE'S REALLY SWEET.

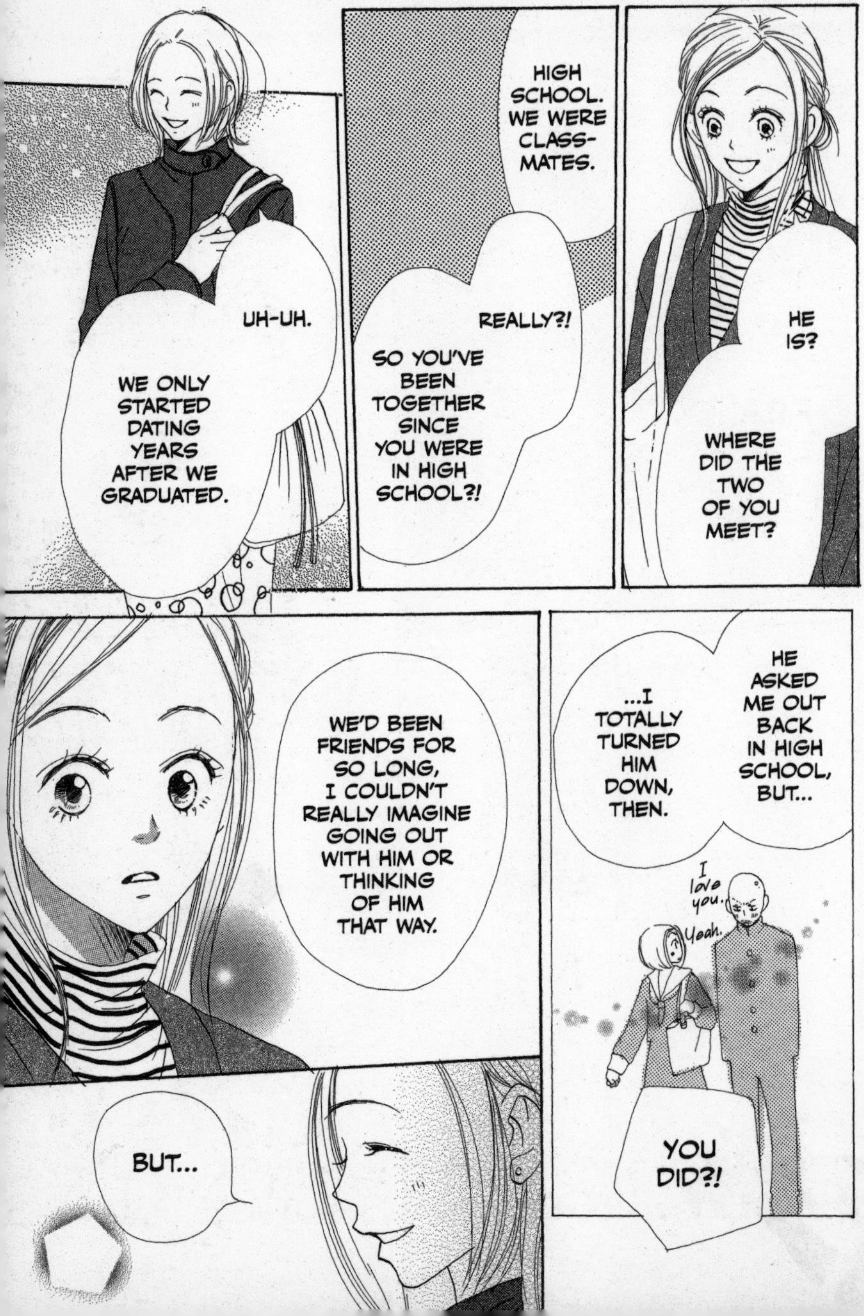
HE IS?
WHERE DID THE TWO OF YOU MEET?
HIGH SCHOOL. WE WERE CLASS-MATES.
REALLY?!
SO YOU'VE BEEN TOGETHER SINCE YOU WERE IN HIGH SCHOOL?!
UH-UH.
WE ONLY STARTED DATING YEARS AFTER WE GRADUATED.
HE ASKED ME OUT BACK IN HIGH SCHOOL, BUT...
...I TOTALLY TURNED HIM DOWN, THEN.
I love you.
Yeah.
YOU DID?!
WE'D BEEN FRIENDS FOR SO LONG, I COULDN'T REALLY IMAGINE GOING OUT WITH HIM OR THINKING OF HIM THAT WAY.
BUT...

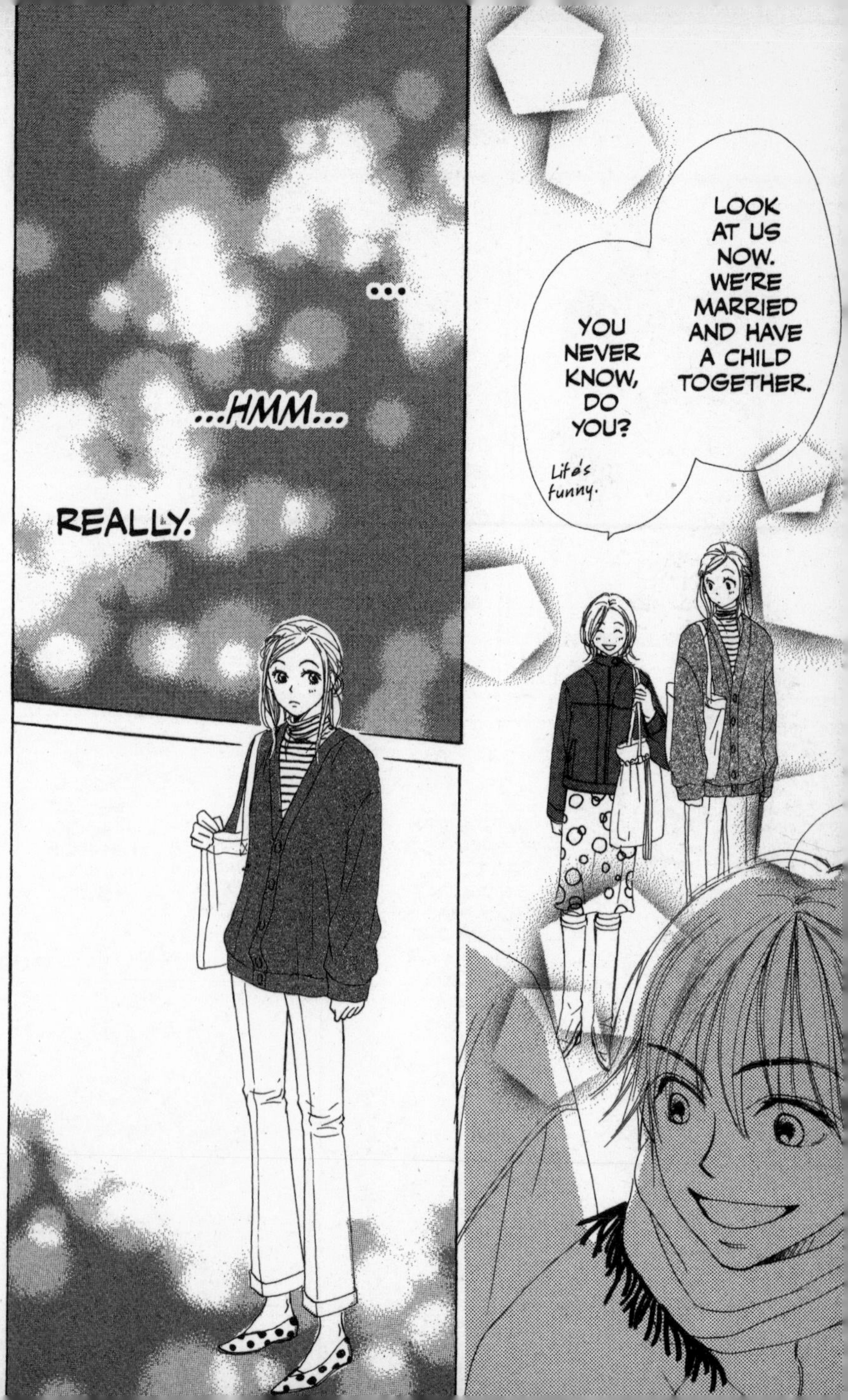
LOOK AT US NOW. WE'RE MARRIED AND HAVE A CHILD TOGETHER.
YOU NEVER KNOW, DO YOU?
Life's funny.
...
...HMM...
REALLY.

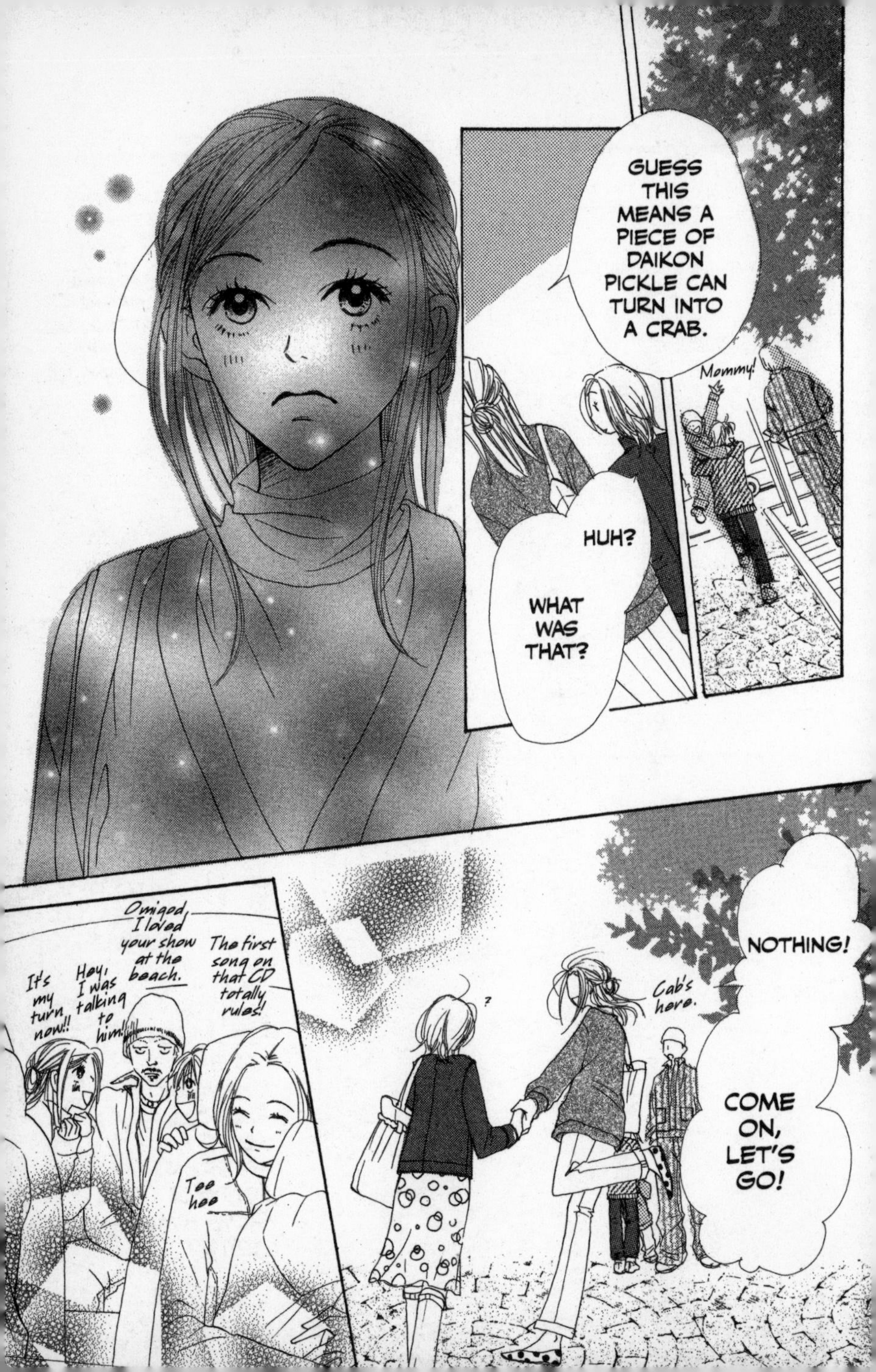
GUESS THIS MEANS A PIECE OF DAIKON PICKLE CAN TURN INTO A CRAB.
Mommy!
HUH?
WHAT WAS THAT?
NOTHING!
Cab's here.
COME ON, LET'S GO!
The first song on that CD totally rules!
Omigod, I loved your show at the beach.
Hey, I was talking to him!!
It's my turn now!!
Tee hee

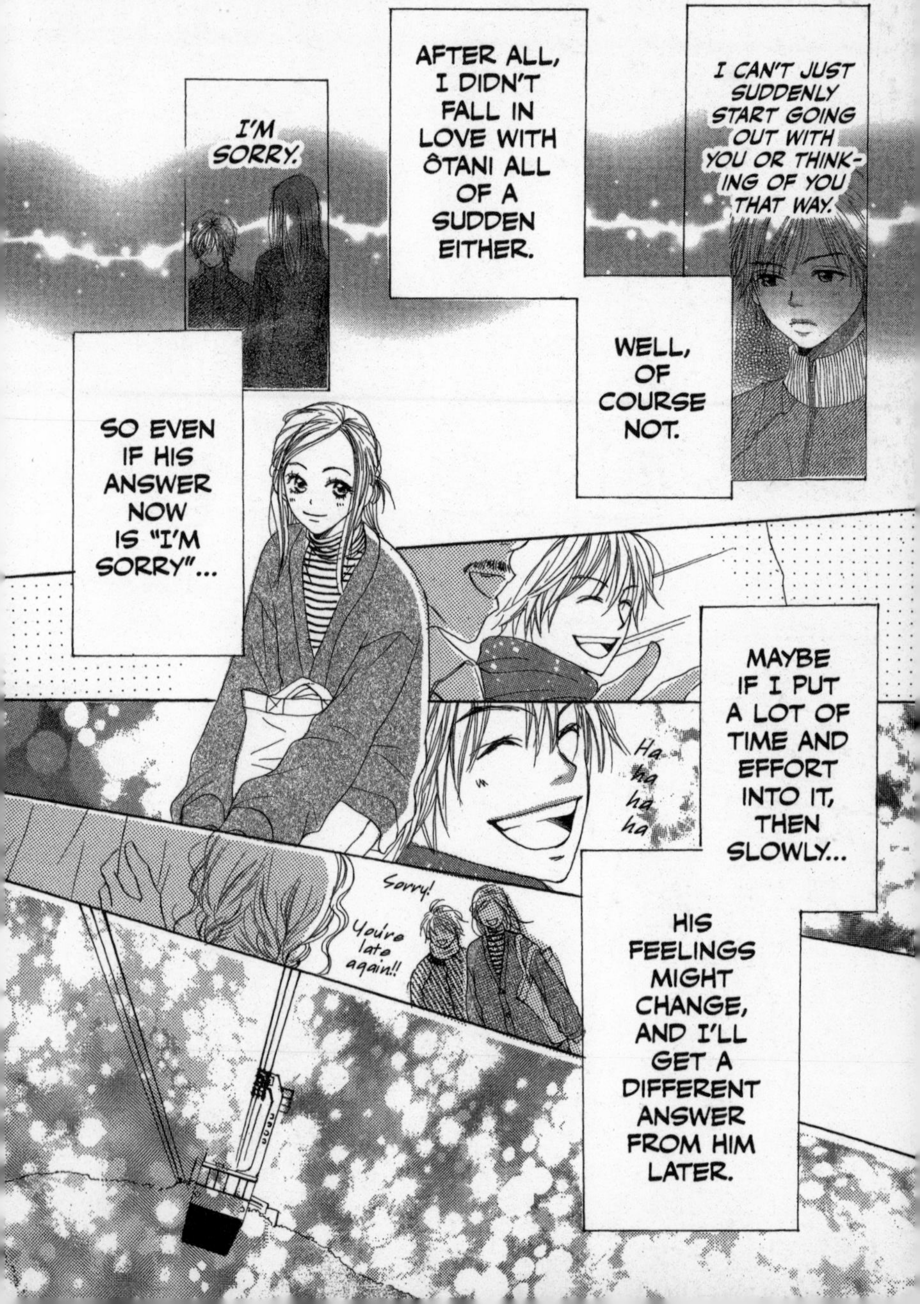
I CAN'T JUST SUDDENLY START GOING OUT WITH YOU OR THINKING OF YOU THAT WAY.
WELL, OF COURSE NOT.
AFTER ALL, I DIDN'T FALL IN LOVE WITH ÔTANI ALL OF A SUDDEN EITHER.
I'M SORRY.
SO EVEN IF HIS ANSWER NOW IS "I'M SORRY"...
MAYBE IF I PUT A LOT OF TIME AND EFFORT INTO IT, THEN SLOWLY...
Ha ha ha ha
HIS FEELINGS MIGHT CHANGE, AND I'LL GET A DIFFERENT ANSWER FROM HIM LATER.
Sorry!
You're late again!!

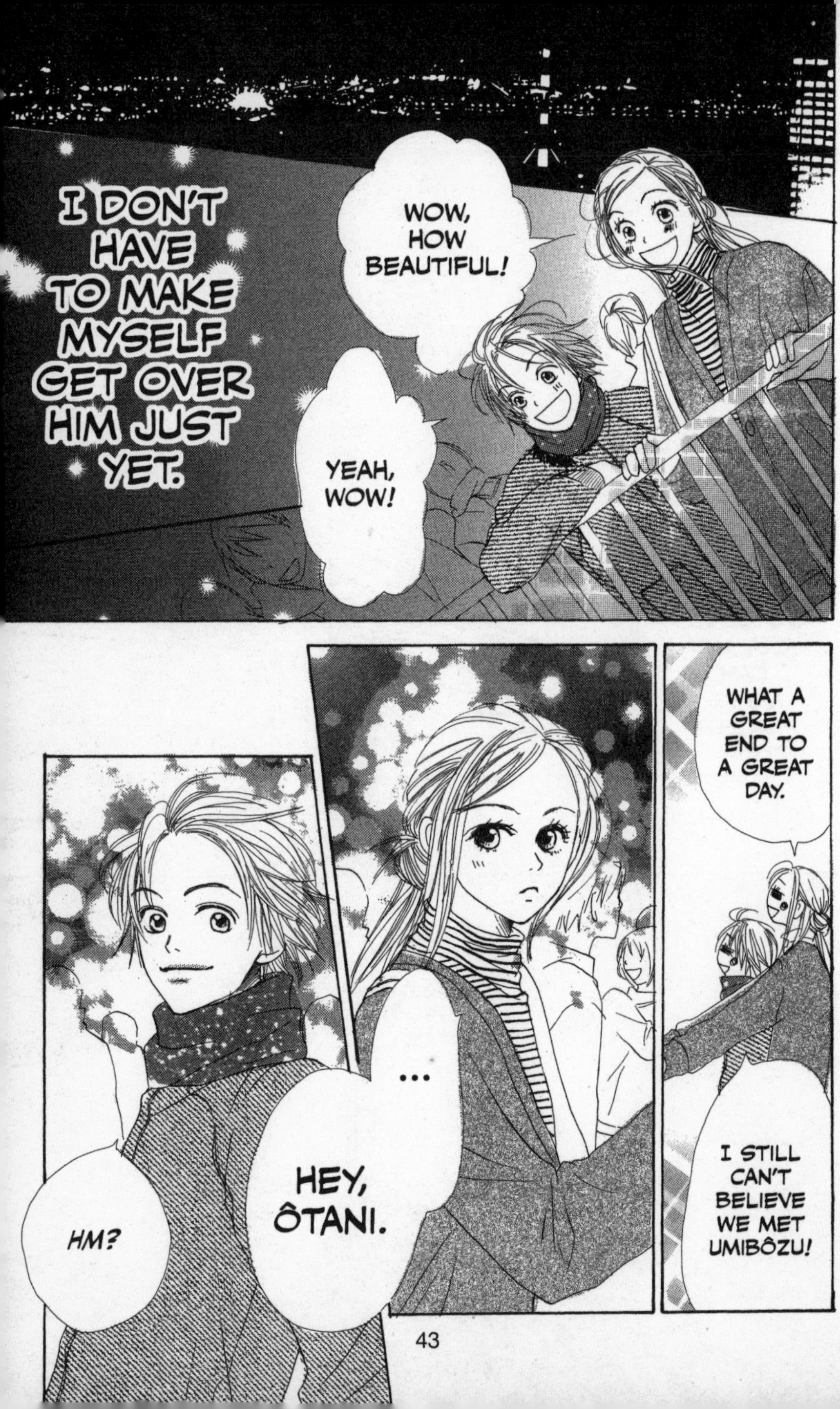
WOW, HOW BEAUTIFUL!
YEAH, WOW!
I DON'T HAVE TO MAKE MYSELF GET OVER HIM JUST YET.
WHAT A GREAT END TO A GREAT DAY.
I STILL CAN'T BELIEVE WE MET UMIBÔZU!
...
HEY, ÔTANI.
HM?

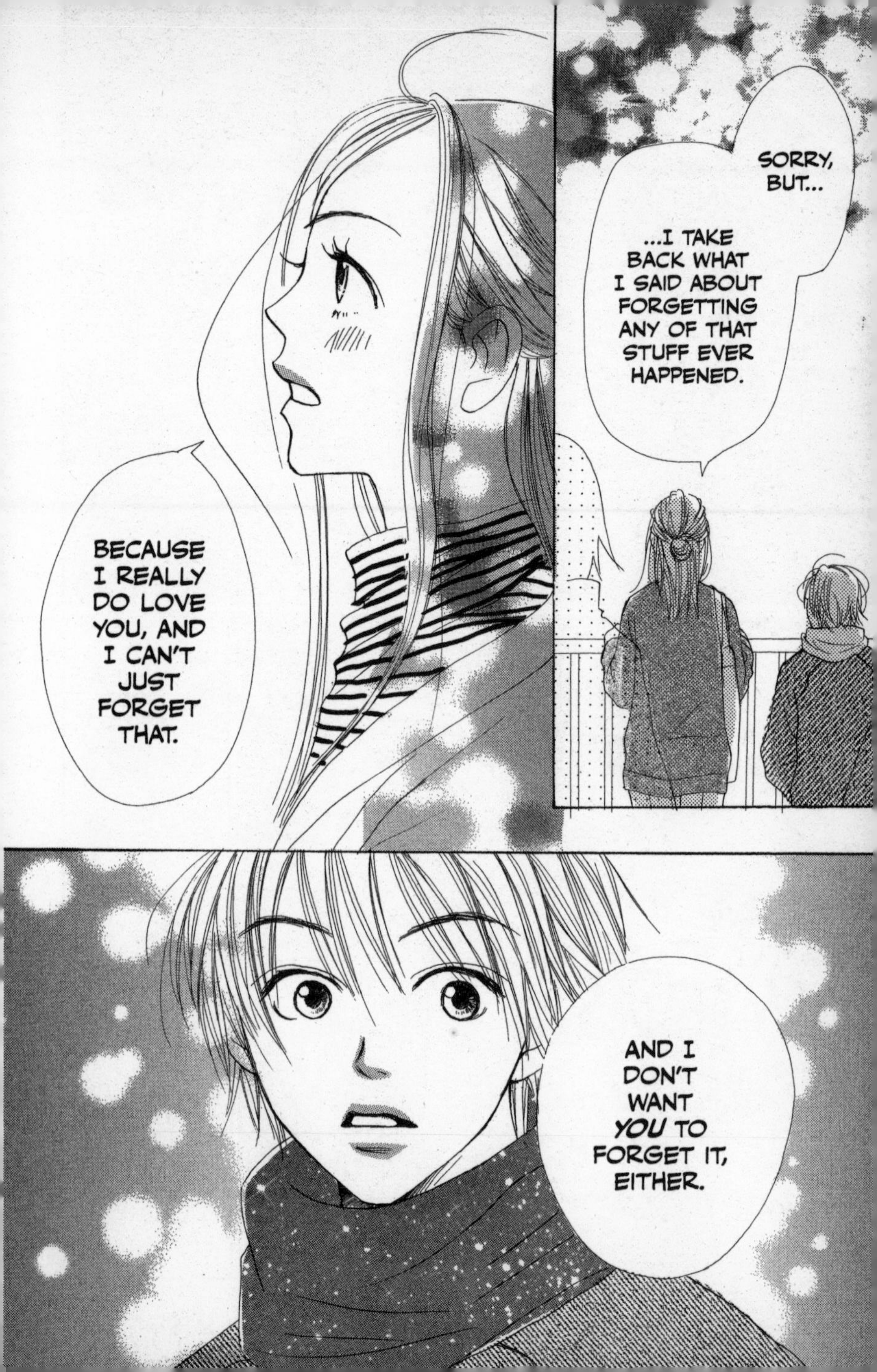
SORRY, BUT...
...I TAKE BACK WHAT I SAID ABOUT FORGETTING ANY OF THAT STUFF EVER HAPPENED.
BECAUSE I REALLY DO LOVE YOU, AND I CAN'T JUST FORGET THAT.
AND I DON'T WANT *YOU* TO FORGET IT, EITHER.

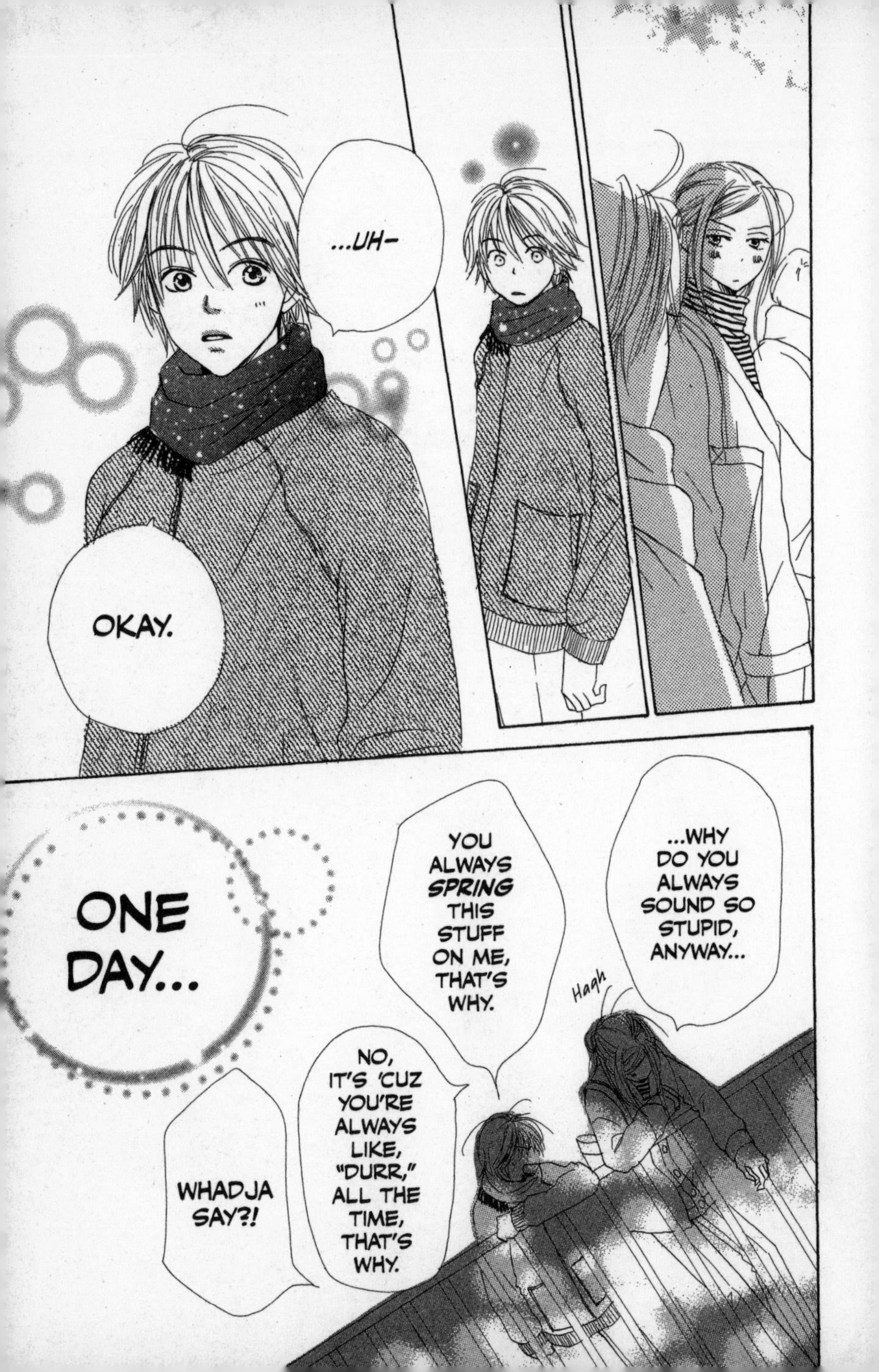
...UH-
OKAY.
ONE DAY...
...WHY DO YOU ALWAYS SOUND SO STUPID, ANYWAY...
Haqh
YOU ALWAYS *SPRING* THIS STUFF ON ME, THAT'S WHY.
NO, IT'S 'CUZ YOU'RE ALWAYS LIKE, "DURR," ALL THE TIME, THAT'S WHY.
WHADJA SAY?!

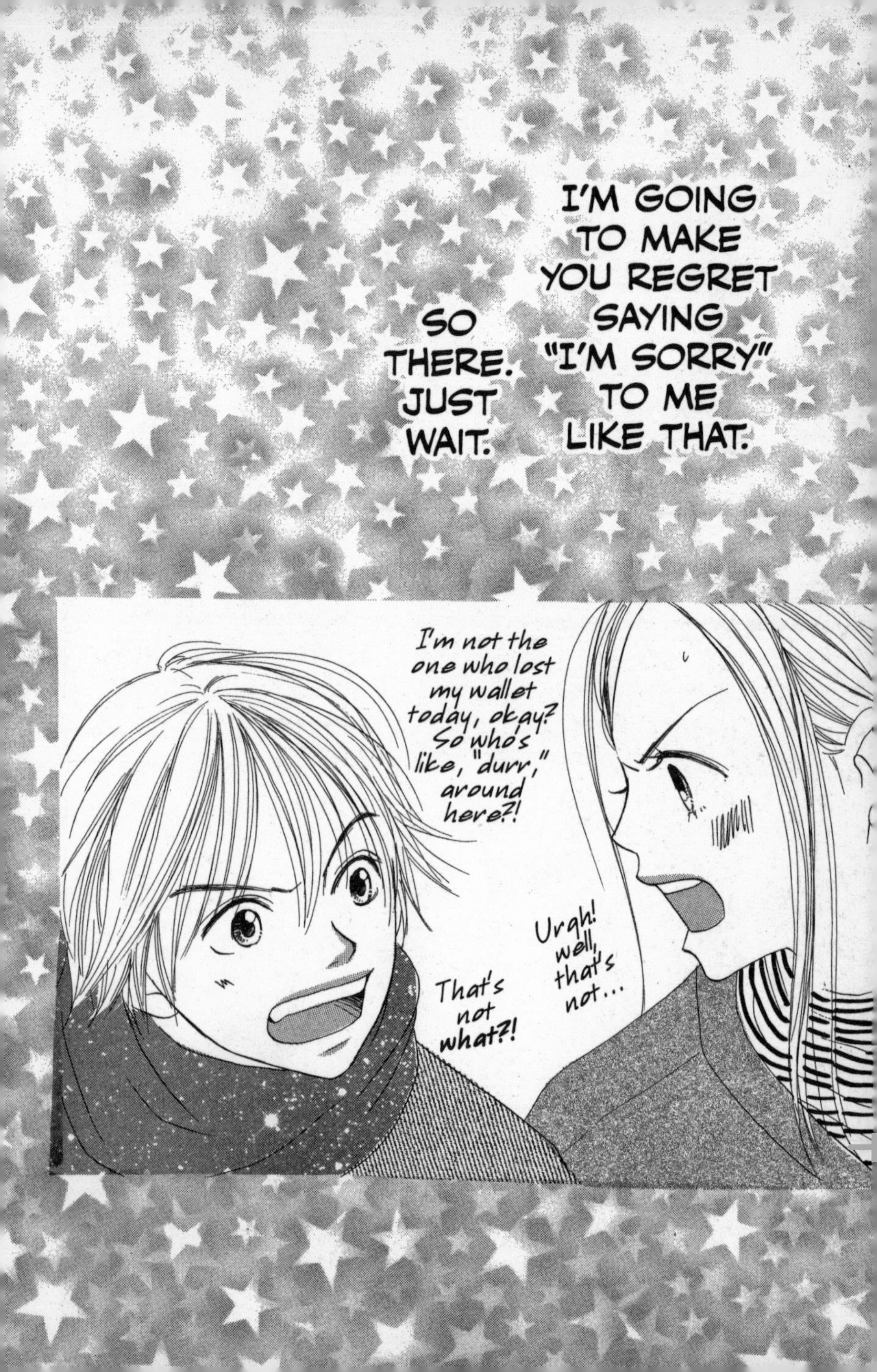
I'M GOING TO MAKE YOU REGRET SAYING "I'M SORRY" TO ME LIKE THAT.
SO THERE. JUST WAIT.
I'm not the one who lost my wallet today, okay? So who's like, "durr," around here?!
Urgh! well, that's not...
That's not what?!

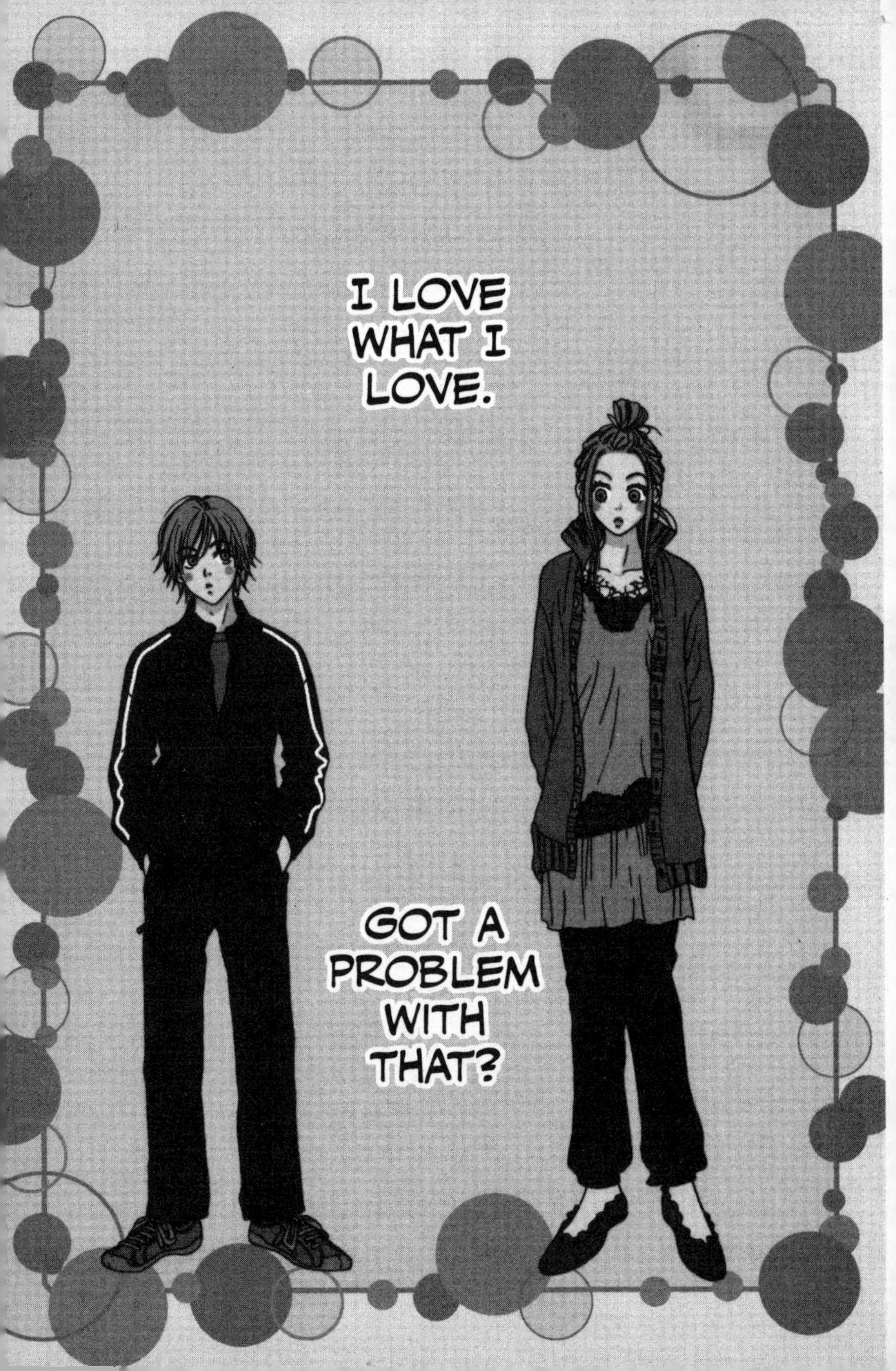
I LOVE WHAT I LOVE.
GOT A PROBLEM WITH THAT?

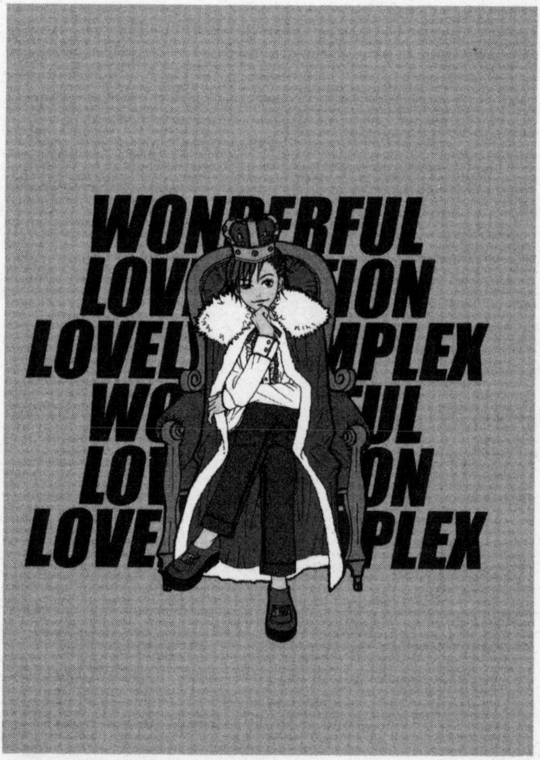
WONDERFUL
LOV ION
LOVEL MPLEX
WO UL
LO ON
LOVE PLEX

CHAPTER 18

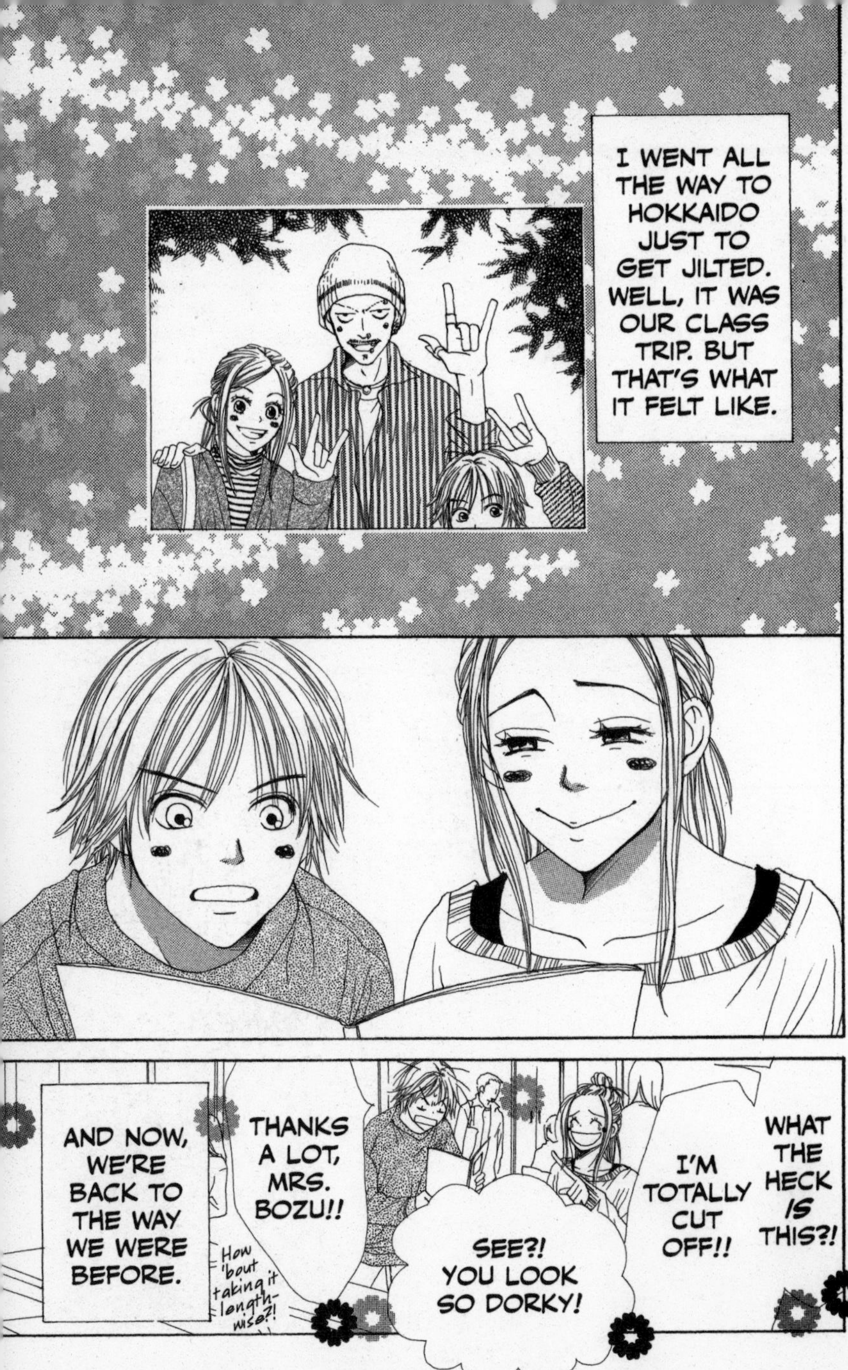
I WENT ALL THE WAY TO HOKKAIDO JUST TO GET JILTED. WELL, IT WAS OUR CLASS TRIP. BUT THAT'S WHAT IT FELT LIKE.
WHAT THE HECK *IS* THIS?!
I'M TOTALLY CUT OFF!!
SEE?! YOU LOOK SO DORKY!
THANKS A LOT, MRS. BOZU!!
How 'bout taking it length-wise?!
AND NOW, WE'RE BACK TO THE WAY WE WERE BEFORE.

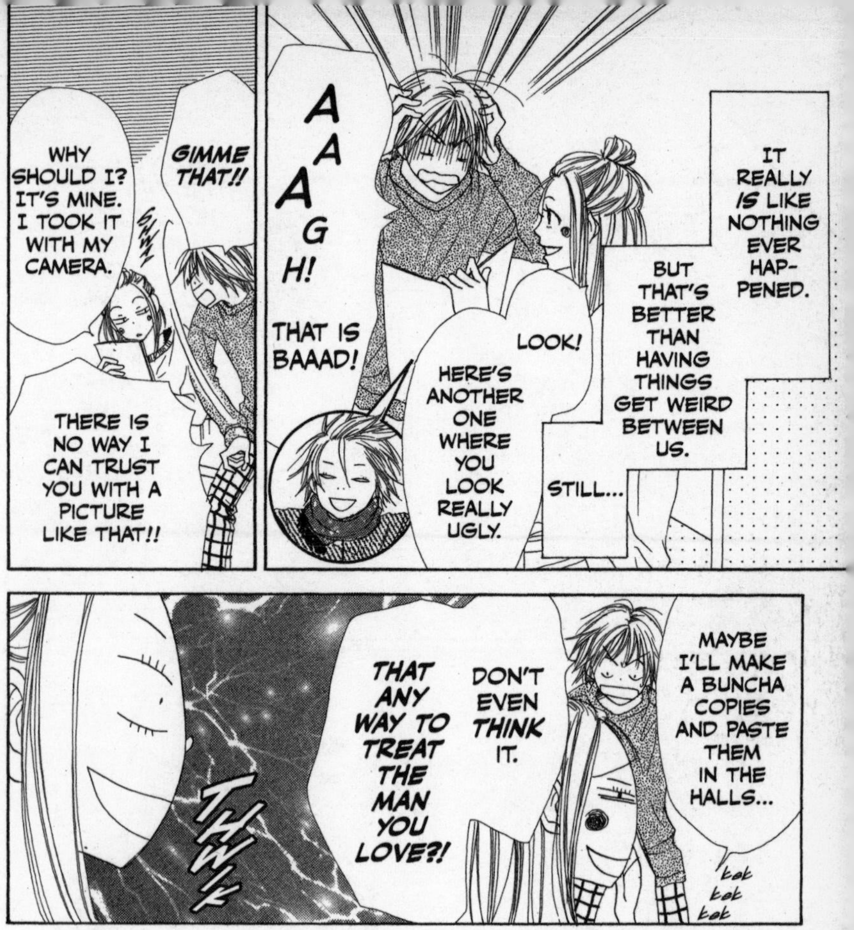
IT REALLY *IS* LIKE NOTHING EVER HAPPENED.
BUT THAT'S BETTER THAN HAVING THINGS GET WEIRD BETWEEN US.
STILL...
LOOK!
HERE'S ANOTHER ONE WHERE YOU LOOK REALLY UGLY.
AAAGH!
THAT IS BAAAD!
GIMME THAT!!
WHY SHOULD I? IT'S MINE. I TOOK IT WITH MY CAMERA.
THERE IS NO WAY I CAN TRUST YOU WITH A PICTURE LIKE THAT!!
MAYBE I'LL MAKE A BUNCHA COPIES AND PASTE THEM IN THE HALLS...
kak kak kak
DON'T EVEN *THINK* IT.
THAT ANY WAY TO TREAT THE MAN YOU LOVE?!
THWIK

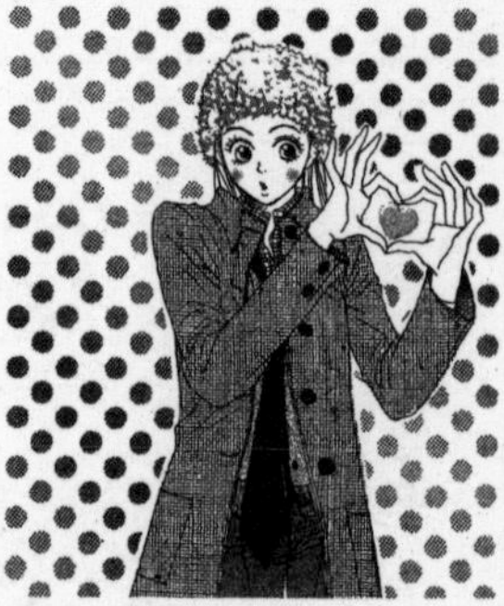

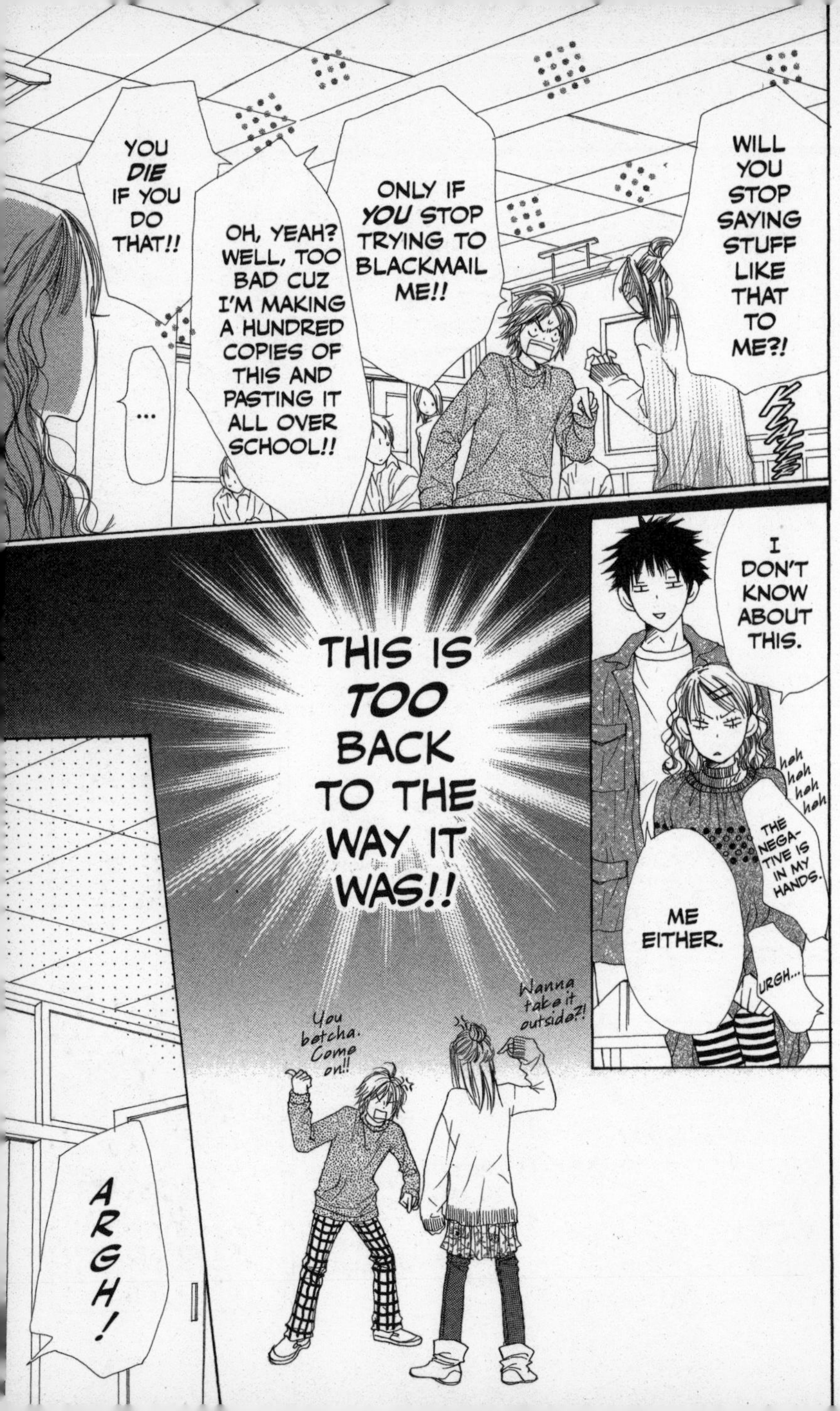
WILL YOU STOP SAYING STUFF LIKE THAT TO ME?!
ONLY IF *YOU* STOP TRYING TO BLACKMAIL ME!!
OH, YEAH? WELL, TOO BAD CUZ I'M MAKING A HUNDRED COPIES OF THIS AND PASTING IT ALL OVER SCHOOL!!
YOU *DIE* IF YOU DO THAT!!
...
I DON'T KNOW ABOUT THIS.
heh heh heh heh
THE NEGATIVE IS IN MY HANDS.
ME EITHER.
URGH...
THIS IS *TOO* BACK TO THE WAY IT WAS!!
Wanna take it outside?!
You betcha. Come on!!
ARGH!

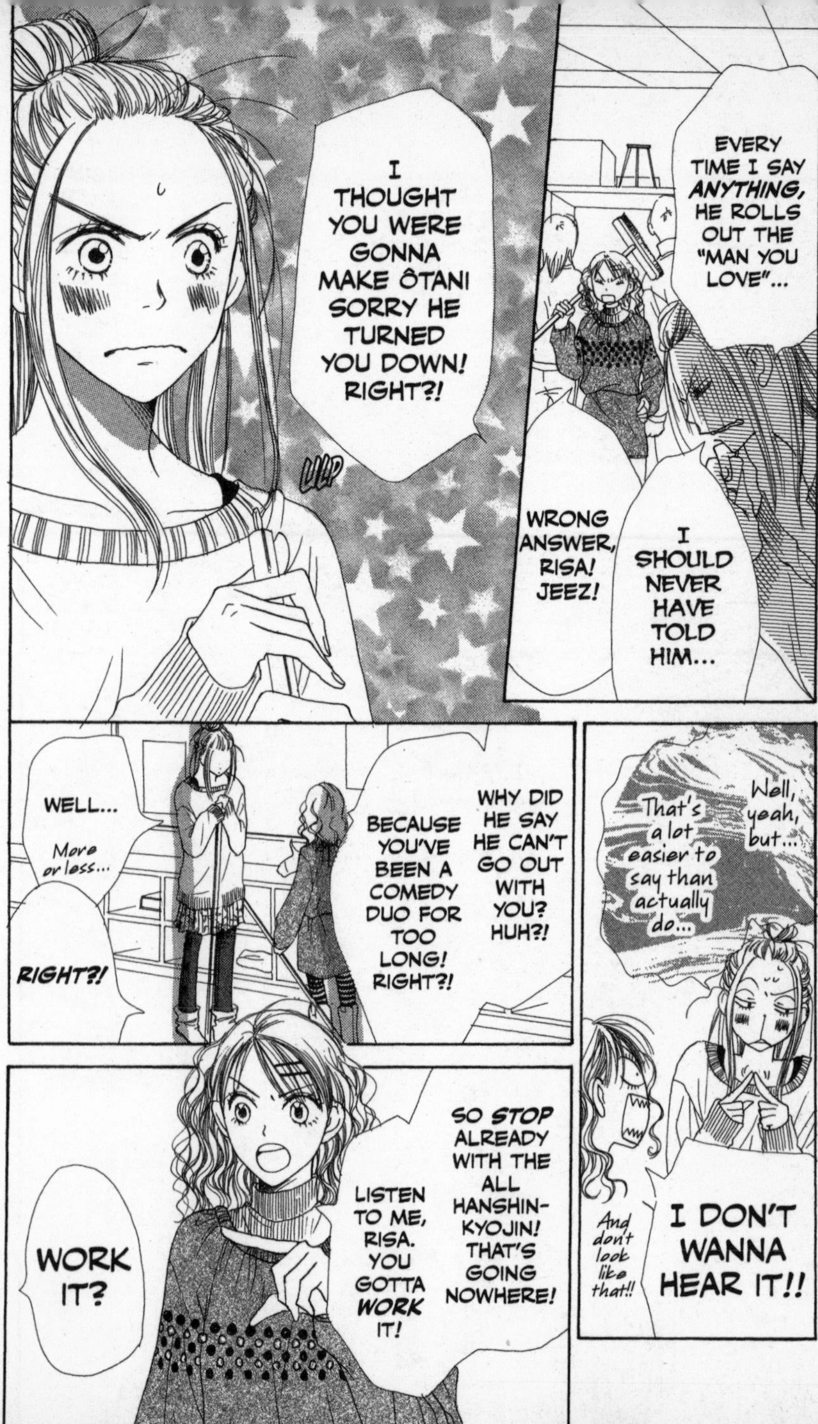
EVERY TIME I SAY *ANYTHING,* HE ROLLS OUT THE "MAN YOU LOVE"...
I SHOULD NEVER HAVE TOLD HIM...
WRONG ANSWER, RISA! JEEZ!
I THOUGHT YOU WERE GONNA MAKE ÔTANI SORRY HE TURNED YOU DOWN! RIGHT?!
ULP
Well, yeah, but...
That's a lot easier to say than actually do...
I DON'T WANNA HEAR IT!!
And don't look like that!!
WHY DID HE SAY HE CAN'T GO OUT WITH YOU? HUH?!
BECAUSE YOU'VE BEEN A COMEDY DUO FOR TOO LONG! RIGHT?!
WELL...
More or less...
RIGHT?!
SO *STOP* ALREADY WITH THE ALL HANSHIN-KYOJIN! THAT'S GOING NOWHERE!
LISTEN TO ME, RISA. YOU GOTTA *WORK* IT!
WORK IT?

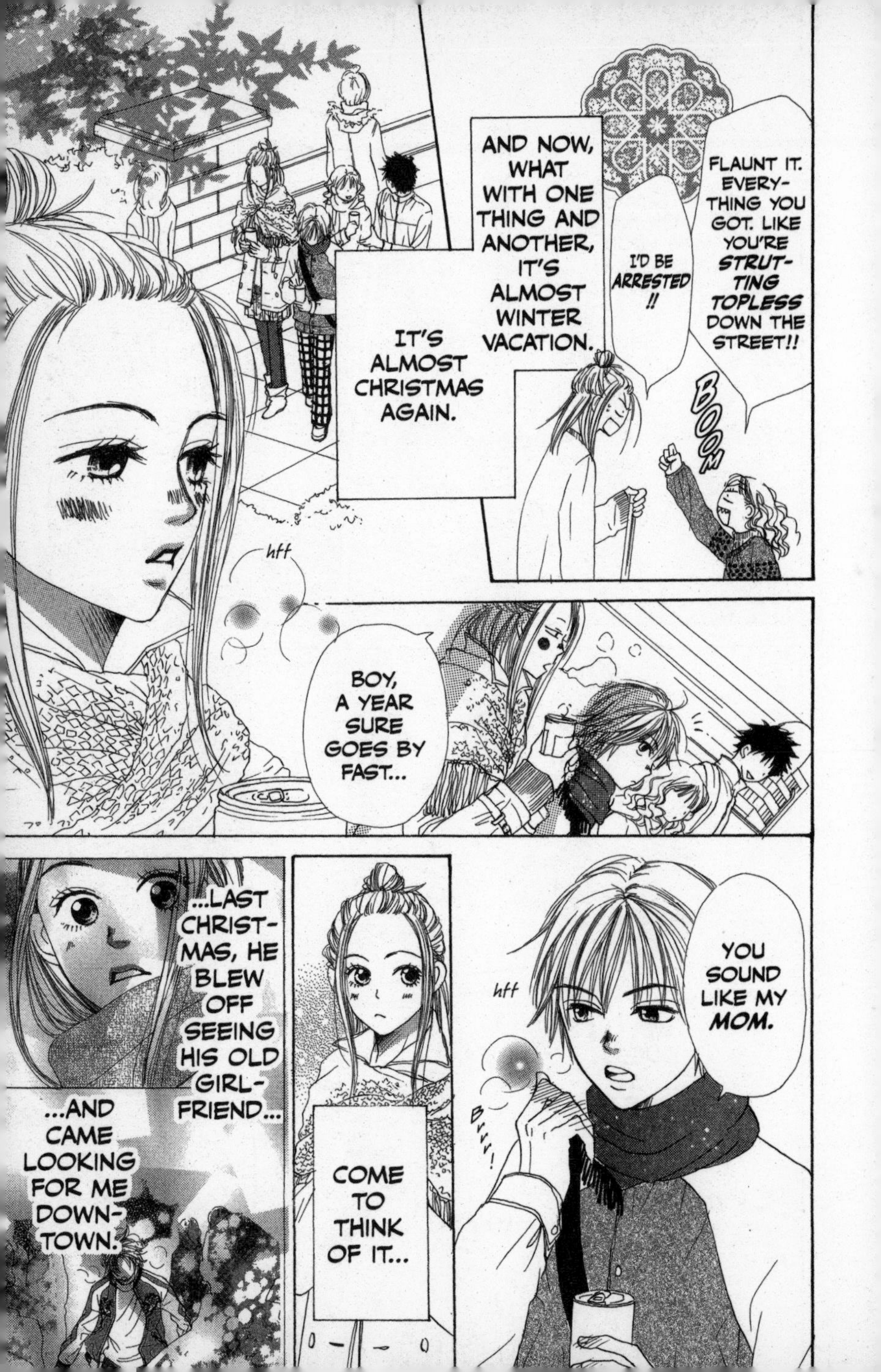

AND NOW, WHAT WITH ONE THING AND ANOTHER, IT'S ALMOST WINTER VACATION.
FLAUNT IT. EVERYTHING YOU GOT. LIKE YOU'RE STRUTTING TOPLESS DOWN THE STREET!!
BOOM
I'D BE ARRESTED!!
IT'S ALMOST CHRISTMAS AGAIN.
BOY, A YEAR SURE GOES BY FAST...
hff
YOU SOUND LIKE MY MOM.
hff
Bvvv!
COME TO THINK OF IT...
...LAST CHRISTMAS, HE BLEW OFF SEEING HIS OLD GIRLFRIEND...
...AND CAME LOOKING FOR ME DOWNTOWN.

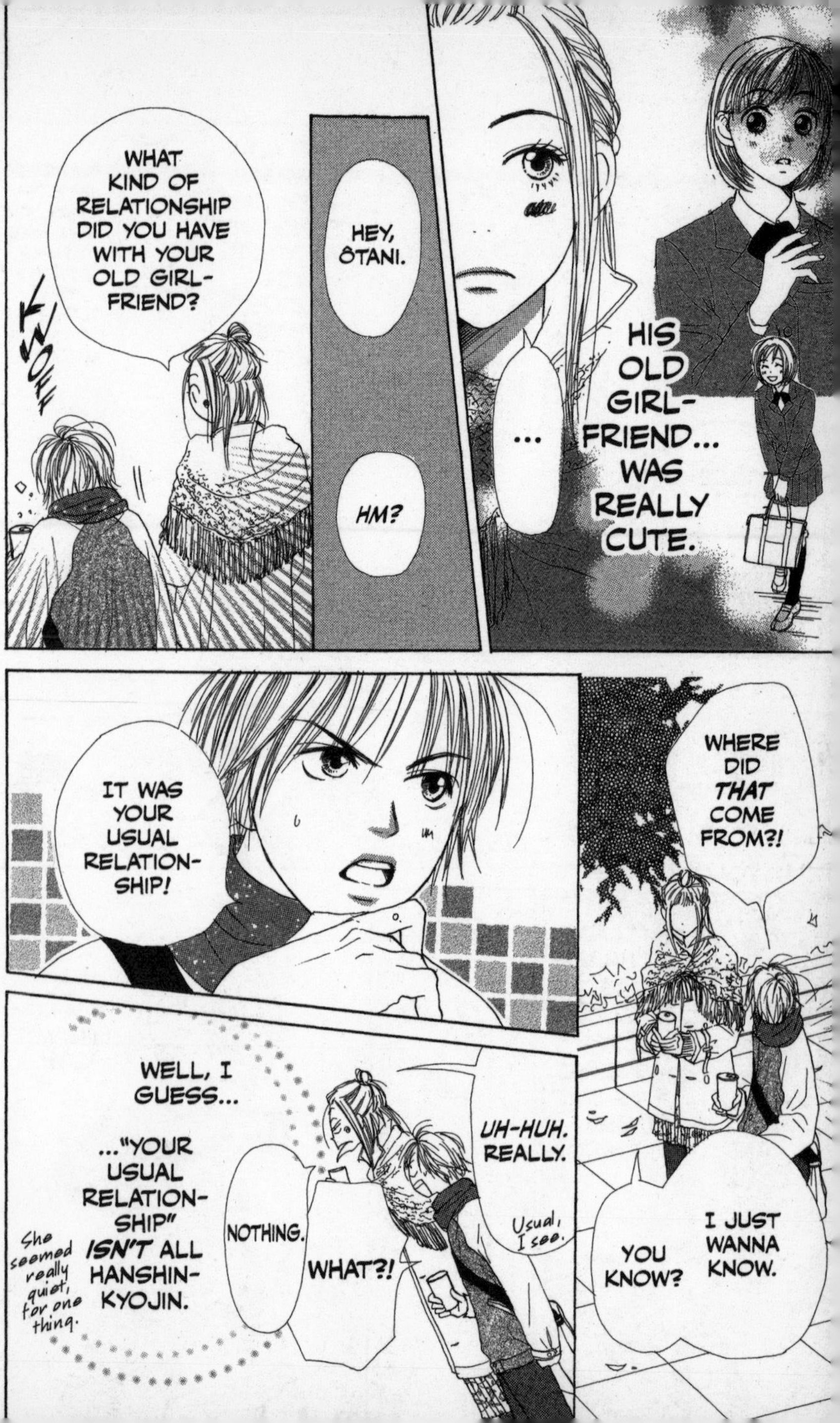
HIS OLD GIRL-FRIEND... WAS REALLY CUTE.
...
HEY, ŌTANI.
HM?
WHAT KIND OF RELATIONSHIP DID YOU HAVE WITH YOUR OLD GIRL-FRIEND?
KWOFF
WHERE DID *THAT* COME FROM?!
I JUST WANNA KNOW.
YOU KNOW?
IT WAS YOUR USUAL RELATION-SHIP!
UH-HUH. REALLY.
Usual, I see.
NOTHING.
WHAT?!
WELL, I GUESS...
..."YOUR USUAL RELATION-SHIP" *ISN'T* ALL HANSHIN-KYOJIN.
She seemed really quiet, for one thing.

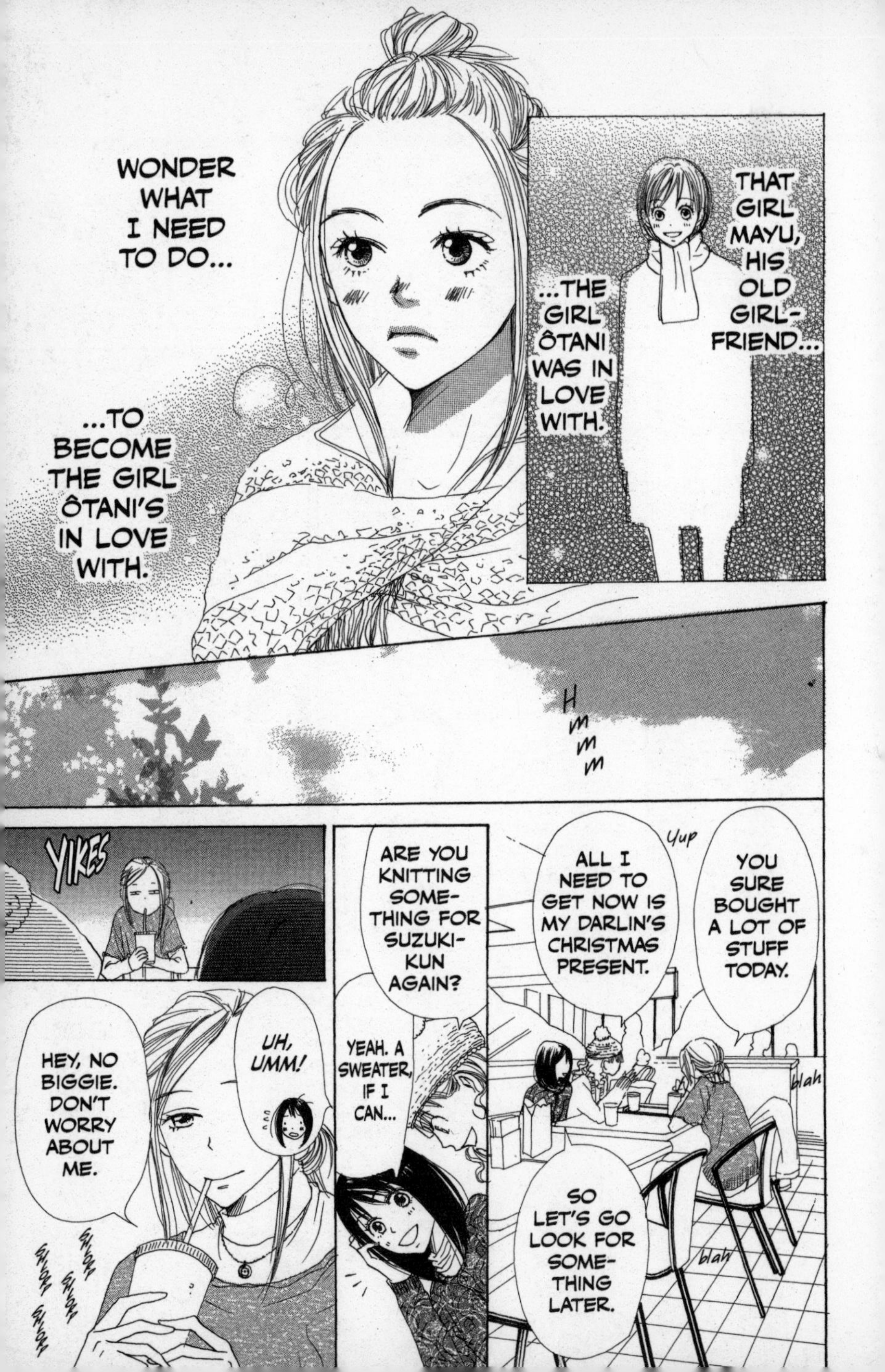
THAT GIRL MAYU, HIS OLD GIRLFRIEND...
...THE GIRL ÔTANI WAS IN LOVE WITH.
WONDER WHAT I NEED TO DO...
...TO BECOME THE GIRL ÔTANI'S IN LOVE WITH.
Hmmm
YOU SURE BOUGHT A LOT OF STUFF TODAY.
Yup
ALL I NEED TO GET NOW IS MY DARLIN'S CHRISTMAS PRESENT.
blah
blah
SO LET'S GO LOOK FOR SOMETHING LATER.
ARE YOU KNITTING SOMETHING FOR SUZUKI-KUN AGAIN?
YEAH. A SWEATER, IF I CAN...
YIKES
UH, UMM!
HEY, NO BIGGIE. DON'T WORRY ABOUT ME.

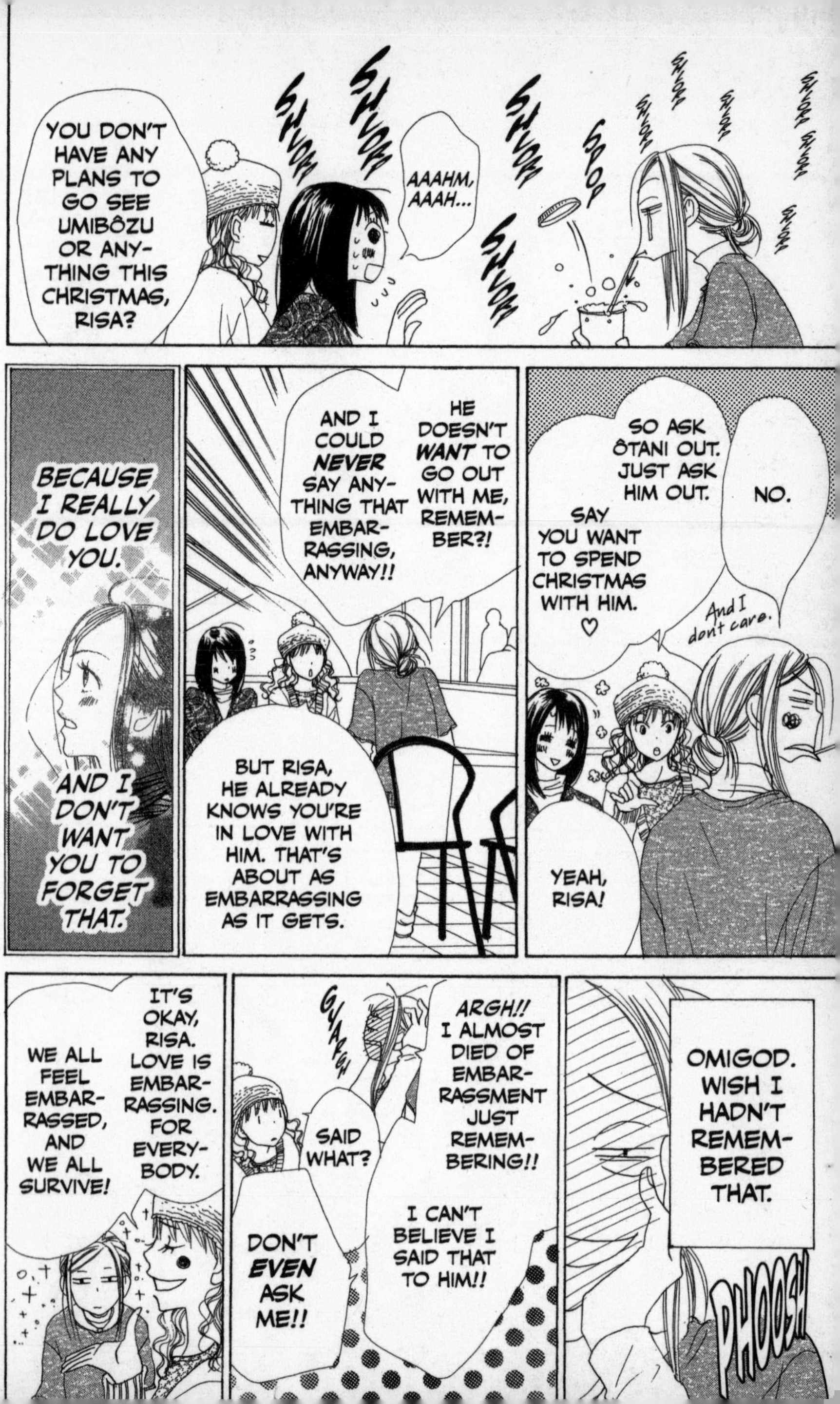
SHWOM
SHWOM
SHWOM
SHWOM
AAAHM, AAAH...
YOU DON'T HAVE ANY PLANS TO GO SEE UMIBÔZU OR ANYTHING THIS CHRISTMAS, RISA?
NO.
SO ASK ŌTANI OUT. JUST ASK HIM OUT.
SAY YOU WANT TO SPEND CHRISTMAS WITH HIM. ♡
And I don't care.
YEAH, RISA!
HE DOESN'T WANT TO GO OUT WITH ME, REMEMBER?!
AND I COULD NEVER SAY ANYTHING THAT EMBARRASSING, ANYWAY!!
BUT RISA, HE ALREADY KNOWS YOU'RE IN LOVE WITH HIM. THAT'S ABOUT AS EMBARRASSING AS IT GETS.
BECAUSE I REALLY DO LOVE YOU.
AND I DON'T WANT YOU TO FORGET THAT.
OMIGOD. WISH I HADN'T REMEMBERED THAT.
PHOOSH
ARGH!! I ALMOST DIED OF EMBARRASSMENT JUST REMEMBERING!!
SAID WHAT?
I CAN'T BELIEVE I SAID THAT TO HIM!!
DON'T EVEN ASK ME!!
IT'S OKAY, RISA. LOVE IS EMBARRASSING. FOR EVERYBODY.
WE ALL FEEL EMBARRASSED, AND WE ALL SURVIVE!

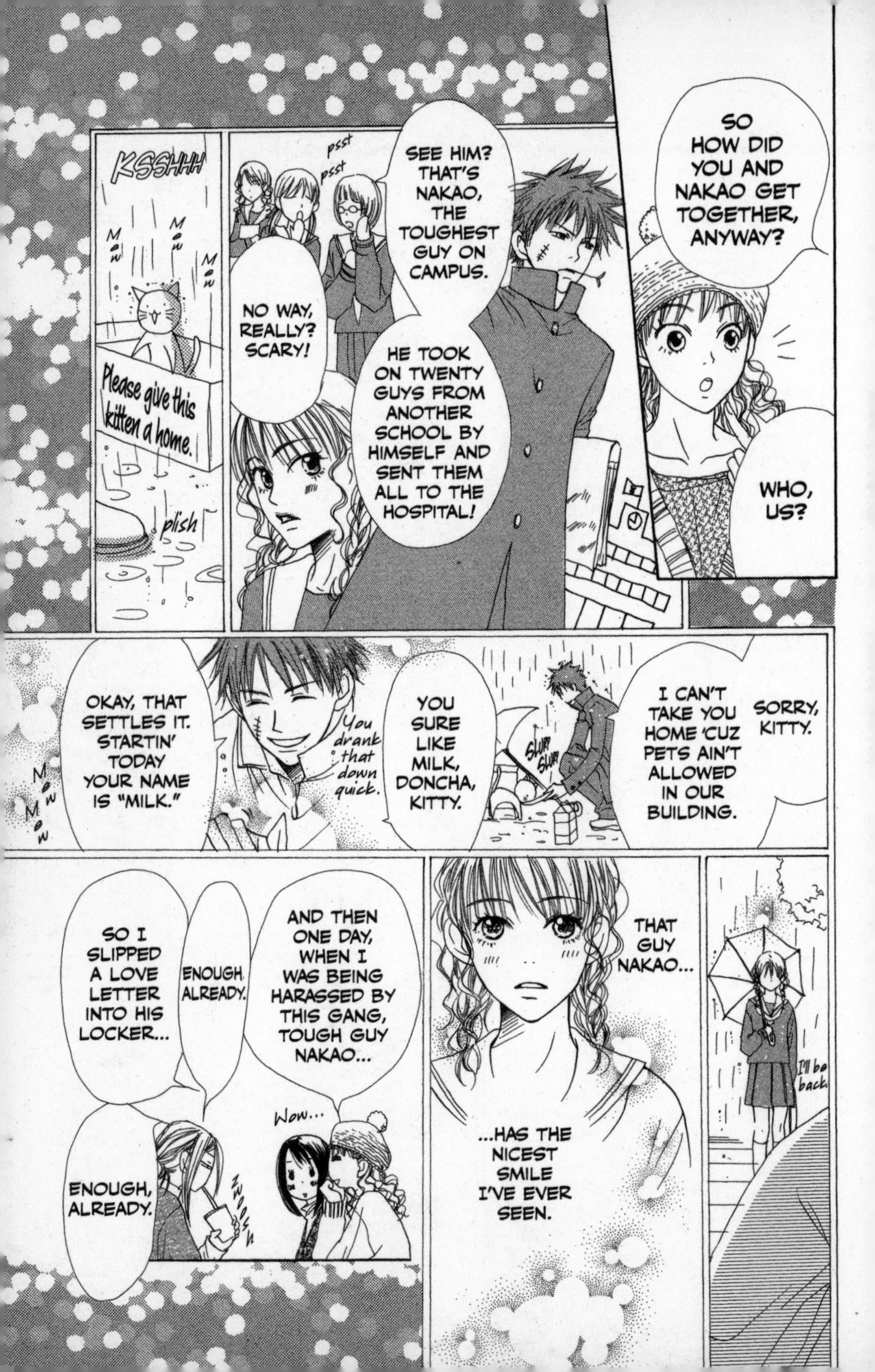
SO HOW DID YOU AND NAKAO GET TOGETHER, ANYWAY?
WHO, US?
SEE HIM? THAT'S NAKAO, THE TOUGHEST GUY ON CAMPUS.
psst
psst
NO WAY, REALLY? SCARY!
HE TOOK ON TWENTY GUYS FROM ANOTHER SCHOOL BY HIMSELF AND SENT THEM ALL TO THE HOSPITAL!
KSSHHH
Mew
Mew
Mew
Please give this kitten a home.
plish
SORRY, KITTY.
I CAN'T TAKE YOU HOME 'CUZ PETS AIN'T ALLOWED IN OUR BUILDING.
SLURP SLURP
YOU SURE LIKE MILK, DONCHA, KITTY.
You drank that down quick.
OKAY, THAT SETTLES IT. STARTIN' TODAY YOUR NAME IS "MILK."
Mew
Mew
I'll be back.
THAT GUY NAKAO...
...HAS THE NICEST SMILE I'VE EVER SEEN.
AND THEN ONE DAY, WHEN I WAS BEING HARASSED BY THIS GANG, TOUGH GUY NAKAO...
ENOUGH ALREADY.
SO I SLIPPED A LOVE LETTER INTO HIS LOCKER...
Wow...
ENOUGH, ALREADY.

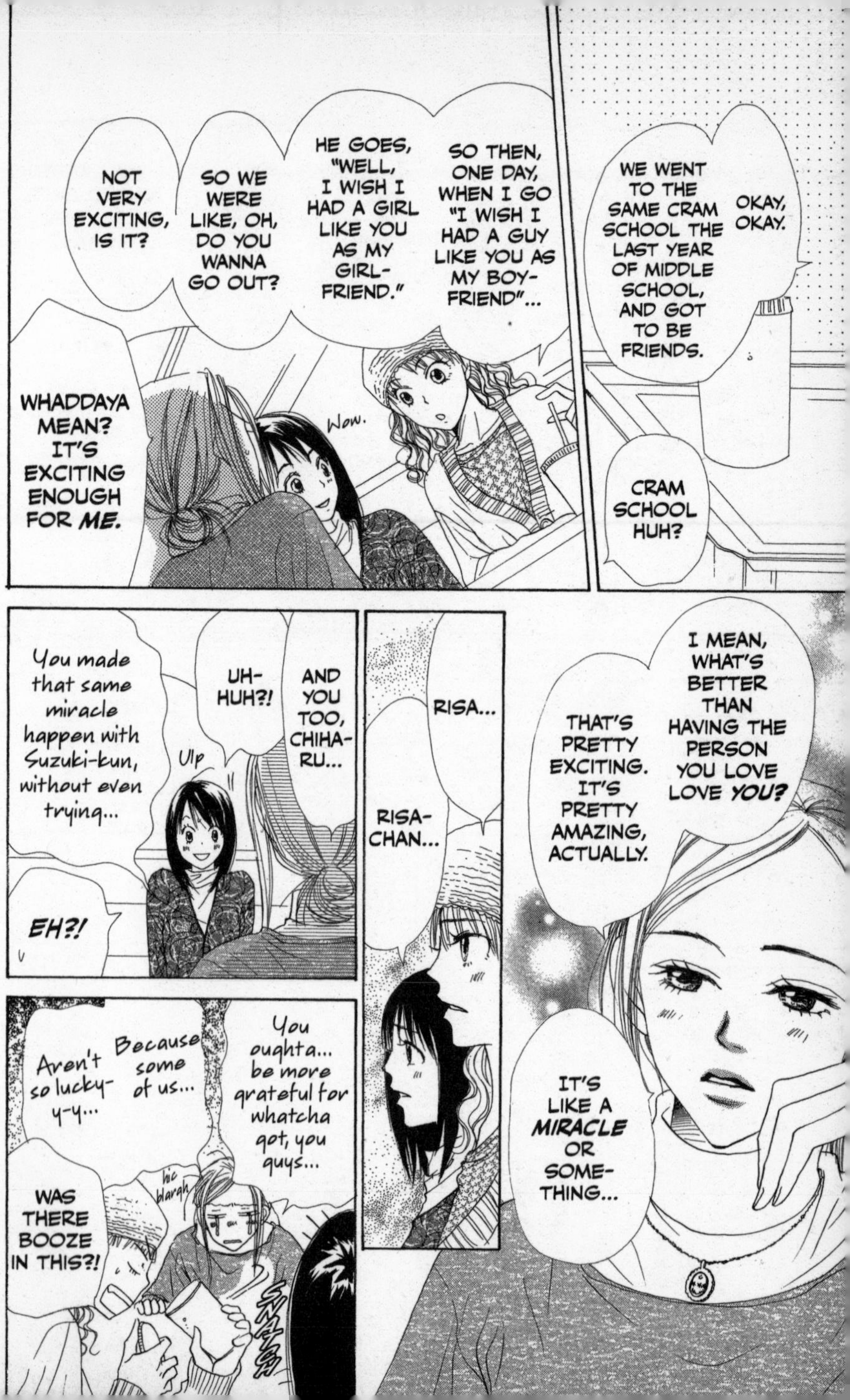

WE WENT TO THE SAME CRAM SCHOOL THE LAST YEAR OF MIDDLE SCHOOL, AND GOT TO BE FRIENDS.
OKAY, OKAY.
CRAM SCHOOL HUH?
SO THEN, ONE DAY, WHEN I GO "I WISH I HAD A GUY LIKE YOU AS MY BOY-FRIEND"...
HE GOES, "WELL, I WISH I HAD A GIRL LIKE YOU AS MY GIRL-FRIEND."
SO WE WERE LIKE, OH, DO YOU WANNA GO OUT?
NOT VERY EXCITING, IS IT?
Wow.
WHADDAYA MEAN? IT'S EXCITING ENOUGH FOR ***ME.***
I MEAN, WHAT'S BETTER THAN HAVING THE PERSON YOU LOVE LOVE ***YOU?***
THAT'S PRETTY EXCITING. IT'S PRETTY AMAZING, ACTUALLY.
IT'S LIKE A ***MIRACLE*** OR SOME-THING...
RISA...
RISA-CHAN...
AND YOU TOO, CHIHA-RU...
UH-HUH?!
Ulp
You made that same miracle happen with Suzuki-kun, without even trying...
EH?!
You oughta... be more grateful for whatcha got, you guys...
Because some of us...
Aren't so lucky-y-y...
hic blargh
WAS THERE BOOZE IN THIS?!
SNATCH

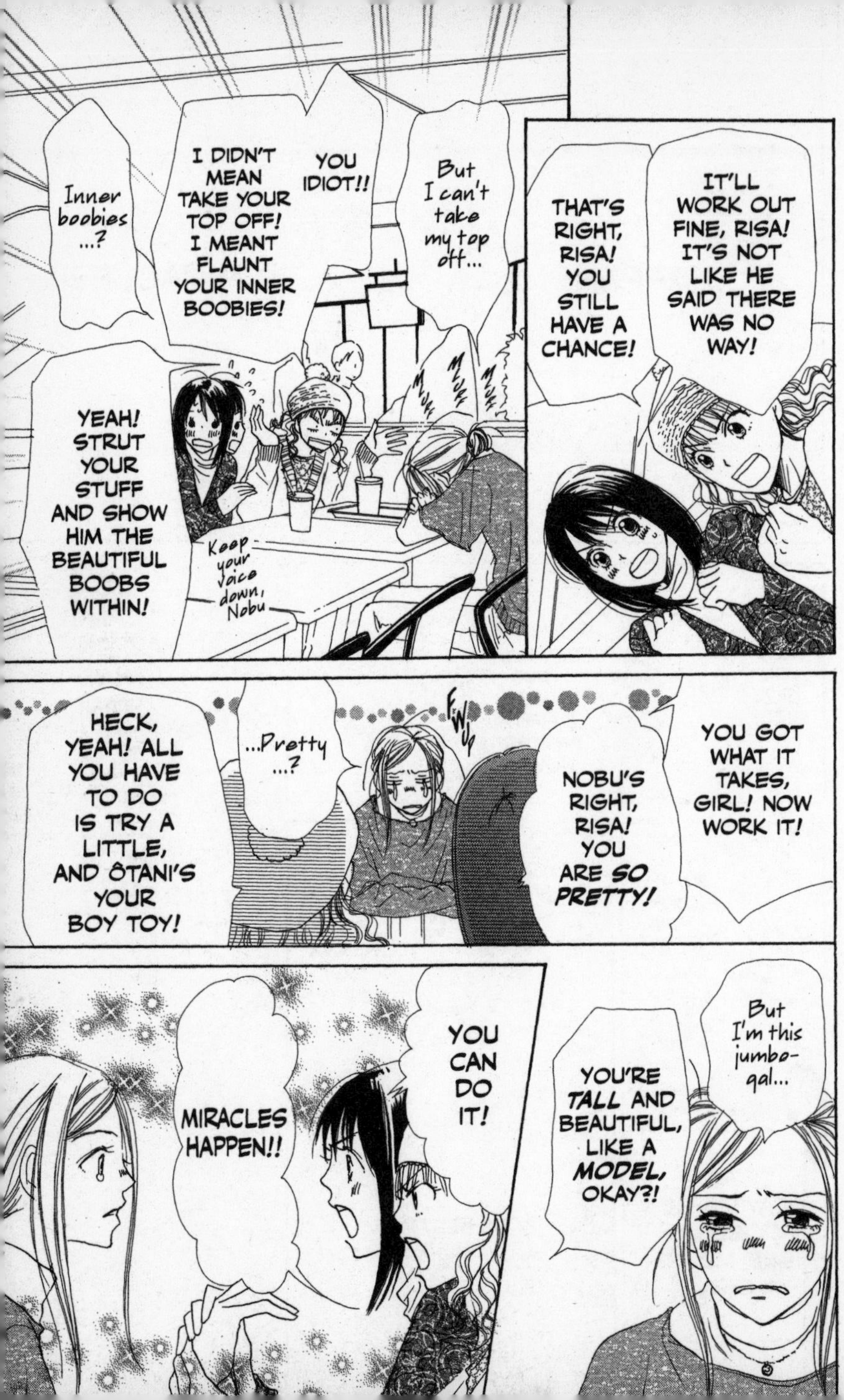
IT'LL WORK OUT FINE, RISA! IT'S NOT LIKE HE SAID THERE WAS NO WAY!
THAT'S RIGHT, RISA! YOU STILL HAVE A CHANCE!
But I can't take my top off...
YOU IDIOT!!
I DIDN'T MEAN TAKE YOUR TOP OFF! I MEANT FLAUNT YOUR INNER BOOBIES!
Inner boobies ...?
MUFF
MUFF
YEAH! STRUT YOUR STUFF AND SHOW HIM THE BEAUTIFUL BOOBS WITHIN!
Keep your voice down, Nobu
YOU GOT WHAT IT TAKES, GIRL! NOW WORK IT!
NOBU'S RIGHT, RISA! YOU ARE *SO PRETTY!*
FWUP
...Pretty ...?
HECK, YEAH! ALL YOU HAVE TO DO IS TRY A LITTLE, AND ŌTANI'S YOUR BOY TOY!
But I'm this jumbo-gal...
YOU'RE *TALL* AND BEAUTIFUL, LIKE A *MODEL*, OKAY?!
YOU CAN DO IT!
MIRACLES HAPPEN!!

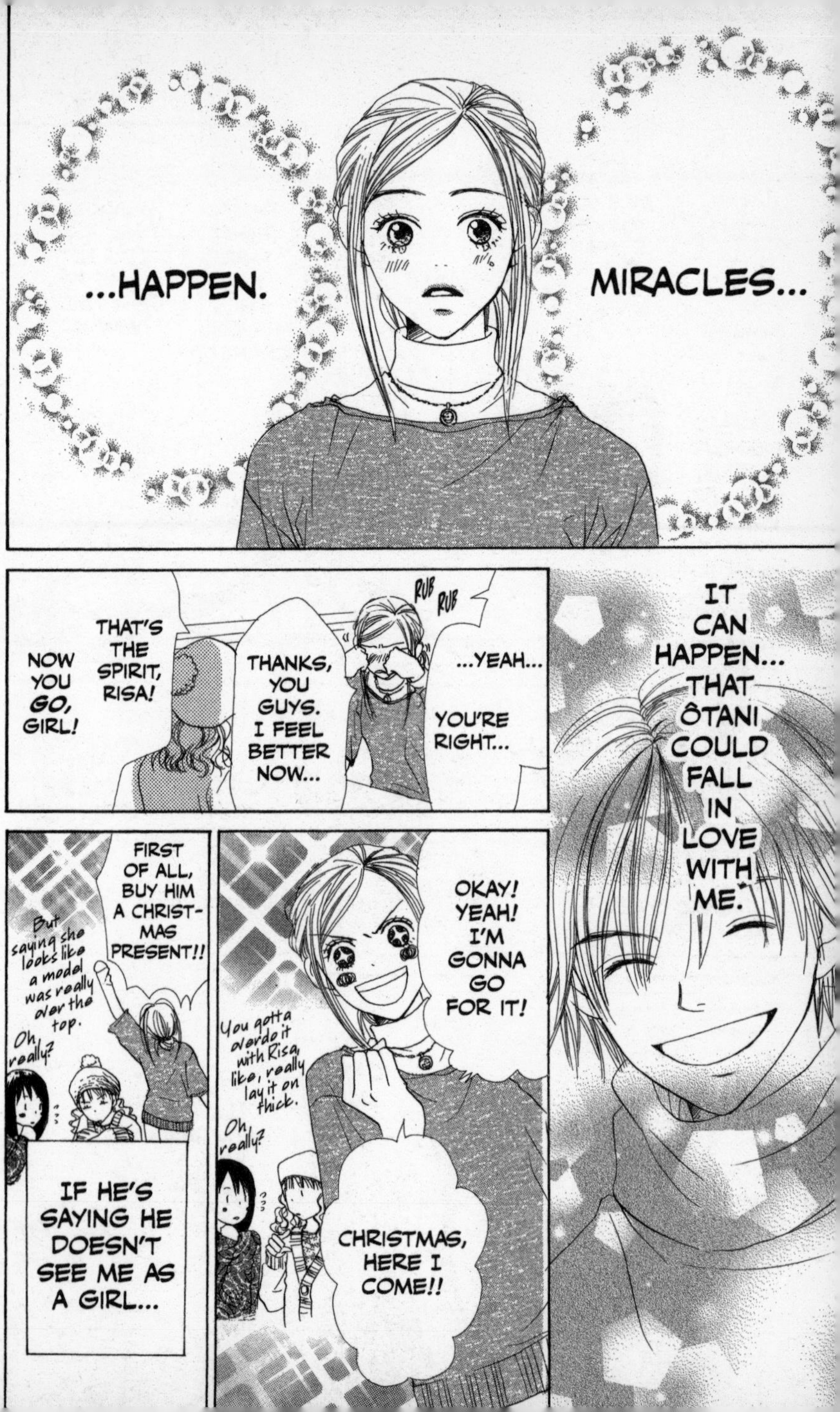

MIRACLES...
...HAPPEN.
IT CAN HAPPEN... THAT ŌTANI COULD FALL IN LOVE WITH ME.
RUB RUB
...YEAH...
YOU'RE RIGHT...
THANKS, YOU GUYS. I FEEL BETTER NOW...
THAT'S THE SPIRIT, RISA!
NOW YOU GO, GIRL!
OKAY! YEAH! I'M GONNA GO FOR IT!
You gotta overdo it with Risa, really like, really lay it on thick.
Oh really?
CHRISTMAS, HERE I COME!!
FIRST OF ALL, BUY HIM A CHRIST-MAS PRESENT!!
But saying she looks like a model was really over the top.
Oh really?
IF HE'S SAYING HE DOESN'T SEE ME AS A GIRL...

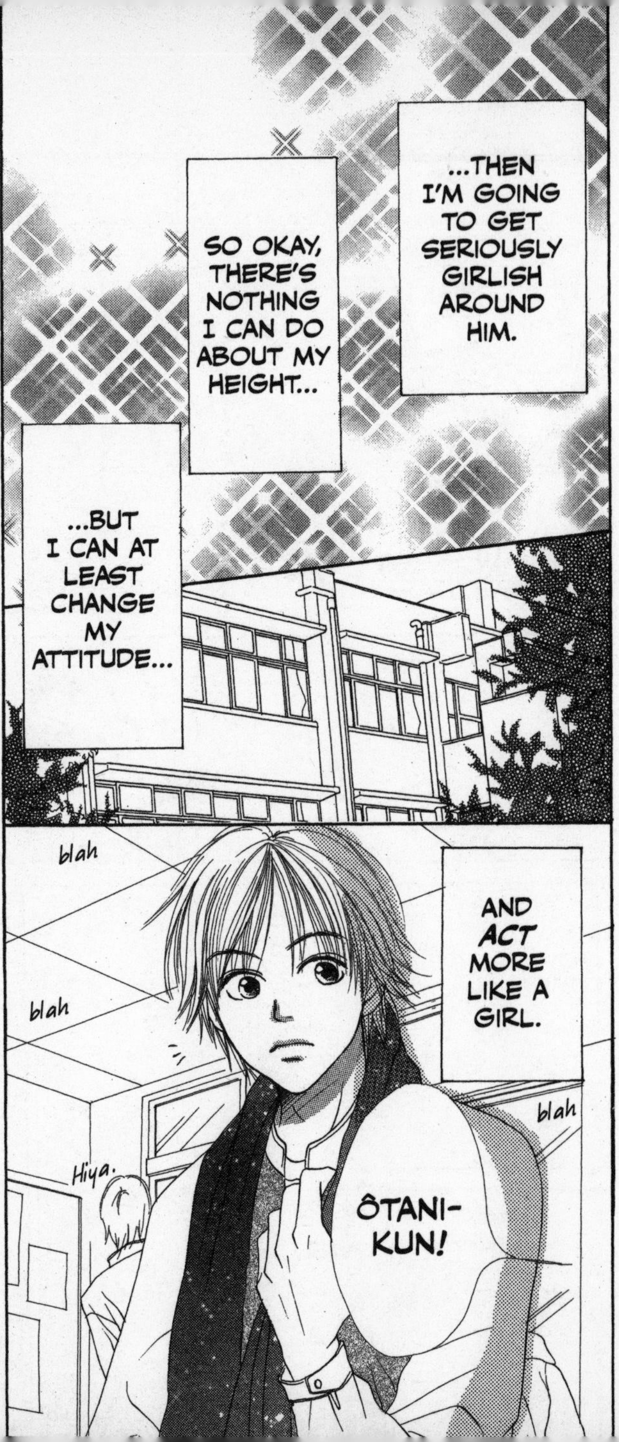
...THEN I'M GOING TO GET SERIOUSLY GIRLISH AROUND HIM.
SO OKAY, THERE'S NOTHING I CAN DO ABOUT MY HEIGHT...
...BUT I CAN AT LEAST CHANGE MY ATTITUDE...
AND ACT MORE LIKE A GIRL.
blah
blah
blah
Hiya.
ÔTANI-KUN!

2

It's been months since I visited the gym where I signed up. Well, let's face it, why would a lazy homebody like me leave the house to go work out? It was never going to happen... But there's a class called "hip hop dancing," and since I love hip hop, I'm hoping to take it someday. I was hopeless at aerobics, though... The thing about aerobics is, it's not physically tiring so much as psychologically draining. Or emotionally scarring. The humiliation of turning the opposite way from everyone else, or the shame when you're facing forward and everyone else is facing backward and your eyes meet is too, too great for words. How does everybody manage to remember the routines?!

I have great respect for Morning Musume. They are amazing! I mean, they all have their dance routines down!!

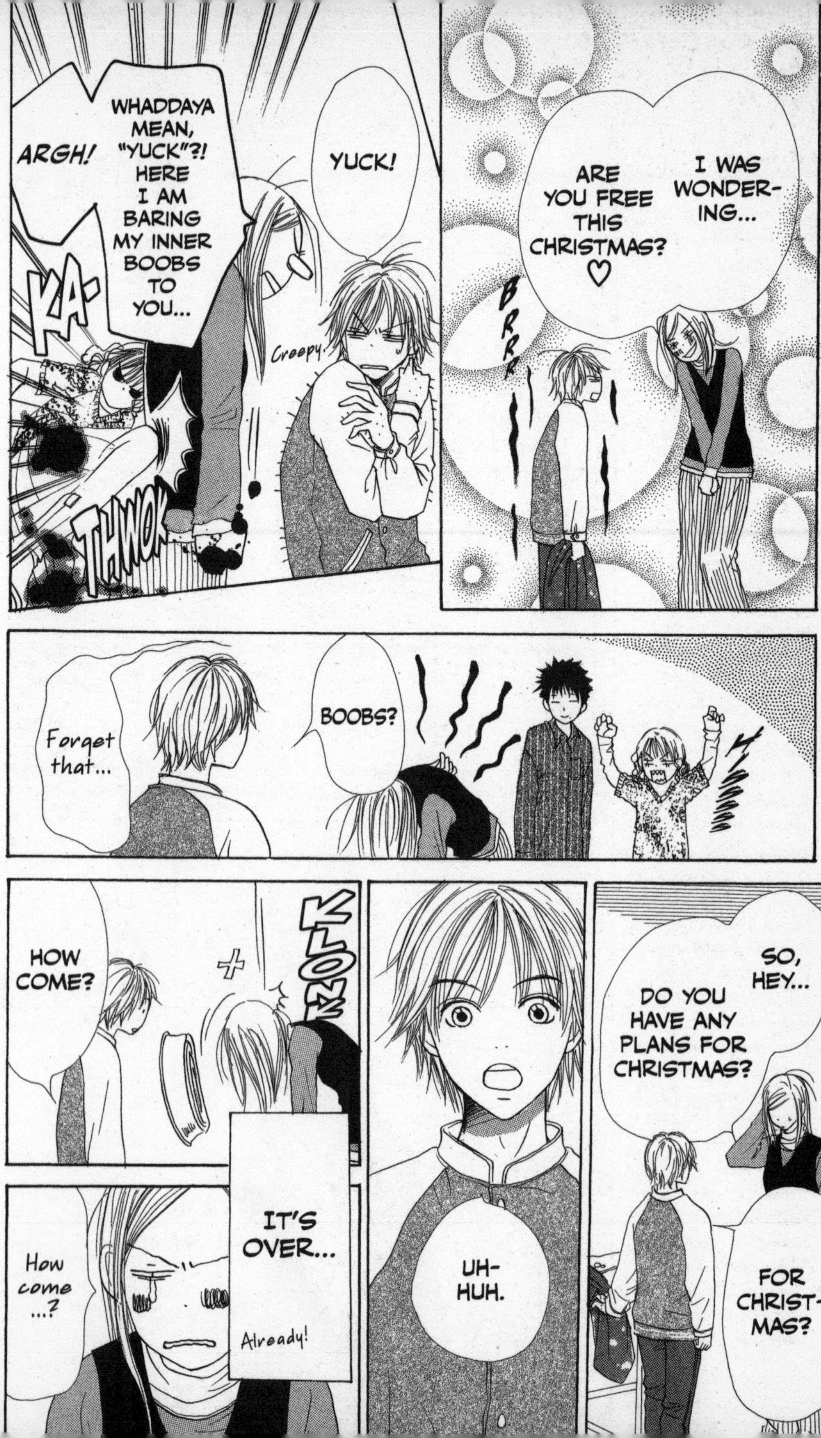
I WAS WONDER-ING...
ARE YOU FREE THIS CHRISTMAS? ♡
BRRR
YUCK!
Creepy.
WHADDAYA MEAN, "YUCK"?! HERE I AM BARING MY INNER BOOBS TO YOU...
ARGH!
KA-
THWOK
BOOBS?
Forget that...
SO, HEY...
DO YOU HAVE ANY PLANS FOR CHRISTMAS?
FOR CHRIST-MAS?
UH-HUH.
KLONK
HOW COME?
IT'S OVER...
Already!
How come ...?

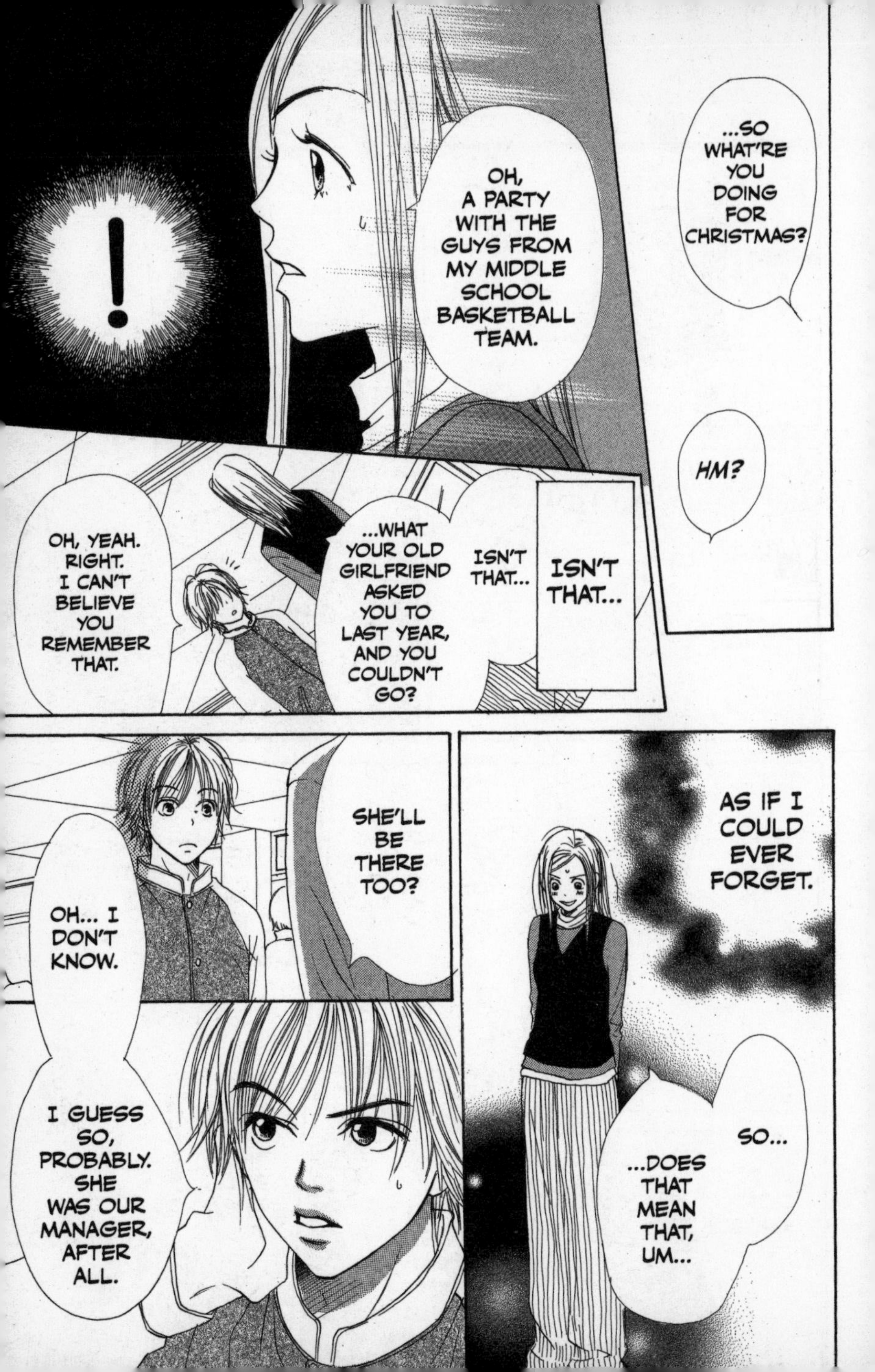
...SO WHAT'RE YOU DOING FOR CHRISTMAS?
HM?
OH, A PARTY WITH THE GUYS FROM MY MIDDLE SCHOOL BASKETBALL TEAM.
!
ISN'T THAT...
ISN'T THAT...
...WHAT YOUR OLD GIRLFRIEND ASKED YOU TO LAST YEAR, AND YOU COULDN'T GO?
OH, YEAH. RIGHT. I CAN'T BELIEVE YOU REMEMBER THAT.
AS IF I COULD EVER FORGET.
SO...
...DOES THAT MEAN THAT, UM...
SHE'LL BE THERE TOO?
OH... I DON'T KNOW.
I GUESS SO, PROBABLY. SHE WAS OUR MANAGER, AFTER ALL.

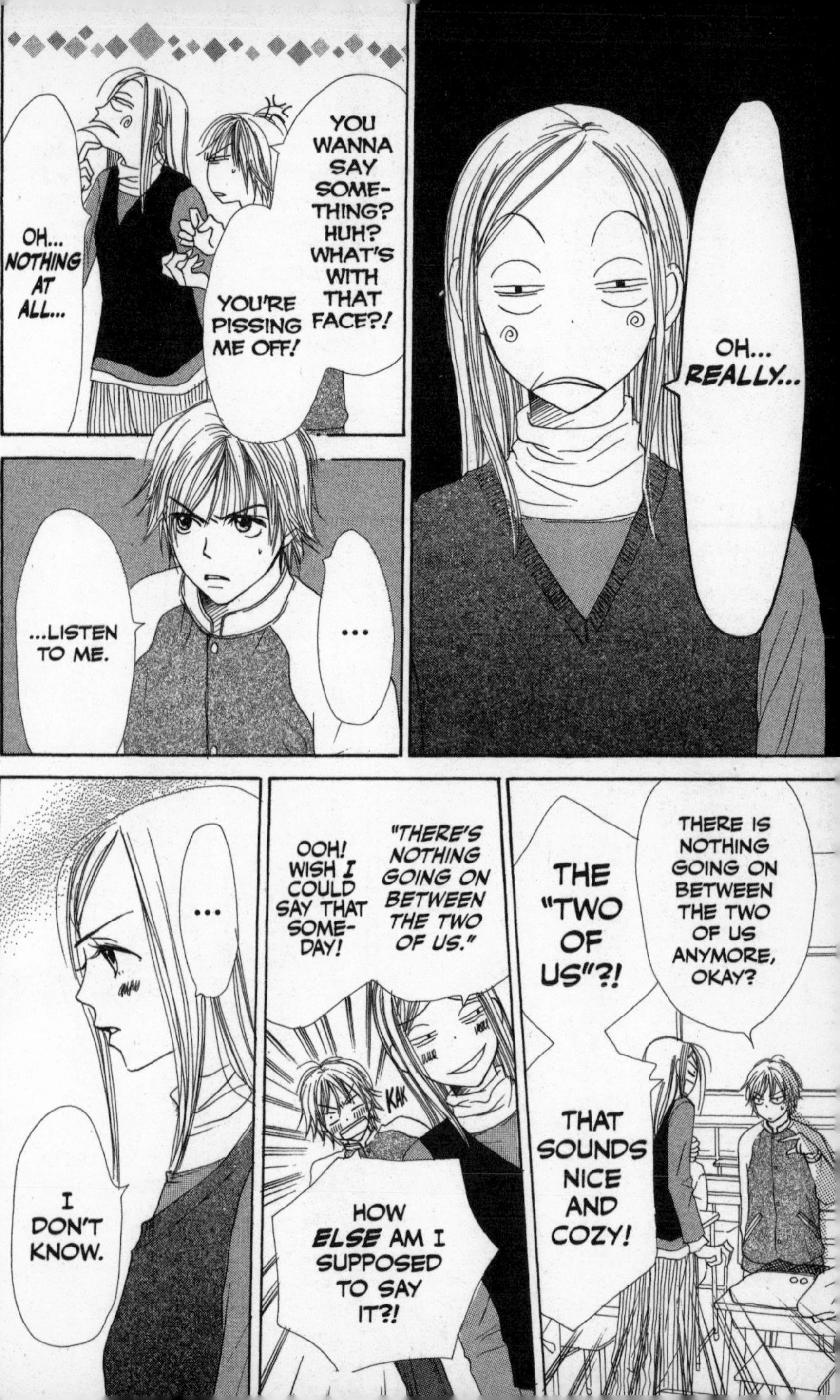
OH... REALLY...
YOU WANNA SAY SOMETHING? HUH? WHAT'S WITH THAT FACE?!
YOU'RE PISSING ME OFF!
OH... NOTHING AT ALL...
...
...LISTEN TO ME.
THERE IS NOTHING GOING ON BETWEEN THE TWO OF US ANYMORE, OKAY?
THE "TWO OF US"?!
THAT SOUNDS NICE AND COZY!
"THERE'S NOTHING GOING ON BETWEEN THE TWO OF US."
OOH! WISH I COULD SAY THAT SOMEDAY!
KAK
HOW ELSE AM I SUPPOSED TO SAY IT?!
...
I DON'T KNOW.

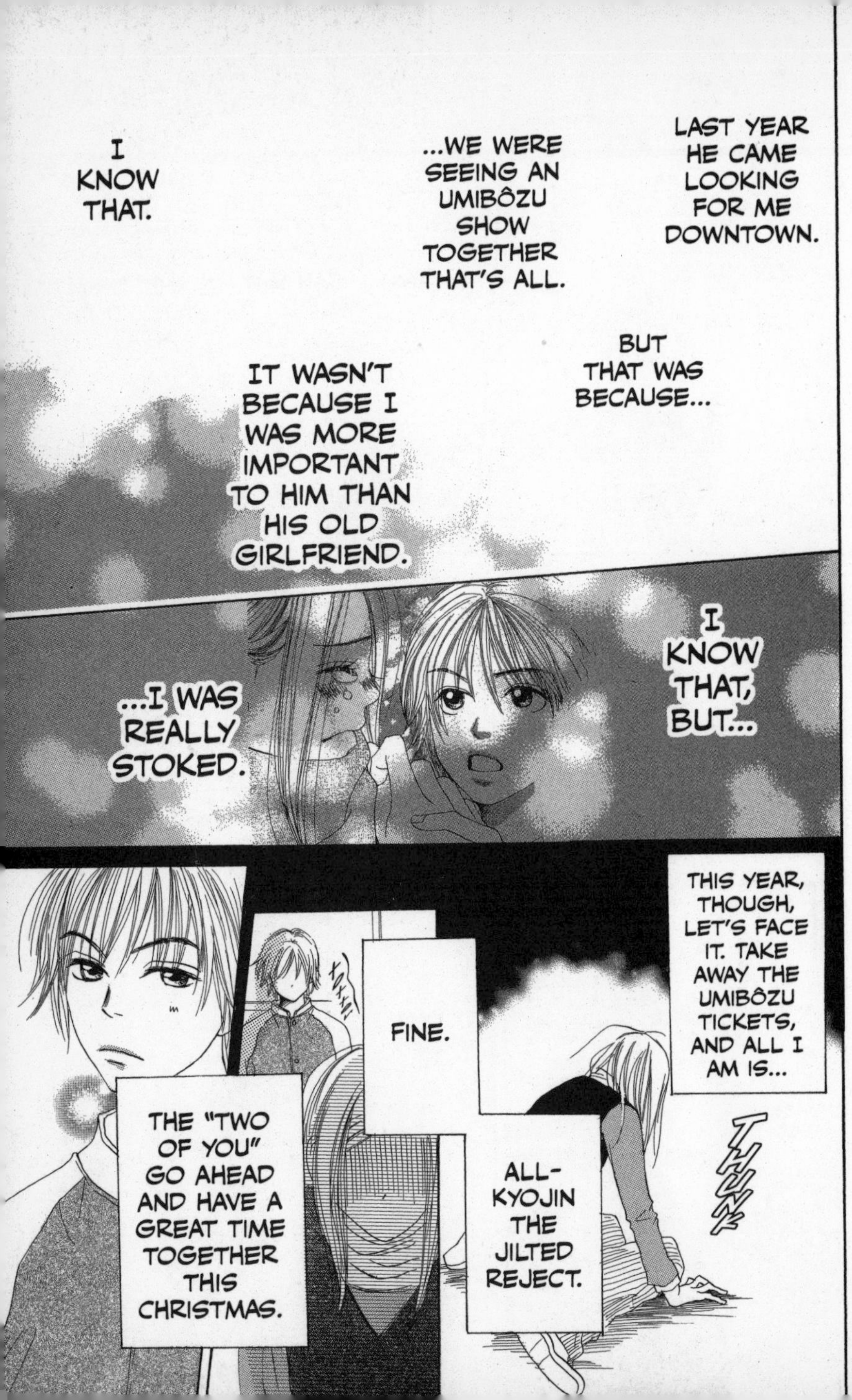
LAST YEAR HE CAME LOOKING FOR ME DOWNTOWN.
...WE WERE SEEING AN UMIBÔZU SHOW TOGETHER THAT'S ALL.
I KNOW THAT.
BUT THAT WAS BECAUSE...
IT WASN'T BECAUSE I WAS MORE IMPORTANT TO HIM THAN HIS OLD GIRLFRIEND.
I KNOW THAT, BUT...
...I WAS REALLY STOKED.
THIS YEAR, THOUGH, LET'S FACE IT. TAKE AWAY THE UMIBÔZU TICKETS, AND ALL I AM IS...
THUNK
ALL-KYOJIN THE JILTED REJECT.
FINE.
THE "TWO OF YOU" GO AHEAD AND HAVE A GREAT TIME TOGETHER THIS CHRISTMAS.

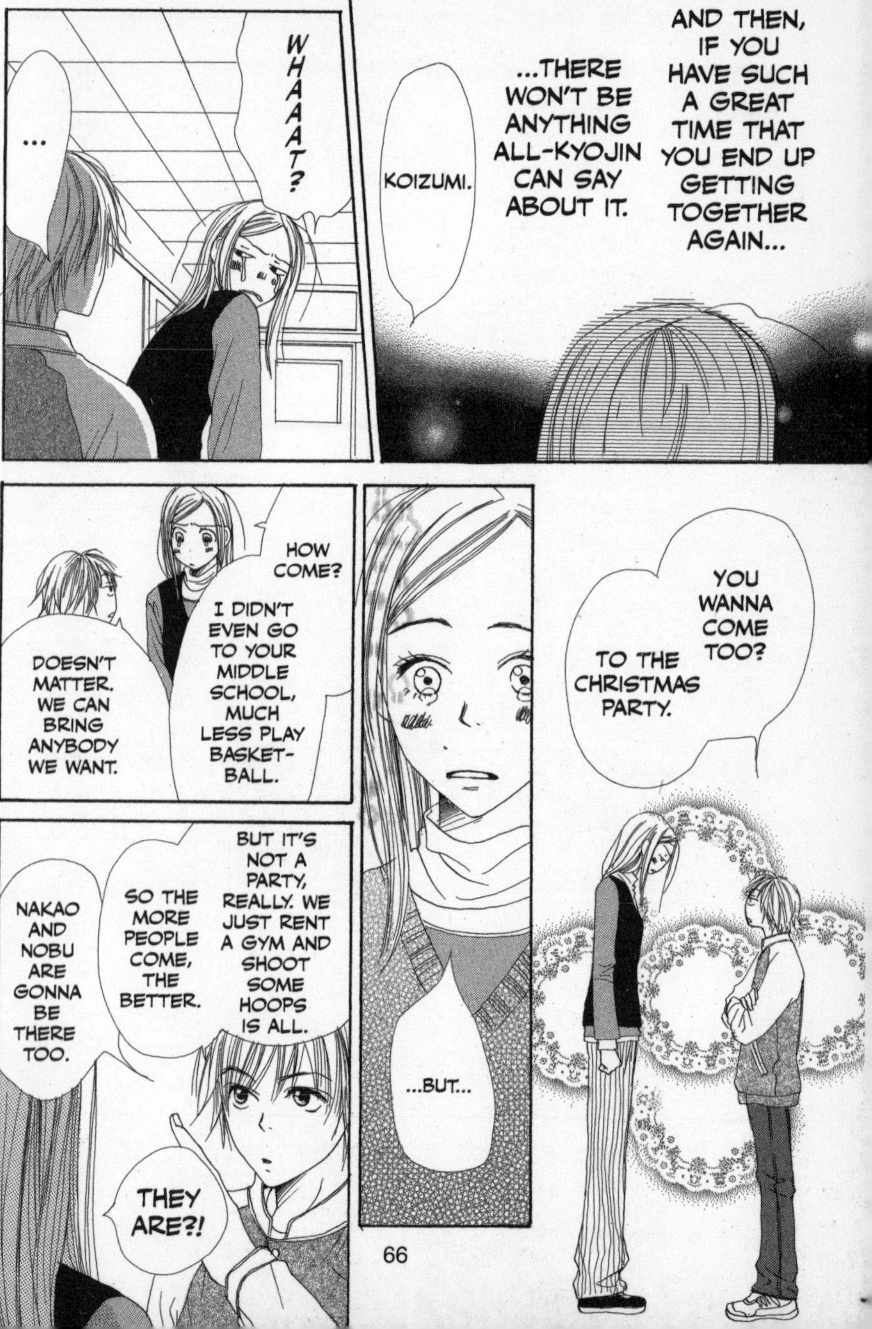
AND THEN, IF YOU HAVE SUCH A GREAT TIME THAT YOU END UP GETTING TOGETHER AGAIN...
...THERE WON'T BE ANYTHING ALL-KYOJIN CAN SAY ABOUT IT.
KOIZUMI.
WHAAAAT?
...
YOU WANNA COME TOO?
TO THE CHRISTMAS PARTY.
...BUT...
HOW COME?
I DIDN'T EVEN GO TO YOUR MIDDLE SCHOOL, MUCH LESS PLAY BASKETBALL.
DOESN'T MATTER. WE CAN BRING ANYBODY WE WANT.
BUT IT'S NOT A PARTY, REALLY. WE JUST RENT A GYM AND SHOOT SOME HOOPS IS ALL.
SO THE MORE PEOPLE COME, THE BETTER.
NAKAO AND NOBU ARE GONNA BE THERE TOO.
THEY ARE?!

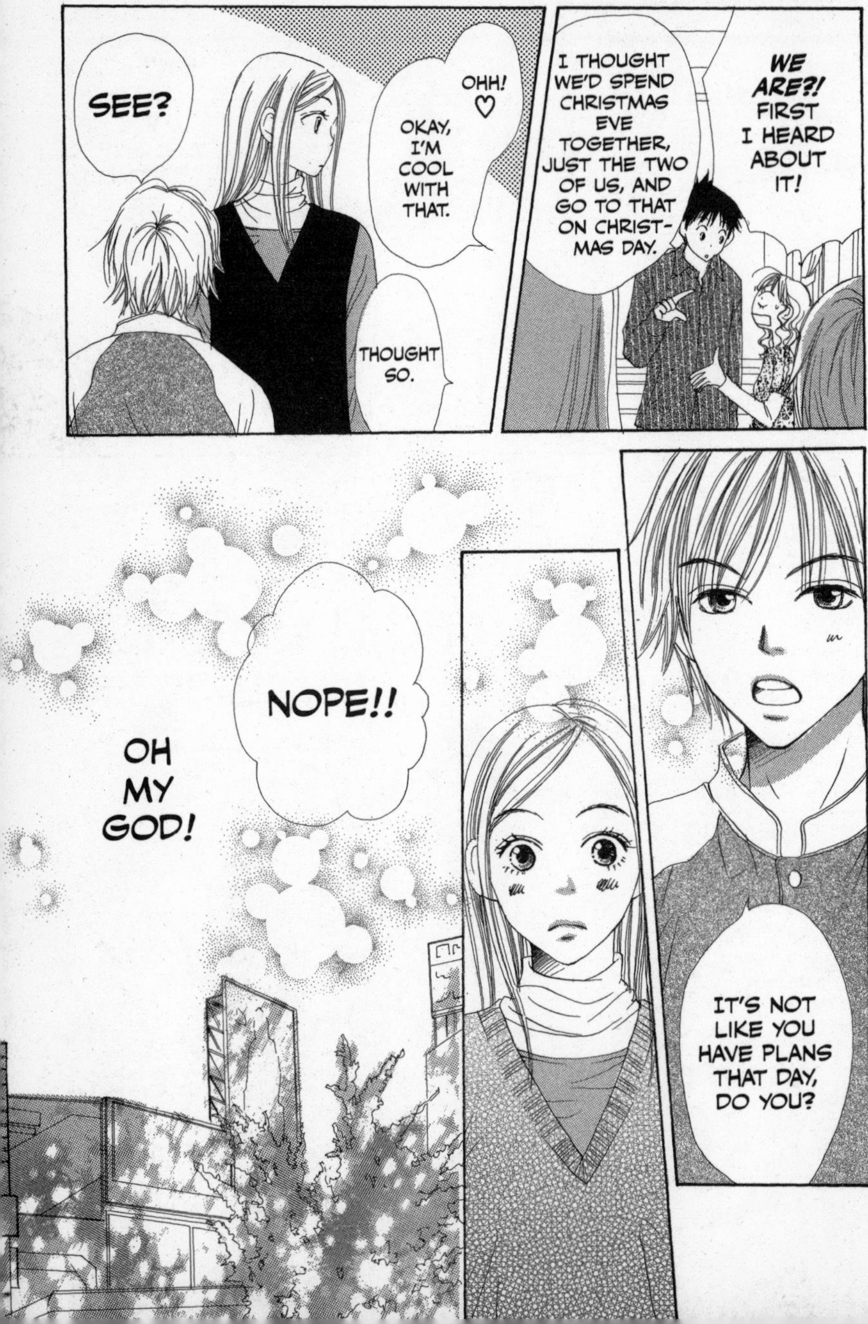
I THOUGHT WE'D SPEND CHRISTMAS EVE TOGETHER, JUST THE TWO OF US, AND GO TO THAT ON CHRISTMAS DAY.
WE ARE?! FIRST I HEARD ABOUT IT!
OHH! ♡
OKAY, I'M COOL WITH THAT.
SEE?
THOUGHT SO.
IT'S NOT LIKE YOU HAVE PLANS THAT DAY, DO YOU?
NOPE!!
OH MY GOD!

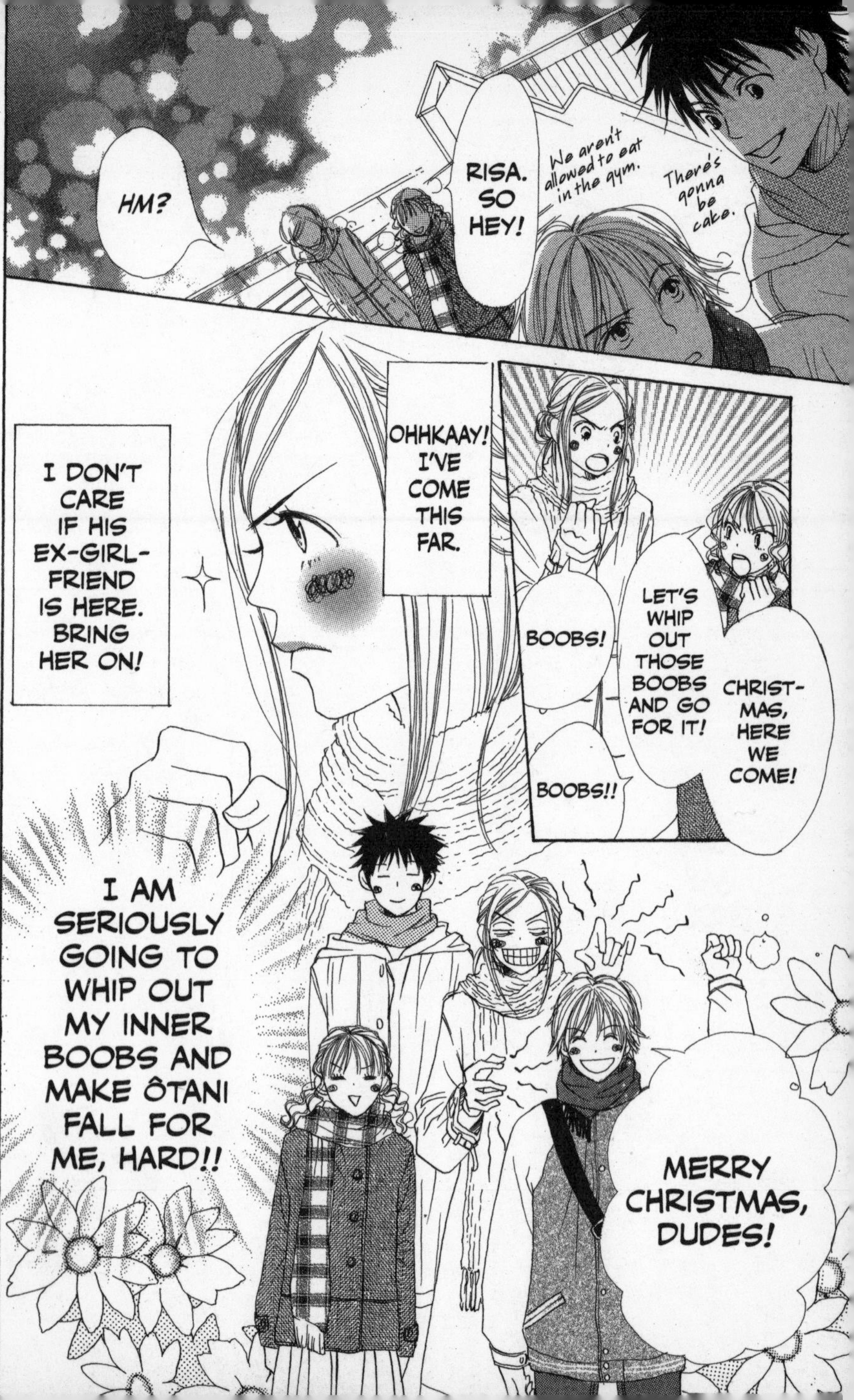
There's gonna be cake.
We aren't allowed to eat in the gym.
RISA. SO HEY!
HM?
CHRISTMAS, HERE WE COME!
LET'S WHIP OUT THOSE BOOBS AND GO FOR IT!
BOOBS!
BOOBS!!
OHHKAAY! I'VE COME THIS FAR.
I DON'T CARE IF HIS EX-GIRLFRIEND IS HERE. BRING HER ON!
MERRY CHRISTMAS, DUDES!
I AM SERIOUSLY GOING TO WHIP OUT MY INNER BOOBS AND MAKE ÔTANI FALL FOR ME, HARD!!

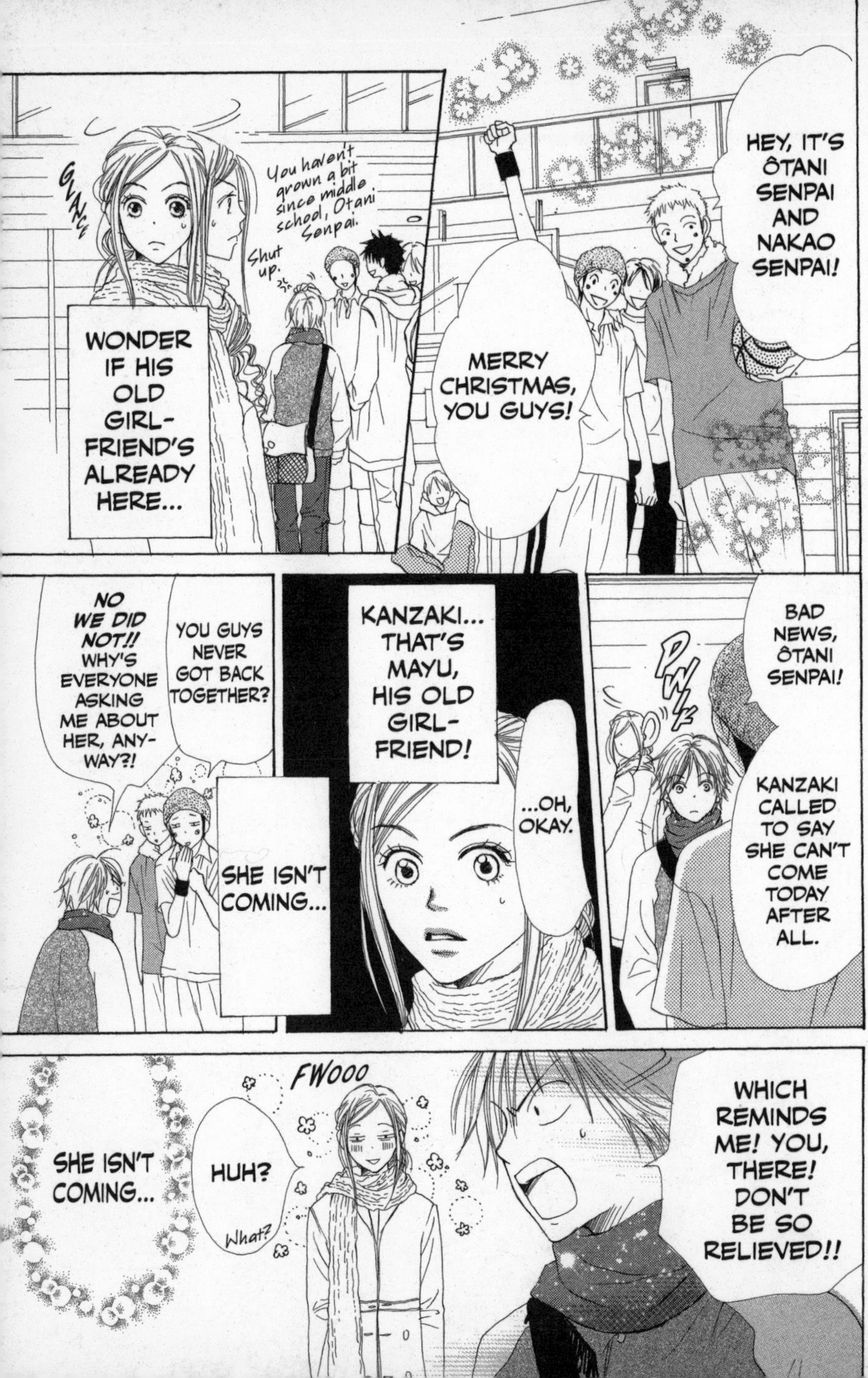
HEY, IT'S ÔTANI SENPAI AND NAKAO SENPAI!
MERRY CHRISTMAS, YOU GUYS!
GLANCE
You haven't grown a bit since middle school, Otani Senpai.
Shut up.
WONDER IF HIS OLD GIRL-FRIEND'S ALREADY HERE...
BAD NEWS, ÔTANI SENPAI!
KANZAKI CALLED TO SAY SHE CAN'T COME TODAY AFTER ALL.
KANZAKI... THAT'S MAYU, HIS OLD GIRL-FRIEND!
...OH, OKAY.
SHE ISN'T COMING...
YOU GUYS NEVER GOT BACK TOGETHER?
NO WE DID NOT!! WHY'S EVERYONE ASKING ME ABOUT HER, ANY-WAY?!
WHICH REMINDS ME! YOU, THERE! DON'T BE SO RELIEVED!!
FWOOO
HUH?
What?
SHE ISN'T COMING...

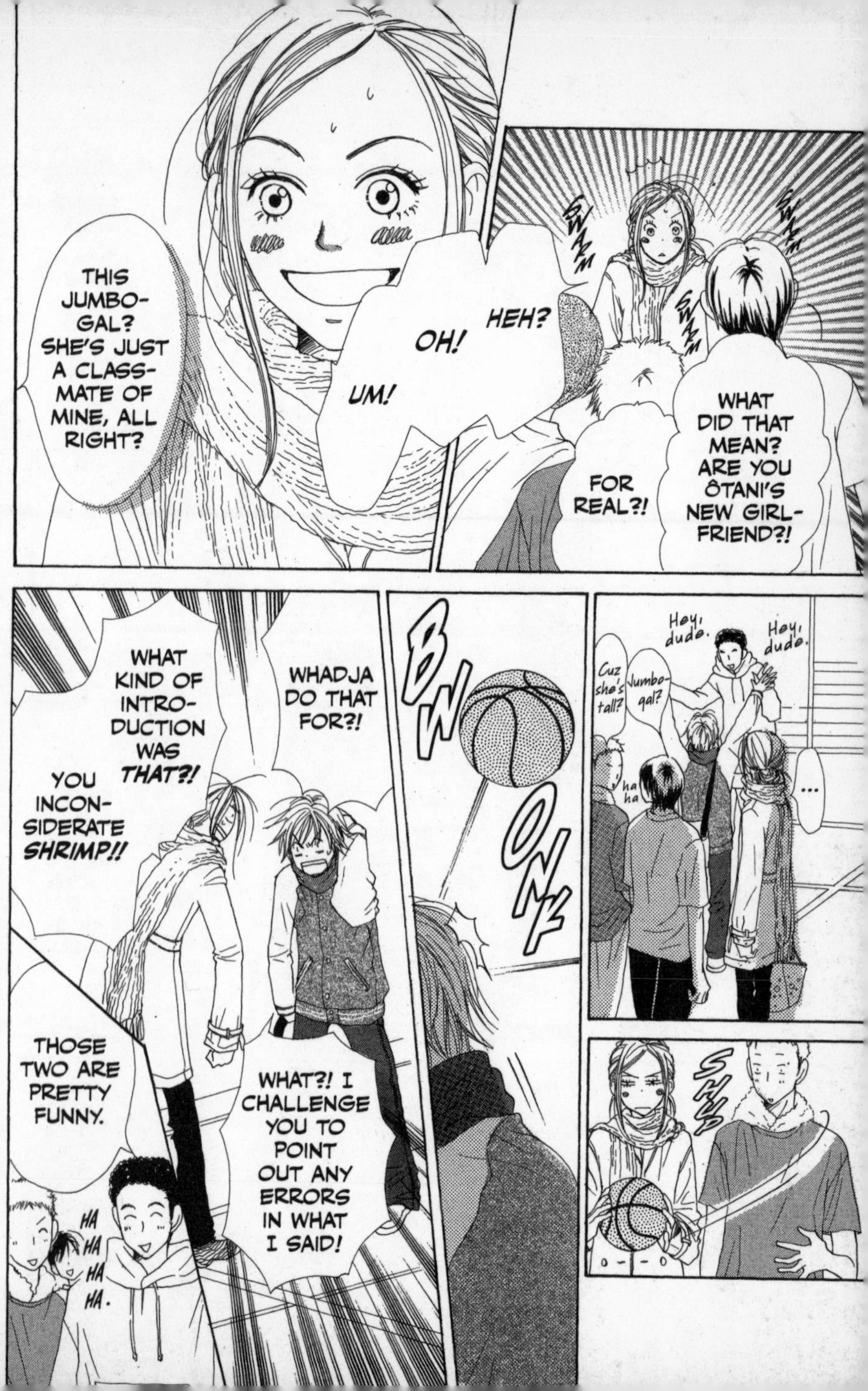
SWARM
SWARM
SWARM
WHAT DID THAT MEAN? ARE YOU ÔTANI'S NEW GIRLFRIEND?!
FOR REAL?!
HEH?
OH!
UM!
THIS JUMBO-GAL? SHE'S JUST A CLASSMATE OF MINE, ALL RIGHT?
Hey, dude.
Hey, dude.
Jumbo-gal?
Cuz she's tall?
ha ha
...
SHWP
BWONNG
WHAT KIND OF INTRODUCTION WAS THAT?!
YOU INCONSIDERATE SHRIMP!!
WHADJA DO THAT FOR?!
WHAT?! I CHALLENGE YOU TO POINT OUT ANY ERRORS IN WHAT I SAID!
THOSE TWO ARE PRETTY FUNNY.
HA HA HA HA.

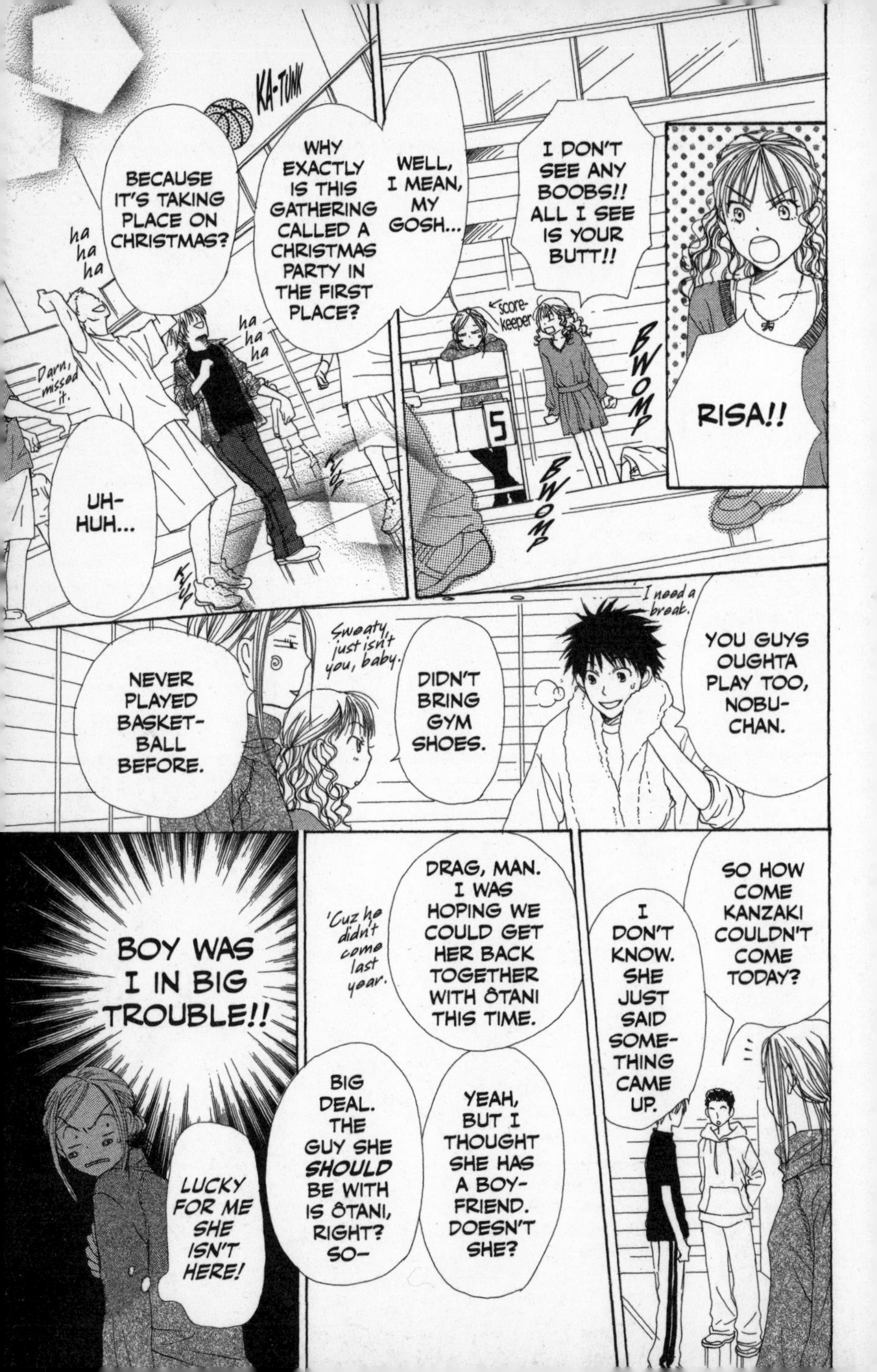
RISA!!
I DON'T SEE ANY BOOBS!! ALL I SEE IS YOUR BUTT!!
score-keeper
BWOMP
BWOMP
WELL, I MEAN, MY GOSH...
WHY EXACTLY IS THIS GATHERING CALLED A CHRISTMAS PARTY IN THE FIRST PLACE?
KA-TUNK
BECAUSE IT'S TAKING PLACE ON CHRISTMAS?
ha ha ha
ha ha ha
Darn, missed it.
UH-HUH...
YOU GUYS OUGHTA PLAY TOO, NOBU-CHAN.
I need a break.
DIDN'T BRING GYM SHOES.
Sweaty just isn't you, baby.
NEVER PLAYED BASKETBALL BEFORE.
SO HOW COME KANZAKI COULDN'T COME TODAY?
I DON'T KNOW. SHE JUST SAID SOMETHING CAME UP.
DRAG, MAN. I WAS HOPING WE COULD GET HER BACK TOGETHER WITH ŌTANI THIS TIME.
'Cuz he didn't come last year.
YEAH, BUT I THOUGHT SHE HAS A BOYFRIEND. DOESN'T SHE?
BIG DEAL. THE GUY SHE *SHOULD* BE WITH IS ŌTANI, RIGHT? SO-
BOY WAS I IN BIG TROUBLE!!
LUCKY FOR ME SHE ISN'T HERE!

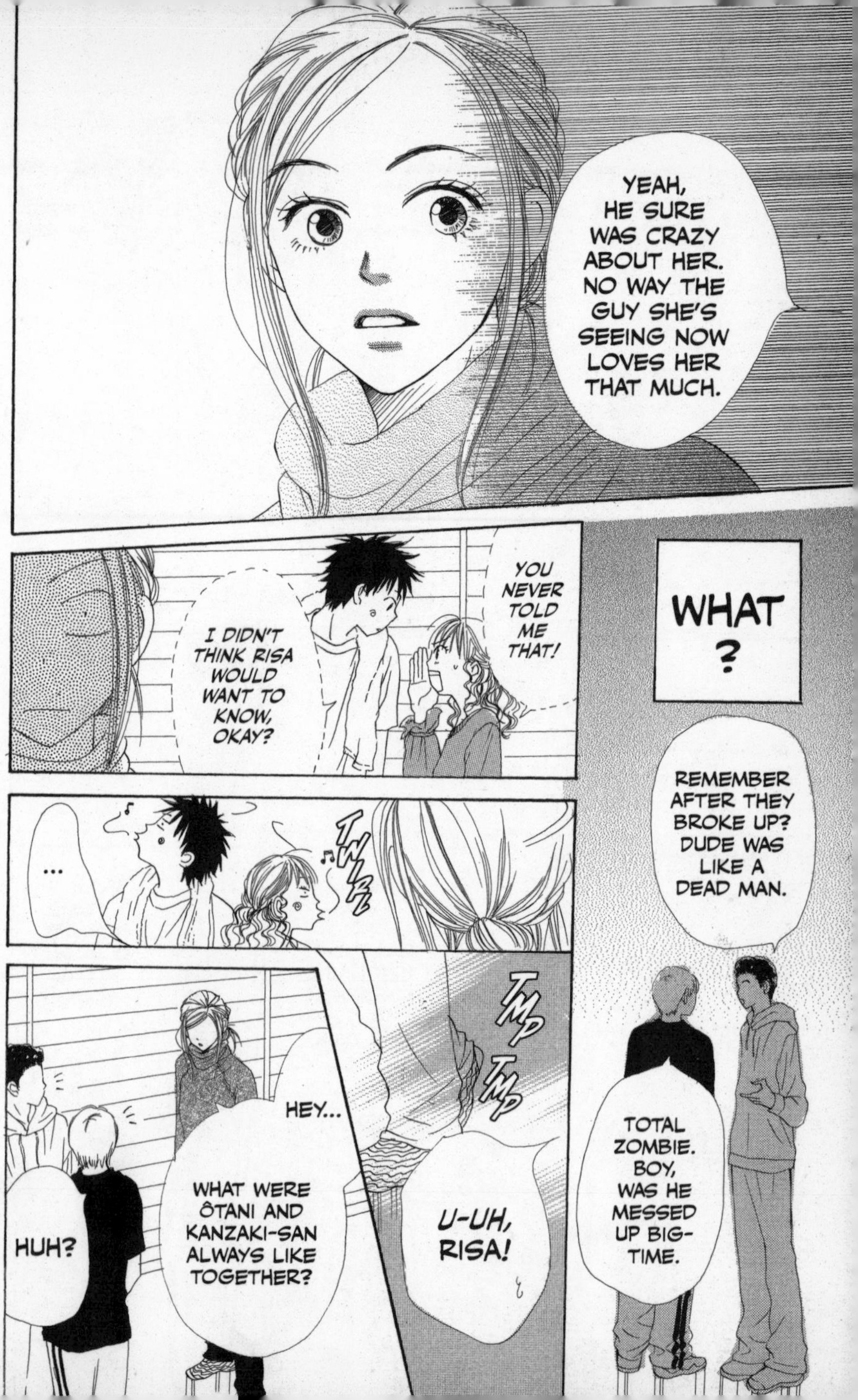
YEAH, HE SURE WAS CRAZY ABOUT HER. NO WAY THE GUY SHE'S SEEING NOW LOVES HER THAT MUCH.
WHAT?
REMEMBER AFTER THEY BROKE UP? DUDE WAS LIKE A DEAD MAN.
TOTAL ZOMBIE. BOY, WAS HE MESSED UP BIG-TIME.
YOU NEVER TOLD ME THAT!
I DIDN'T THINK RISA WOULD WANT TO KNOW, OKAY?
...
TMP TMP
U-UH, RISA!
HEY...
WHAT WERE ÔTANI AND KANZAKI-SAN ALWAYS LIKE TOGETHER?
HUH?

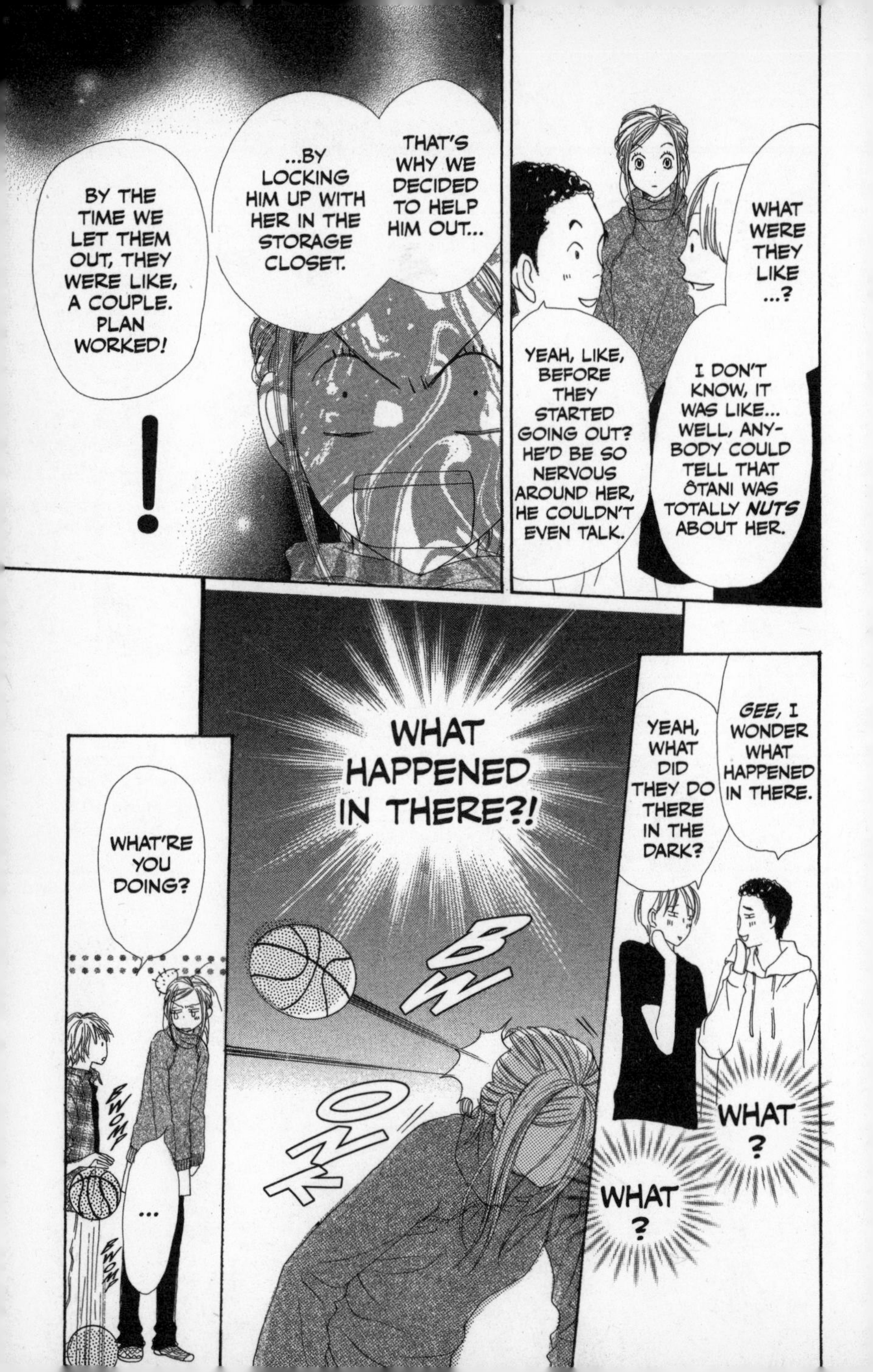
WHAT WERE THEY LIKE ...?
I DON'T KNOW, IT WAS LIKE... WELL, ANYBODY COULD TELL THAT ŌTANI WAS TOTALLY ***NUTS*** ABOUT HER.
YEAH, LIKE, BEFORE THEY STARTED GOING OUT? HE'D BE SO NERVOUS AROUND HER, HE COULDN'T EVEN TALK.
THAT'S WHY WE DECIDED TO HELP HIM OUT...
...BY LOCKING HIM UP WITH HER IN THE STORAGE CLOSET.
BY THE TIME WE LET THEM OUT, THEY WERE LIKE, A COUPLE. PLAN WORKED!
!
GEE, I WONDER WHAT HAPPENED IN THERE.
YEAH, WHAT DID THEY DO THERE IN THE DARK?
WHAT?
WHAT?
WHAT HAPPENED IN THERE?!
BWONK
WHAT'RE YOU DOING?
...
BWOM
BWOM

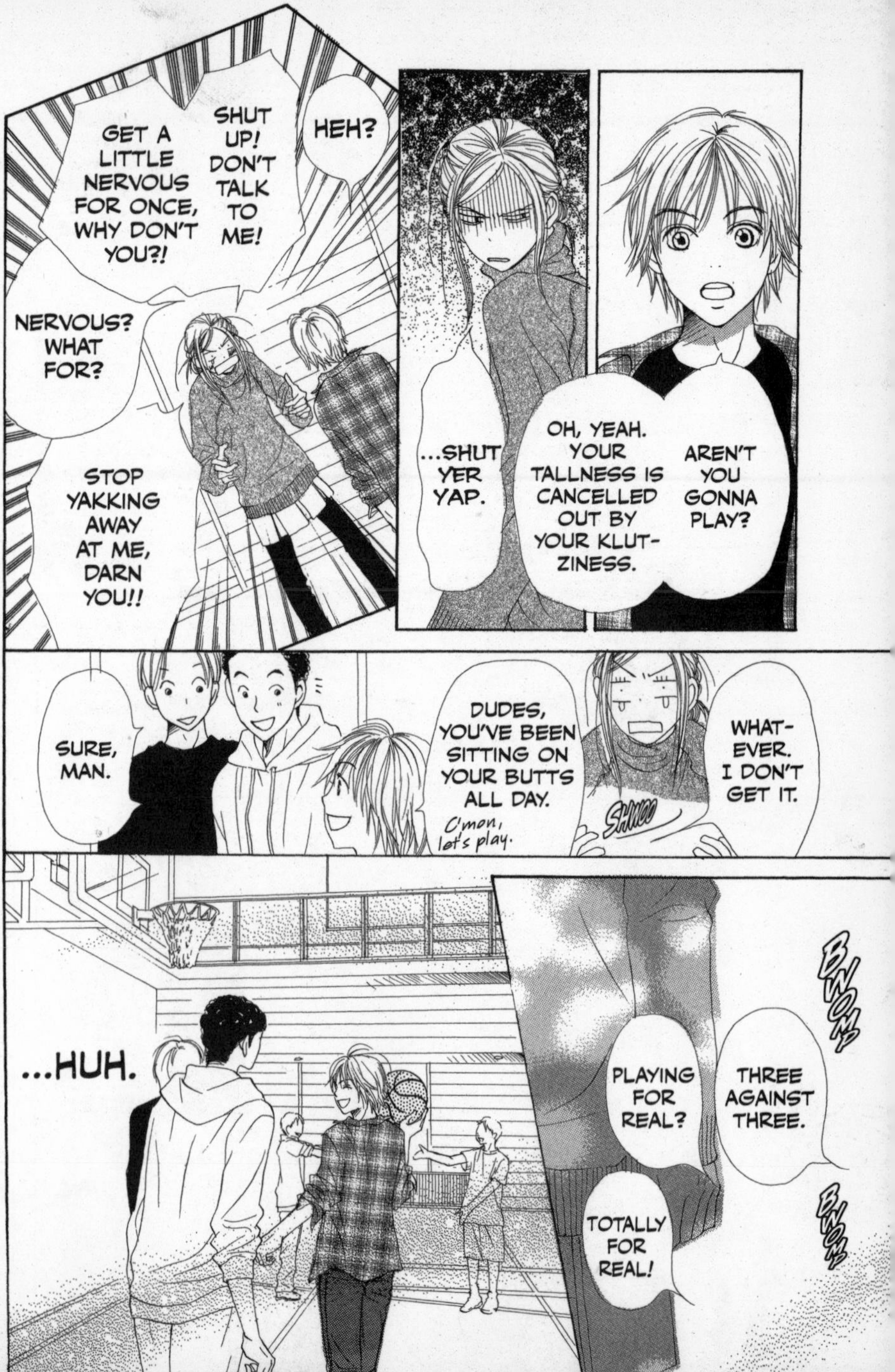
AREN'T YOU GONNA PLAY?
OH, YEAH. YOUR TALLNESS IS CANCELLED OUT BY YOUR KLUTZINESS.
...SHUT YER YAP.
HEH?
SHUT UP! DON'T TALK TO ME!
GET A LITTLE NERVOUS FOR ONCE, WHY DON'T YOU?!
NERVOUS? WHAT FOR?
STOP YAKKING AWAY AT ME, DARN YOU!!
WHATEVER. I DON'T GET IT.
SHWOO
DUDES, YOU'VE BEEN SITTING ON YOUR BUTTS ALL DAY.
C'mon, let's play.
SURE, MAN.
BNOM
BNOM
THREE AGAINST THREE.
PLAYING FOR REAL?
TOTALLY FOR REAL!
...HUH.

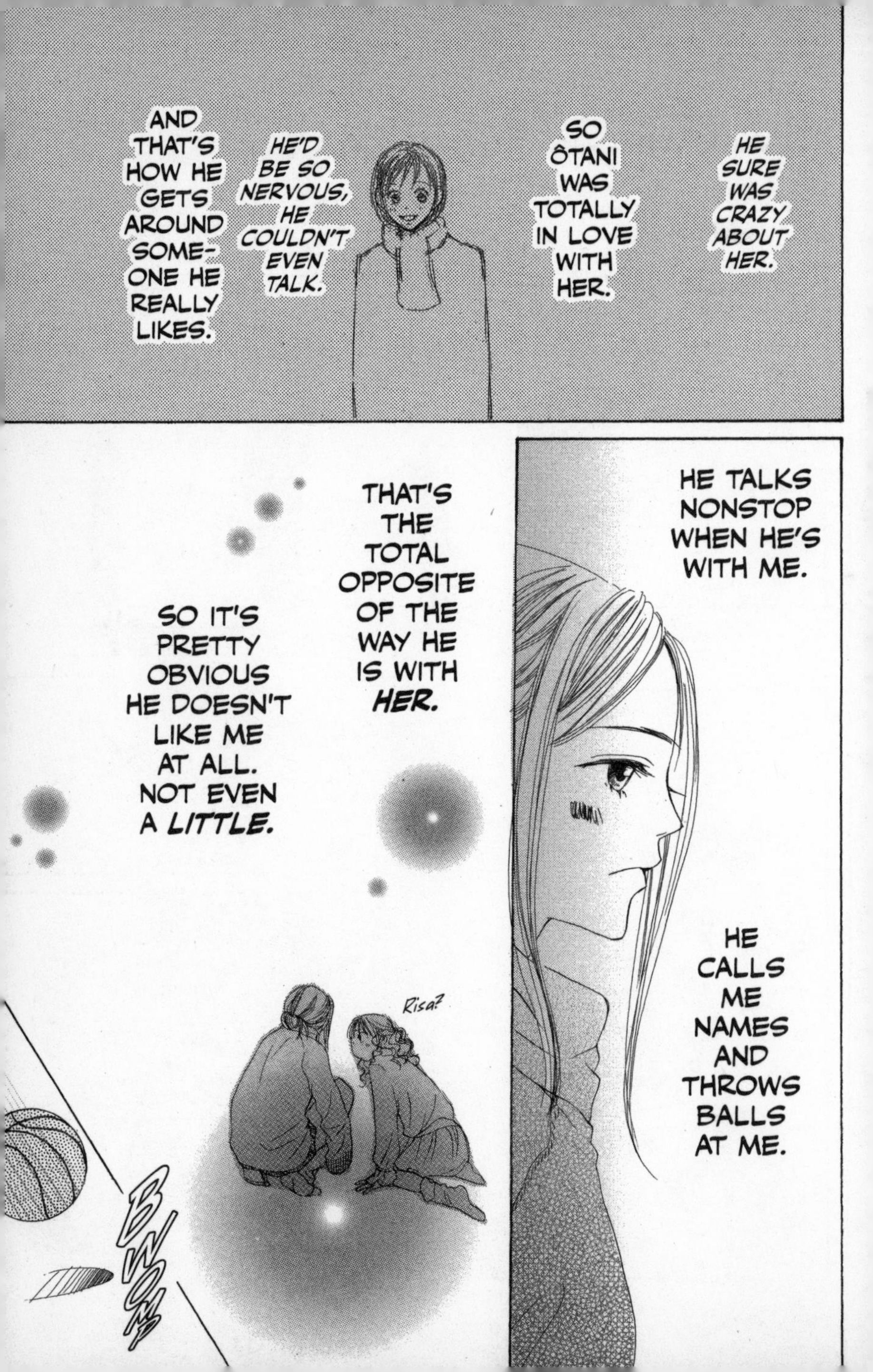
HE SURE WAS CRAZY ABOUT HER.
SO ÔTANI WAS TOTALLY IN LOVE WITH HER.
HE'D BE SO NERVOUS, HE COULDN'T EVEN TALK.
AND THAT'S HOW HE GETS AROUND SOME-ONE HE REALLY LIKES.
HE TALKS NONSTOP WHEN HE'S WITH ME.
HE CALLS ME NAMES AND THROWS BALLS AT ME.
THAT'S THE TOTAL OPPOSITE OF THE WAY HE IS WITH *HER.*
SO IT'S PRETTY OBVIOUS HE DOESN'T LIKE ME AT ALL. NOT EVEN A *LITTLE.*
Risa?
BWOMP

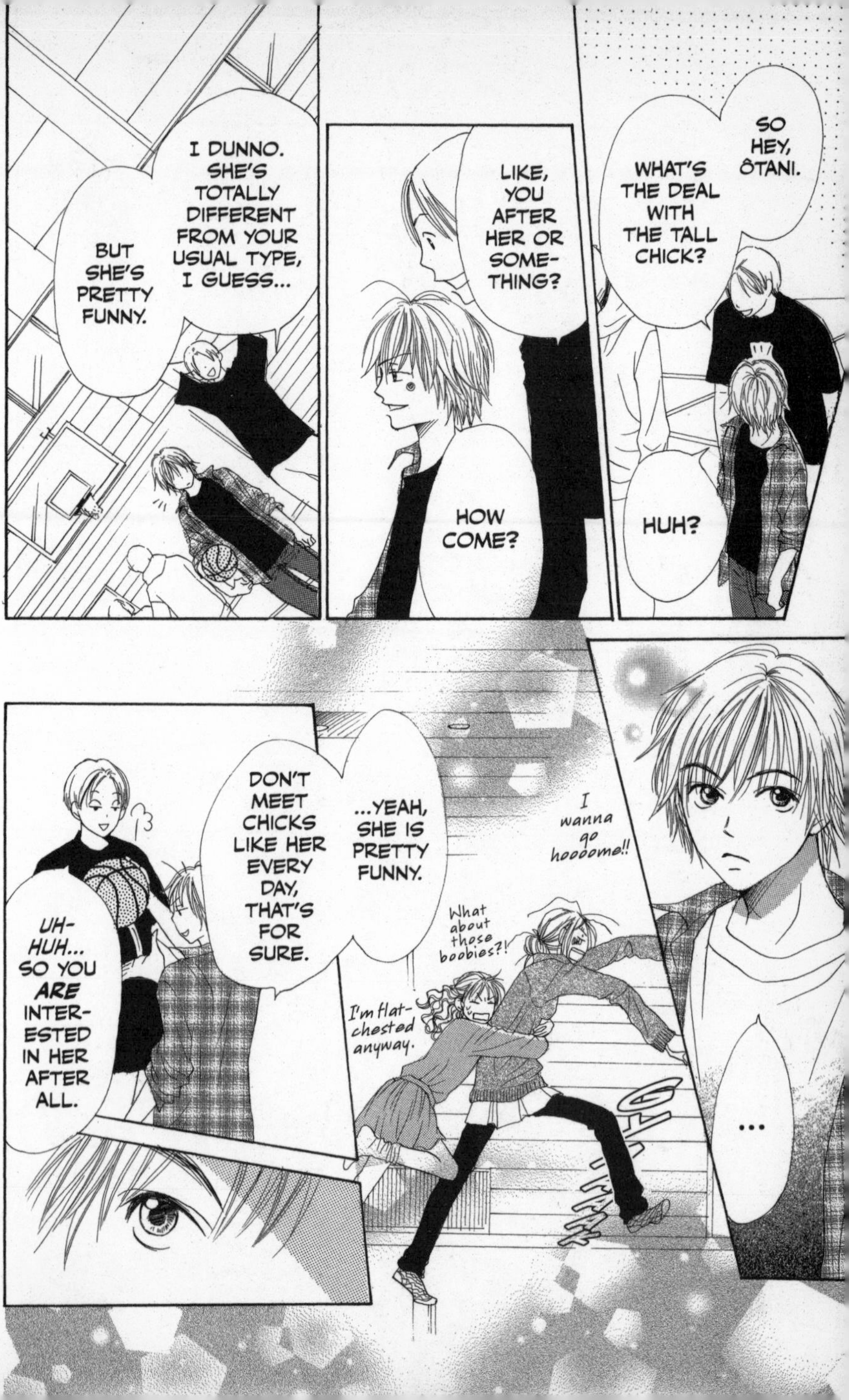
SO HEY, ŌTANI.
WHAT'S THE DEAL WITH THE TALL CHICK?
HUH?
LIKE, YOU AFTER HER OR SOME-THING?
HOW COME?
I DUNNO. SHE'S TOTALLY DIFFERENT FROM YOUR USUAL TYPE, I GUESS...
BUT SHE'S PRETTY FUNNY.
...
I wanna go hoooome!!
What about those boobies?!
I'm flat-chested anyway.
...YEAH, SHE IS PRETTY FUNNY.
DON'T MEET CHICKS LIKE HER EVERY DAY, THAT'S FOR SURE.
UH-HUH... SO YOU ARE INTERESTED IN HER AFTER ALL.

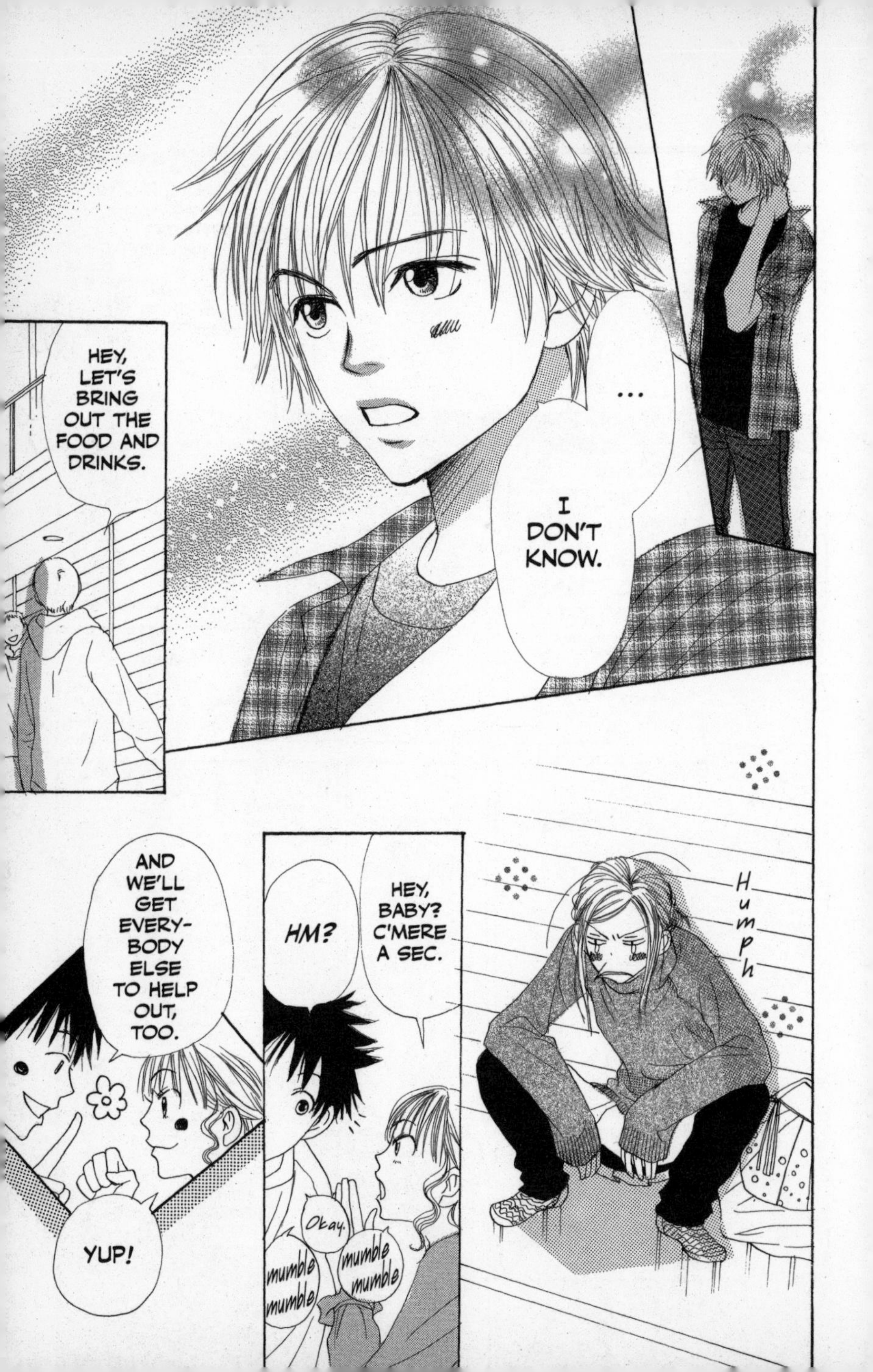
...
I DON'T KNOW.
HEY, LET'S BRING OUT THE FOOD AND DRINKS.
Humph
HEY, BABY? C'MERE A SEC.
HM?
Okay.
mumble mumble
mumble mumble
AND WE'LL GET EVERYBODY ELSE TO HELP OUT, TOO.
YUP!

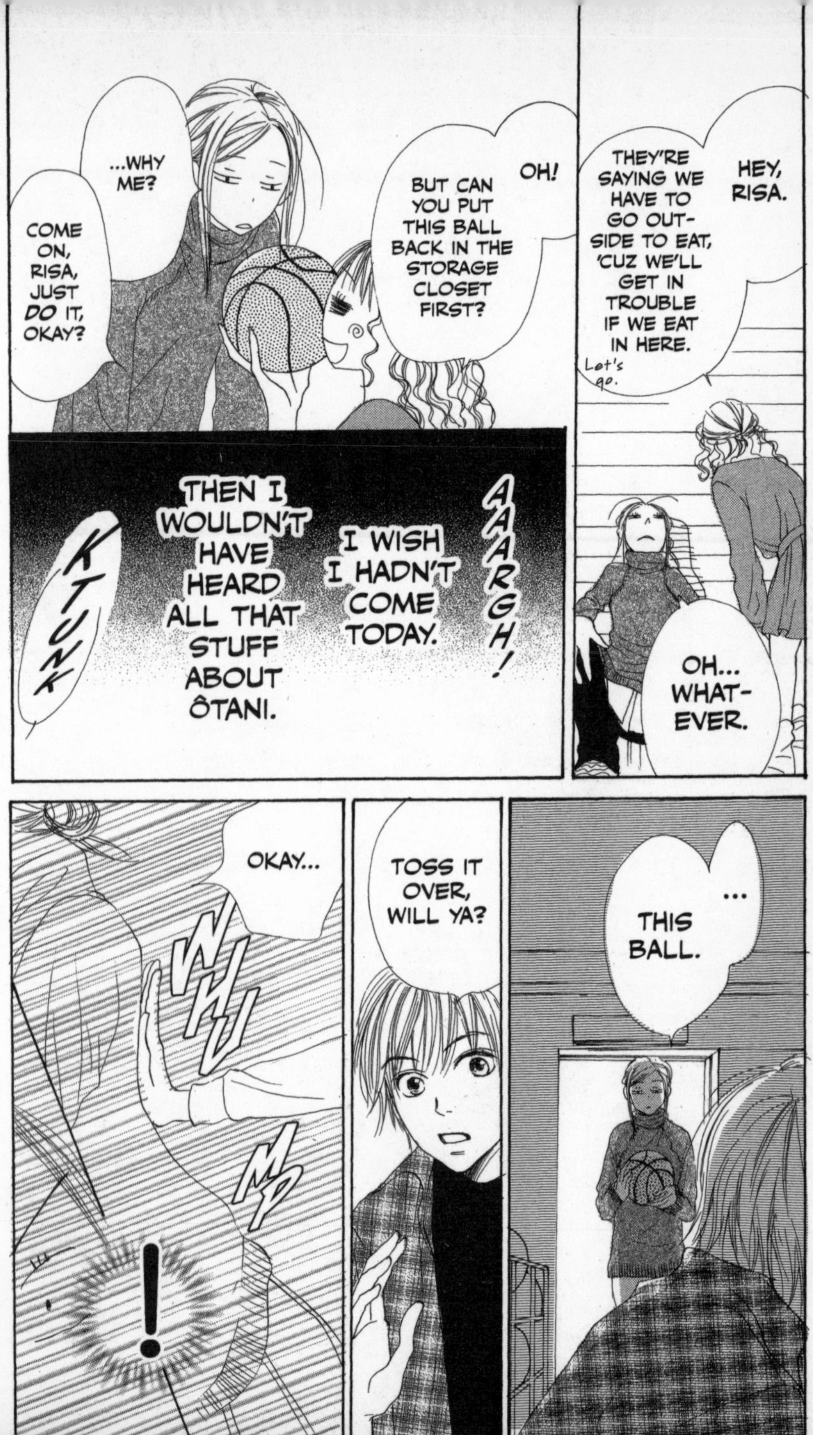
HEY, RISA.
THEY'RE SAYING WE HAVE TO GO OUTSIDE TO EAT, 'CUZ WE'LL GET IN TROUBLE IF WE EAT IN HERE.
Let's go.
OH... WHATEVER.
OH!
BUT CAN YOU PUT THIS BALL BACK IN THE STORAGE CLOSET FIRST?
...WHY ME?
COME ON, RISA, JUST DO IT, OKAY?
AAAARGH!
I WISH I HADN'T COME TODAY.
THEN I WOULDN'T HAVE HEARD ALL THAT STUFF ABOUT ÔTANI.
KTUNK
...
THIS BALL.
TOSS IT OVER, WILL YA?
OKAY...
WHUMP
!

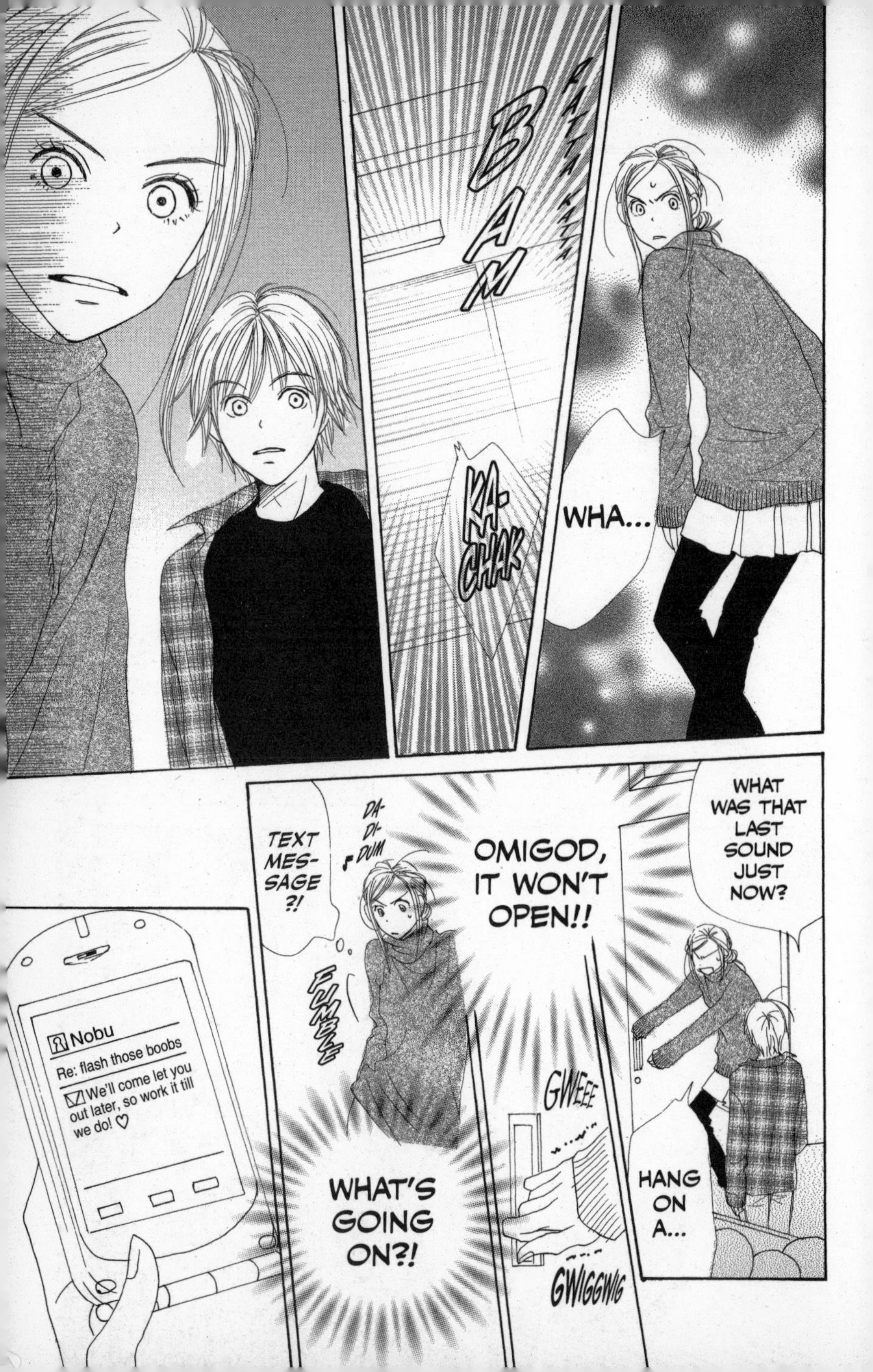
WHA...
RATTA KATTA
BAM
KA-CHAK
WHAT WAS THAT LAST SOUND JUST NOW?
HANG ON A...
OMIGOD, IT WON'T OPEN!!
GWEEE
GWIGGWIG
DA-DI-DUM
TEXT MES-SAGE?!
FUMBLE
WHAT'S GOING ON?!
Nobu
Re: flash those boobs
We'll come let you out later, so work it till we do! ♡

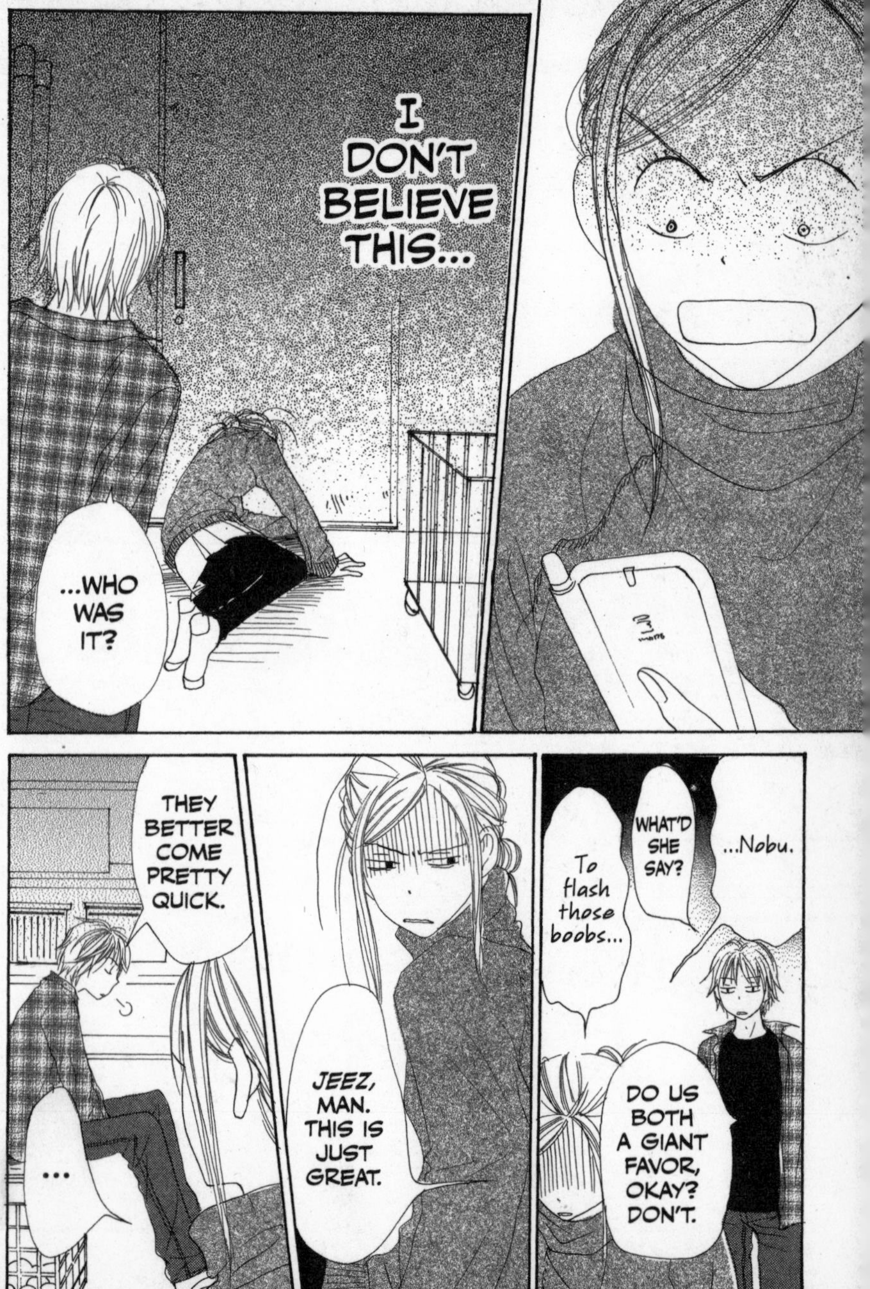
I DON'T BELIEVE THIS...
...WHO WAS IT?
...Nobu.
WHAT'D SHE SAY?
To flash those boobs...
DO US BOTH A GIANT FAVOR, OKAY? DON'T.
JEEZ, MAN. THIS IS JUST GREAT.
THEY BETTER COME PRETTY QUICK.
...

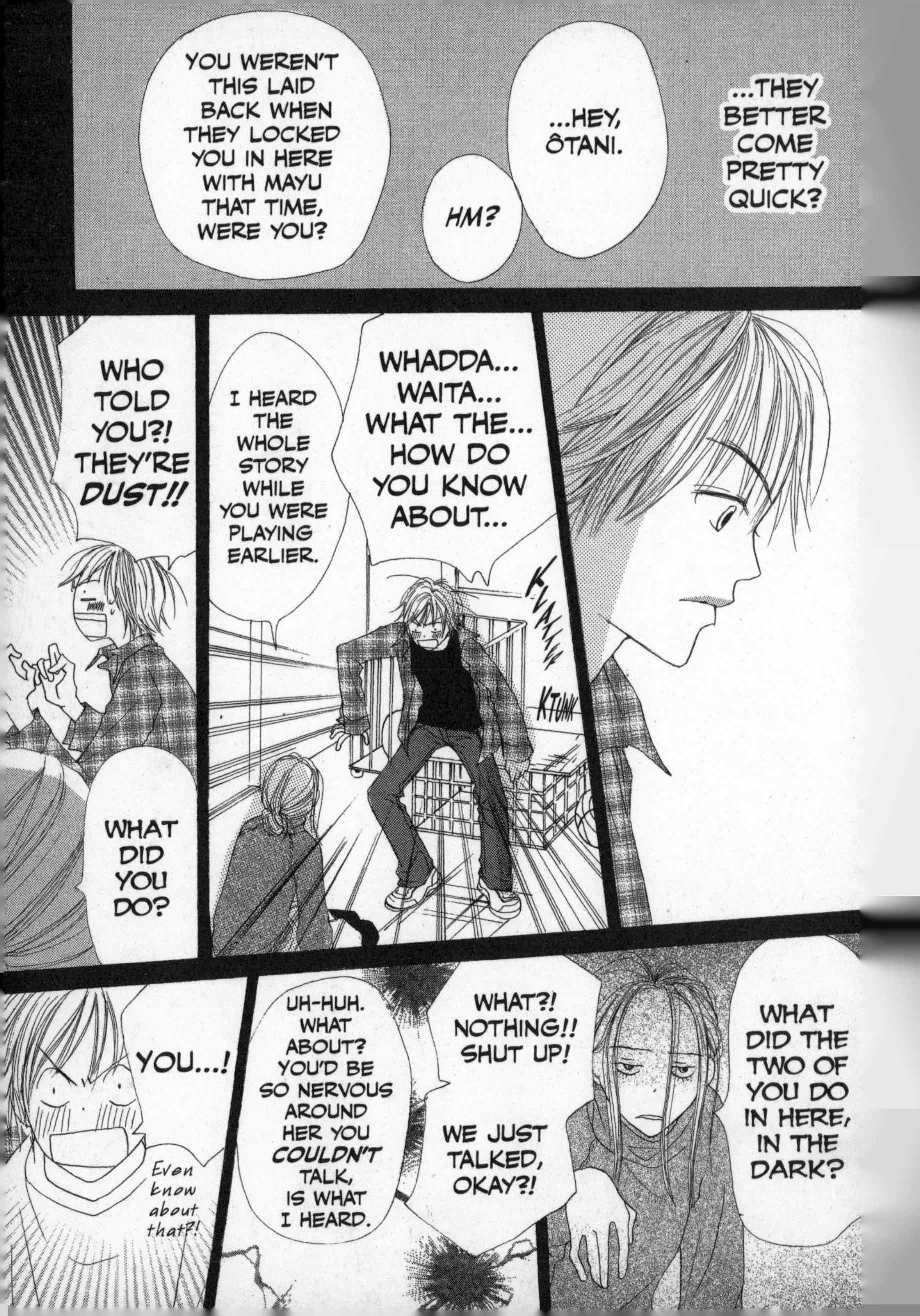
...THEY BETTER COME PRETTY QUICK?
...HEY, ÔTANI.
HM?
YOU WEREN'T THIS LAID BACK WHEN THEY LOCKED YOU IN HERE WITH MAYU THAT TIME, WERE YOU?
WHADDA... WAITA... WHAT THE... HOW DO YOU KNOW ABOUT...
KTUNK
I HEARD THE WHOLE STORY WHILE YOU WERE PLAYING EARLIER.
WHO TOLD YOU?! THEY'RE DUST!!
WHAT DID YOU DO?
WHAT DID THE TWO OF YOU DO IN HERE, IN THE DARK?
WHAT?! NOTHING!! SHUT UP!
WE JUST TALKED, OKAY?!
UH-HUH. WHAT ABOUT? YOU'D BE SO NERVOUS AROUND HER YOU COULDN'T TALK, IS WHAT I HEARD.
YOU...!
Even know about that?!

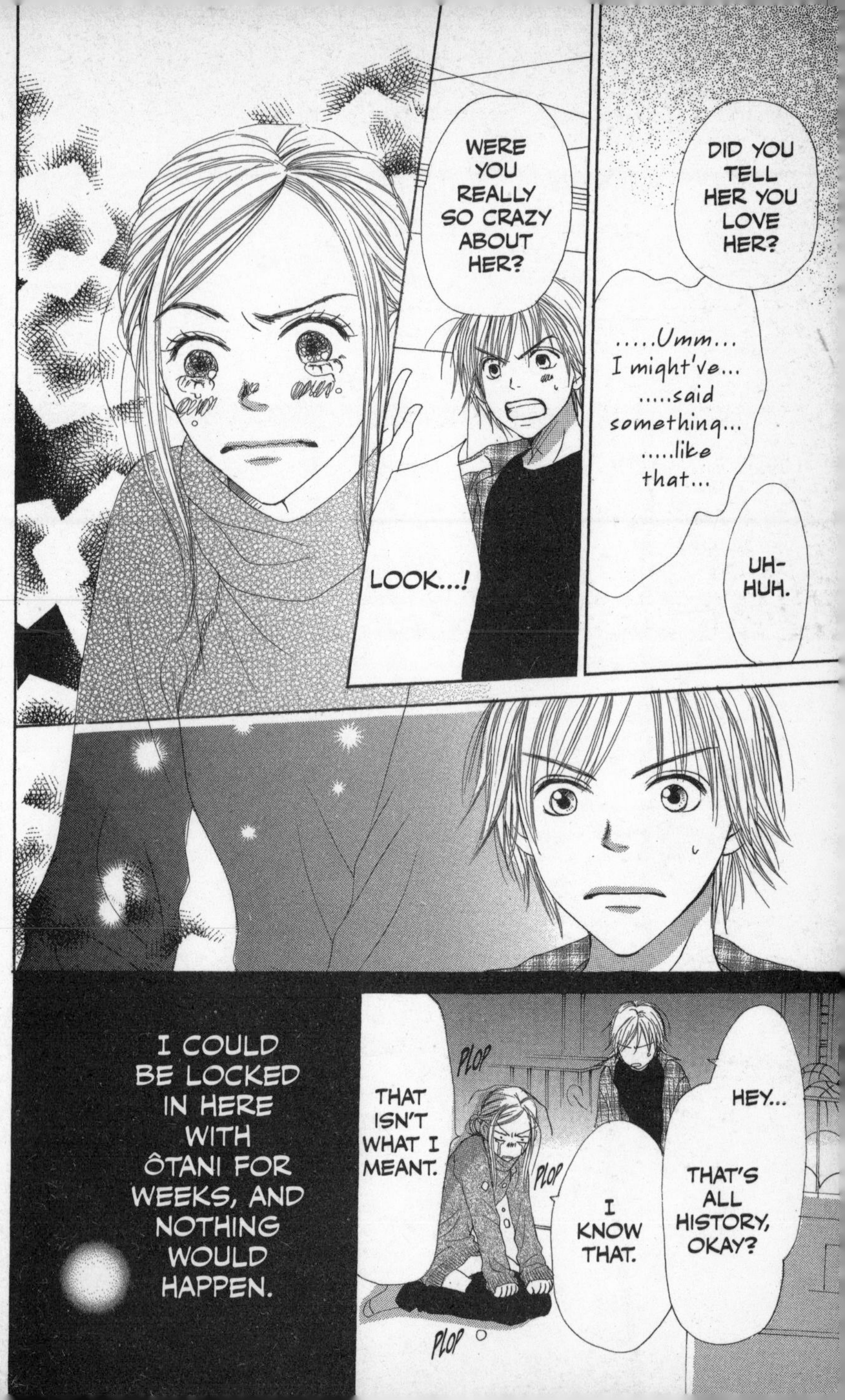
DID YOU TELL HER YOU LOVE HER?
.....Umm... I might've... .....said something... .....like that...
UH-HUH.
WERE YOU REALLY SO CRAZY ABOUT HER?
LOOK...!
HEY...
THAT'S ALL HISTORY, OKAY?
I KNOW THAT.
PLOP
PLOP
PLOP
THAT ISN'T WHAT I MEANT.
I COULD BE LOCKED IN HERE WITH ÔTANI FOR WEEKS, AND NOTHING WOULD HAPPEN.

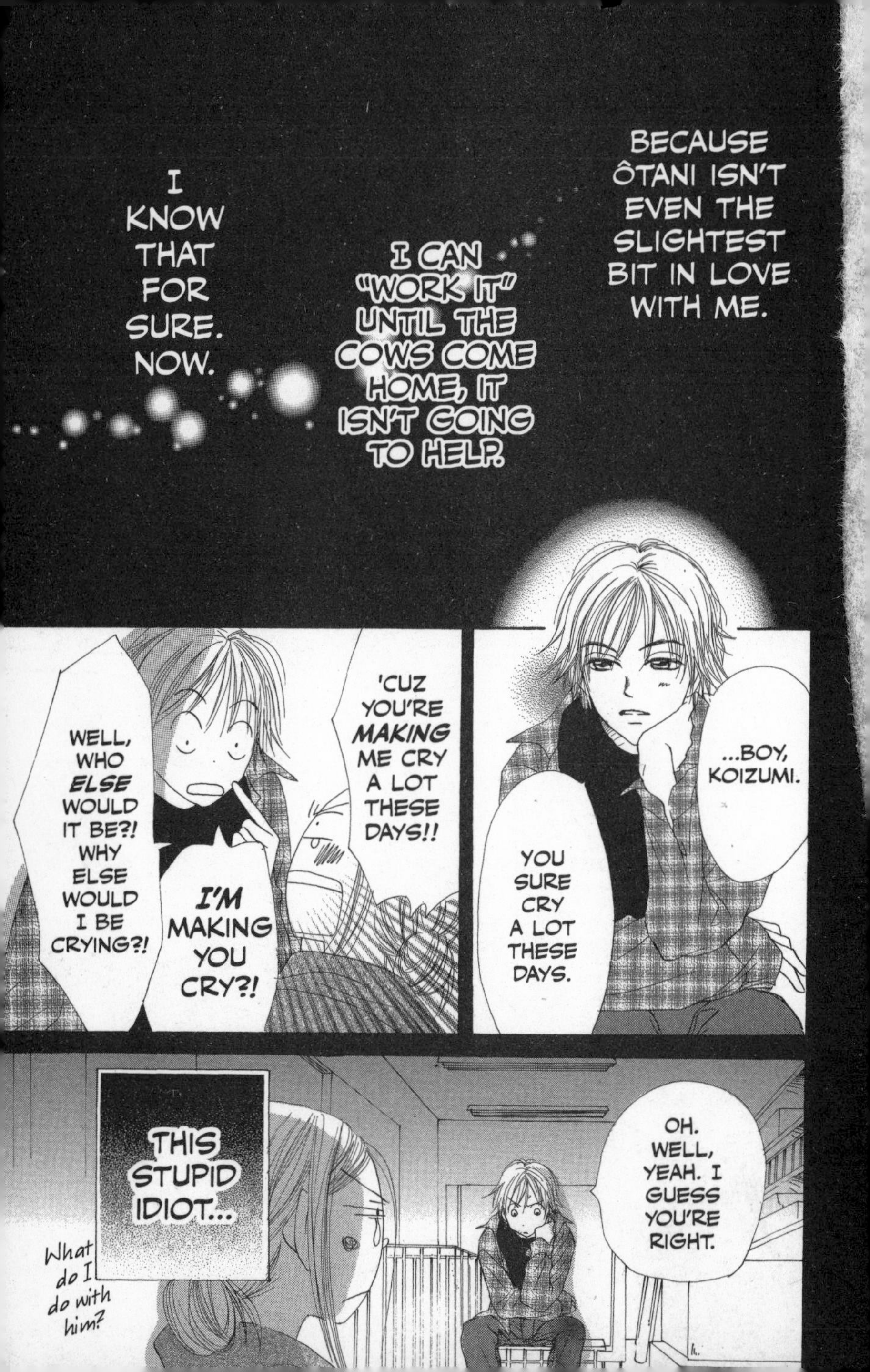
BECAUSE ÔTANI ISN'T EVEN THE SLIGHTEST BIT IN LOVE WITH ME.
I CAN "WORK IT" UNTIL THE COWS COME HOME, IT ISN'T GOING TO HELP.
I KNOW THAT FOR SURE. NOW.
...BOY, KOIZUMI.
YOU SURE CRY A LOT THESE DAYS.
'CUZ YOU'RE *MAKING* ME CRY A LOT THESE DAYS!!
I'M MAKING YOU CRY?!
WELL, WHO *ELSE* WOULD IT BE?! WHY ELSE WOULD I BE CRYING?!
OH. WELL, YEAH. I GUESS YOU'RE RIGHT.
THIS STUPID IDIOT...
What do I do with him?

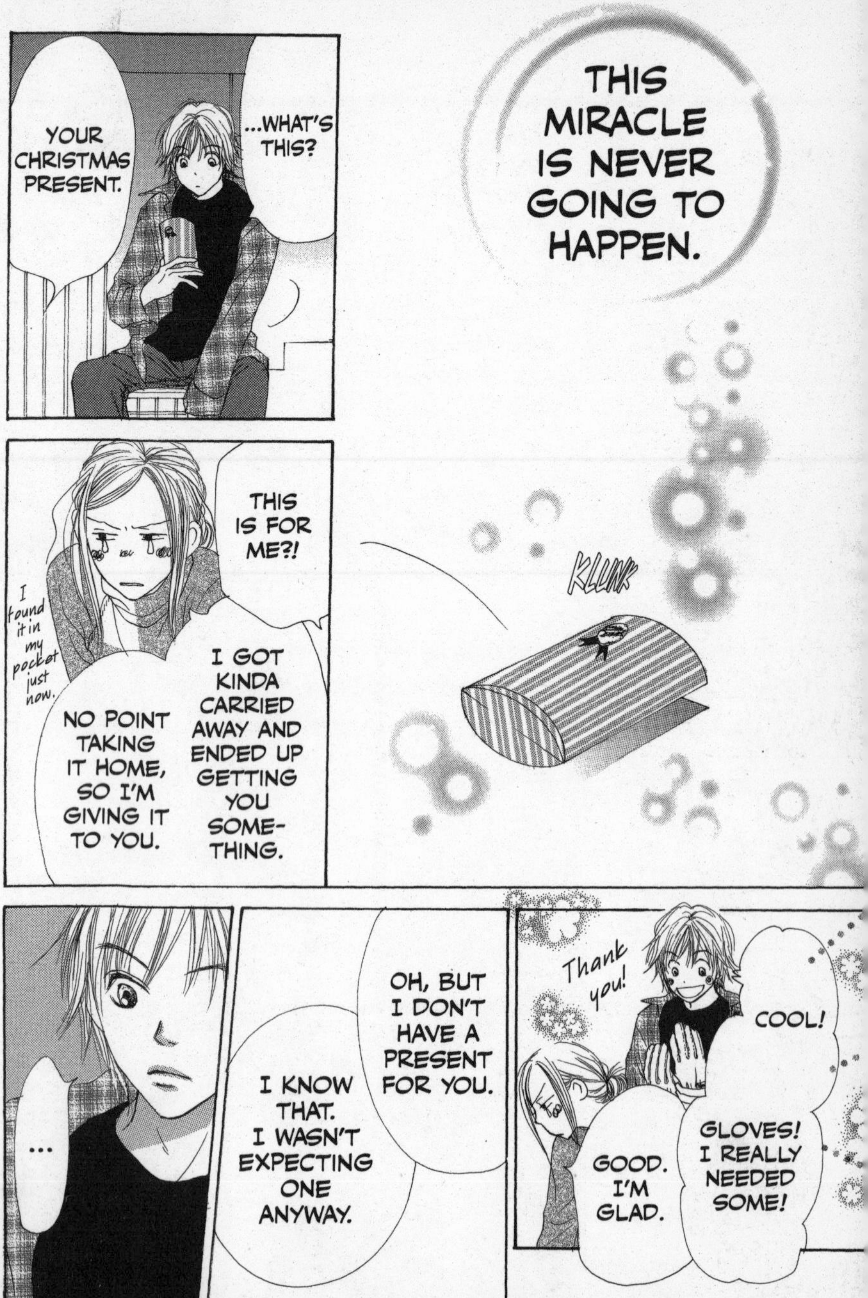
THIS MIRACLE IS NEVER GOING TO HAPPEN.
...WHAT'S THIS?
YOUR CHRISTMAS PRESENT.
KLUNK
THIS IS FOR ME?!
I GOT KINDA CARRIED AWAY AND ENDED UP GETTING YOU SOME-THING.
NO POINT TAKING IT HOME, SO I'M GIVING IT TO YOU.
I found it in my pocket just now.
Thank you!
COOL!
GLOVES! I REALLY NEEDED SOME!
GOOD. I'M GLAD.
OH, BUT I DON'T HAVE A PRESENT FOR YOU.
I KNOW THAT. I WASN'T EXPECTING ONE ANYWAY.
...

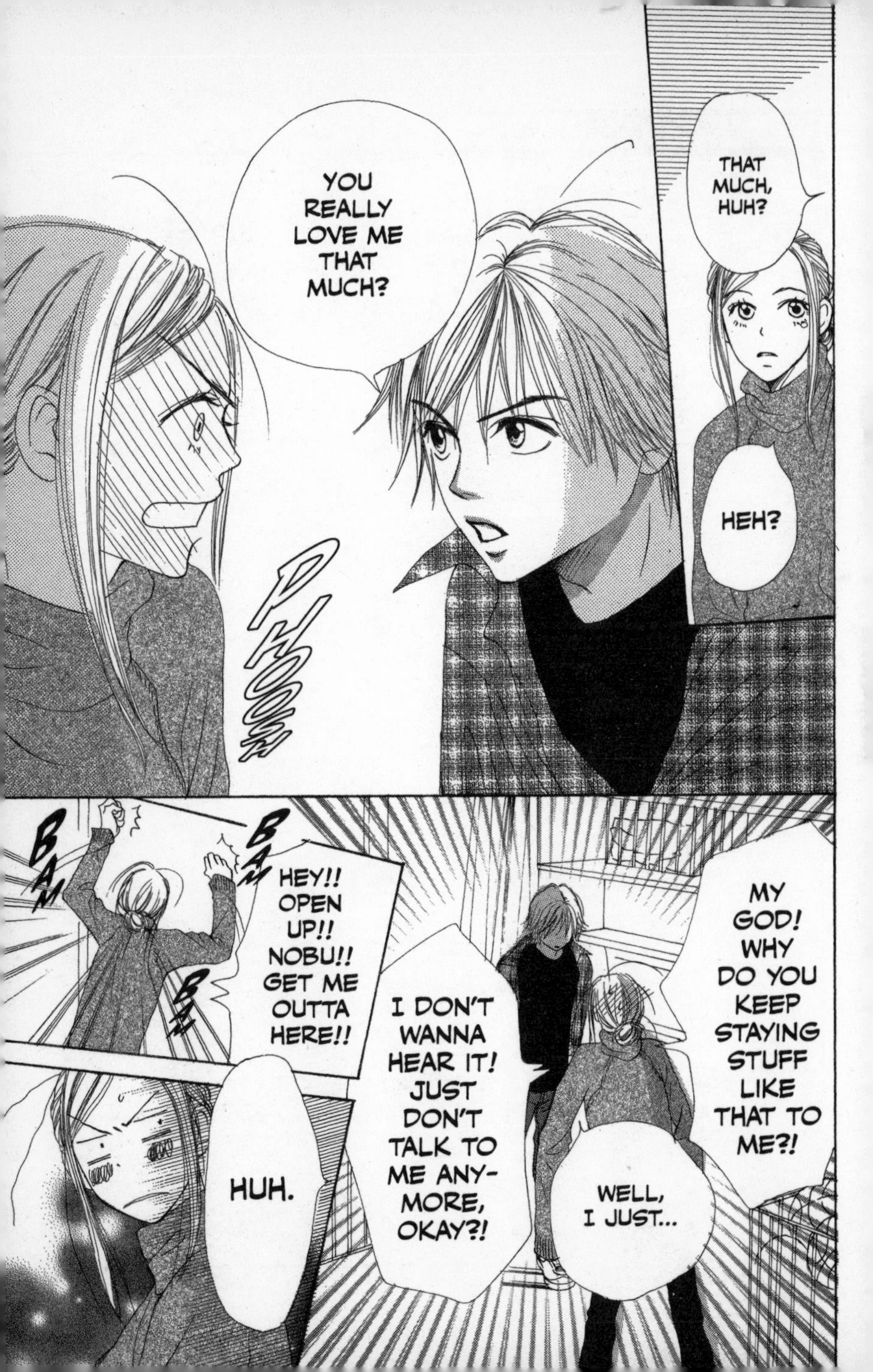
THAT MUCH, HUH?
HEH?
YOU REALLY LOVE ME THAT MUCH?
MY GOD! WHY DO YOU KEEP STAYING STUFF LIKE THAT TO ME?!
WELL, I JUST...
I DON'T WANNA HEAR IT! JUST DON'T TALK TO ME ANY-MORE, OKAY?!
HUH.
HEY!! OPEN UP!! NOBU!! GET ME OUTTA HERE!!
BAM
BAM
BAM

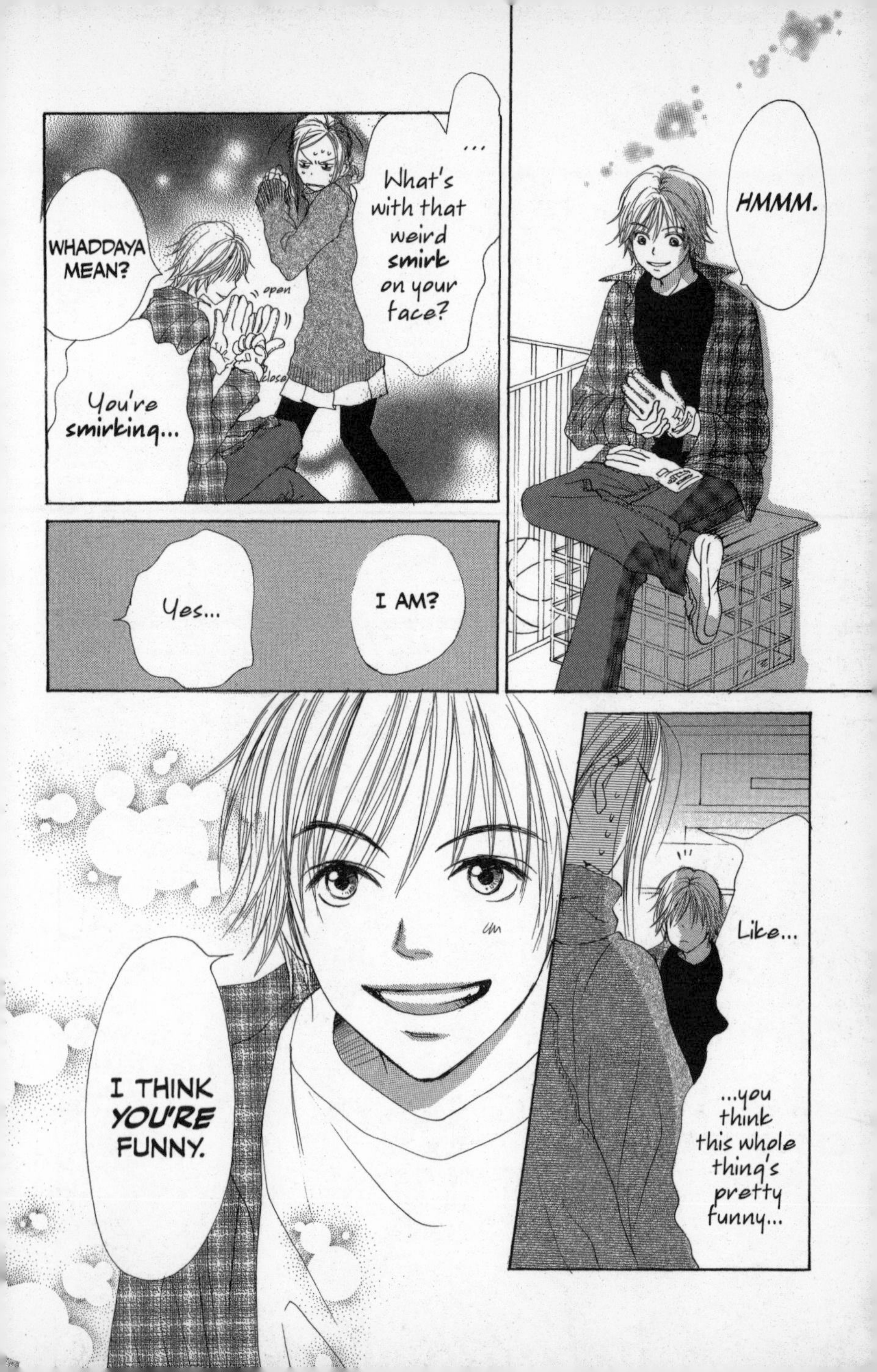
HMMM.
...
What's with that weird smirk on your face?
WHADDAYA MEAN?
open
close
You're smirking...
I AM?
Yes...
Like...
...you think this whole thing's pretty funny...
I THINK YOU'RE FUNNY.

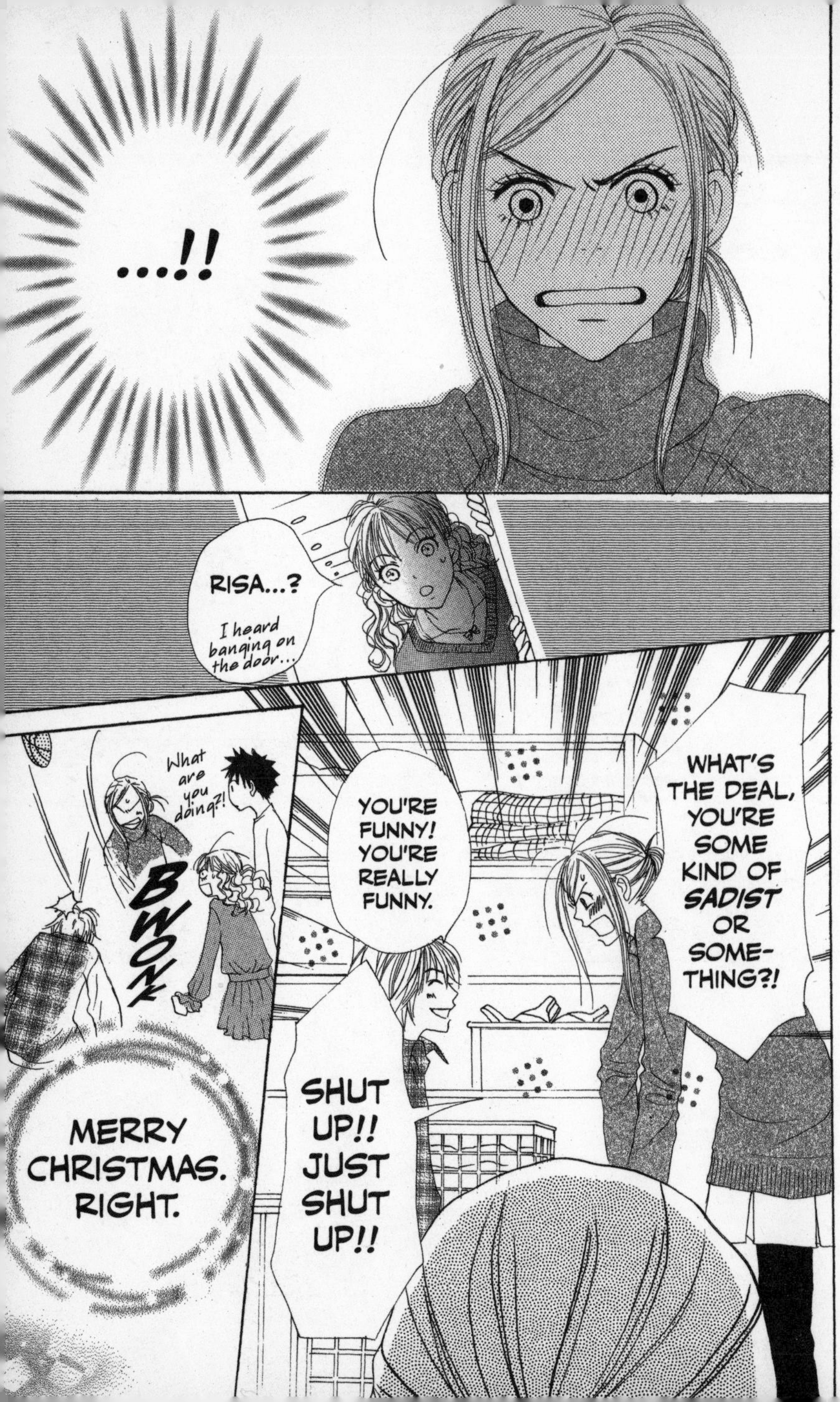
...!!
RISA...?
I heard banging on the door...
WHAT'S THE DEAL, YOU'RE SOME KIND OF SADIST OR SOMETHING?!
YOU'RE FUNNY! YOU'RE REALLY FUNNY.
SHUT UP!! JUST SHUT UP!!
What are you doing?!
BWONK
MERRY CHRISTMAS. RIGHT.

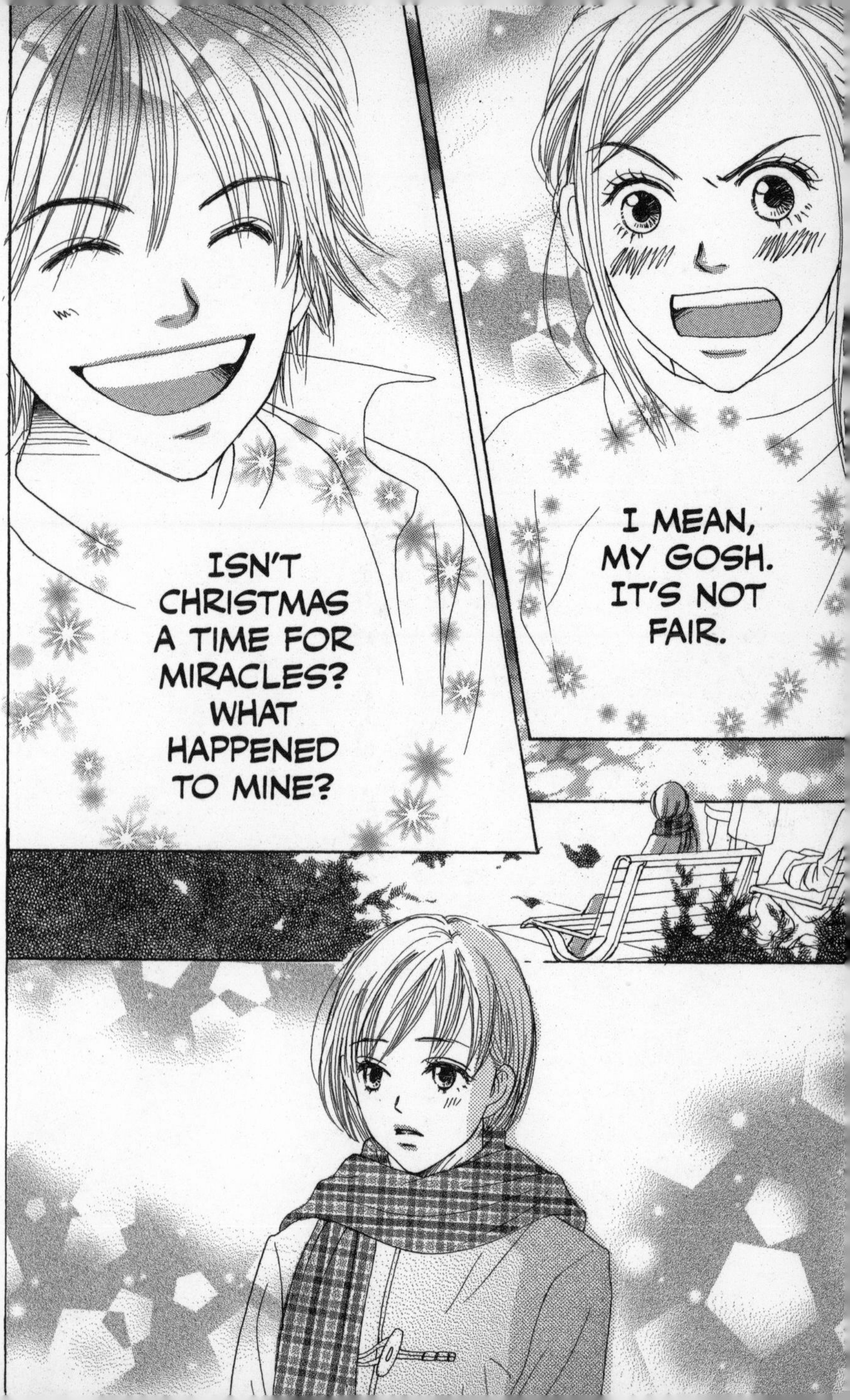
I MEAN, MY GOSH. IT'S NOT FAIR.
ISN'T CHRISTMAS A TIME FOR MIRACLES? WHAT HAPPENED TO MINE?

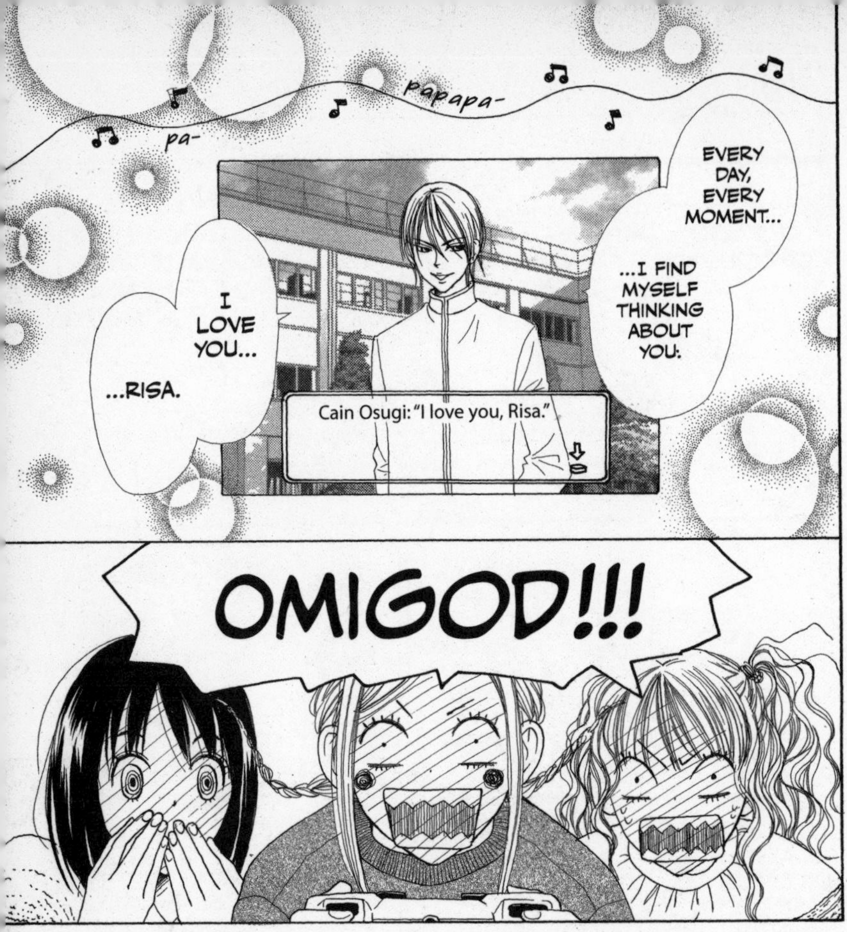
pa-
papapa-
EVERY DAY, EVERY MOMENT...
...I FIND MYSELF THINKING ABOUT YOU.
I LOVE YOU...
...RISA.
Cain Osugi: "I love you, Risa."
OMIGOD!!!

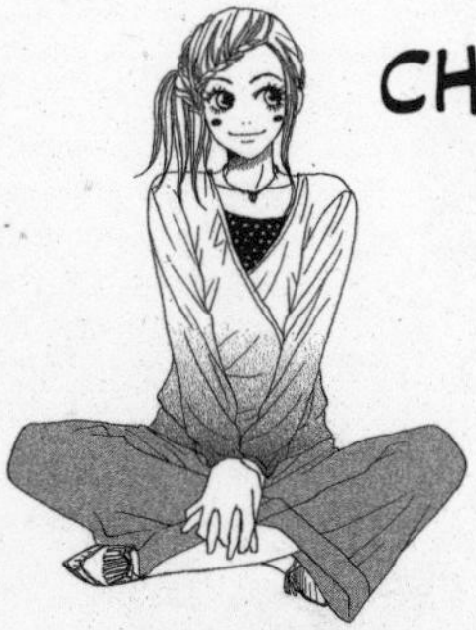

CHAPTER 19

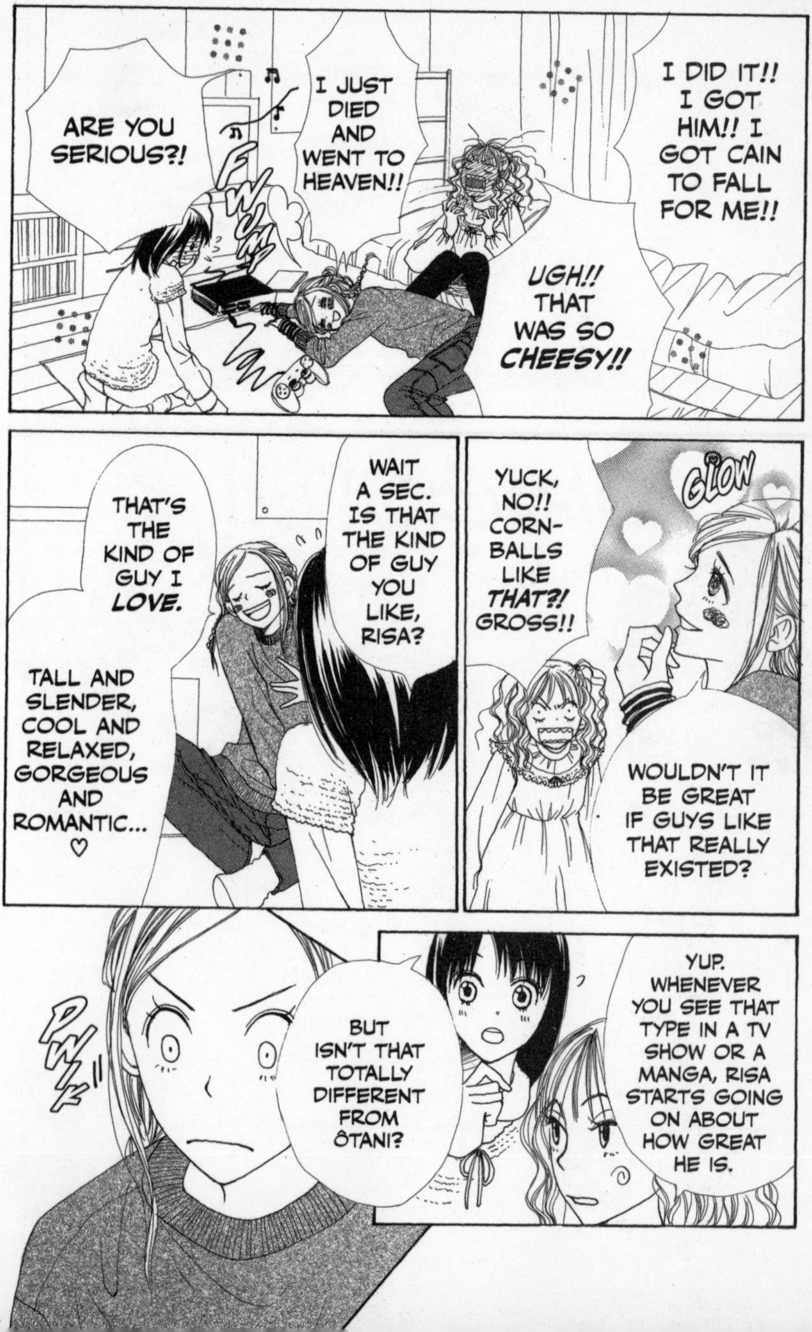
I DID IT!! I GOT HIM!! I GOT CAIN TO FALL FOR ME!!
UGH!! THAT WAS SO CHEESY!!
I JUST DIED AND WENT TO HEAVEN!!
ARE YOU SERIOUS?!
GLOW
WOULDN'T IT BE GREAT IF GUYS LIKE THAT REALLY EXISTED?
YUCK, NO!! CORN-BALLS LIKE THAT?! GROSS!!
WAIT A SEC. IS THAT THE KIND OF GUY YOU LIKE, RISA?
THAT'S THE KIND OF GUY I LOVE.
TALL AND SLENDER, COOL AND RELAXED, GORGEOUS AND ROMANTIC... ♡
YUP. WHENEVER YOU SEE THAT TYPE IN A TV SHOW OR A MANGA, RISA STARTS GOING ON ABOUT HOW GREAT HE IS.
BUT ISN'T THAT TOTALLY DIFFERENT FROM ŌTANI?

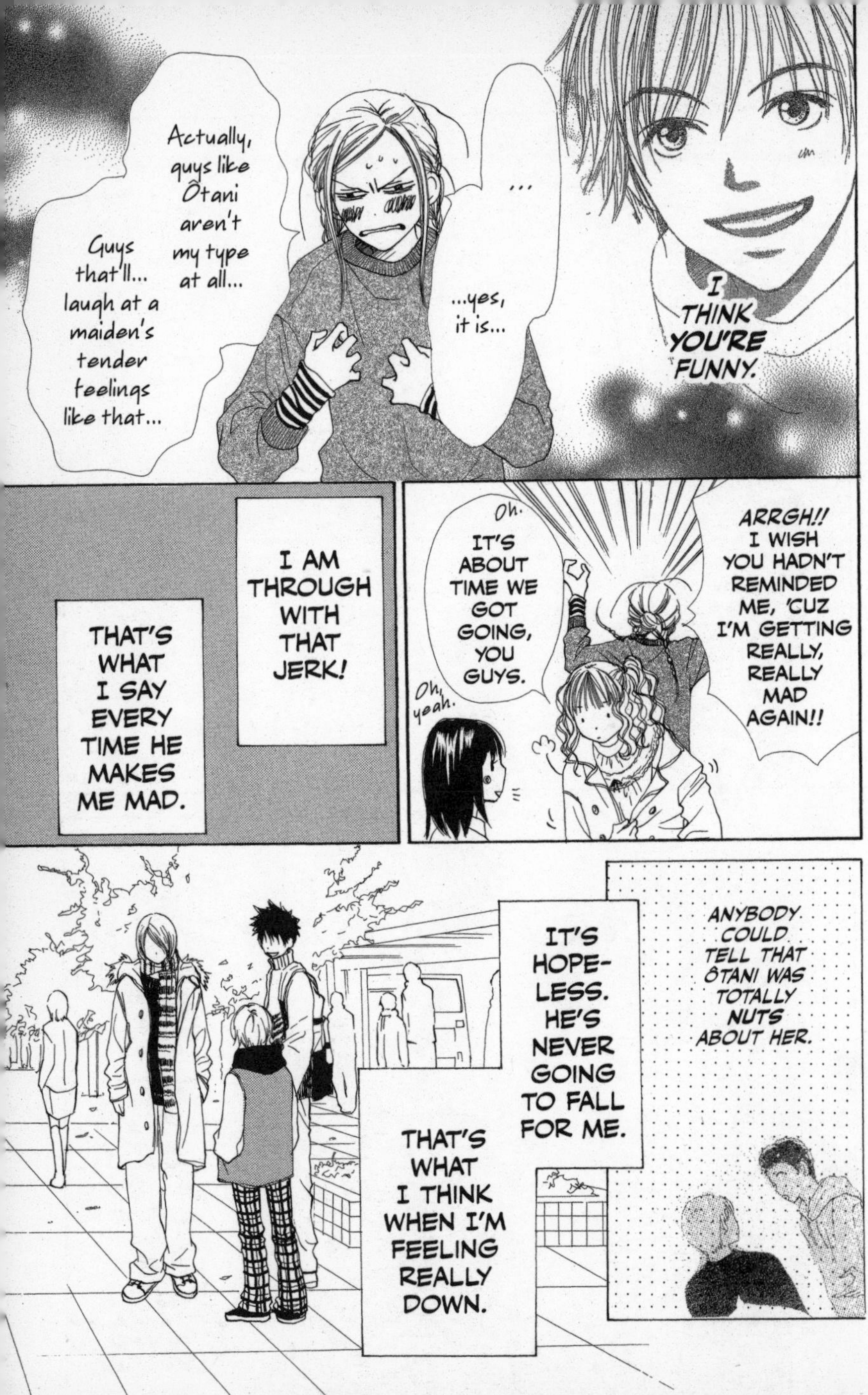
I THINK YOU'RE FUNNY.
um
...
...yes, it is...
Actually, guys like Ōtani aren't my type at all...
Guys that'll... laugh at a maiden's tender feelings like that...
ARRGH!! I WISH YOU HADN'T REMINDED ME, 'CUZ I'M GETTING REALLY, REALLY MAD AGAIN!!
Oh. IT'S ABOUT TIME WE GOT GOING, YOU GUYS.
Oh, yeah.
I AM THROUGH WITH THAT JERK!
THAT'S WHAT I SAY EVERY TIME HE MAKES ME MAD.
ANYBODY COULD TELL THAT ŌTANI WAS TOTALLY NUTS ABOUT HER.
IT'S HOPE-LESS. HE'S NEVER GOING TO FALL FOR ME.
THAT'S WHAT I THINK WHEN I'M FEELING REALLY DOWN.

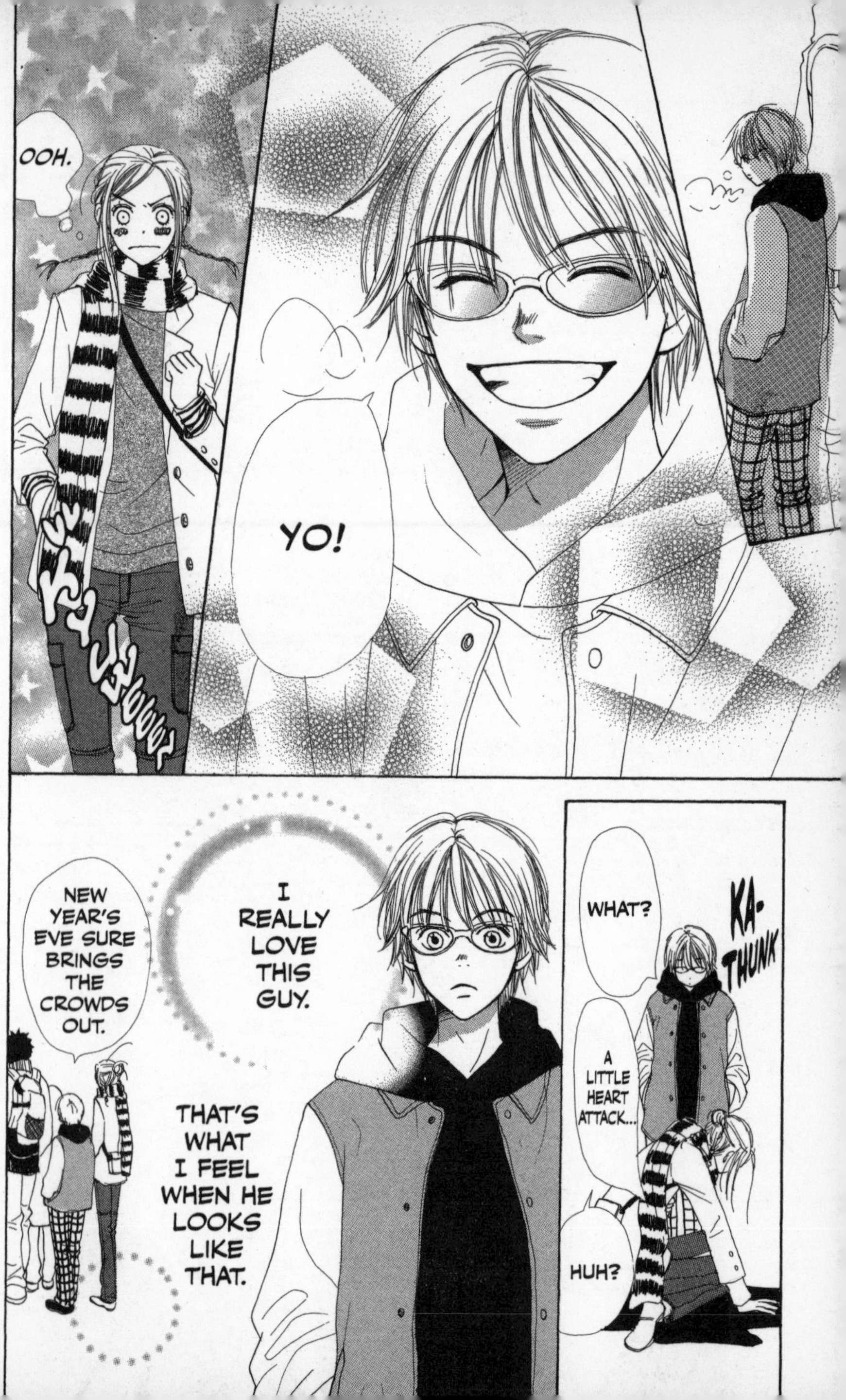
OOH.
YO!
WHAT?
KA-THUNK
A LITTLE HEART ATTACK...
HUH?
I REALLY LOVE THIS GUY.
THAT'S WHAT I FEEL WHEN HE LOOKS LIKE THAT.
NEW YEAR'S EVE SURE BRINGS THE CROWDS OUT.

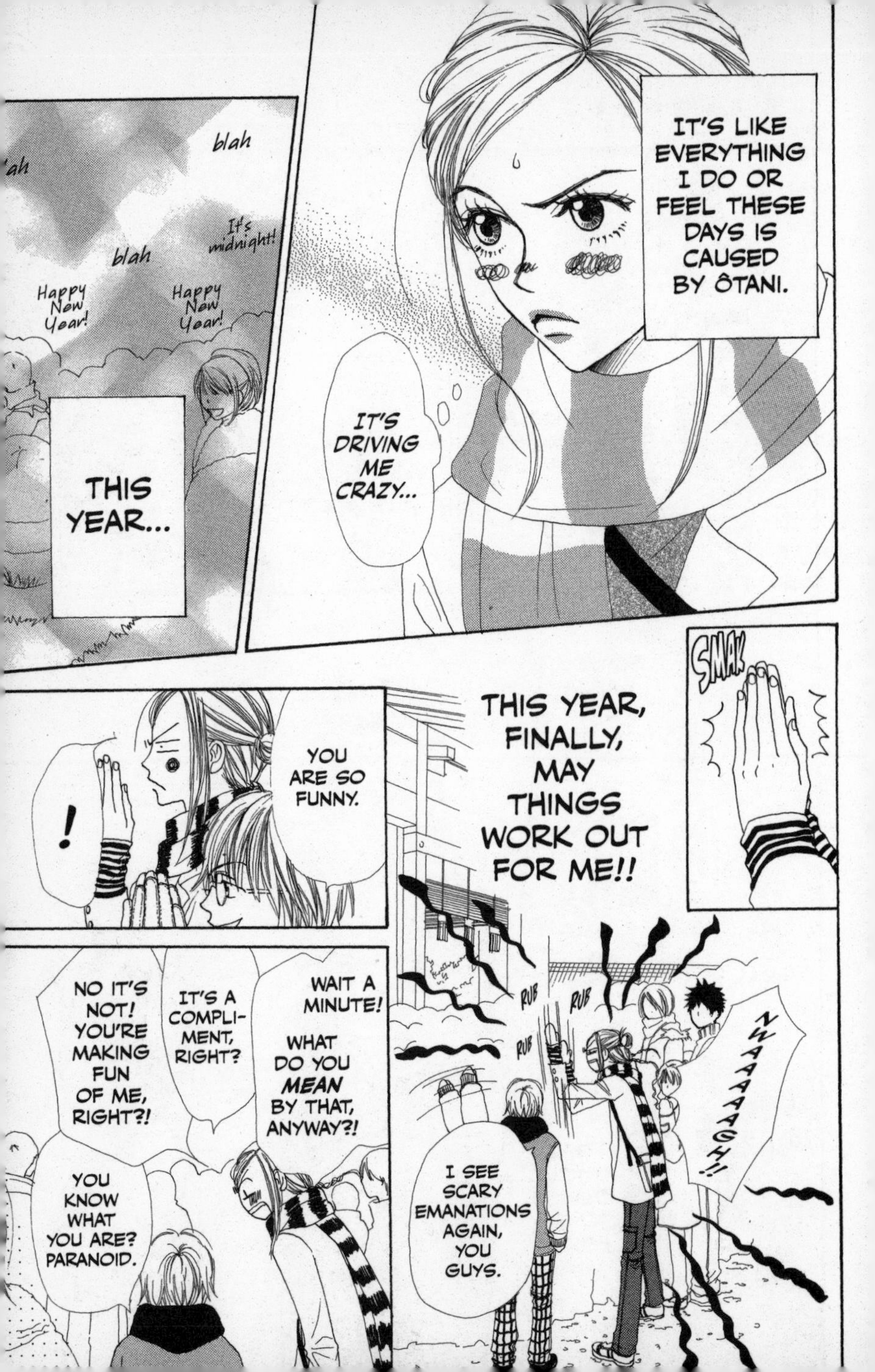
IT'S LIKE EVERYTHING I DO OR FEEL THESE DAYS IS CAUSED BY ÔTANI.
IT'S DRIVING ME CRAZY...
blah
It's midnight!
blah
Happy New Year!
Happy New Year!
THIS YEAR...
SMAK
THIS YEAR, FINALLY, MAY THINGS WORK OUT FOR ME!!
YOU ARE SO FUNNY.
!
NWAAAAAAGH!!
RUB
RUB
RUB
I SEE SCARY EMANATIONS AGAIN, YOU GUYS.
WAIT A MINUTE!
WHAT DO YOU *MEAN* BY THAT, ANYWAY?!
IT'S A COMPLI-MENT, RIGHT?
NO IT'S NOT! YOU'RE MAKING FUN OF ME, RIGHT?!
YOU KNOW WHAT YOU ARE? PARANOID.

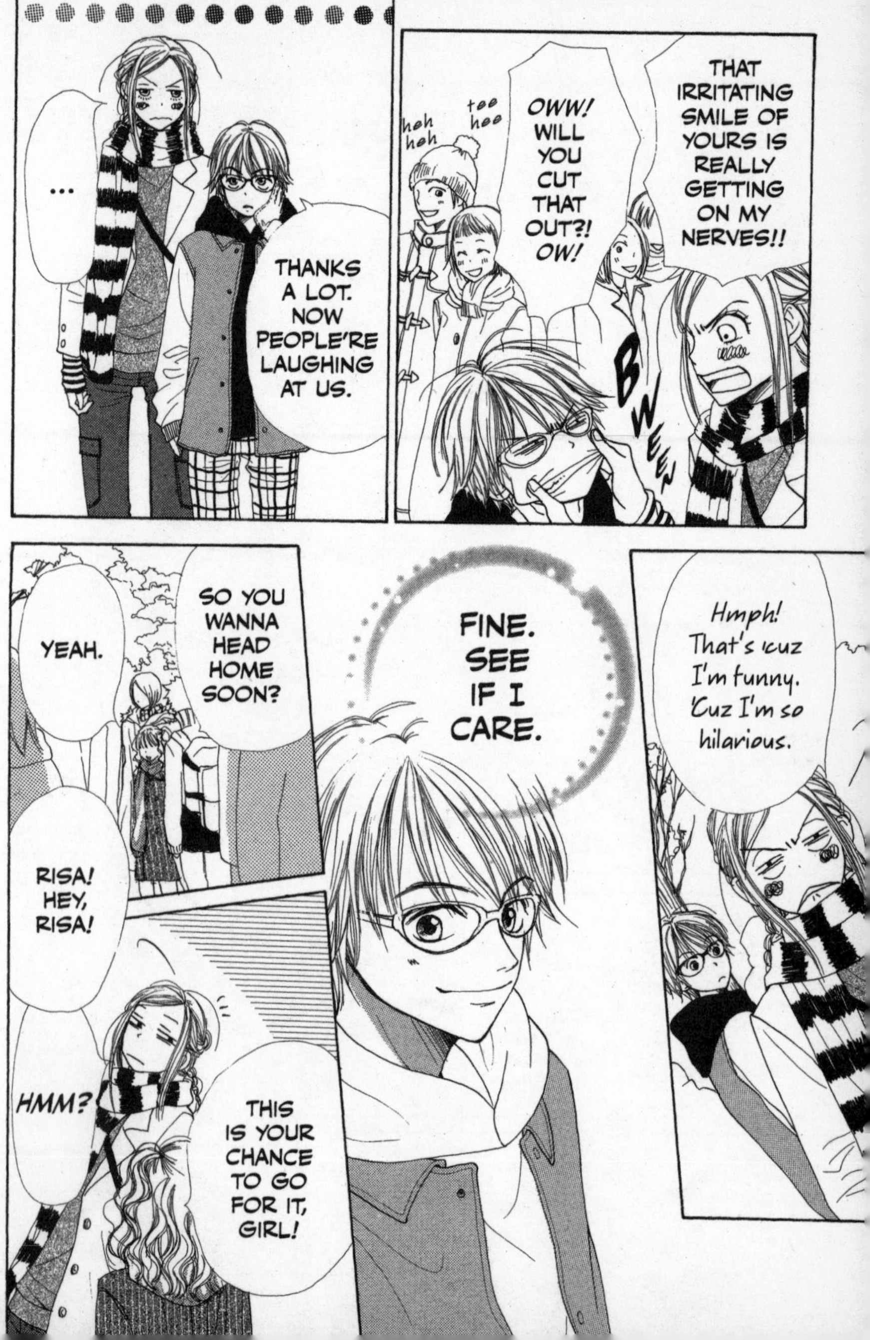
THAT IRRITATING SMILE OF YOURS IS REALLY GETTING ON MY NERVES!!
BWEEN
OWW! WILL YOU CUT THAT OUT?! OW!
tee hee
heh heh
...
THANKS A LOT. NOW PEOPLE'RE LAUGHING AT US.
Hmph! That's 'cuz I'm funny. 'Cuz I'm so hilarious.
FINE. SEE IF I CARE.
SO YOU WANNA HEAD HOME SOON?
YEAH.
RISA! HEY, RISA!
HMM?
THIS IS YOUR CHANCE TO GO FOR IT, GIRL!

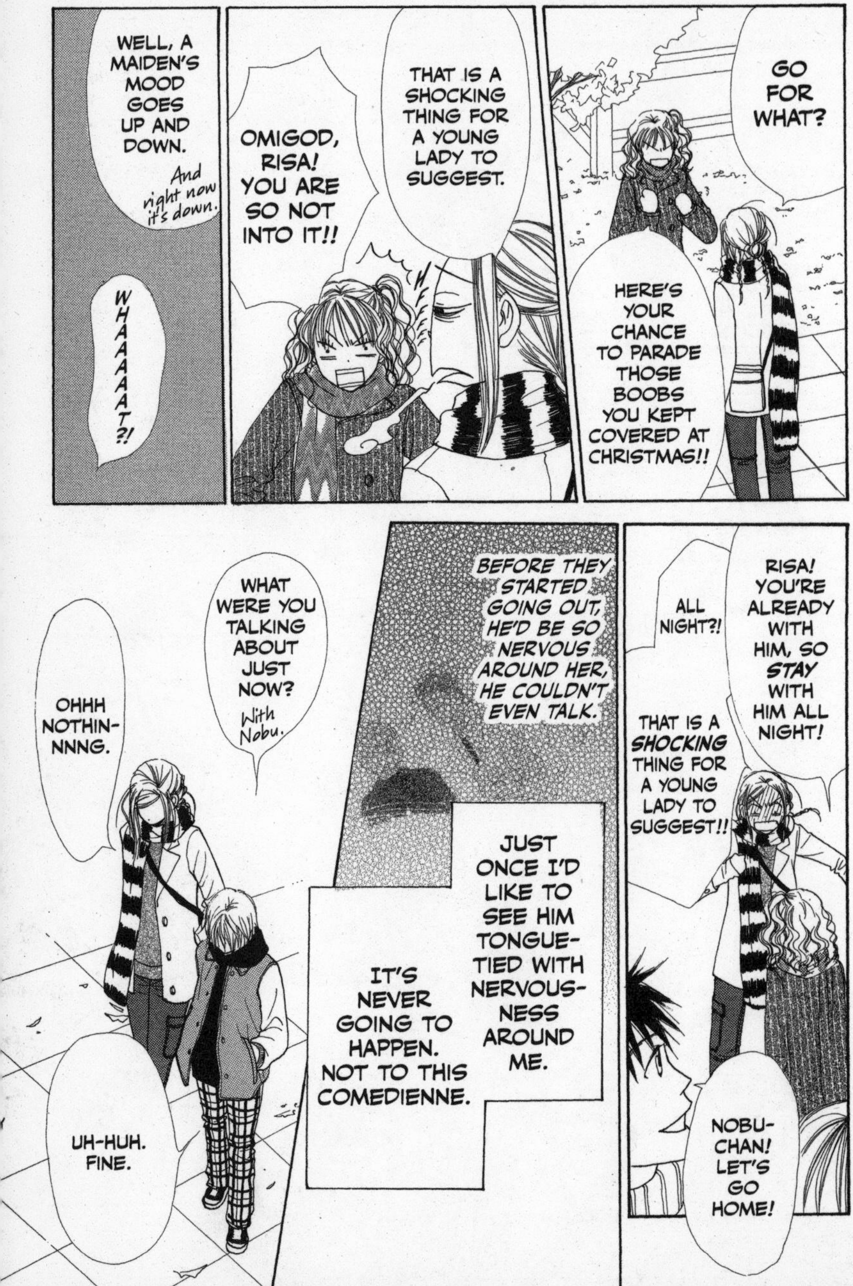
GO FOR WHAT?
HERE'S YOUR CHANCE TO PARADE THOSE BOOBS YOU KEPT COVERED AT CHRISTMAS!!
THAT IS A SHOCKING THING FOR A YOUNG LADY TO SUGGEST.
OMIGOD, RISA! YOU ARE SO NOT INTO IT!!
WELL, A MAIDEN'S MOOD GOES UP AND DOWN.
And right now it's down.
WHAAAAAAAT?!
RISA! YOU'RE ALREADY WITH HIM, SO STAY WITH HIM ALL NIGHT!
ALL NIGHT?!
THAT IS A SHOCKING THING FOR A YOUNG LADY TO SUGGEST!!
NOBU-CHAN! LET'S GO HOME!
BEFORE THEY STARTED GOING OUT, HE'D BE SO NERVOUS AROUND HER, HE COULDN'T EVEN TALK.
JUST ONCE I'D LIKE TO SEE HIM TONGUE-TIED WITH NERVOUSNESS AROUND ME.
IT'S NEVER GOING TO HAPPEN. NOT TO THIS COMEDIENNE.
WHAT WERE YOU TALKING ABOUT JUST NOW?
With Nobu.
OHHH NOTHIN-NNNG.
UH-HUH. FINE.

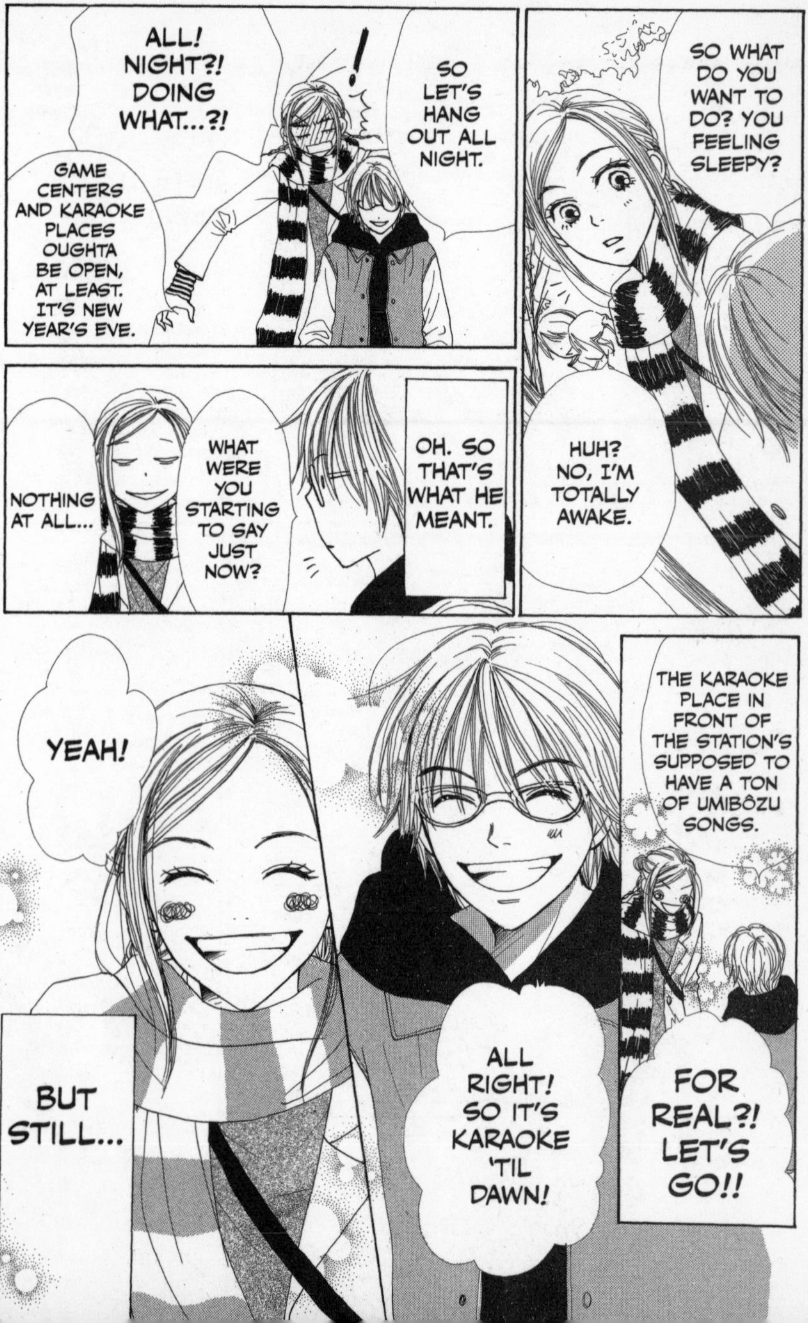
SO WHAT DO YOU WANT TO DO? YOU FEELING SLEEPY?
HUH? NO, I'M TOTALLY AWAKE.
SO LET'S HANG OUT ALL NIGHT.
!
ALL! NIGHT?! DOING WHAT...?!
GAME CENTERS AND KARAOKE PLACES OUGHTA BE OPEN, AT LEAST. IT'S NEW YEAR'S EVE.
OH. SO THAT'S WHAT HE MEANT.
WHAT WERE YOU STARTING TO SAY JUST NOW?
NOTHING AT ALL...
THE KARAOKE PLACE IN FRONT OF THE STATION'S SUPPOSED TO HAVE A TON OF UMIBÔZU SONGS.
FOR REAL?! LET'S GO!!
ALL RIGHT! SO IT'S KARAOKE 'TIL DAWN!
YEAH!
BUT STILL...

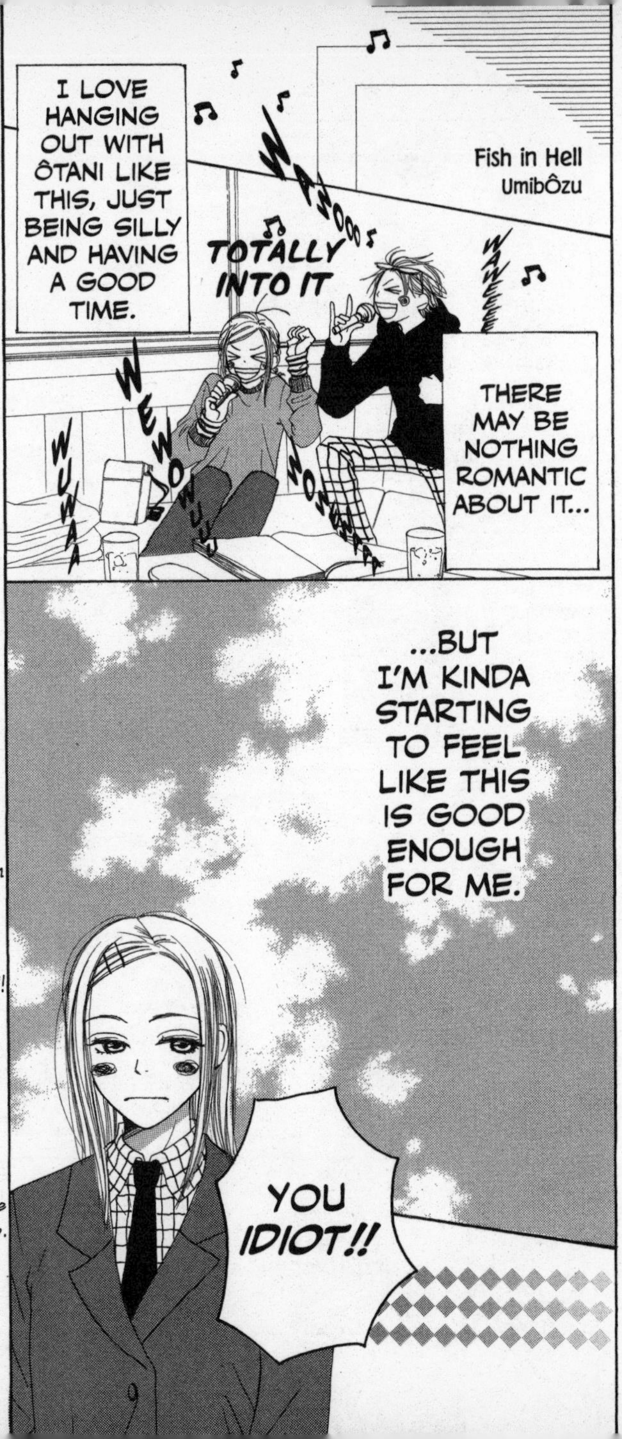
Fish in Hell
UmibÔzu
I LOVE HANGING OUT WITH ÔTANI LIKE THIS, JUST BEING SILLY AND HAVING A GOOD TIME.
TOTALLY INTO IT
THERE MAY BE NOTHING ROMANTIC ABOUT IT...
...BUT I'M KINDA STARTING TO FEEL LIKE THIS IS GOOD ENOUGH FOR ME.
YOU IDIOT!!

3

Thank you for all the letters and emails! I read every single one I get. Sorry I can't answer them, though!!

Gosh, you all draw so well... You blow me away.

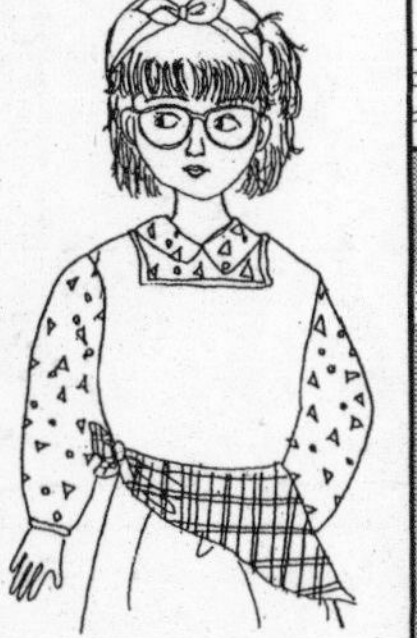

This ↑ by the way is a self-portrait I drew in sixth grade. I found it in our yearbook.

...what's with that ribbon-tied bandana?! And that weird pattern on the shirt?!

I've never worn glasses...so I guess those are supposed to be sunglasses. That scarf around the waist bothers me, too. Who would ever wear that...?

And what's this person looking at, anyway...?

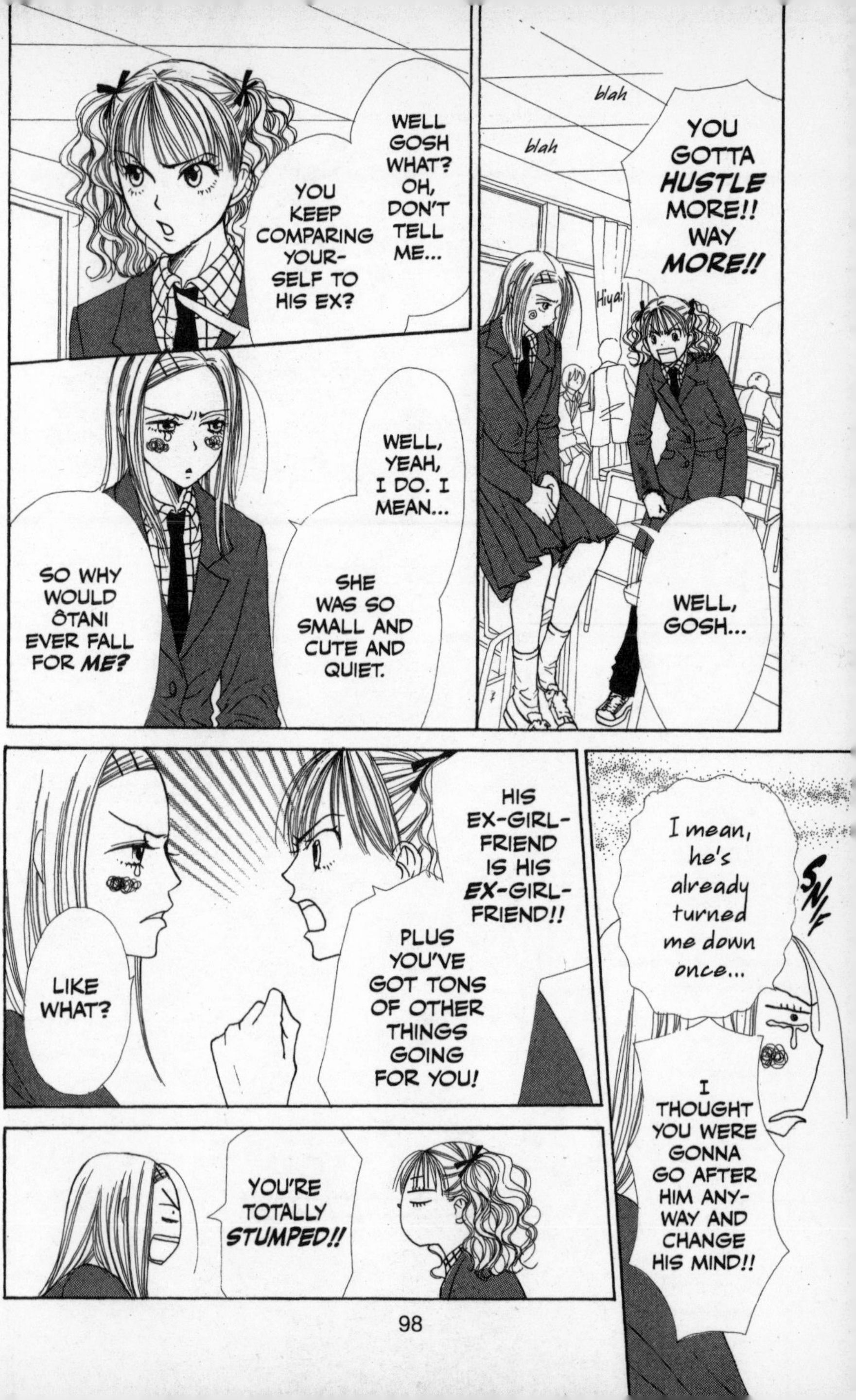
blah
blah
YOU GOTTA HUSTLE MORE!! WAY MORE!!
Hiya!
WELL, GOSH...
WELL GOSH WHAT? OH, DON'T TELL ME...
YOU KEEP COMPARING YOUR-SELF TO HIS EX?
WELL, YEAH, I DO. I MEAN...
SHE WAS SO SMALL AND CUTE AND QUIET.
SO WHY WOULD ÔTANI EVER FALL FOR ME?
I mean, he's already turned me down once...
SNIF
I THOUGHT YOU WERE GONNA GO AFTER HIM ANY-WAY AND CHANGE HIS MIND!!
HIS EX-GIRL-FRIEND IS HIS EX-GIRL-FRIEND!!
PLUS YOU'VE GOT TONS OF OTHER THINGS GOING FOR YOU!
LIKE WHAT?
YOU'RE TOTALLY STUMPED!!

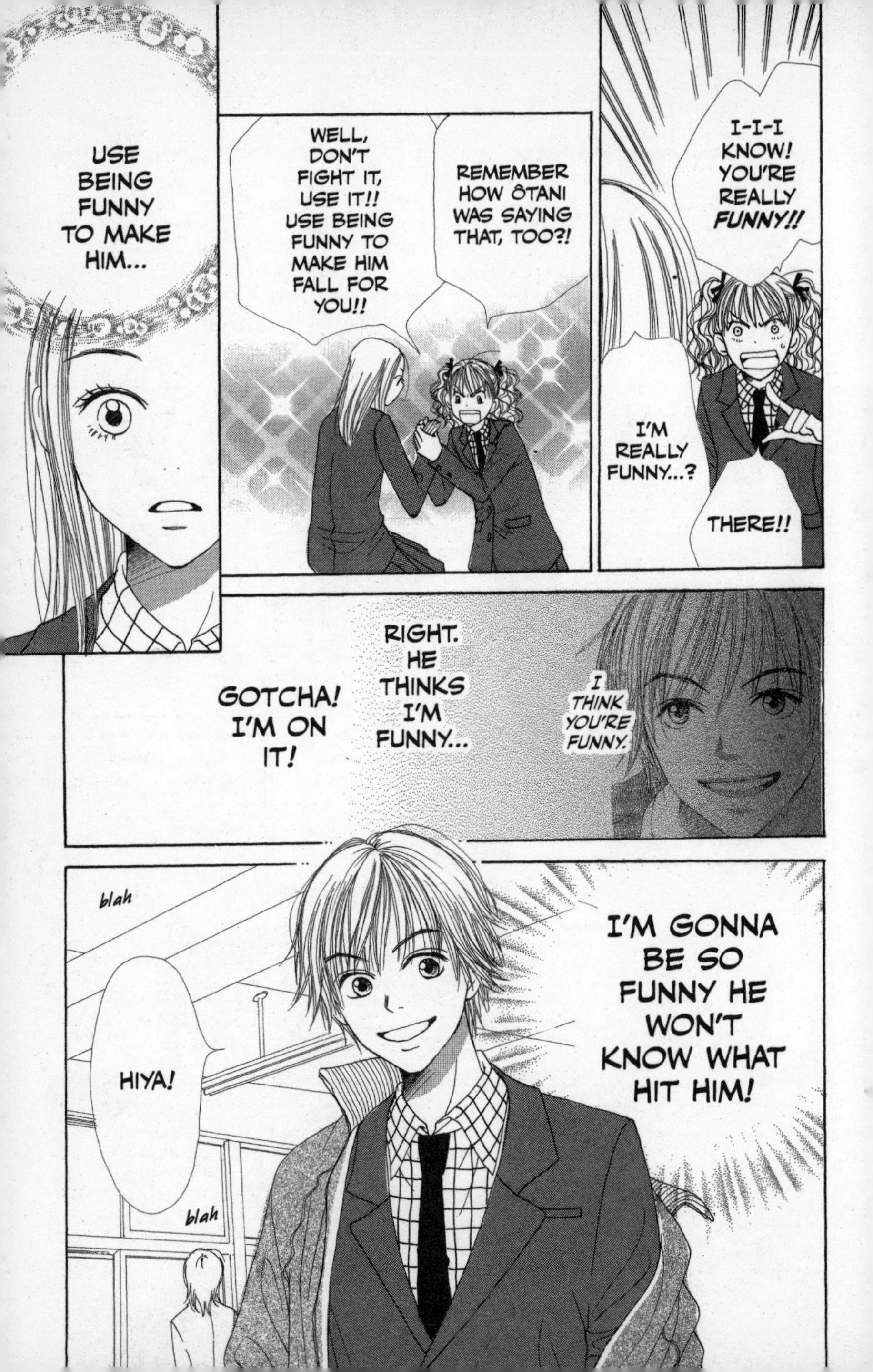
I-I-I KNOW! YOU'RE REALLY FUNNY!!
I'M REALLY FUNNY...?
THERE!!
REMEMBER HOW ÔTANI WAS SAYING THAT, TOO?!
WELL, DON'T FIGHT IT, USE IT!! USE BEING FUNNY TO MAKE HIM FALL FOR YOU!!
USE BEING FUNNY TO MAKE HIM...
I THINK YOU'RE FUNNY.
RIGHT. HE THINKS I'M FUNNY...
GOTCHA! I'M ON IT!
I'M GONNA BE SO FUNNY HE WON'T KNOW WHAT HIT HIM!
blah
HIYA!
blah

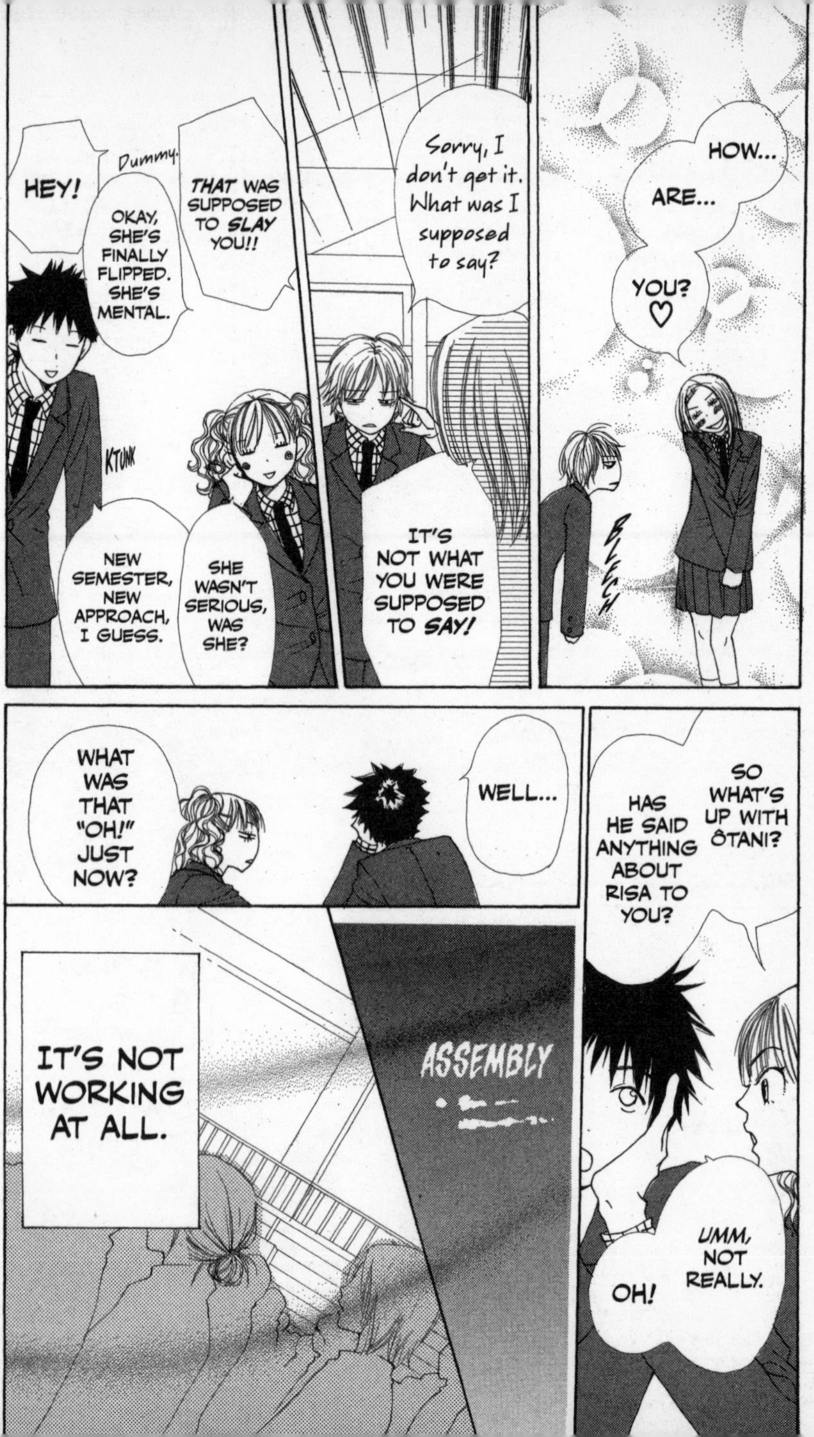
HOW...
ARE...
YOU? ♡
BLECH
Sorry, I don't get it. What was I supposed to say?
IT'S NOT WHAT YOU WERE SUPPOSED TO SAY!
HEY!
THAT WAS SUPPOSED TO SLAY YOU!!
Dummy.
OKAY, SHE'S FINALLY FLIPPED. SHE'S MENTAL.
KTUNK
SHE WASN'T SERIOUS, WAS SHE?
NEW SEMESTER, NEW APPROACH, I GUESS.
SO WHAT'S UP WITH ŌTANI?
HAS HE SAID ANYTHING ABOUT RISA TO YOU?
UMM, NOT REALLY.
OH!
WELL...
WHAT WAS THAT "OH!" JUST NOW?
ASSEMBLY
IT'S NOT WORKING AT ALL.

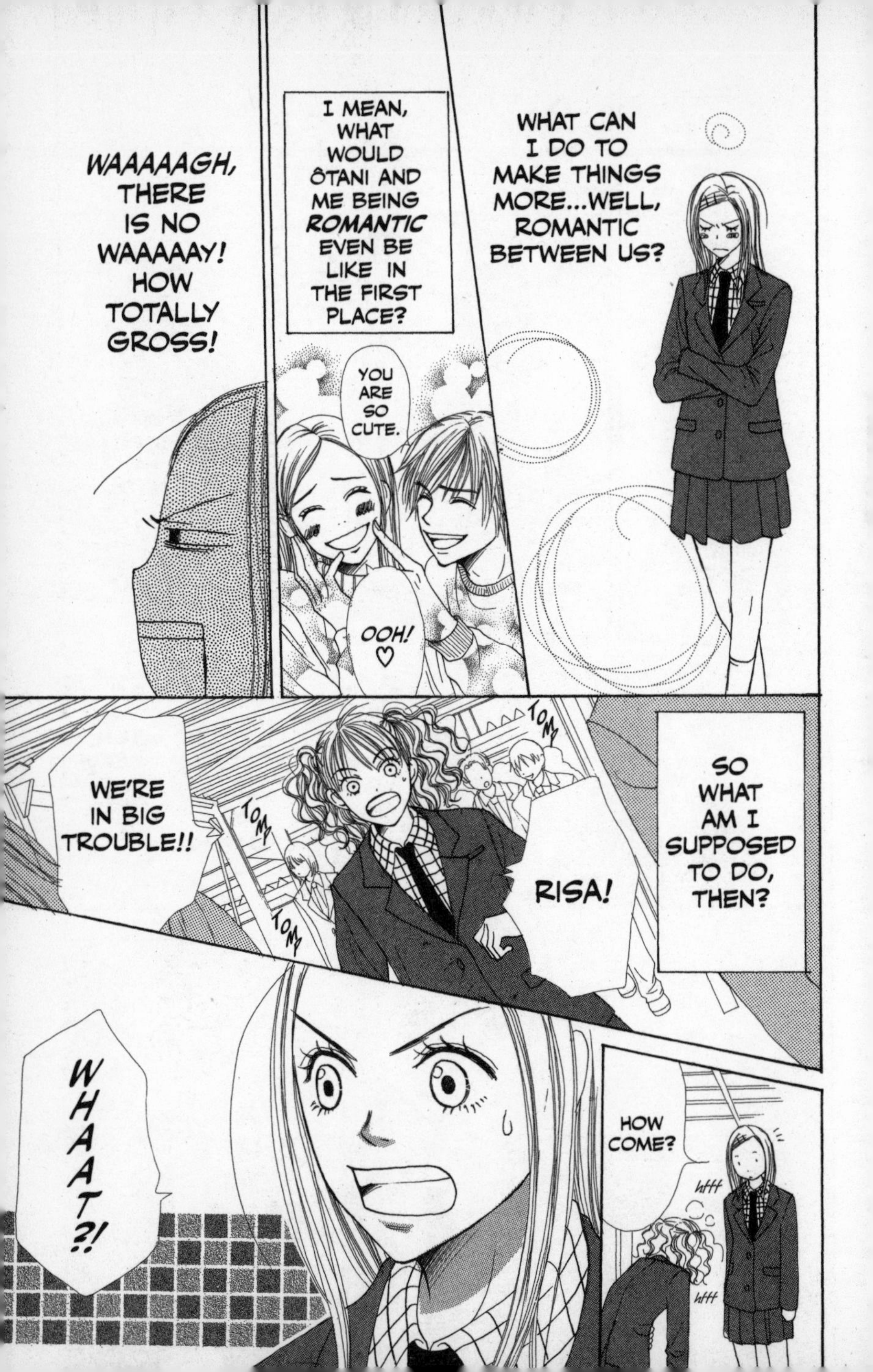
WHAT CAN I DO TO MAKE THINGS MORE...WELL, ROMANTIC BETWEEN US?
I MEAN, WHAT WOULD ŌTANI AND ME BEING *ROMANTIC* EVEN BE LIKE IN THE FIRST PLACE?
YOU ARE SO CUTE.
OOH! ♡
WAAAAAGH, THERE IS NO WAAAAAY! HOW TOTALLY GROSS!
SO WHAT AM I SUPPOSED TO DO, THEN?
TOM
RISA!
TOM
TOM
WE'RE IN BIG TROUBLE!!
HOW COME?
hfff
hfff
WHAAT?!

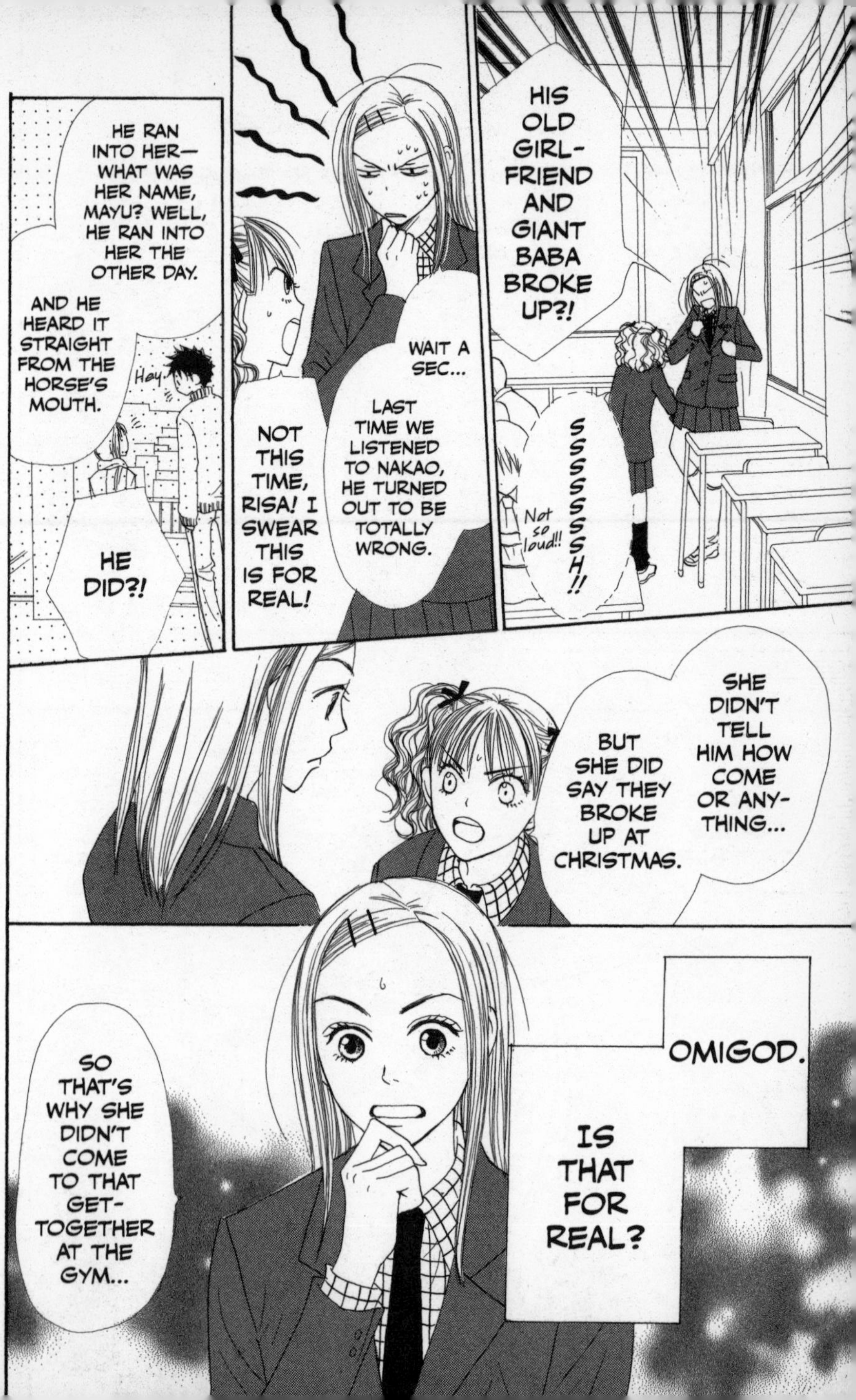
HIS OLD GIRL-FRIEND AND GIANT BABA BROKE UP?!
SSSSSSSH!!
Not so loud!!
WAIT A SEC... LAST TIME WE LISTENED TO NAKAO, HE TURNED OUT TO BE TOTALLY WRONG.
NOT THIS TIME, RISA! I SWEAR THIS IS FOR REAL!
HE RAN INTO HER—WHAT WAS HER NAME, MAYU? WELL, HE RAN INTO HER THE OTHER DAY.
AND HE HEARD IT STRAIGHT FROM THE HORSE'S MOUTH.
Hey.
HE DID?!
SHE DIDN'T TELL HIM HOW COME OR ANY-THING...
BUT SHE DID SAY THEY BROKE UP AT CHRISTMAS.
OMIGOD.
IS THAT FOR REAL?
SO THAT'S WHY SHE DIDN'T COME TO THAT GET-TOGETHER AT THE GYM...

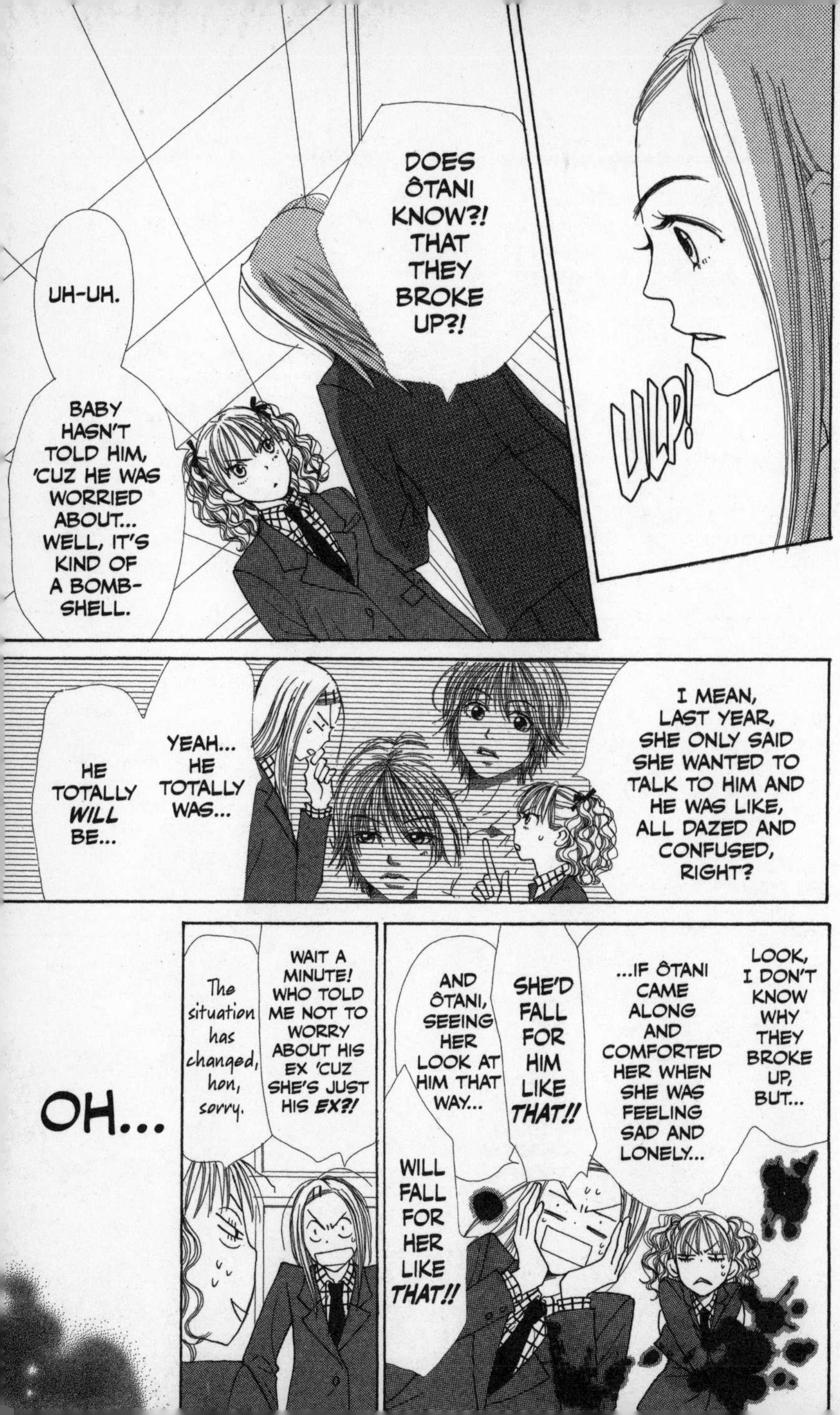
ULP!
DOES ŌTANI KNOW?! THAT THEY BROKE UP?!
UH-UH.
BABY HASN'T TOLD HIM, 'CUZ HE WAS WORRIED ABOUT... WELL, IT'S KIND OF A BOMB-SHELL.
I MEAN, LAST YEAR, SHE ONLY SAID SHE WANTED TO TALK TO HIM AND HE WAS LIKE, ALL DAZED AND CONFUSED, RIGHT?
YEAH... HE TOTALLY WAS...
HE TOTALLY *WILL* BE...
LOOK, I DON'T KNOW WHY THEY BROKE UP, BUT...
...IF ŌTANI CAME ALONG AND COMFORTED HER WHEN SHE WAS FEELING SAD AND LONELY...
SHE'D FALL FOR HIM LIKE *THAT!!*
AND ŌTANI, SEEING HER LOOK AT HIM THAT WAY...
WILL FALL FOR HER LIKE *THAT!!*
WAIT A MINUTE! WHO TOLD ME NOT TO WORRY ABOUT HIS EX 'CUZ SHE'S JUST HIS *EX?!*
The situation has changed, hon, sorry.
OH...

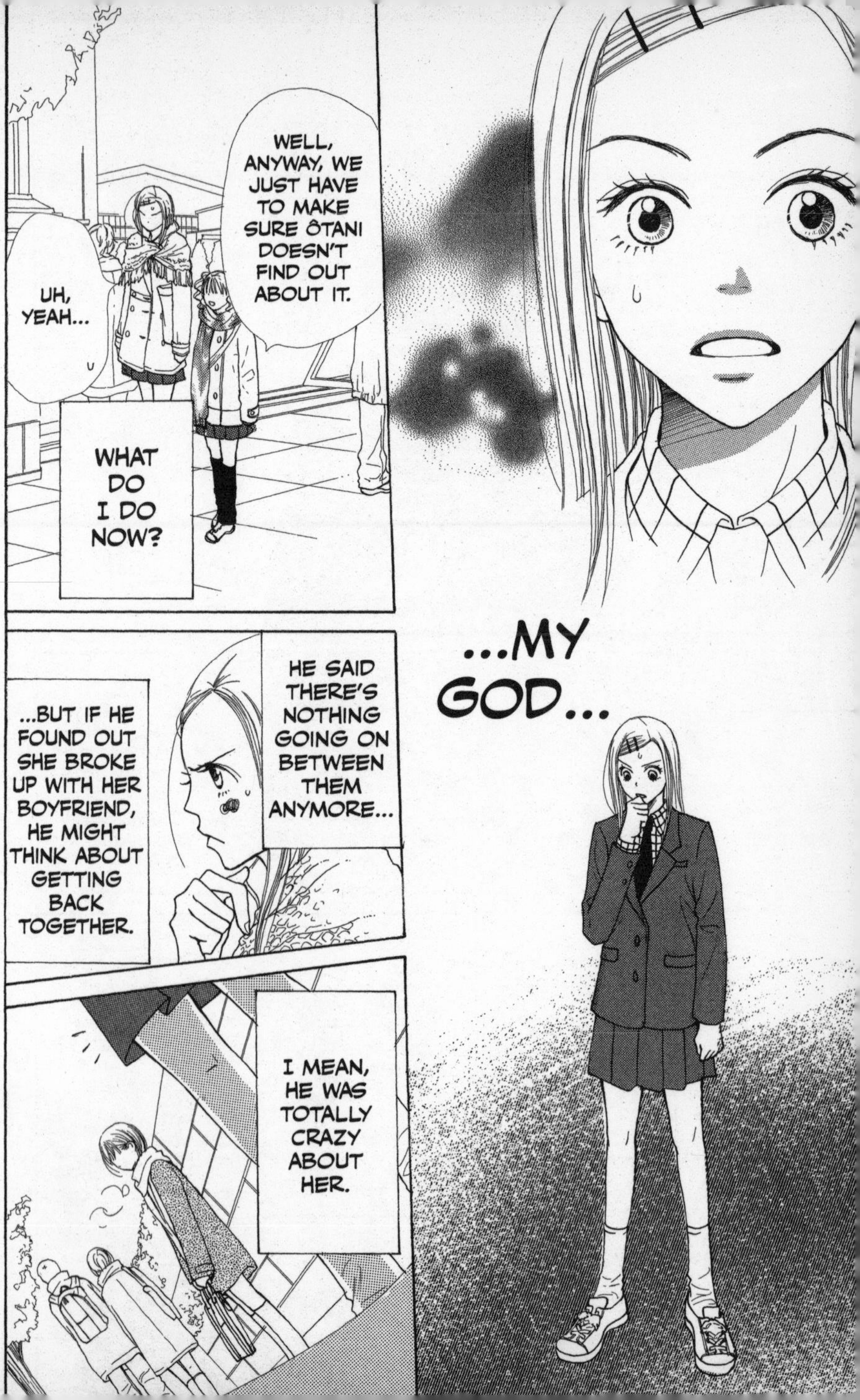
...MY GOD...
WELL, ANYWAY, WE JUST HAVE TO MAKE SURE ÔTANI DOESN'T FIND OUT ABOUT IT.
UH, YEAH...
WHAT DO I DO NOW?
HE SAID THERE'S NOTHING GOING ON BETWEEN THEM ANYMORE...
...BUT IF HE FOUND OUT SHE BROKE UP WITH HER BOYFRIEND, HE MIGHT THINK ABOUT GETTING BACK TOGETHER.
I MEAN, HE WAS TOTALLY CRAZY ABOUT HER.

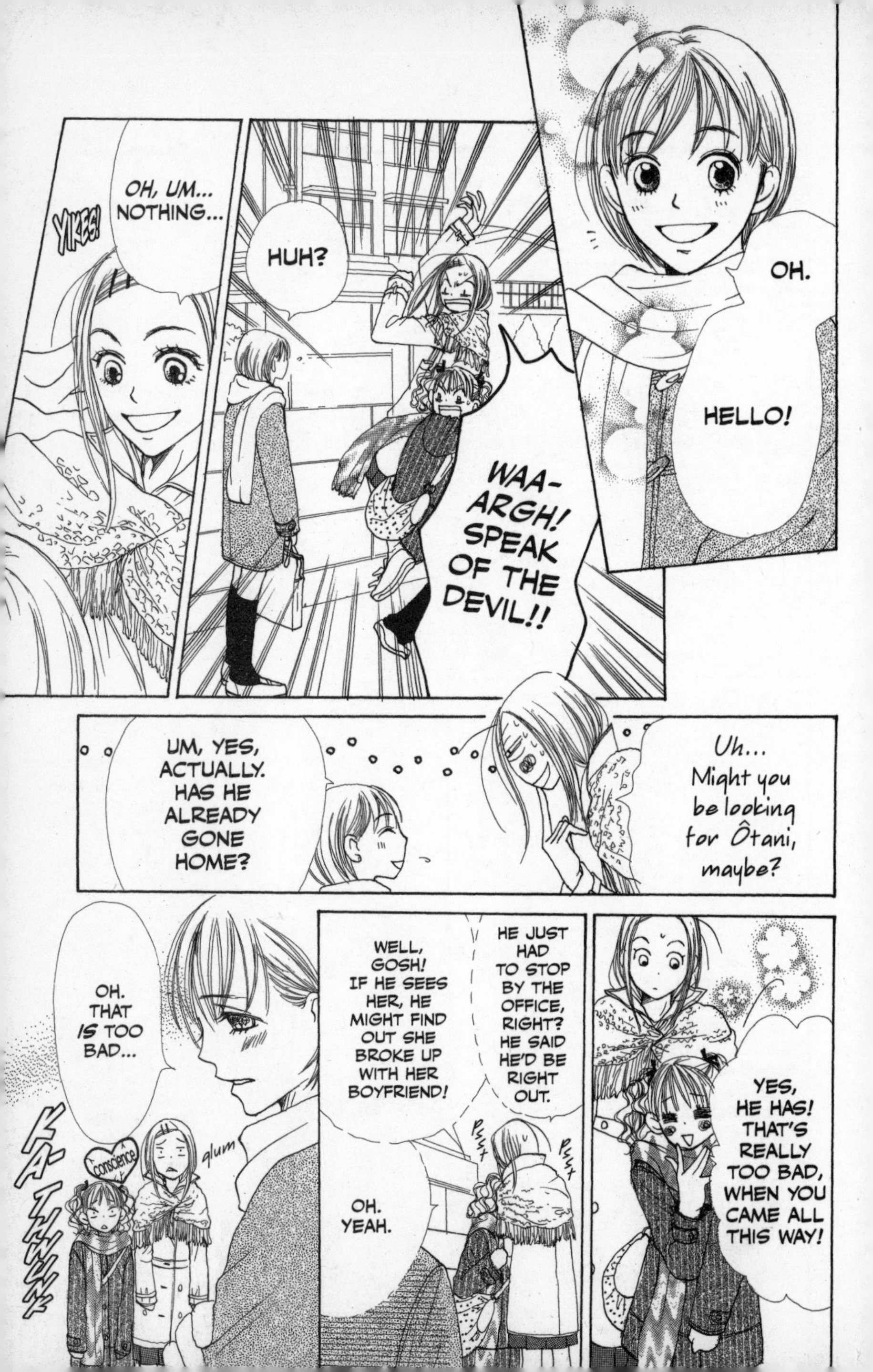
OH.
HELLO!
HUH?
WAA-ARGH! SPEAK OF THE DEVIL!!
YIKES!
OH, UM... NOTHING...
Uh... Might you be looking for Ôtani, maybe?
UM, YES, ACTUALLY. HAS HE ALREADY GONE HOME?
YES, HE HAS! THAT'S REALLY TOO BAD, WHEN YOU CAME ALL THIS WAY!
HE JUST HAD TO STOP BY THE OFFICE, RIGHT? HE SAID HE'D BE RIGHT OUT.
WELL, GOSH! IF HE SEES HER, HE MIGHT FIND OUT SHE BROKE UP WITH HER BOYFRIEND!
PSST
PSST
OH. YEAH.
OH. THAT IS TOO BAD...
conscience
glum
KA-THUNK

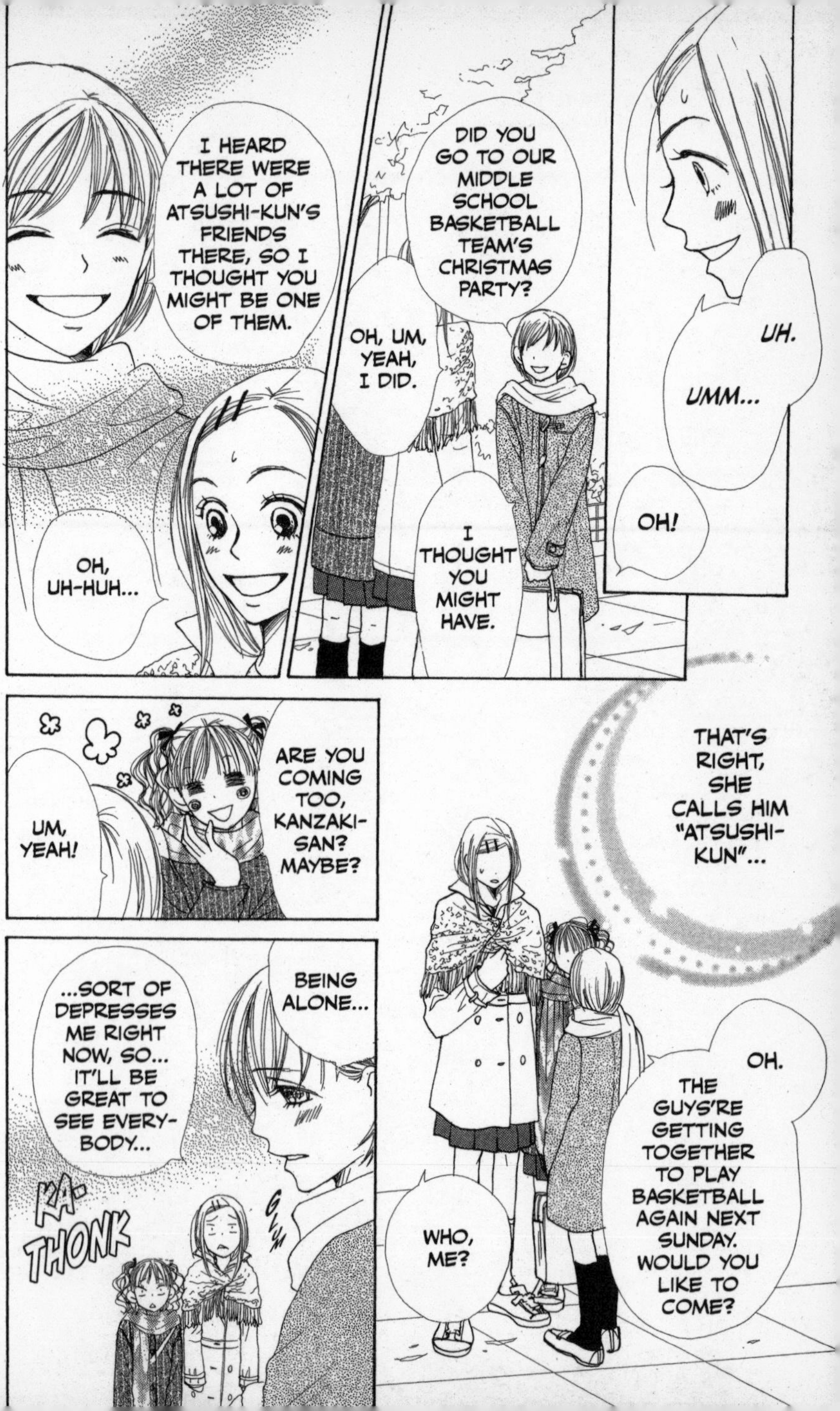
UH.
UMM...
OH!
DID YOU GO TO OUR MIDDLE SCHOOL BASKETBALL TEAM'S CHRISTMAS PARTY?
OH, UM, YEAH, I DID.
I THOUGHT YOU MIGHT HAVE.
I HEARD THERE WERE A LOT OF ATSUSHI-KUN'S FRIENDS THERE, SO I THOUGHT YOU MIGHT BE ONE OF THEM.
OH, UH-HUH...
THAT'S RIGHT, SHE CALLS HIM "ATSUSHI-KUN"...
OH. THE GUYS'RE GETTING TOGETHER TO PLAY BASKETBALL AGAIN NEXT SUNDAY. WOULD YOU LIKE TO COME?
WHO, ME?
ARE YOU COMING TOO, KANZAKI-SAN? MAYBE?
UM, YEAH!
BEING ALONE...
...SORT OF DEPRESSES ME RIGHT NOW, SO... IT'LL BE GREAT TO SEE EVERY-BODY...
GLUM
KA-THONK

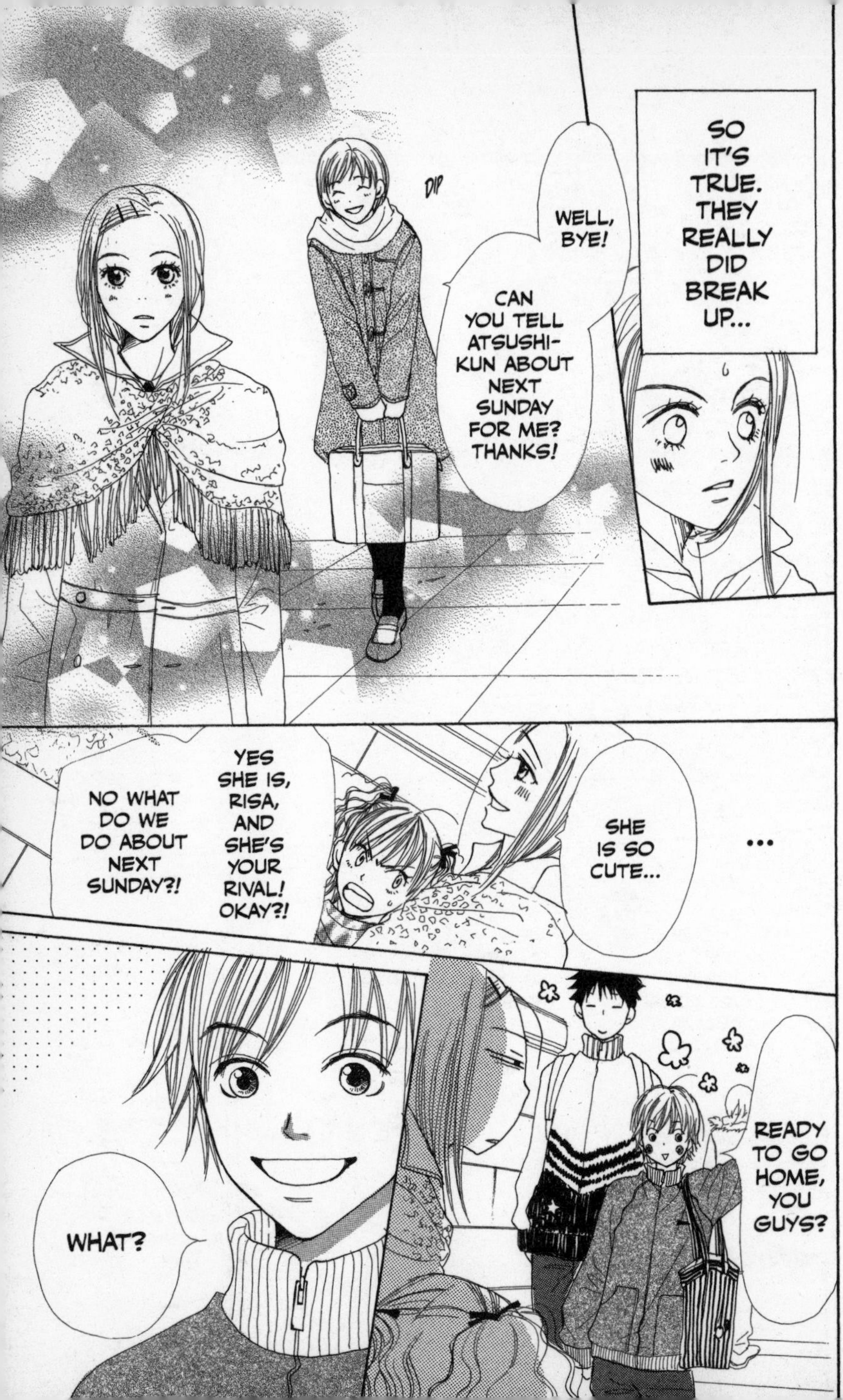
SO IT'S TRUE. THEY REALLY DID BREAK UP...
WELL, BYE!
CAN YOU TELL ATSUSHI-KUN ABOUT NEXT SUNDAY FOR ME? THANKS!
DIP
...
SHE IS SO CUTE...
YES SHE IS, RISA, AND SHE'S YOUR RIVAL! OKAY?!
NO WHAT DO WE DO ABOUT NEXT SUNDAY?!
READY TO GO HOME, YOU GUYS?
WHAT?

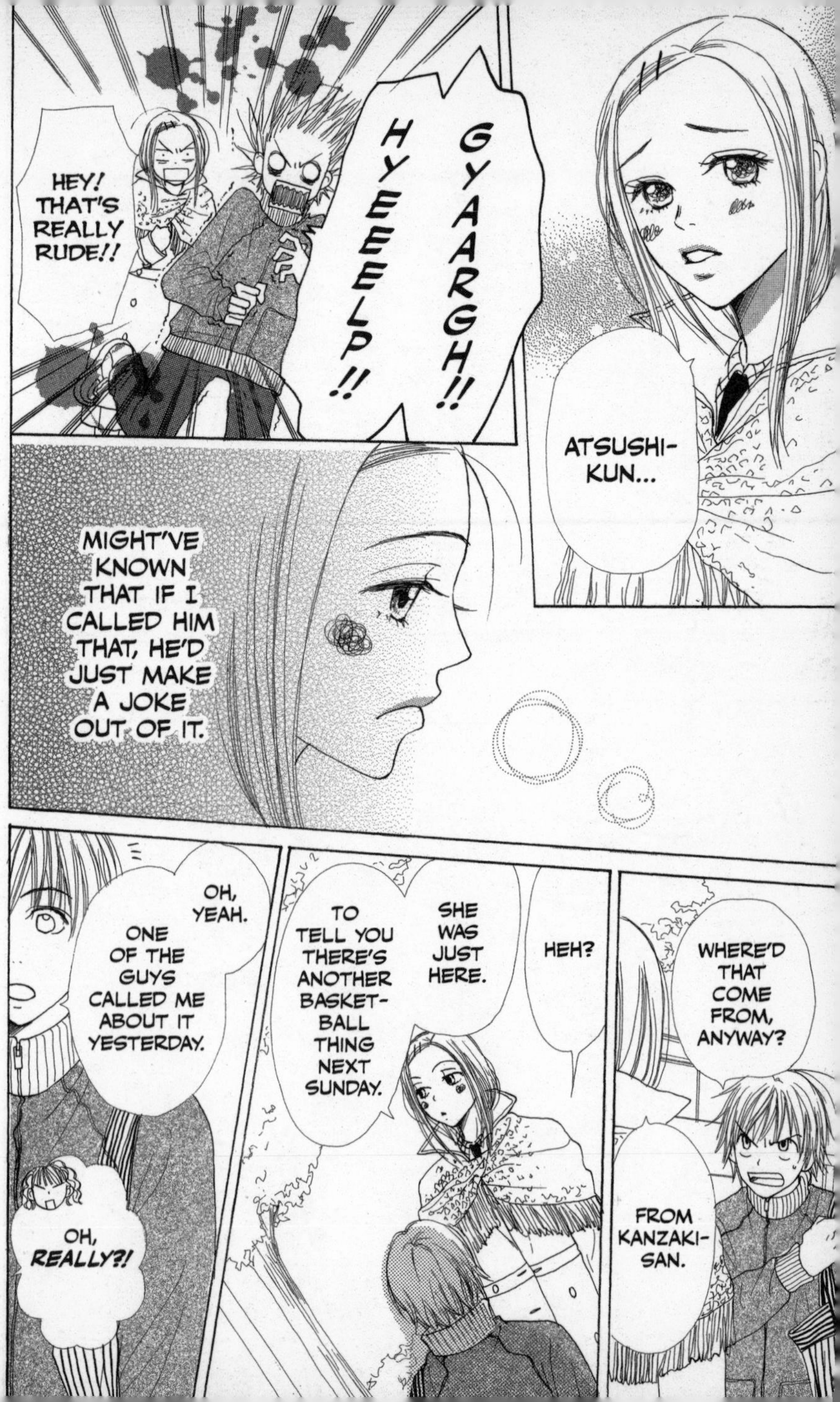
ATSUSHI-KUN...
GYAARGH!!
HYEEEELP!!
HEY! THAT'S REALLY RUDE!!
MIGHT'VE KNOWN THAT IF I CALLED HIM THAT, HE'D JUST MAKE A JOKE OUT OF IT.
WHERE'D THAT COME FROM, ANYWAY?
FROM KANZAKI-SAN.
HEH?
SHE WAS JUST HERE.
TO TELL YOU THERE'S ANOTHER BASKET-BALL THING NEXT SUNDAY.
OH, YEAH.
ONE OF THE GUYS CALLED ME ABOUT IT YESTERDAY.
OH, *REALLY?!*

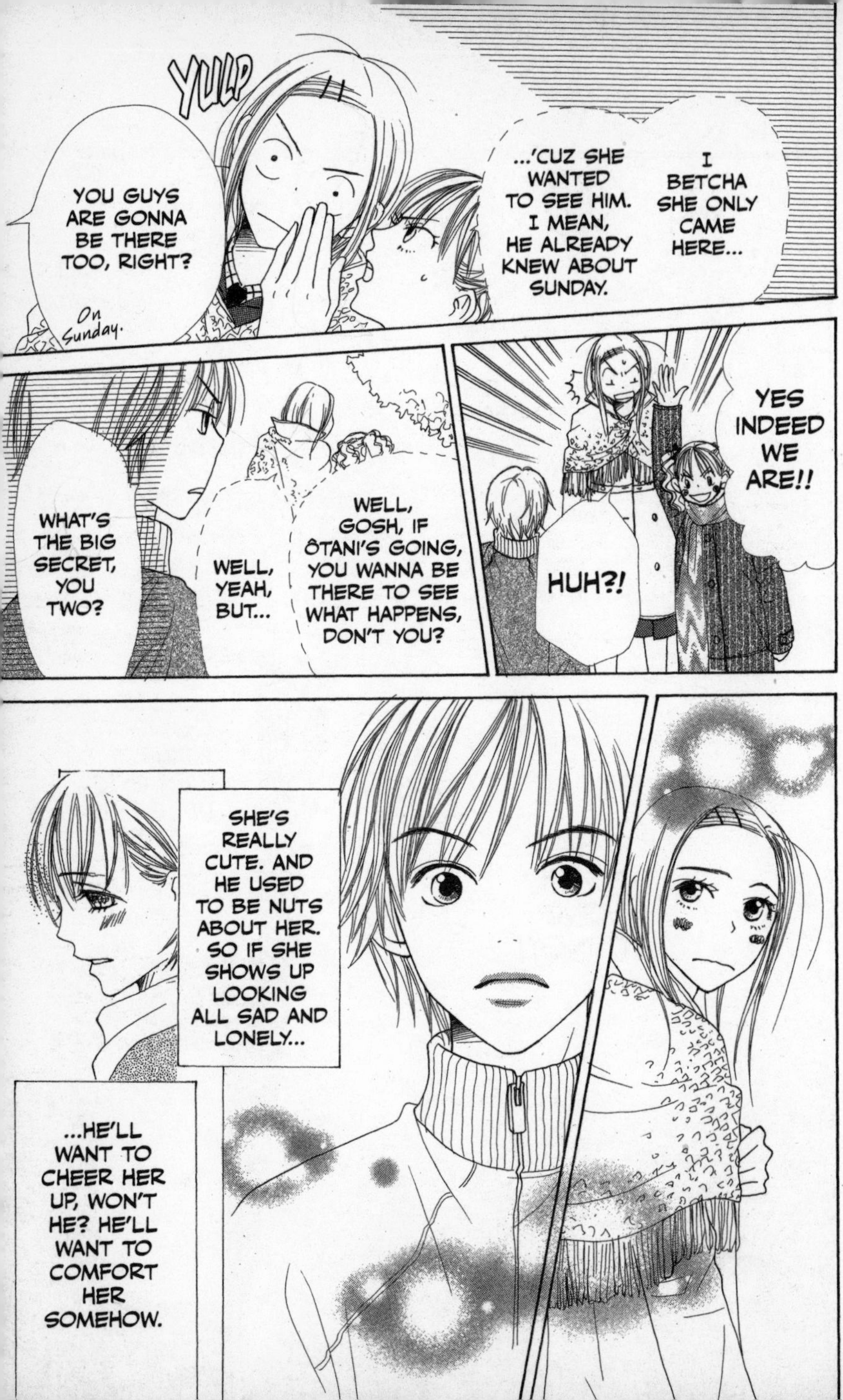
I BETCHA SHE ONLY CAME HERE...
...'CUZ SHE WANTED TO SEE HIM. I MEAN, HE ALREADY KNEW ABOUT SUNDAY.
YULP
YOU GUYS ARE GONNA BE THERE TOO, RIGHT?
On Sunday.
YES INDEED WE ARE!!
HUH?!
WELL, GOSH, IF ÔTANI'S GOING, YOU WANNA BE THERE TO SEE WHAT HAPPENS, DON'T YOU?
WELL, YEAH, BUT...
WHAT'S THE BIG SECRET, YOU TWO?
SHE'S REALLY CUTE. AND HE USED TO BE NUTS ABOUT HER. SO IF SHE SHOWS UP LOOKING ALL SAD AND LONELY...
...HE'LL WANT TO CHEER HER UP, WON'T HE? HE'LL WANT TO COMFORT HER SOMEHOW.

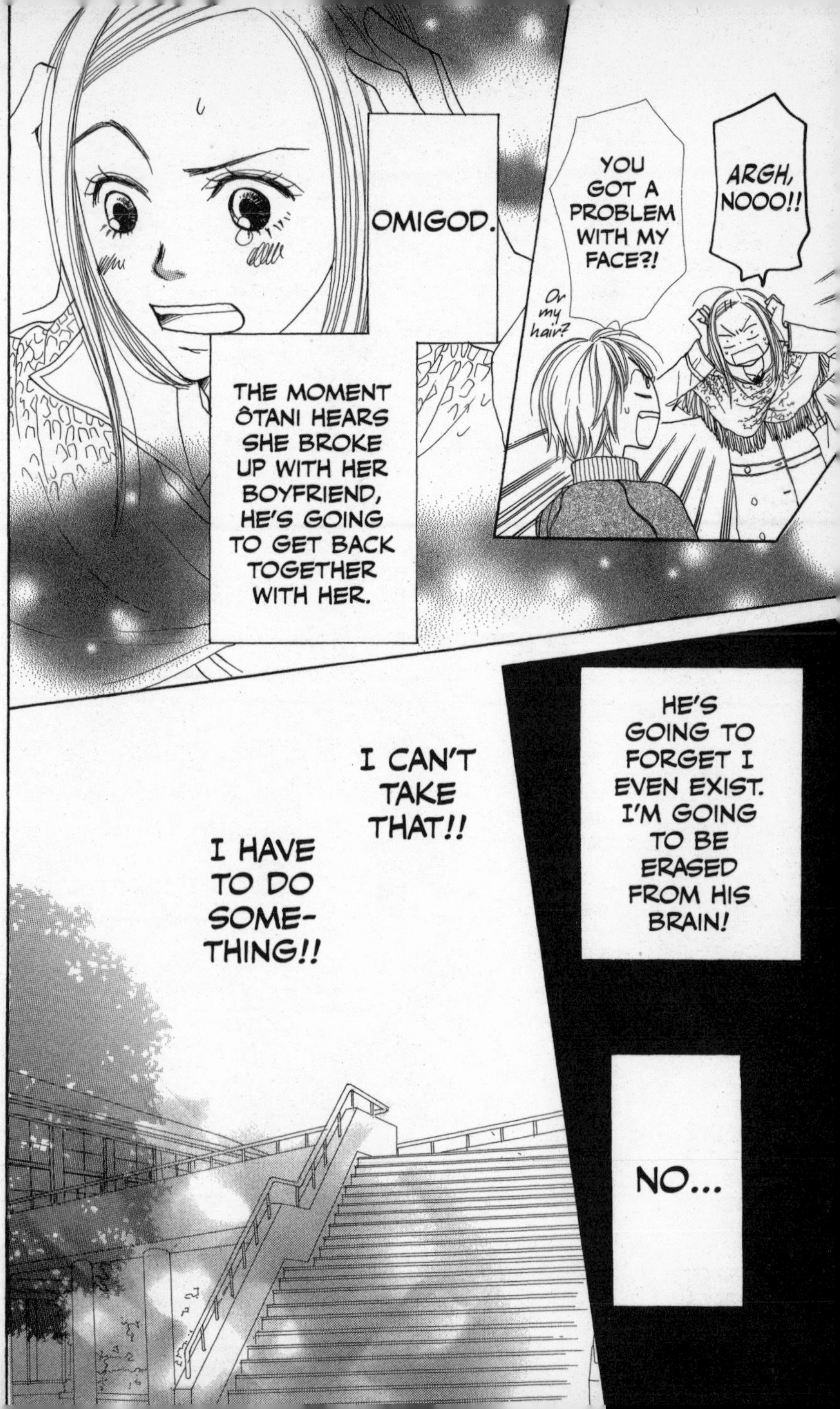
ARGH, NOOO!!
YOU GOT A PROBLEM WITH MY FACE?!
Or my hair?
OMIGOD.
THE MOMENT ÔTANI HEARS SHE BROKE UP WITH HER BOYFRIEND, HE'S GOING TO GET BACK TOGETHER WITH HER.
HE'S GOING TO FORGET I EVEN EXIST. I'M GOING TO BE ERASED FROM HIS BRAIN!
NO...
I CAN'T TAKE THAT!!
I HAVE TO DO SOME-THING!!

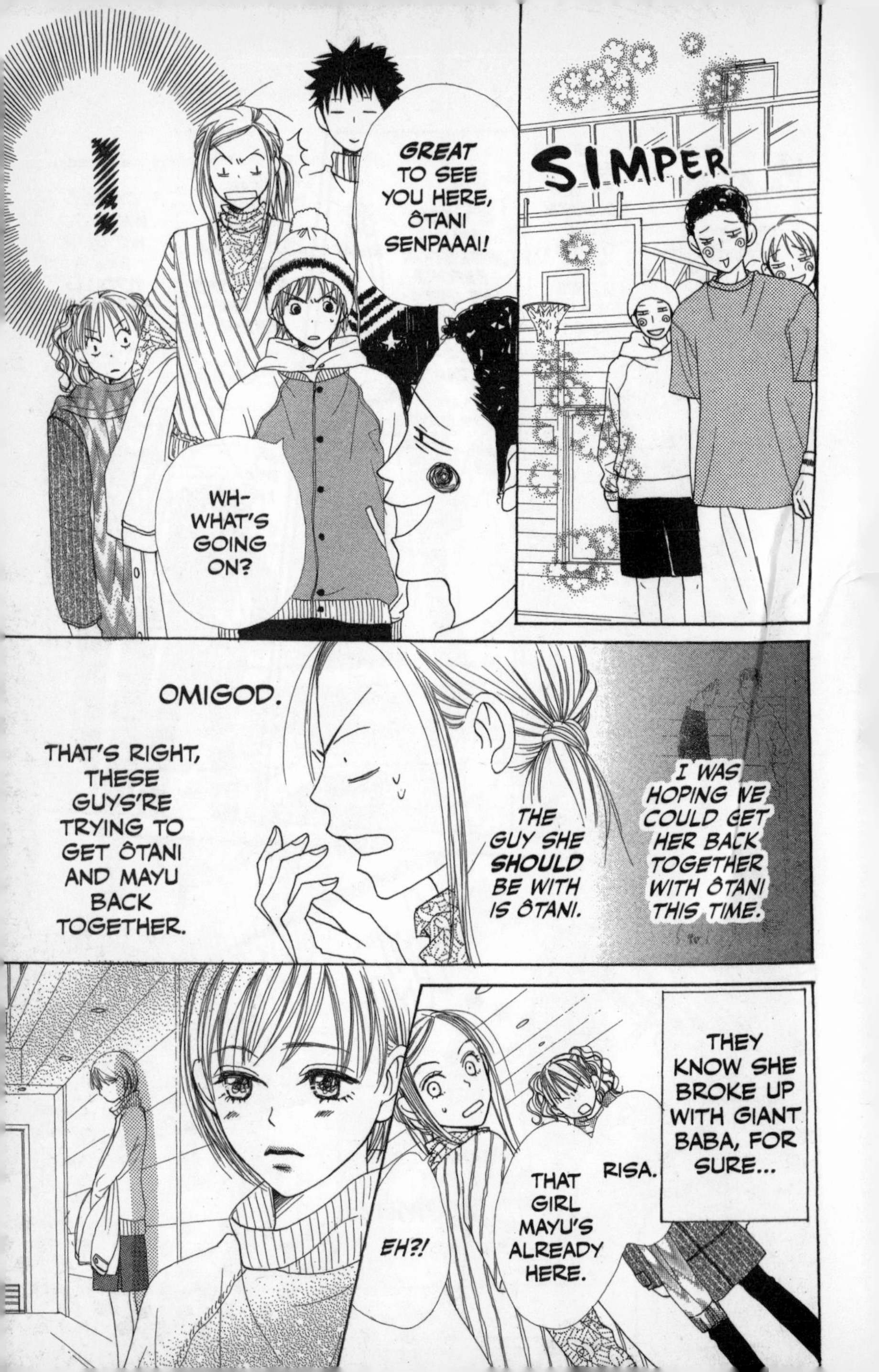
SIMPER
GREAT TO SEE YOU HERE, ÔTANI SENPAAAI!
WH- WHAT'S GOING ON?
I WAS HOPING WE COULD GET HER BACK TOGETHER WITH ÔTANI THIS TIME.
THE GUY SHE SHOULD BE WITH IS ÔTANI.
OMIGOD.
THAT'S RIGHT, THESE GUYS'RE TRYING TO GET ÔTANI AND MAYU BACK TOGETHER.
THEY KNOW SHE BROKE UP WITH GIANT BABA, FOR SURE...
RISA.
THAT GIRL MAYU'S ALREADY HERE.
EH?!

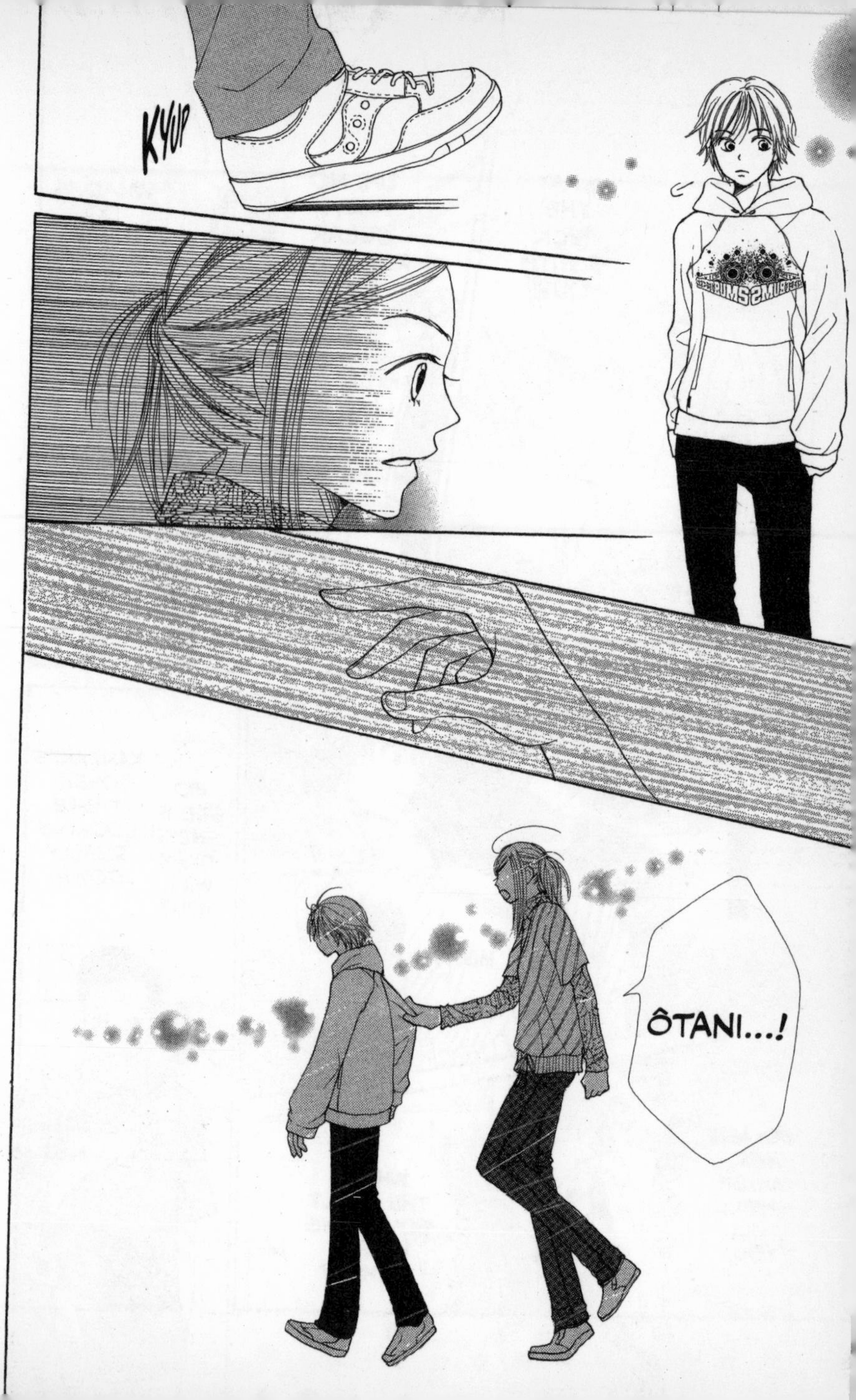
KYUP
ÔTANI...!

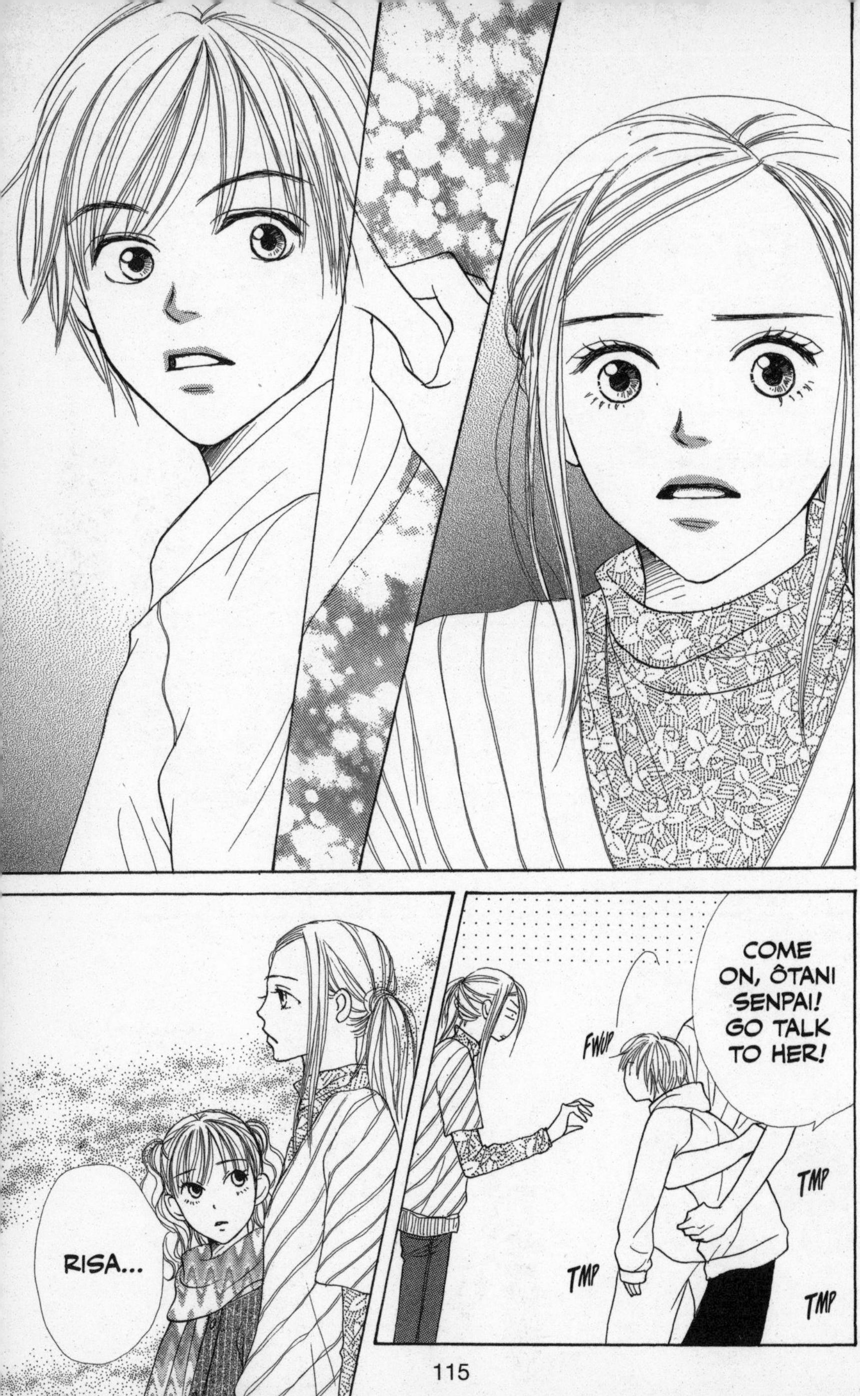
COME ON, ÔTANI SENPAI! GO TALK TO HER!
FWUP
TMP
TMP
TMP
RISA...

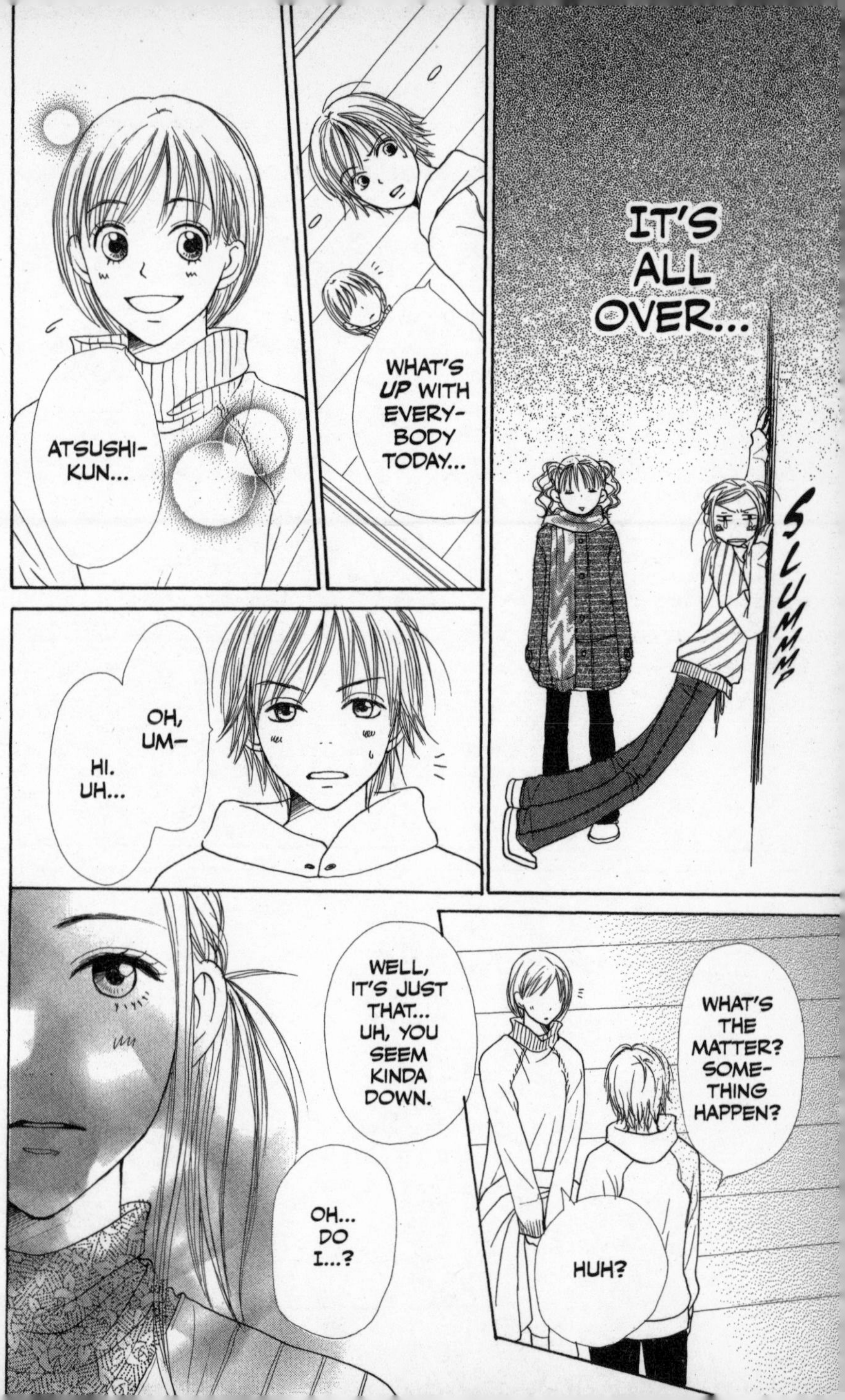
IT'S ALL OVER...
SLUMMMP
WHAT'S UP WITH EVERY-BODY TODAY...
ATSUSHI-KUN...
OH, UM—
HI. UH...
WHAT'S THE MATTER? SOME-THING HAPPEN?
HUH?
WELL, IT'S JUST THAT... UH, YOU SEEM KINDA DOWN.
OH... DO I...?

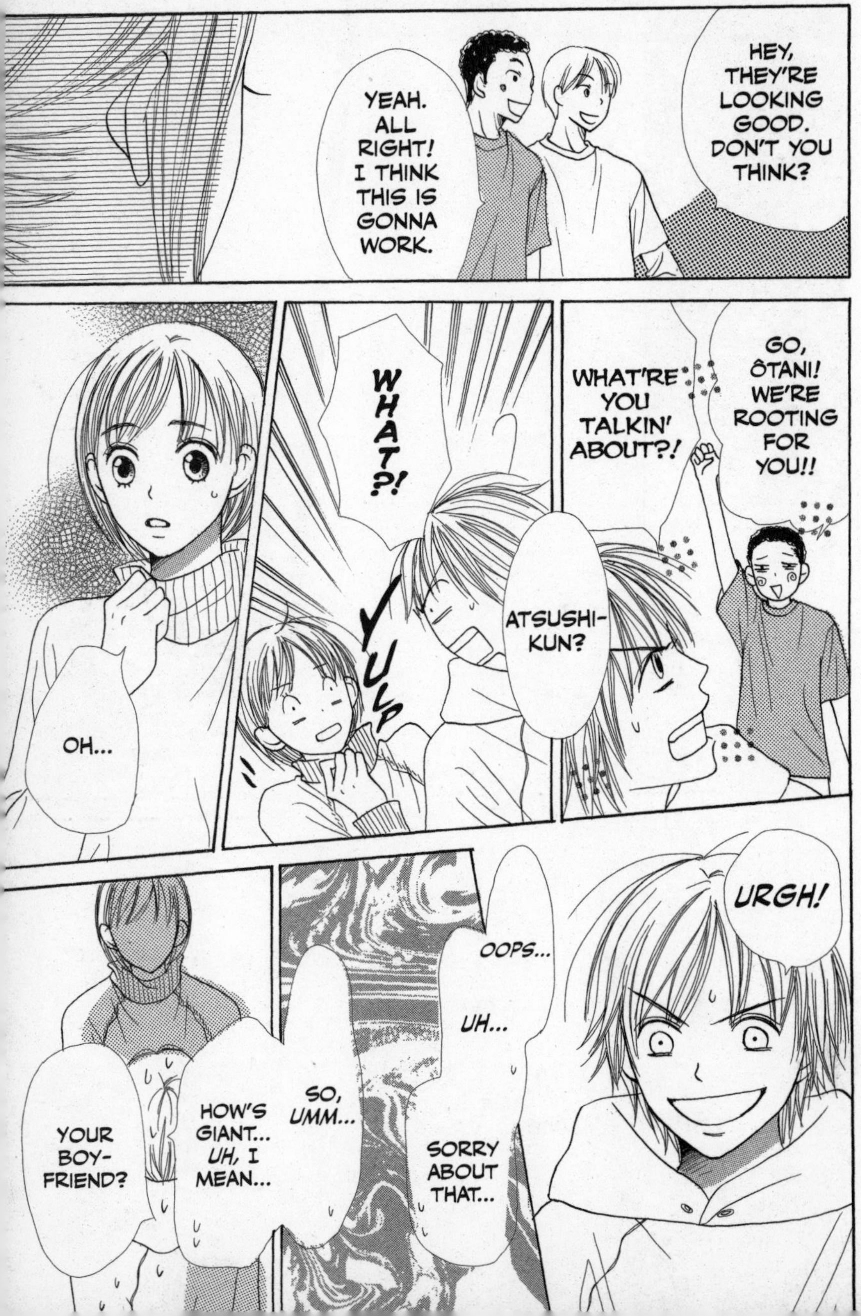
HEY, THEY'RE LOOKING GOOD. DON'T YOU THINK?
YEAH. ALL RIGHT! I THINK THIS IS GONNA WORK.
GO, ÔTANI! WE'RE ROOTING FOR YOU!!
WHAT'RE YOU TALKIN' ABOUT?!
ATSUSHI-KUN?
WHAT?!
OH...
URGH!
OOPS...
UH...
SORRY ABOUT THAT...
SO, UMM...
HOW'S GIANT... UH, I MEAN...
YOUR BOY-FRIEND?

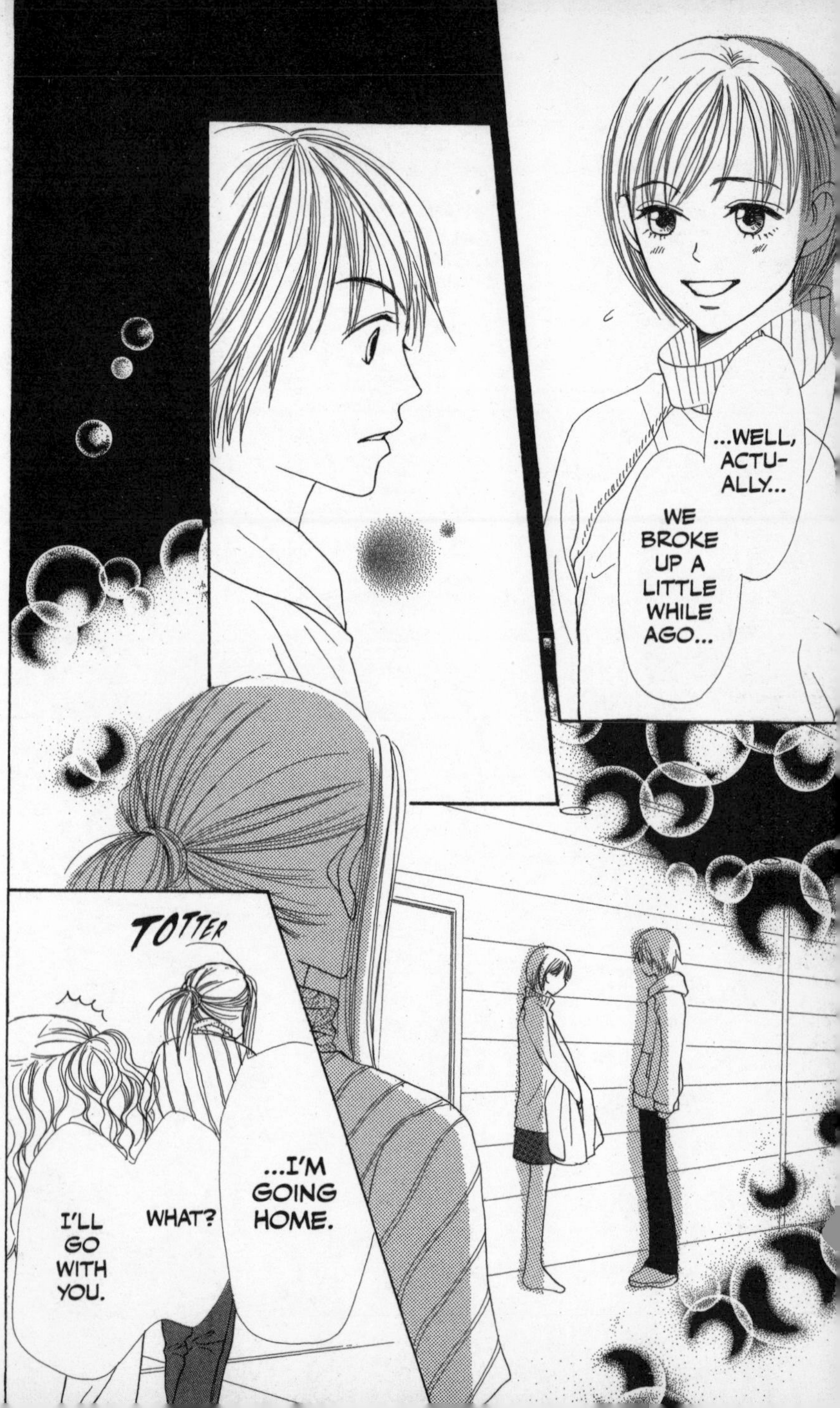
...WELL, ACTU-ALLY...
WE BROKE UP A LITTLE WHILE AGO...
TOTTER
...I'M GOING HOME.
WHAT?
I'LL GO WITH YOU.

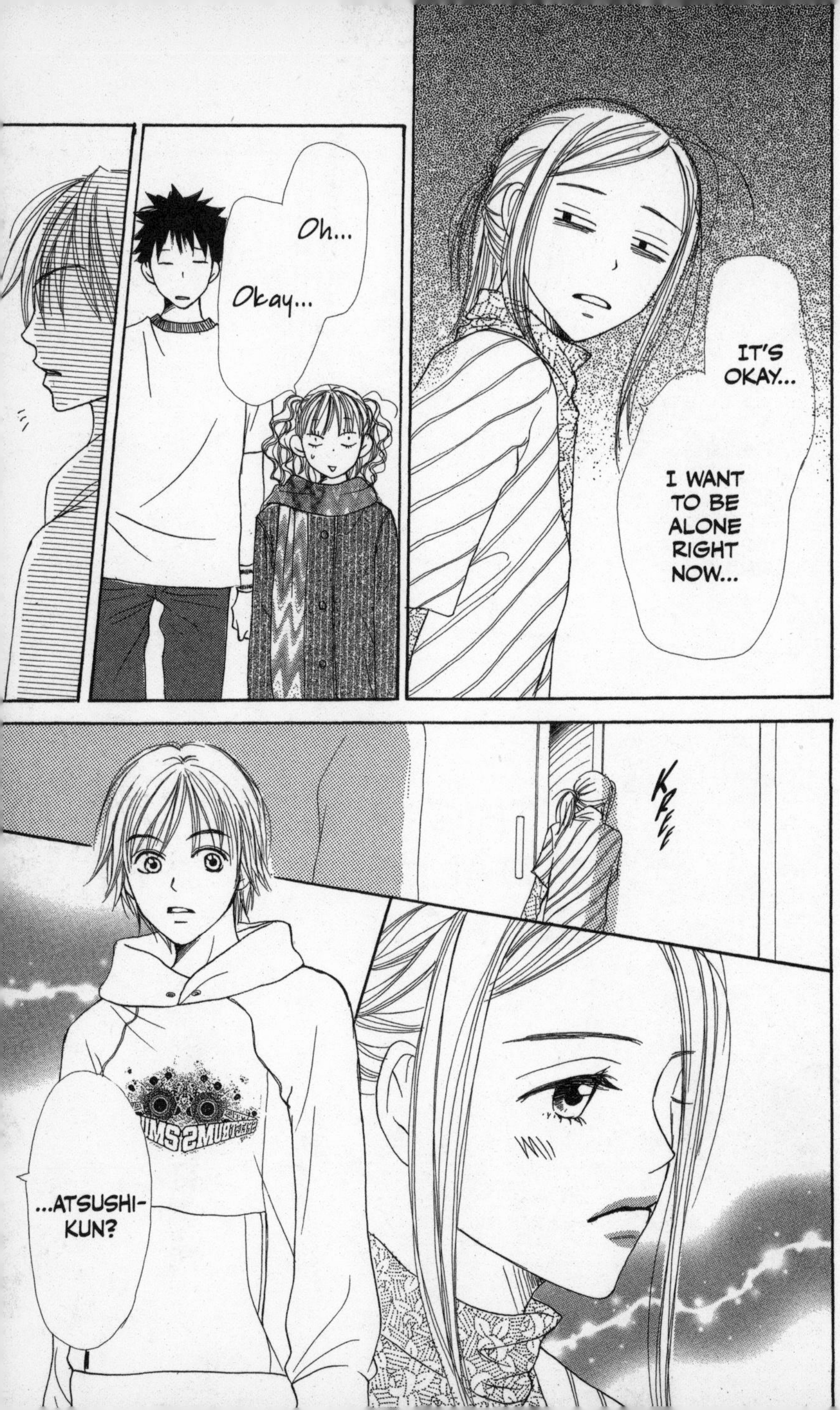
IT'S OKAY... I WANT TO BE ALONE RIGHT NOW...
Oh... Okay...
...ATSUSHI-KUN?

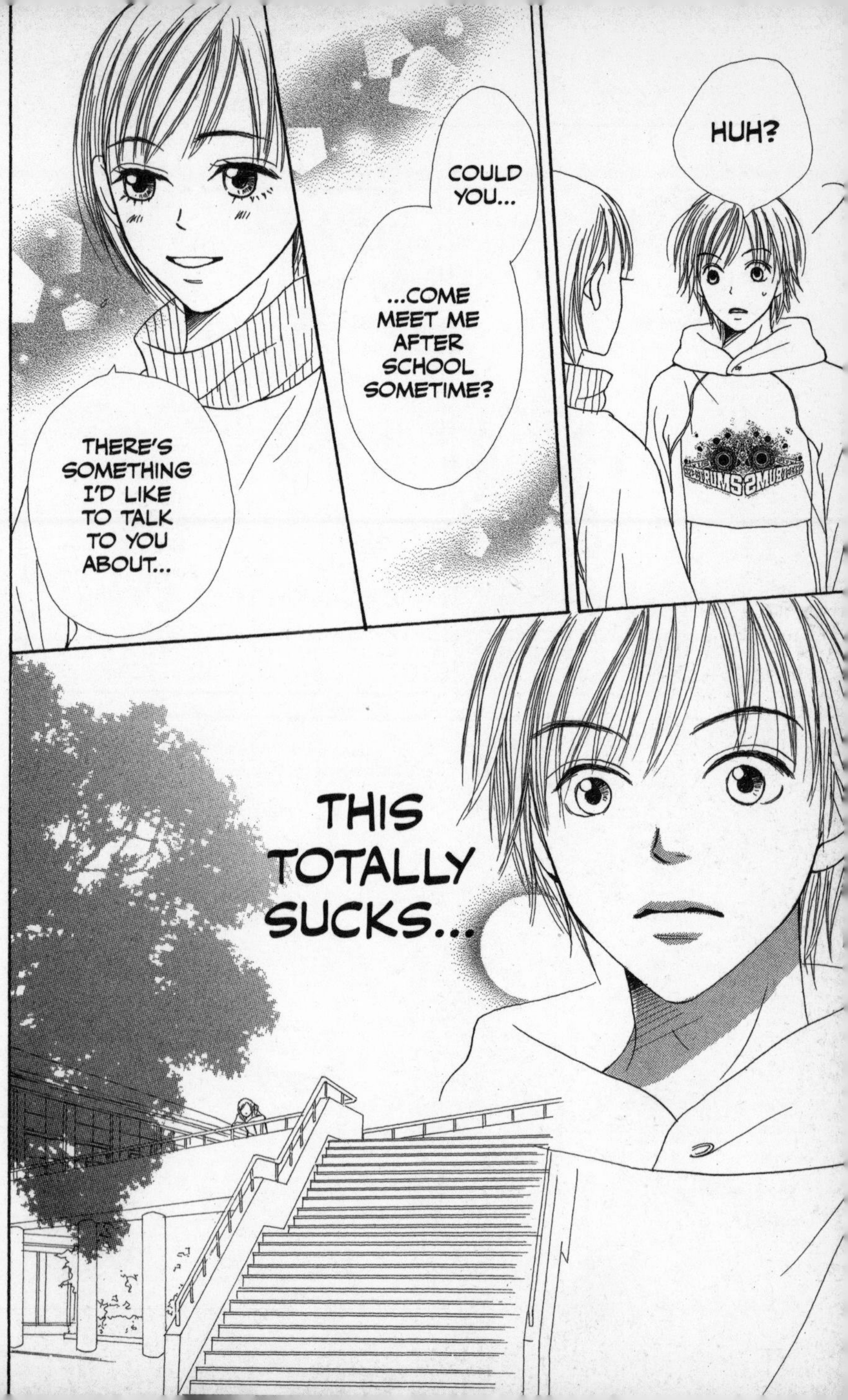
THERE'S SOMETHING I'D LIKE TO TALK TO YOU ABOUT...
COULD YOU...
...COME MEET ME AFTER SCHOOL SOMETIME?
HUH?
THIS TOTALLY SUCKS...

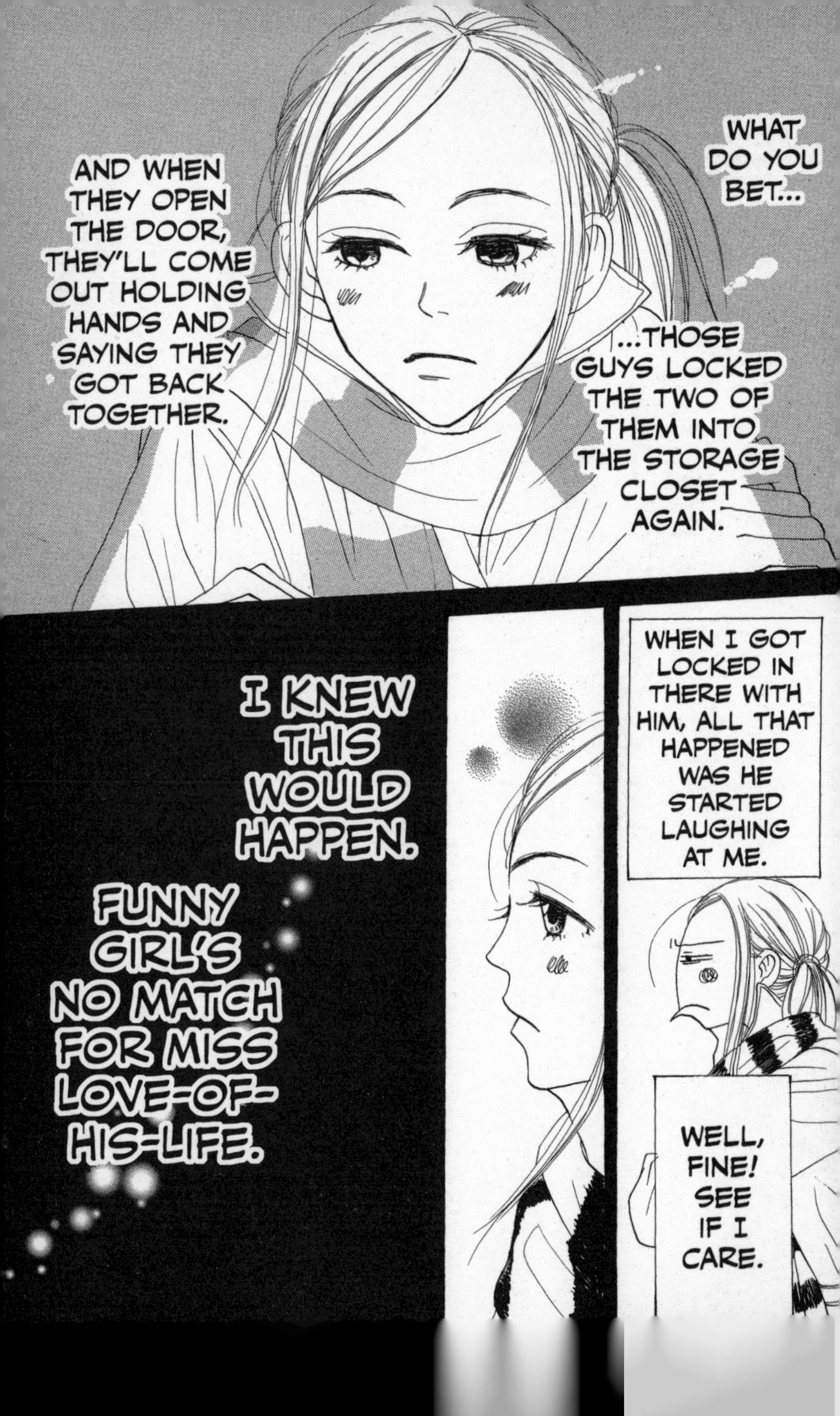
WHAT DO YOU BET...
...THOSE GUYS LOCKED THE TWO OF THEM INTO THE STORAGE CLOSET AGAIN.
AND WHEN THEY OPEN THE DOOR, THEY'LL COME OUT HOLDING HANDS AND SAYING THEY GOT BACK TOGETHER.
WHEN I GOT LOCKED IN THERE WITH HIM, ALL THAT HAPPENED WAS HE STARTED LAUGHING AT ME.
WELL, FINE! SEE IF I CARE.
I KNEW THIS WOULD HAPPEN.
FUNNY GIRL'S NO MATCH FOR MISS LOVE-OF-HIS-LIFE.

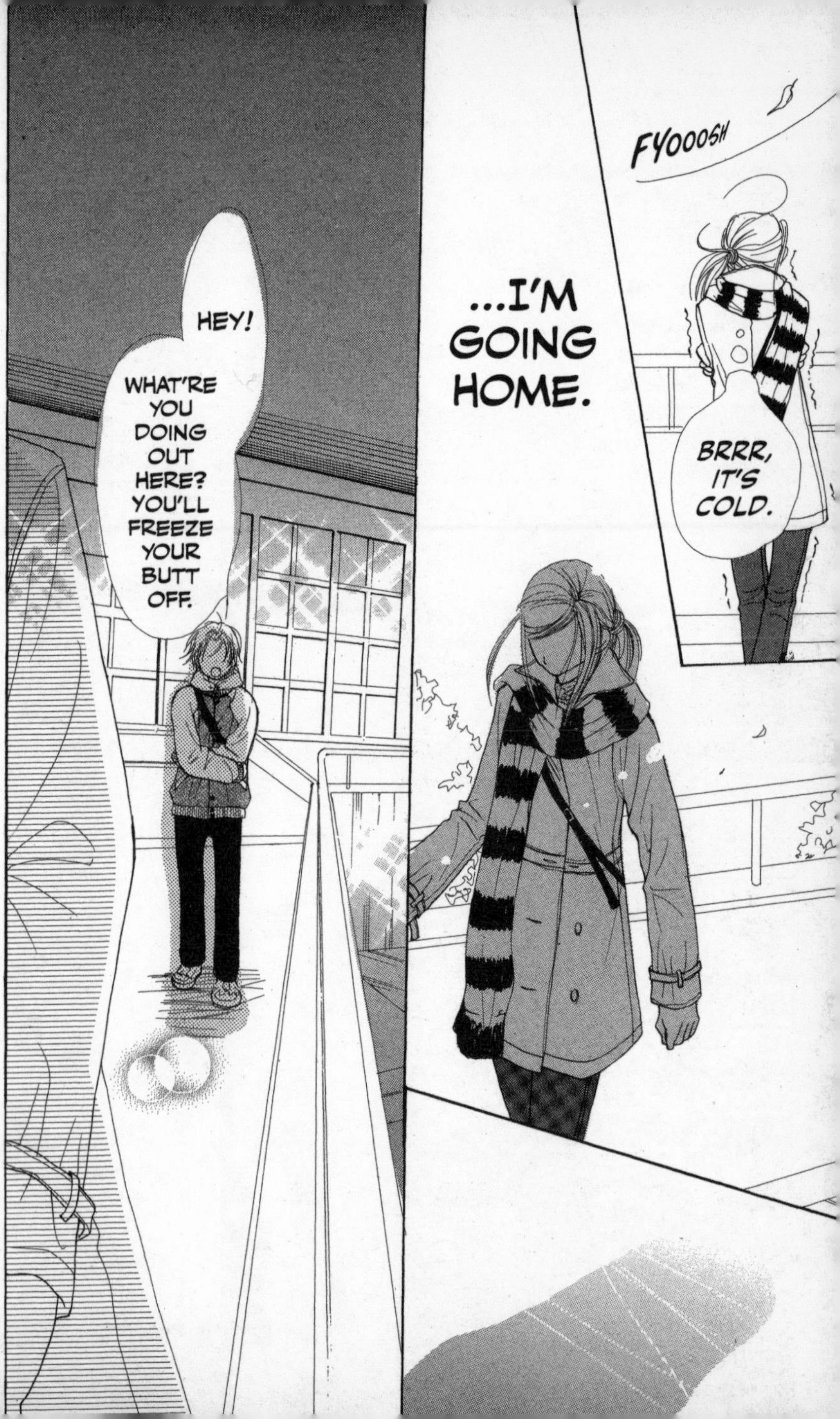
FYOOOSH
BRRR, IT'S COLD.
...I'M GOING HOME.
HEY!
WHAT'RE YOU DOING OUT HERE? YOU'LL FREEZE YOUR BUTT OFF.

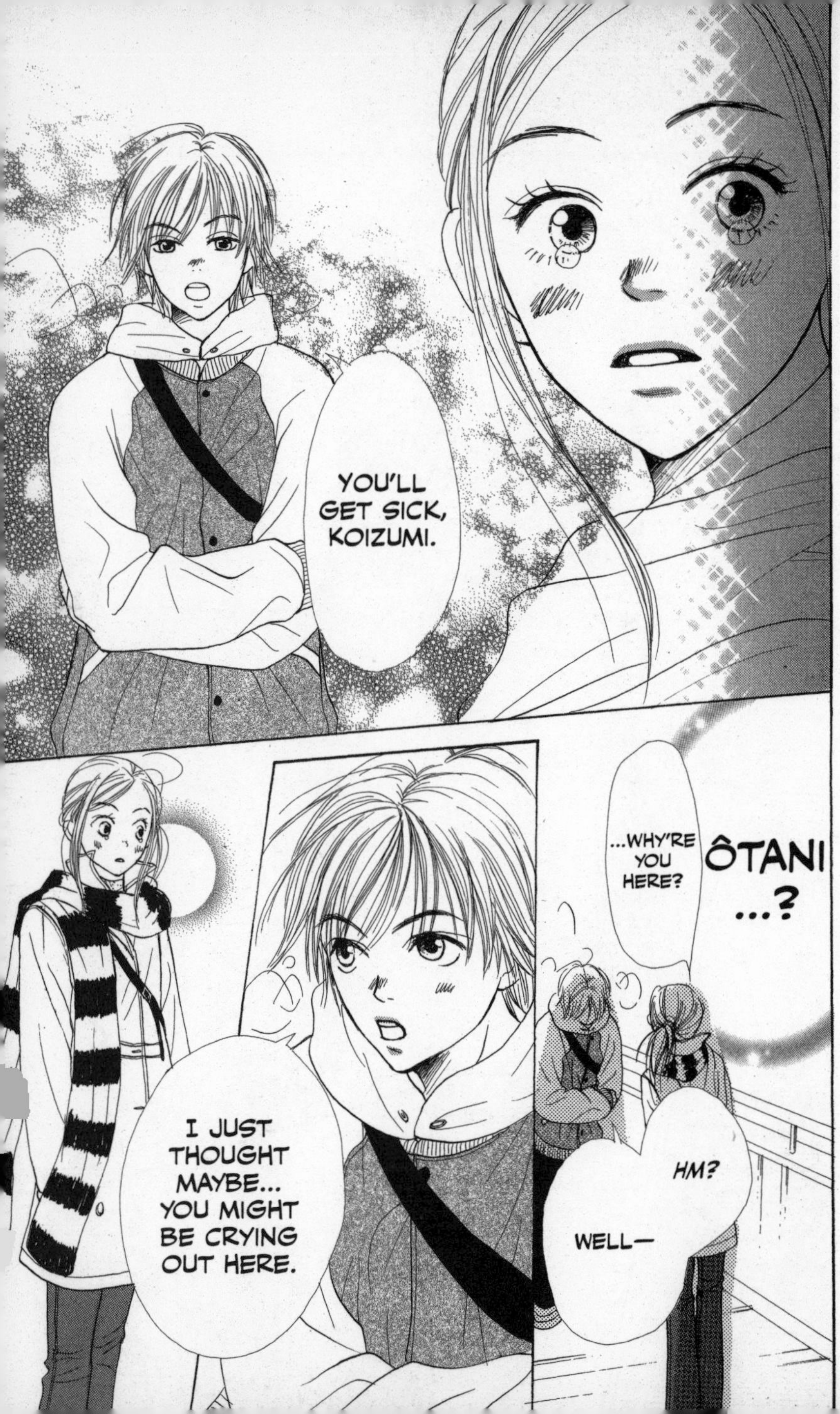
YOU'LL GET SICK, KOIZUMI.
ÔTANI ...?
...WHY'RE YOU HERE?
HM?
WELL—
I JUST THOUGHT MAYBE... YOU MIGHT BE CRYING OUT HERE.

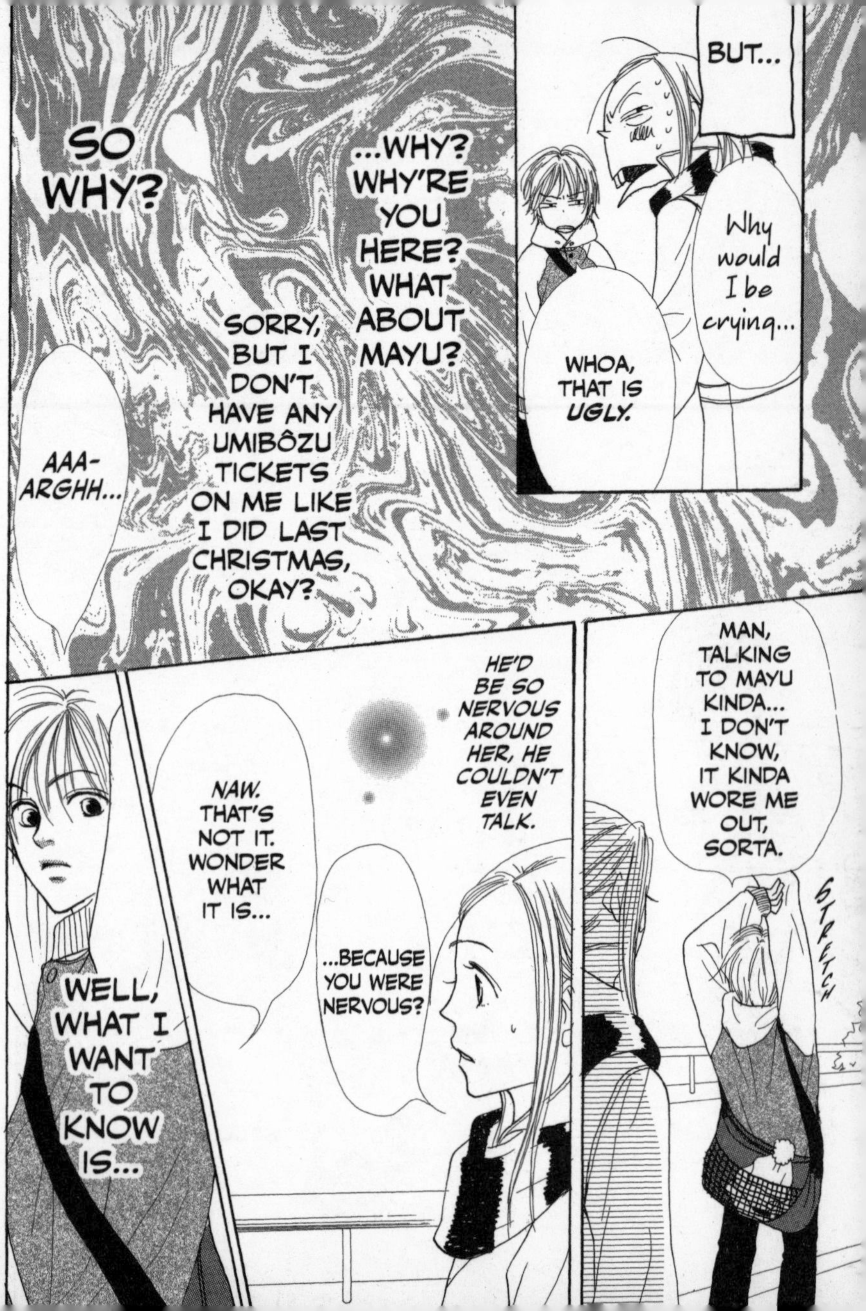
BUT...
Why would I be crying...
WHOA, THAT IS UGLY.
...WHY? WHY'RE YOU HERE? WHAT ABOUT MAYU?
SO WHY?
SORRY, BUT I DON'T HAVE ANY UMIBÔZU TICKETS ON ME LIKE I DID LAST CHRISTMAS, OKAY?
AAA-ARGHH...
MAN, TALKING TO MAYU KINDA... I DON'T KNOW, IT KINDA WORE ME OUT, SORTA.
STRETCH
HE'D BE SO NERVOUS AROUND HER, HE COULDN'T EVEN TALK.
NAW. THAT'S NOT IT. WONDER WHAT IT IS...
...BECAUSE YOU WERE NERVOUS?
WELL, WHAT I WANT TO KNOW IS...

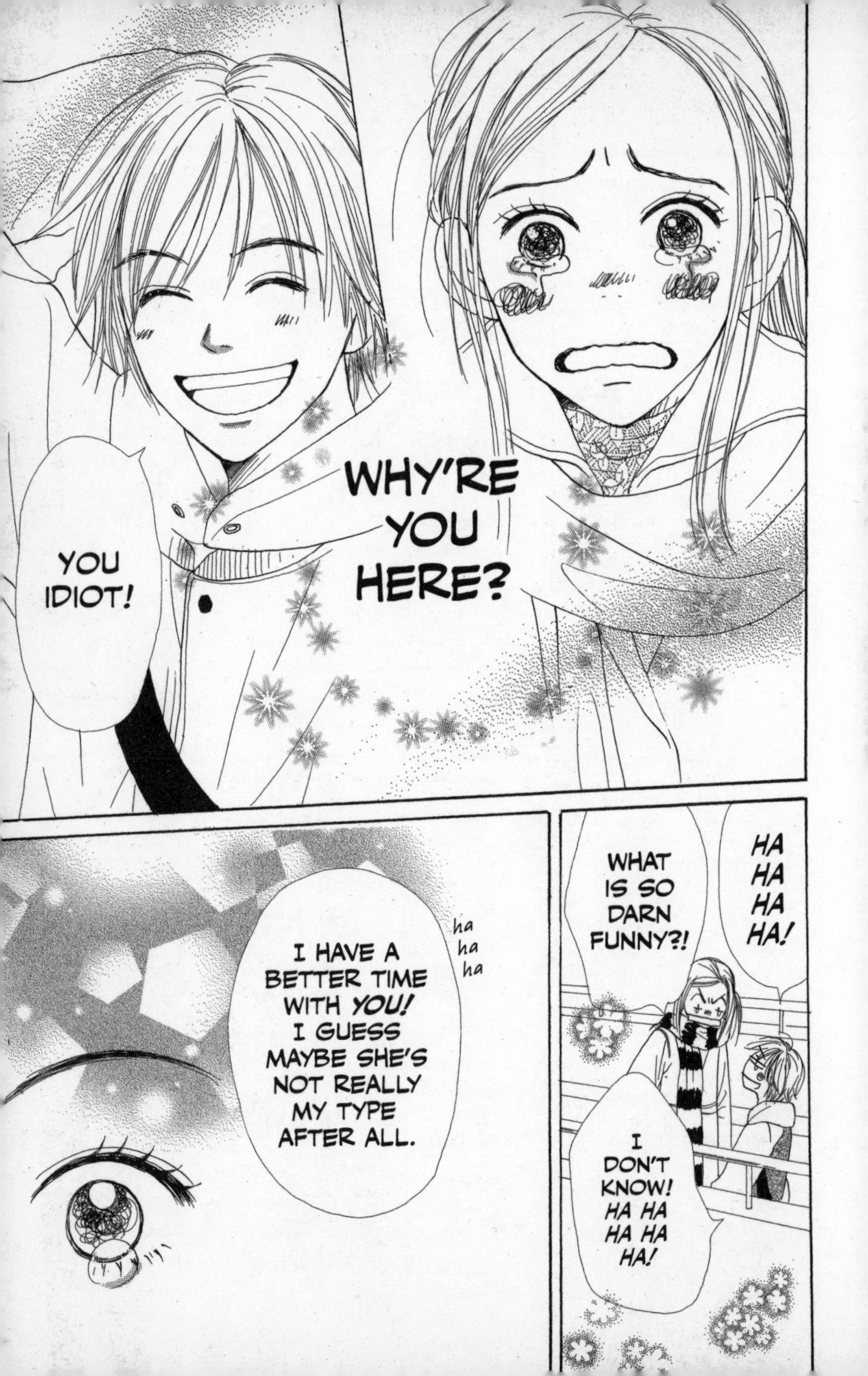
WHY'RE YOU HERE?
YOU IDIOT!
HA HA HA HA!
WHAT IS SO DARN FUNNY?!
I DON'T KNOW! HA HA HA HA HA!
ha ha ha
I HAVE A BETTER TIME WITH YOU! I GUESS MAYBE SHE'S NOT REALLY MY TYPE AFTER ALL.

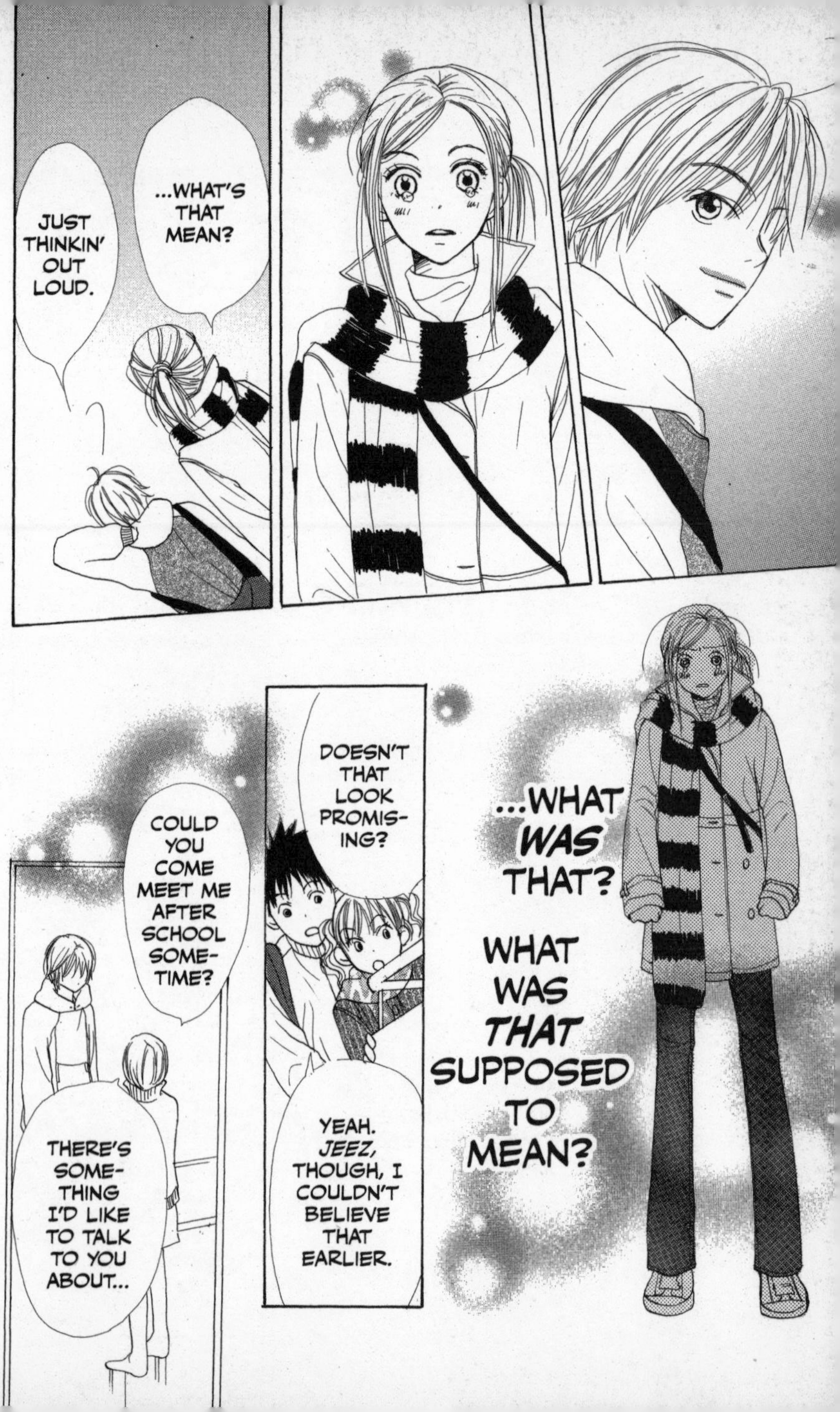
...WHAT'S THAT MEAN?
JUST THINKIN' OUT LOUD.
...WHAT *WAS* THAT?
WHAT WAS *THAT* SUPPOSED TO MEAN?
DOESN'T THAT LOOK PROMIS-ING?
YEAH. *JEEZ,* THOUGH, I COULDN'T BELIEVE THAT EARLIER.
COULD YOU COME MEET ME AFTER SCHOOL SOME-TIME?
THERE'S SOME-THING I'D LIKE TO TALK TO YOU ABOUT...

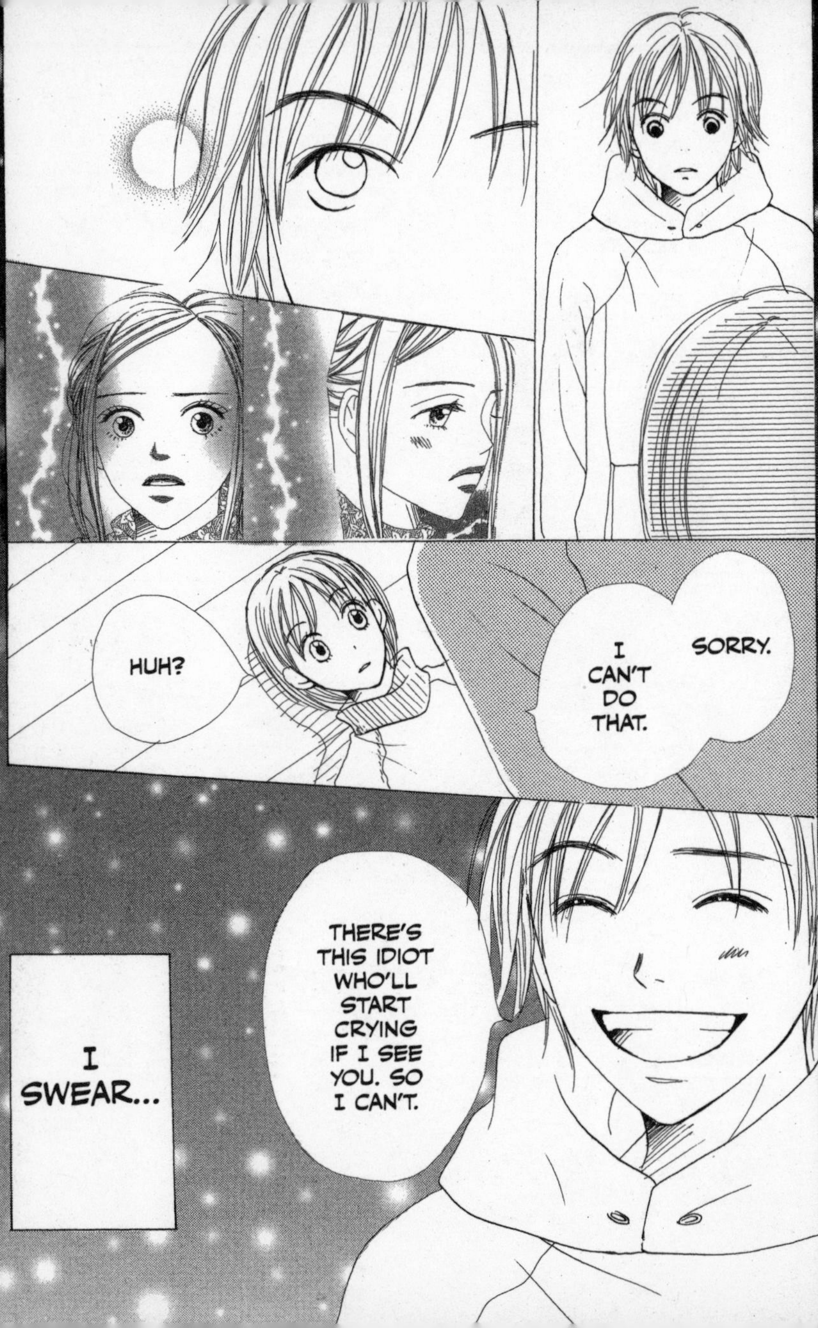
SORRY.
I CAN'T DO THAT.
HUH?
THERE'S THIS IDIOT WHO'LL START CRYING IF I SEE YOU. SO I CAN'T.
I SWEAR...

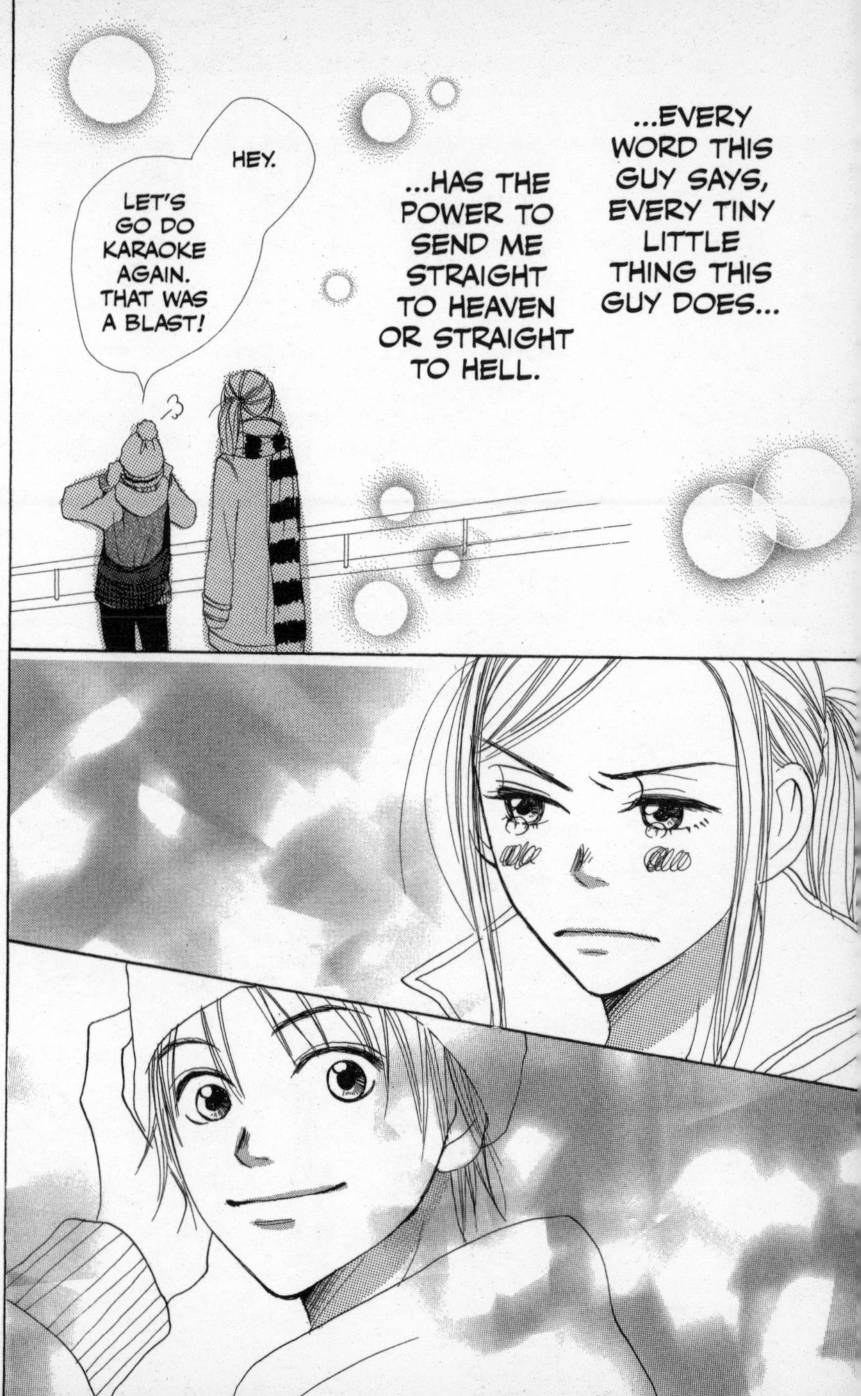
...EVERY WORD THIS GUY SAYS, EVERY TINY LITTLE THING THIS GUY DOES...
...HAS THE POWER TO SEND ME STRAIGHT TO HEAVEN OR STRAIGHT TO HELL.
HEY.
LET'S GO DO KARAOKE AGAIN. THAT WAS A BLAST!

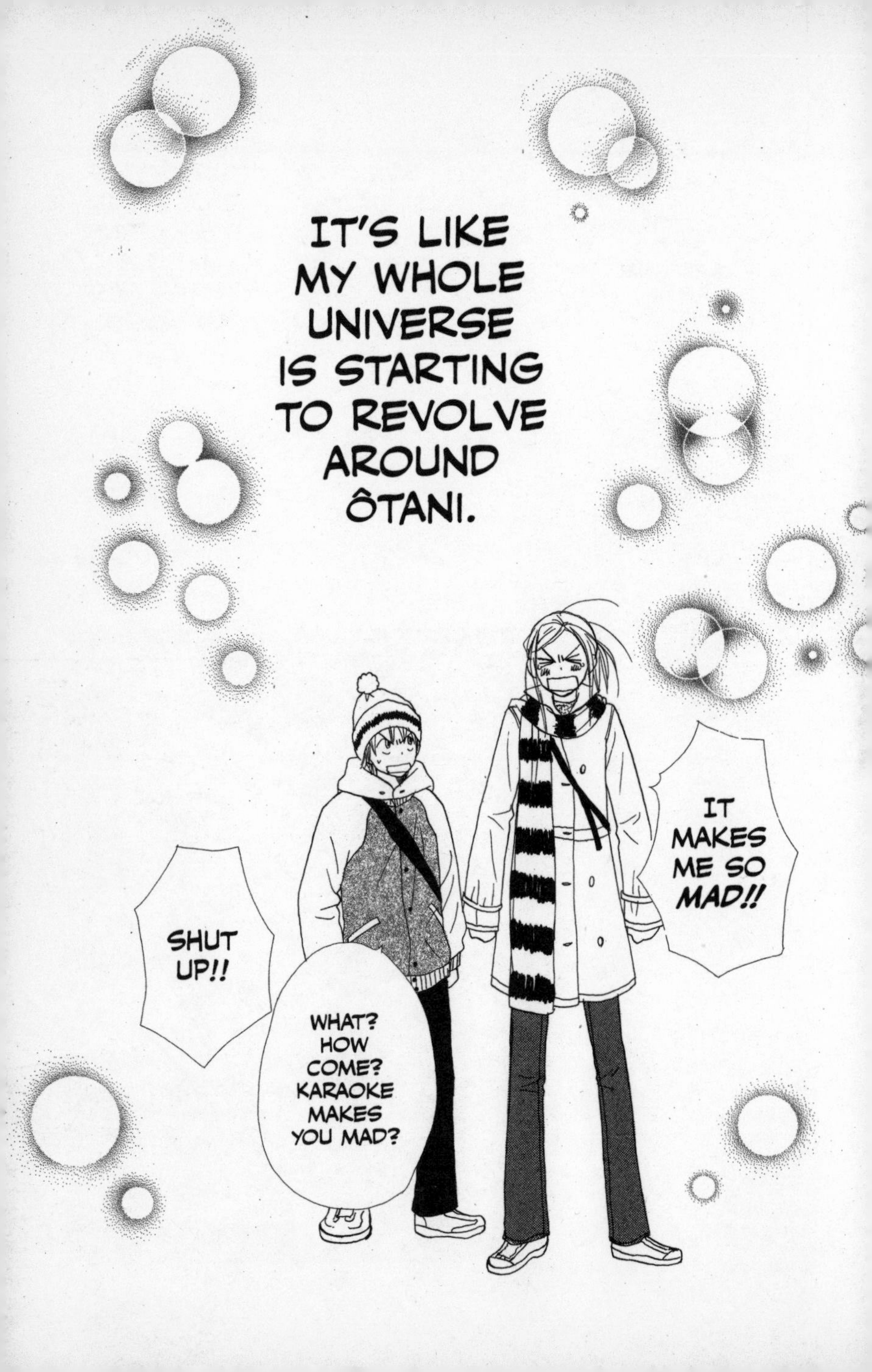
IT'S LIKE MY WHOLE UNIVERSE IS STARTING TO REVOLVE AROUND ÔTANI.
IT MAKES ME SO *MAD!!*
WHAT? HOW COME? KARAOKE MAKES YOU MAD?
SHUT UP!!

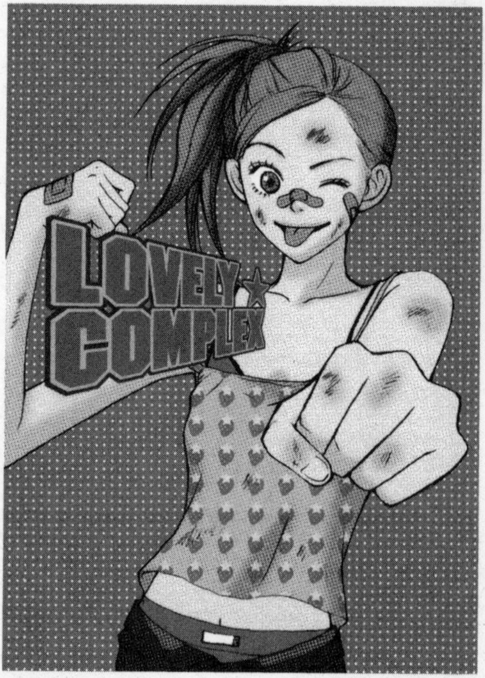
LOVELY★COMPLEX

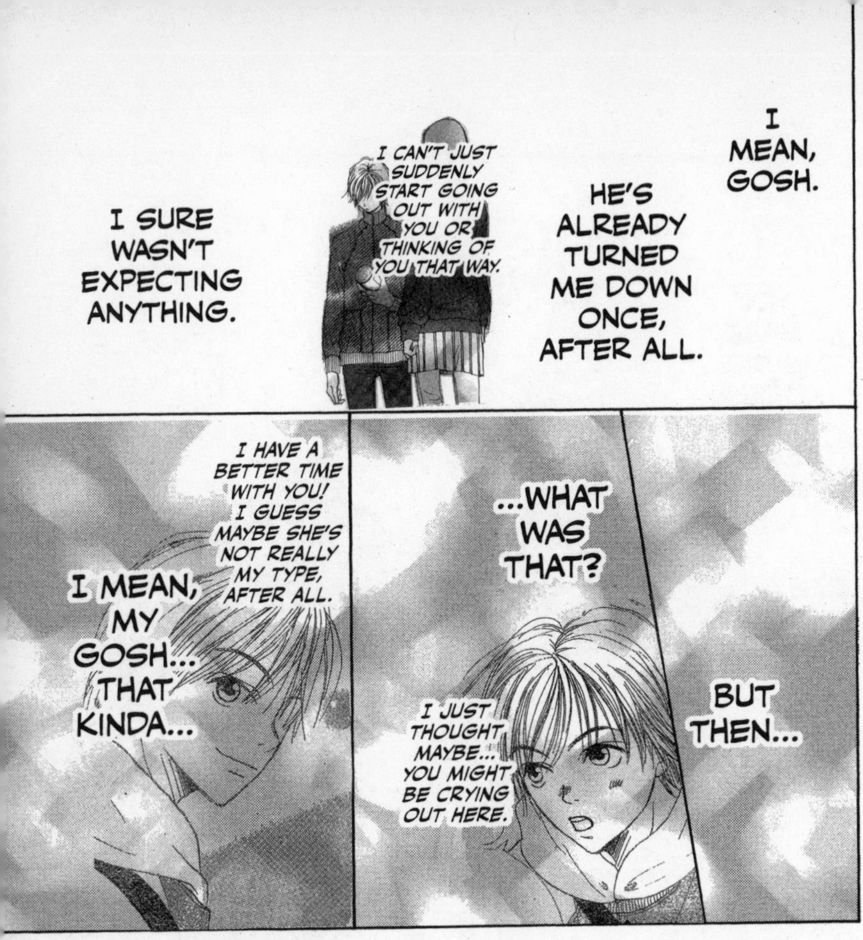
I MEAN, GOSH.
HE'S ALREADY TURNED ME DOWN ONCE, AFTER ALL.
I CAN'T JUST SUDDENLY START GOING OUT WITH YOU OR THINKING OF YOU THAT WAY.
I SURE WASN'T EXPECTING ANYTHING.
BUT THEN...
...WHAT WAS THAT?
I JUST THOUGHT MAYBE... YOU MIGHT BE CRYING OUT HERE.
I HAVE A BETTER TIME WITH YOU! I GUESS MAYBE SHE'S NOT REALLY MY TYPE, AFTER ALL.
I MEAN, MY GOSH... THAT KINDA...

CHAPTER 20

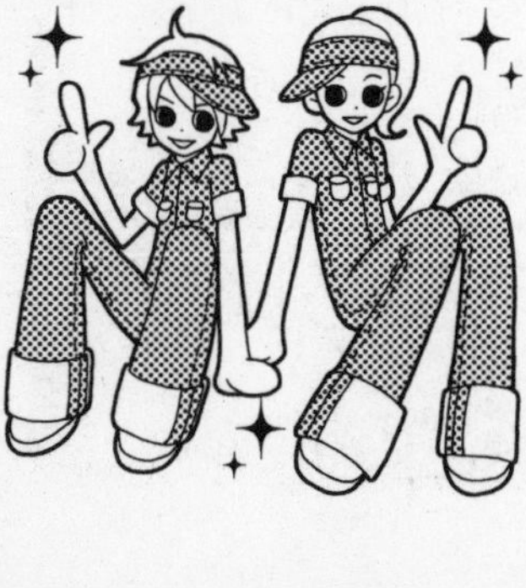

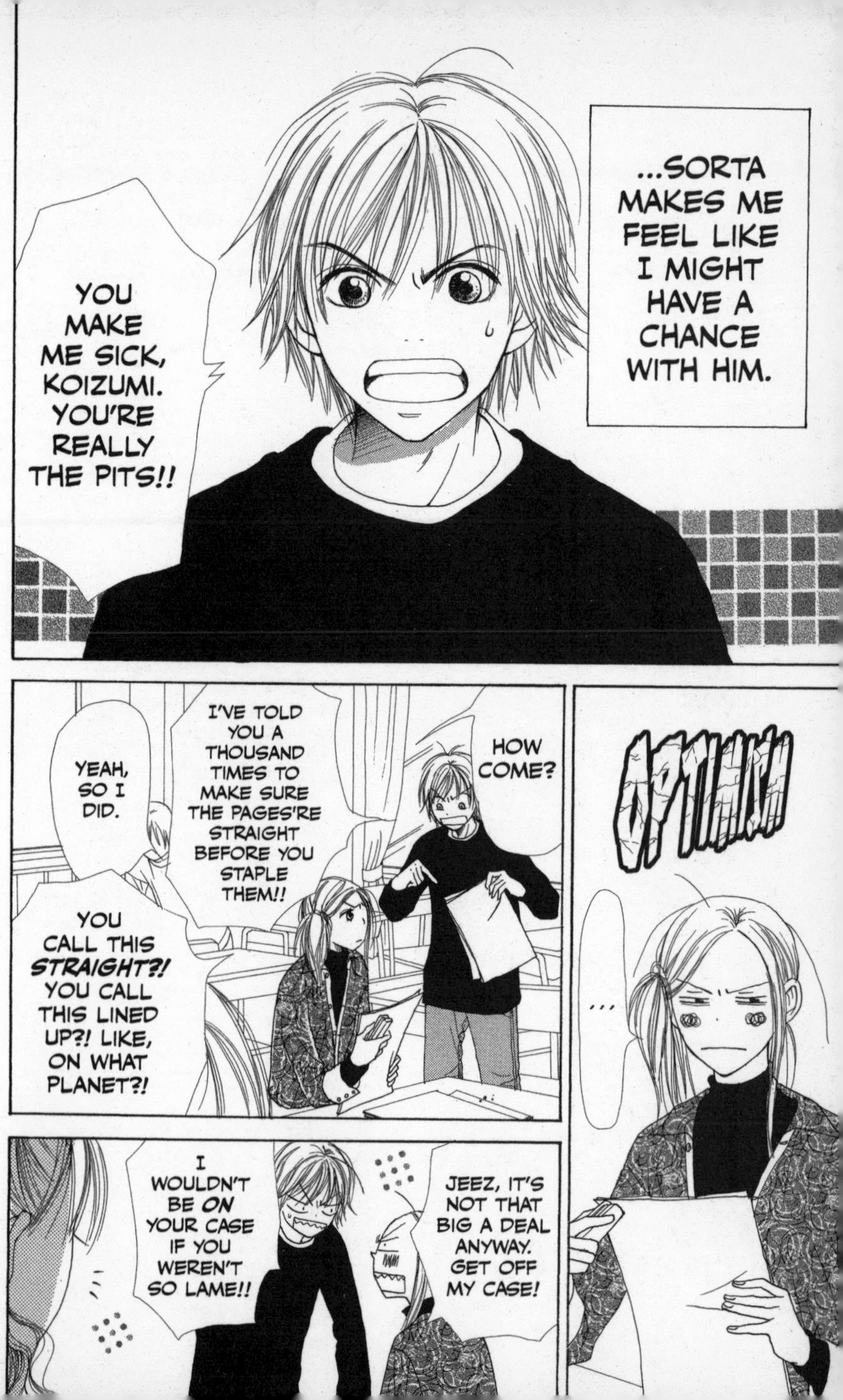
...SORTA MAKES ME FEEL LIKE I MIGHT HAVE A CHANCE WITH HIM.
YOU MAKE ME SICK, KOIZUMI. YOU'RE REALLY THE PITS!!
...
HOW COME?
I'VE TOLD YOU A THOUSAND TIMES TO MAKE SURE THE PAGES'RE STRAIGHT BEFORE YOU STAPLE THEM!!
YEAH, SO I DID.
YOU CALL THIS *STRAIGHT?!* YOU CALL THIS LINED UP?! LIKE, ON WHAT PLANET?!
JEEZ, IT'S NOT THAT BIG A DEAL ANYWAY. GET OFF MY CASE!
I WOULDN'T BE *ON* YOUR CASE IF YOU WEREN'T SO LAME!!

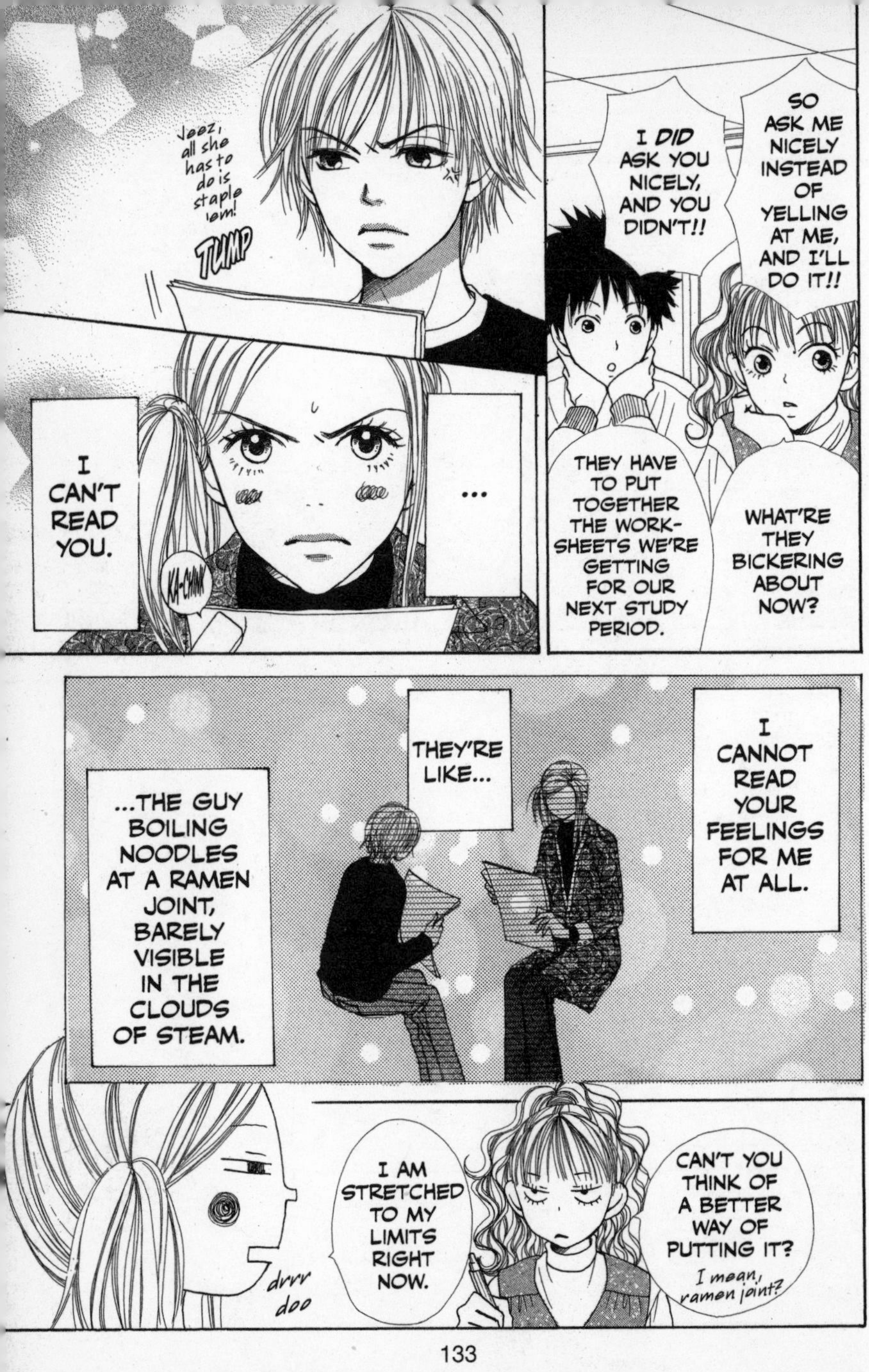
SO ASK ME NICELY INSTEAD OF YELLING AT ME, AND I'LL DO IT!!
I *DID* ASK YOU NICELY, AND YOU DIDN'T!!
WHAT'RE THEY BICKERING ABOUT NOW?
THEY HAVE TO PUT TOGETHER THE WORK-SHEETS WE'RE GETTING FOR OUR NEXT STUDY PERIOD.
Jeez, all she has to do is staple 'em!
TUMP
...
I CAN'T READ YOU.
KA-CHINK
I CANNOT READ YOUR FEELINGS FOR ME AT ALL.
THEY'RE LIKE...
...THE GUY BOILING NOODLES AT A RAMEN JOINT, BARELY VISIBLE IN THE CLOUDS OF STEAM.
CAN'T YOU THINK OF A BETTER WAY OF PUTTING IT?
I mean, ramen joint?
I AM STRETCHED TO MY LIMITS RIGHT NOW.
drrr doo

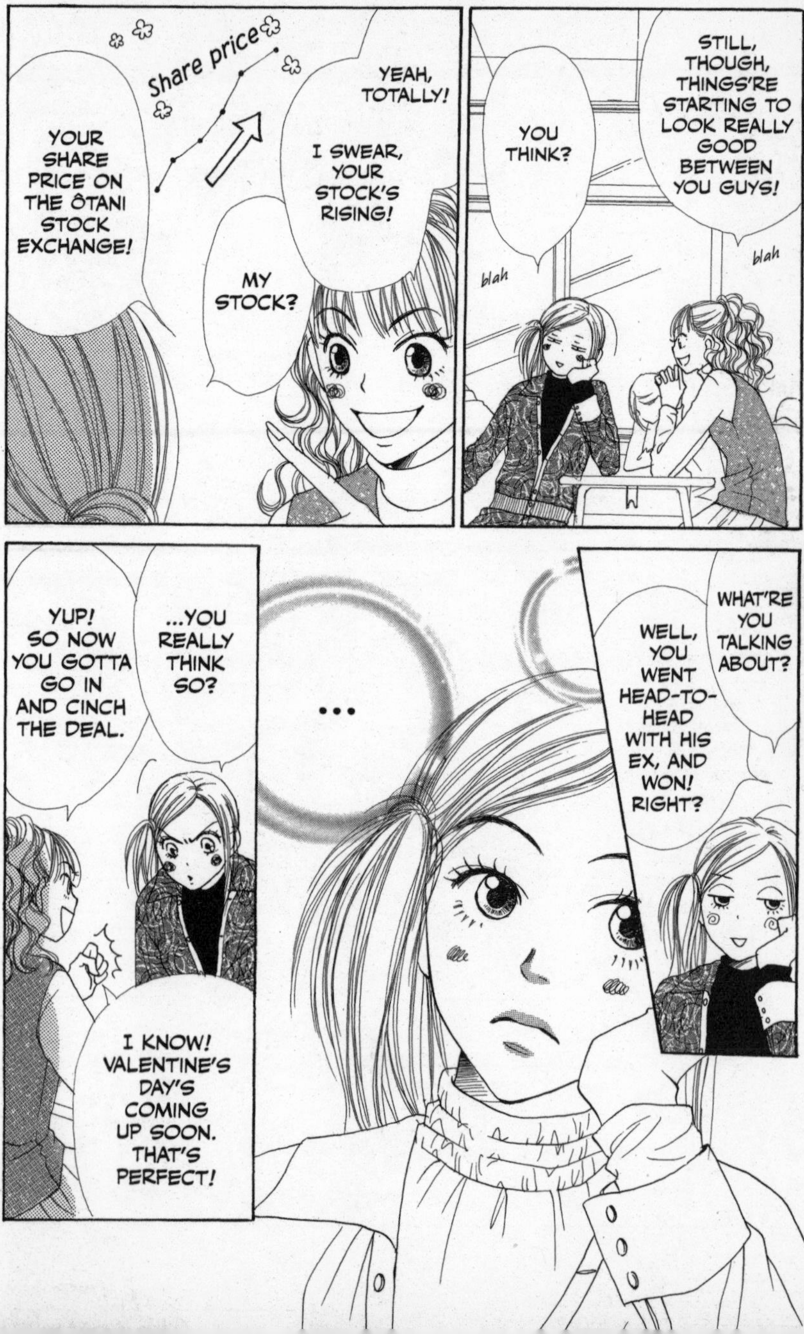
STILL, THOUGH, THINGS'RE STARTING TO LOOK REALLY GOOD BETWEEN YOU GUYS!
YOU THINK?
blah
blah
YEAH, TOTALLY! I SWEAR, YOUR STOCK'S RISING!
Share price
MY STOCK?
YOUR SHARE PRICE ON THE ÔTANI STOCK EXCHANGE!
WHAT'RE YOU TALKING ABOUT?
WELL, YOU WENT HEAD-TO-HEAD WITH HIS EX, AND WON! RIGHT?
...
...YOU REALLY THINK SO?
YUP! SO NOW YOU GOTTA GO IN AND CINCH THE DEAL.
I KNOW! VALENTINE'S DAY'S COMING UP SOON. THAT'S PERFECT!

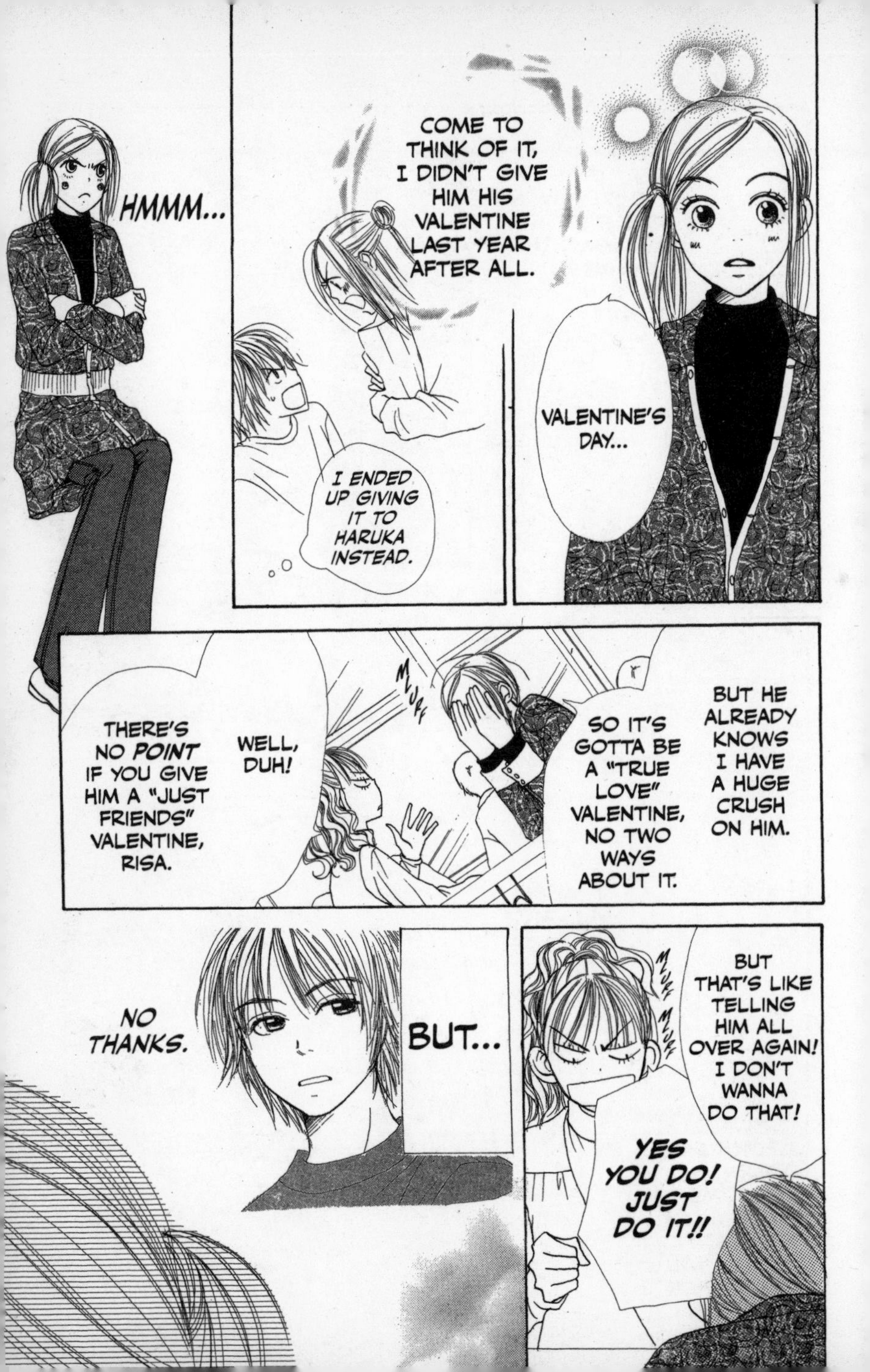
VALENTINE'S DAY...
COME TO THINK OF IT, I DIDN'T GIVE HIM HIS VALENTINE LAST YEAR AFTER ALL.
I ENDED UP GIVING IT TO HARUKA INSTEAD.
HMMM...
BUT HE ALREADY KNOWS I HAVE A HUGE CRUSH ON HIM.
SO IT'S GOTTA BE A "TRUE LOVE" VALENTINE, NO TWO WAYS ABOUT IT.
MUFF
WELL, DUH!
THERE'S NO POINT IF YOU GIVE HIM A "JUST FRIENDS" VALENTINE, RISA.
BUT THAT'S LIKE TELLING HIM ALL OVER AGAIN! I DON'T WANNA DO THAT!
MUFF MUFF
YES YOU DO! JUST DO IT!!
BUT...
NO THANKS.

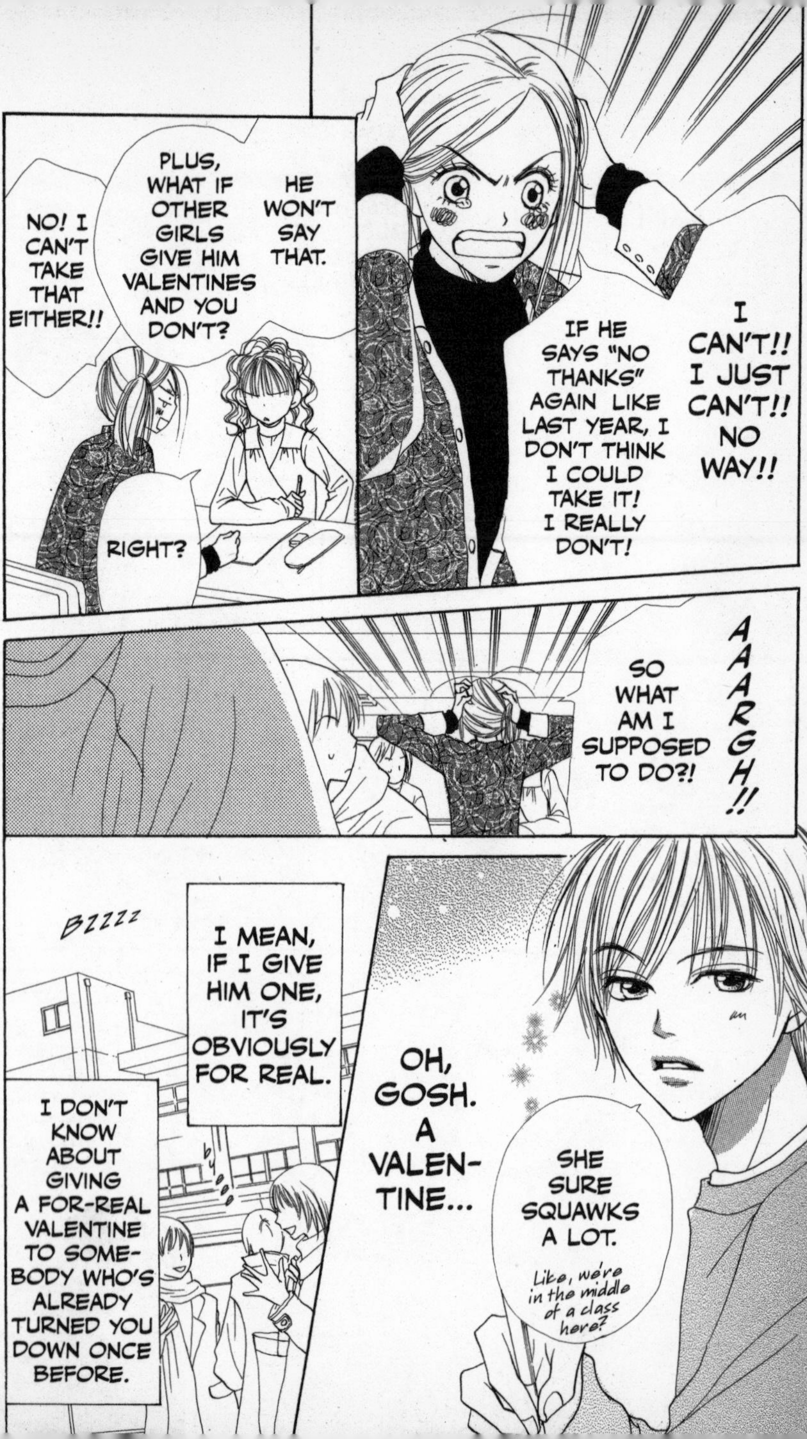
I CAN'T!! I JUST CAN'T!! NO WAY!!
IF HE SAYS "NO THANKS" AGAIN LIKE LAST YEAR, I DON'T THINK I COULD TAKE IT! I REALLY DON'T!
HE WON'T SAY THAT.
PLUS, WHAT IF OTHER GIRLS GIVE HIM VALENTINES AND YOU DON'T?
NO! I CAN'T TAKE THAT EITHER!!
RIGHT?
AAAARGH!!
SO WHAT AM I SUPPOSED TO DO?!
SHE SURE SQUAWKS A LOT.
Like, we're in the middle of a class here?
OH, GOSH. A VALEN-TINE...
I MEAN, IF I GIVE HIM ONE, IT'S OBVIOUSLY FOR REAL.
BZZZZ
I DON'T KNOW ABOUT GIVING A FOR-REAL VALENTINE TO SOME-BODY WHO'S ALREADY TURNED YOU DOWN ONCE BEFORE.

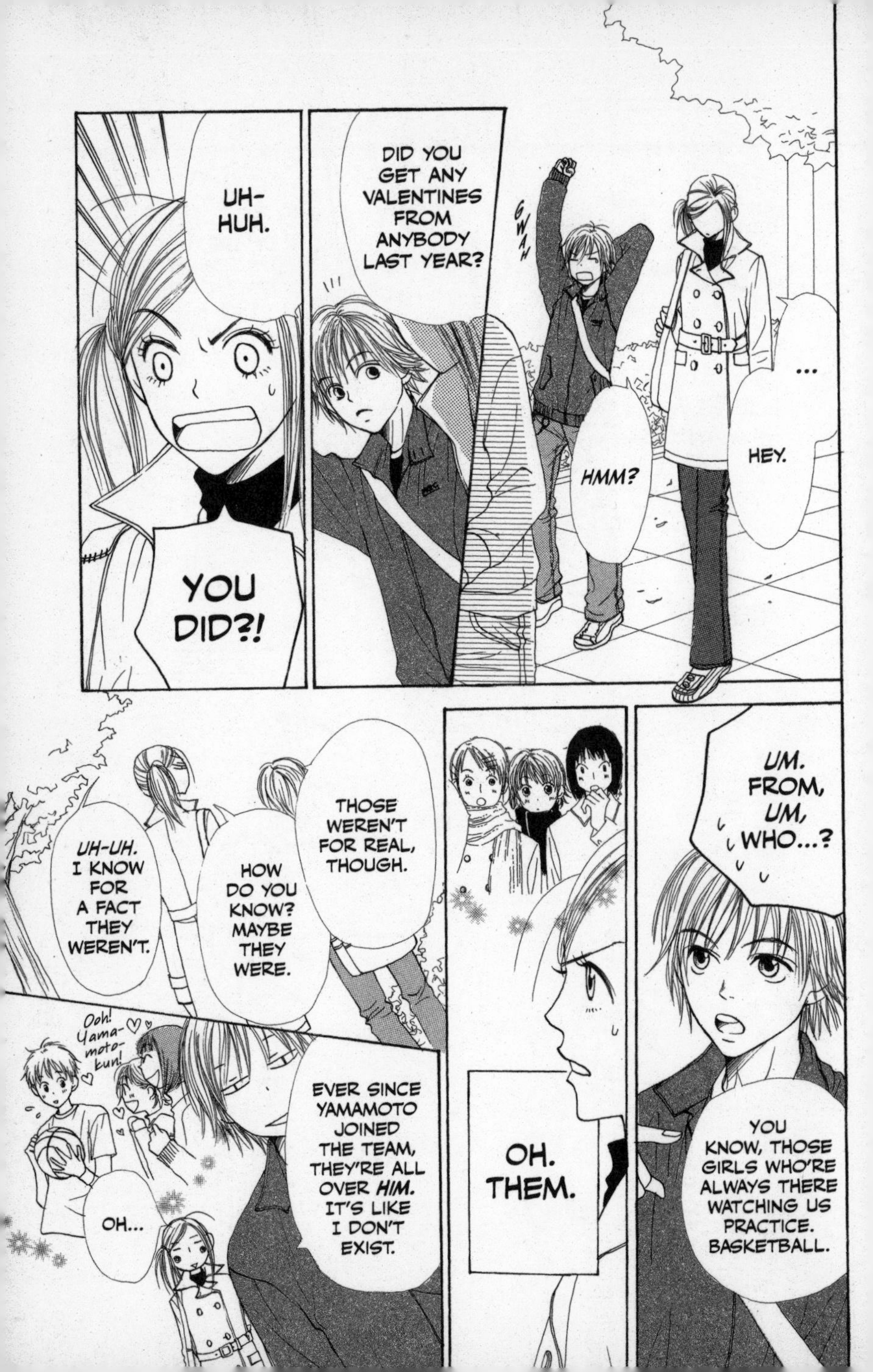
...
HEY.
HMM?
GWAH
DID YOU GET ANY VALENTINES FROM ANYBODY LAST YEAR?
UH-HUH.
YOU DID?!
UM. FROM, UM, WHO...?
YOU KNOW, THOSE GIRLS WHO'RE ALWAYS THERE WATCHING US PRACTICE. BASKETBALL.
OH. THEM.
THOSE WEREN'T FOR REAL, THOUGH.
HOW DO YOU KNOW? MAYBE THEY WERE.
UH-UH. I KNOW FOR A FACT THEY WEREN'T.
EVER SINCE YAMAMOTO JOINED THE TEAM, THEY'RE ALL OVER HIM. IT'S LIKE I DON'T EXIST.
Ooh! Yama-moto-kun!
OH...

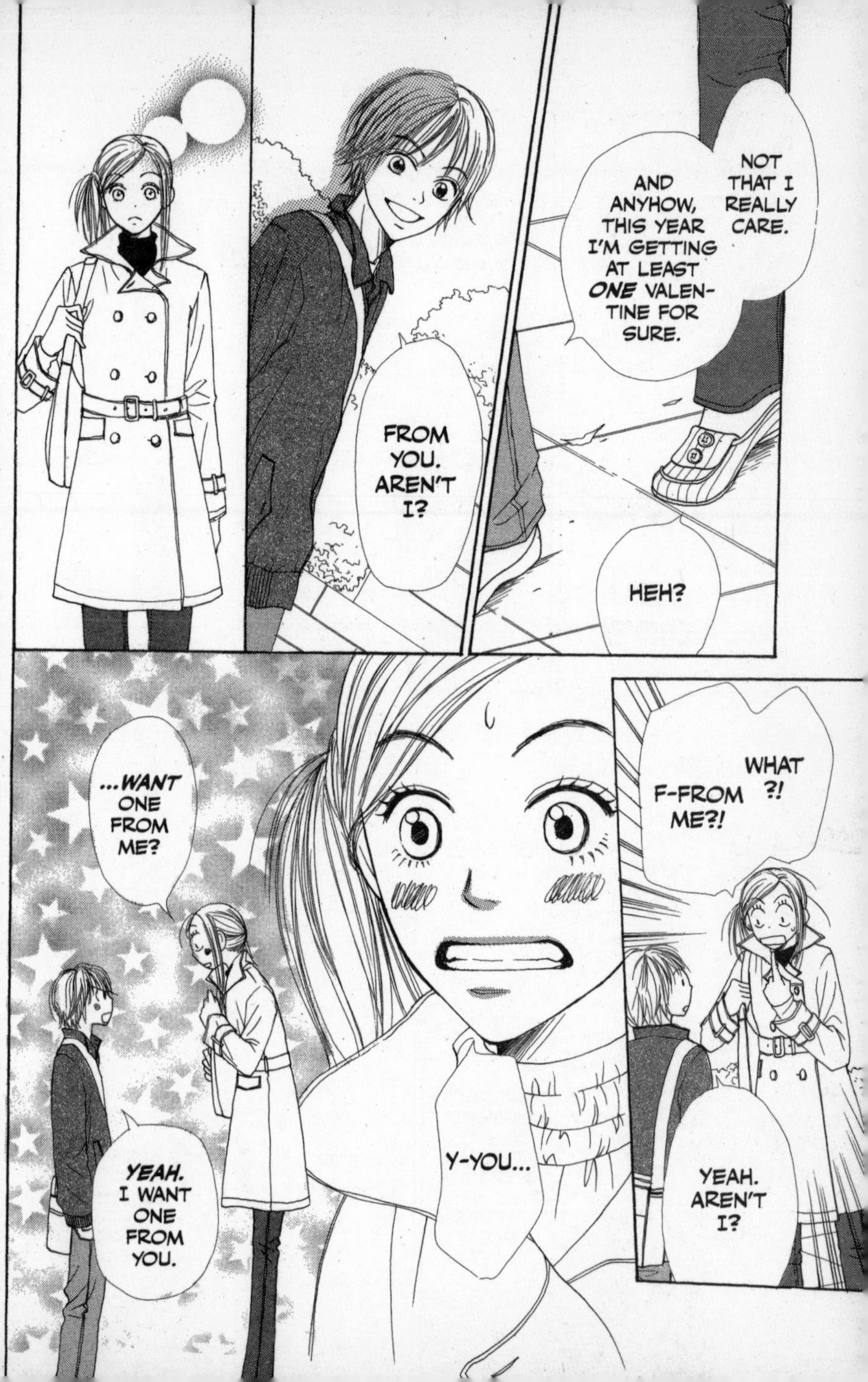
NOT THAT I REALLY CARE.
AND ANYHOW, THIS YEAR I'M GETTING AT LEAST *ONE* VALENTINE FOR SURE.
HEH?
FROM YOU. AREN'T I?
WHAT ?!
F-FROM ME?!
YEAH. AREN'T I?
Y-YOU...
...*WANT* ONE FROM ME?
YEAH. I WANT ONE FROM YOU.

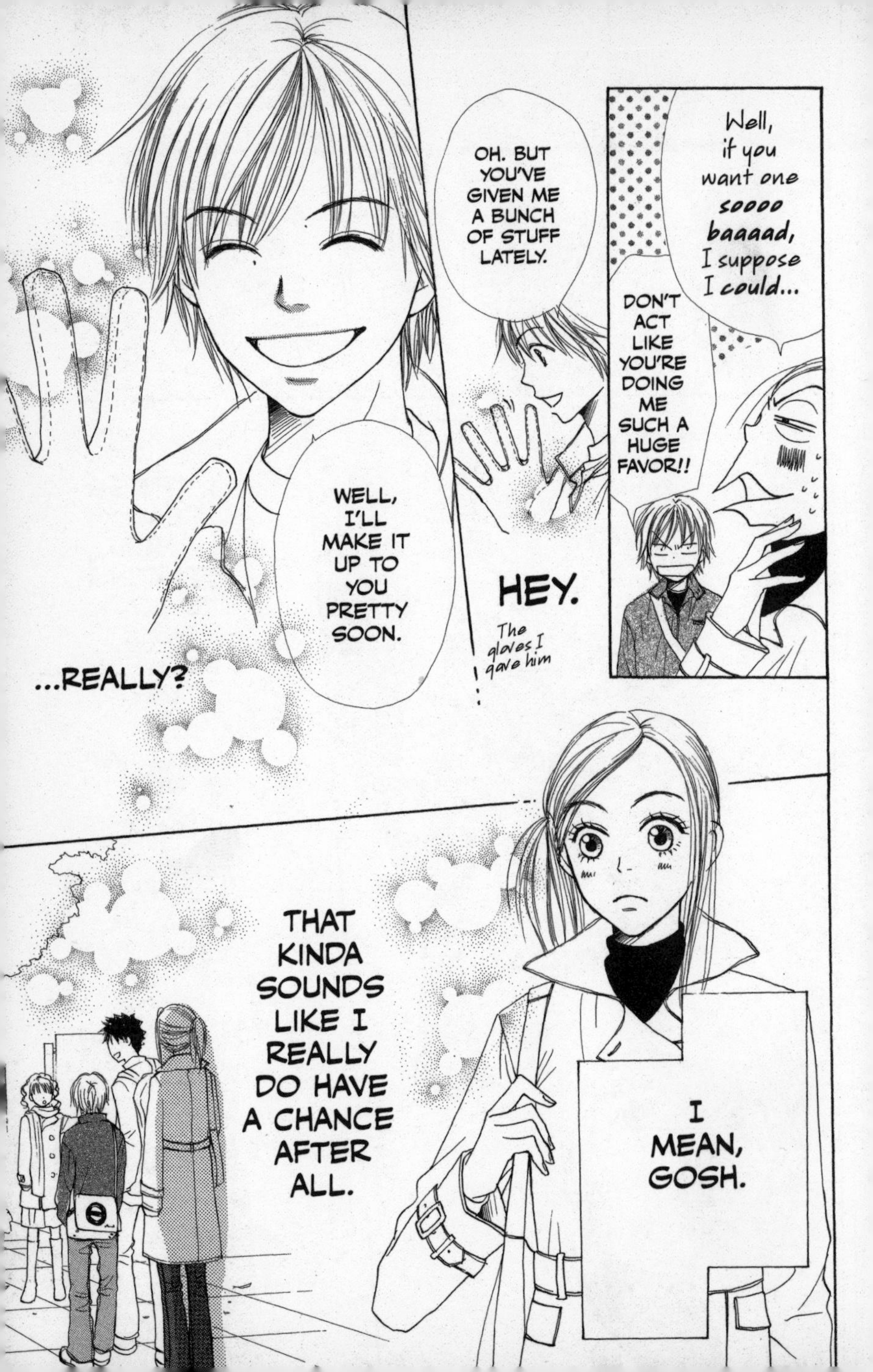
Well, if you want one soooo baaaad, I suppose I could...
DON'T ACT LIKE YOU'RE DOING ME SUCH A HUGE FAVOR!!
OH. BUT YOU'VE GIVEN ME A BUNCH OF STUFF LATELY.
HEY.
The gloves I gave him
WELL, I'LL MAKE IT UP TO YOU PRETTY SOON.
...REALLY?
I MEAN, GOSH.
THAT KINDA SOUNDS LIKE I REALLY DO HAVE A CHANCE AFTER ALL.

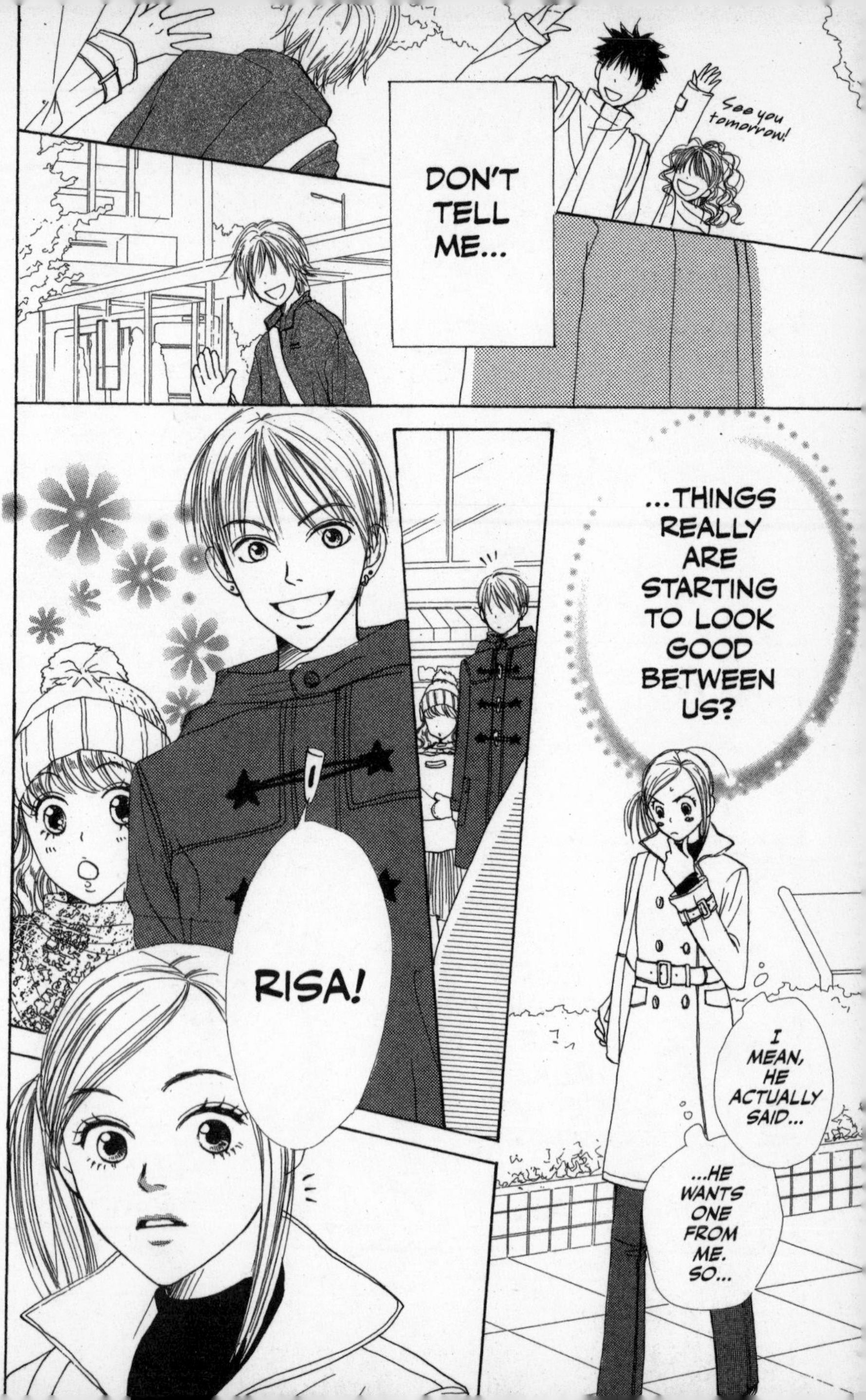
See you tomorrow!
DON'T TELL ME...
...THINGS REALLY ARE STARTING TO LOOK GOOD BETWEEN US?
I MEAN, HE ACTUALLY SAID...
...HE WANTS ONE FROM ME. SO...
RISA!

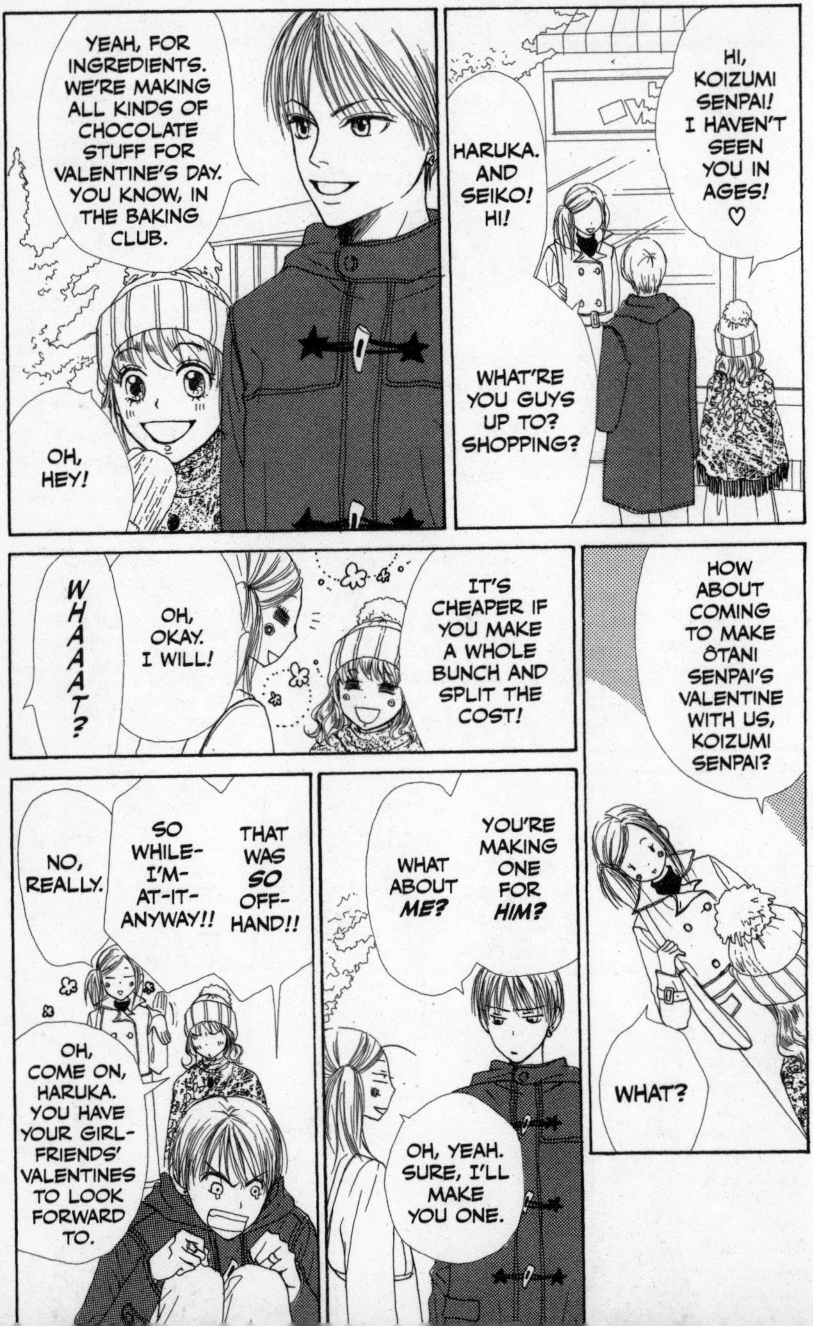
HI, KOIZUMI SENPAI! I HAVEN'T SEEN YOU IN AGES! ♡
HARUKA. AND SEIKO! HI!
WHAT'RE YOU GUYS UP TO? SHOPPING?
YEAH, FOR INGREDIENTS. WE'RE MAKING ALL KINDS OF CHOCOLATE STUFF FOR VALENTINE'S DAY. YOU KNOW, IN THE BAKING CLUB.
OH, HEY!
HOW ABOUT COMING TO MAKE ÔTANI SENPAI'S VALENTINE WITH US, KOIZUMI SENPAI?
WHAT?
IT'S CHEAPER IF YOU MAKE A WHOLE BUNCH AND SPLIT THE COST!
OH, OKAY. I WILL!
WHAAAAT?
YOU'RE MAKING ONE FOR *HIM*?
WHAT ABOUT *ME*?
OH, YEAH. SURE, I'LL MAKE YOU ONE.
THAT WAS *SO* OFF-HAND!!
SO WHILE-I'M-AT-IT-ANYWAY!!
NO, REALLY.
OH, COME ON, HARUKA. YOU HAVE YOUR GIRL-FRIENDS' VALENTINES TO LOOK FORWARD TO.

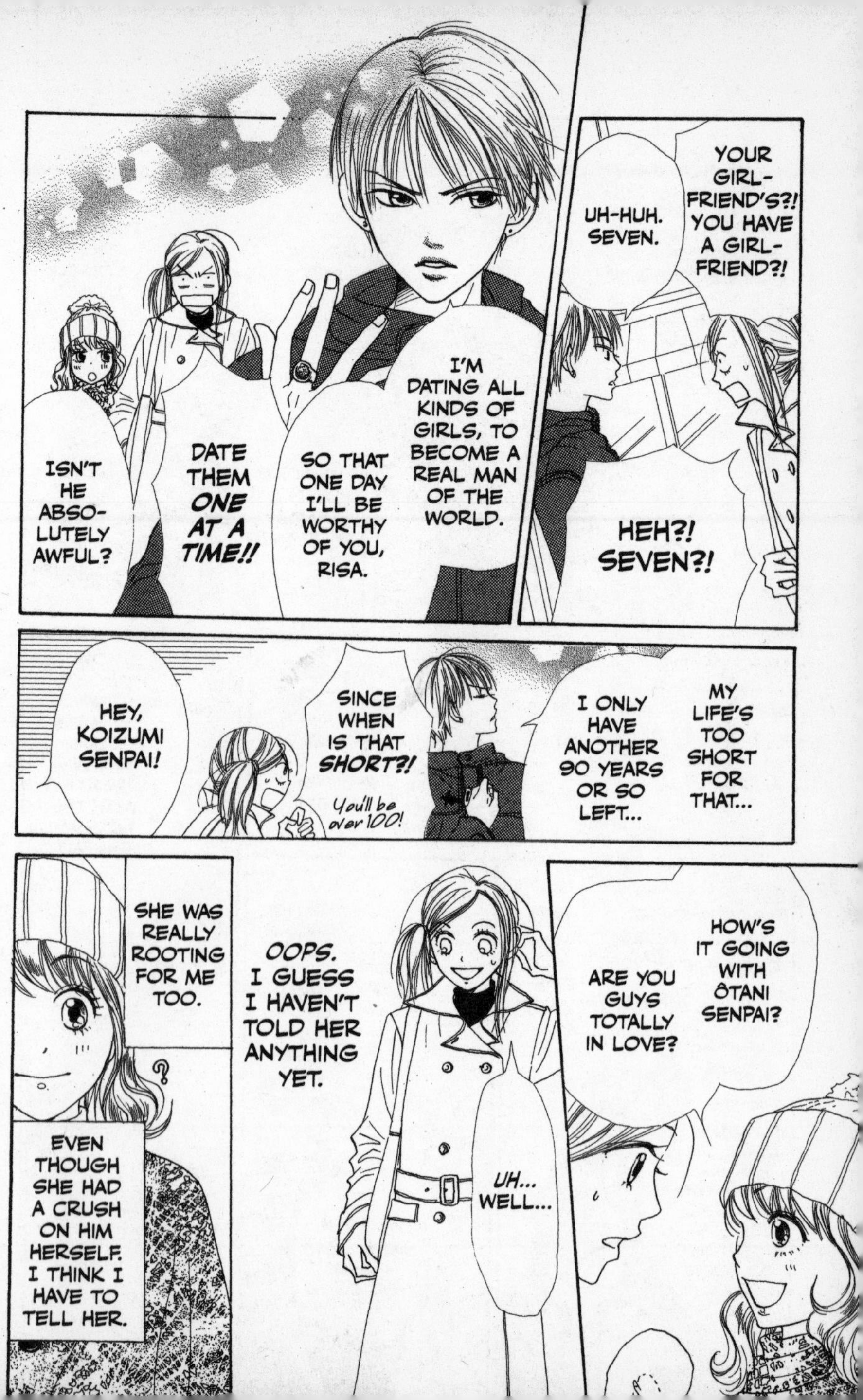
YOUR GIRL-FRIEND'S?! YOU HAVE A GIRL-FRIEND?!
UH-HUH. SEVEN.
HEH?! SEVEN?!
I'M DATING ALL KINDS OF GIRLS, TO BECOME A REAL MAN OF THE WORLD.
SO THAT ONE DAY I'LL BE WORTHY OF YOU, RISA.
DATE THEM ONE AT A TIME!!
ISN'T HE ABSOLUTELY AWFUL?
MY LIFE'S TOO SHORT FOR THAT...
I ONLY HAVE ANOTHER 90 YEARS OR SO LEFT...
SINCE WHEN IS THAT SHORT?!
You'll be over 100!
HEY, KOIZUMI SENPAI!
HOW'S IT GOING WITH ŌTANI SENPAI?
ARE YOU GUYS TOTALLY IN LOVE?
UH... WELL...
OOPS. I GUESS I HAVEN'T TOLD HER ANYTHING YET.
SHE WAS REALLY ROOTING FOR ME TOO.
EVEN THOUGH SHE HAD A CRUSH ON HIM HERSELF. I THINK I HAVE TO TELL HER.

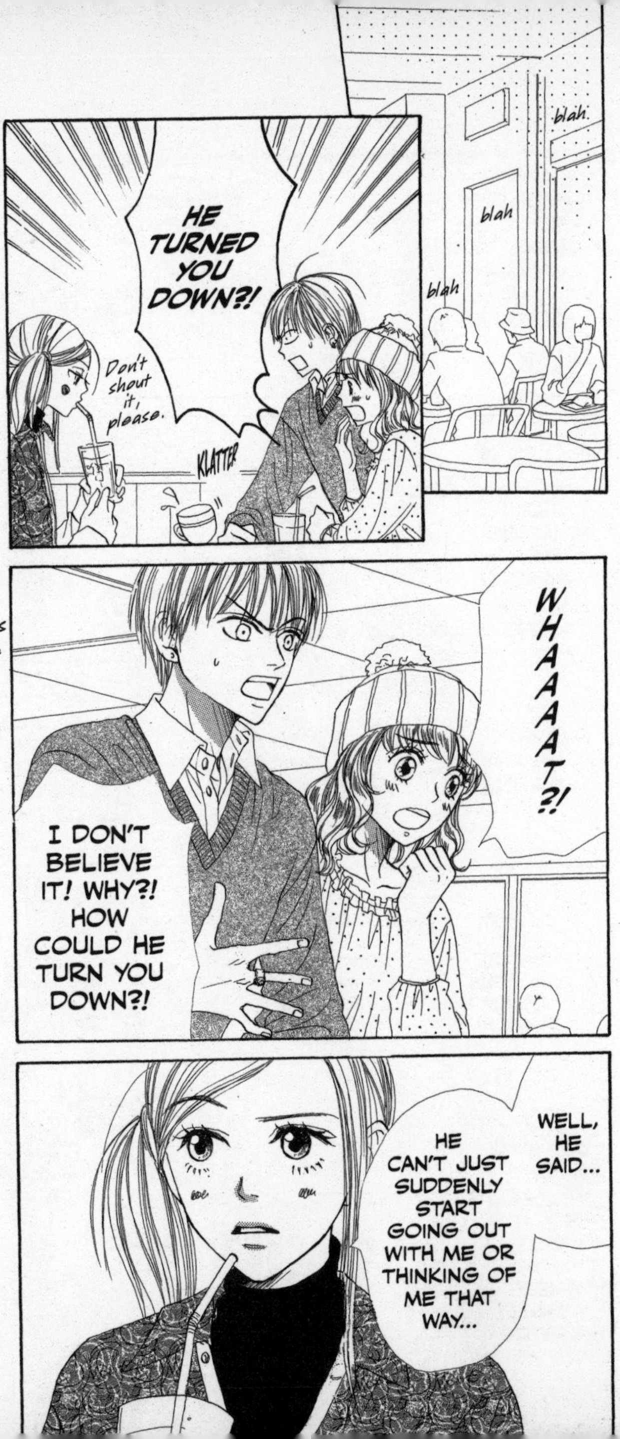
blah
blah
blah
HE TURNED YOU DOWN?!
Don't shout it, please.
KLATTER
WHAAAAAT?!
I DON'T BELIEVE IT! WHY?! HOW COULD HE TURN YOU DOWN?!
WELL, HE SAID...
HE CAN'T JUST SUDDENLY START GOING OUT WITH ME OR THINKING OF ME THAT WAY...

4

So anyway, thank you for reading this again. I really look forward to seeing you all in Vol. 6. Until then, bye! ☆

Aya
May 2003

P.S.
The bonus Page (+4)s in this volume are the characters' profiles that were actually published in Bessatsu Margaret.
Oh, and there's no episode of "24 Hours with the LCPD" this time, because the author, Aya Nakahara Sensei, is away on business. What business? pfff, tee hee

♥Special Thanks♥

Nana Ikebe
Hikari Katayama
Ryosuke Fujii
Nakahara Family
Betsuma Family
and
you

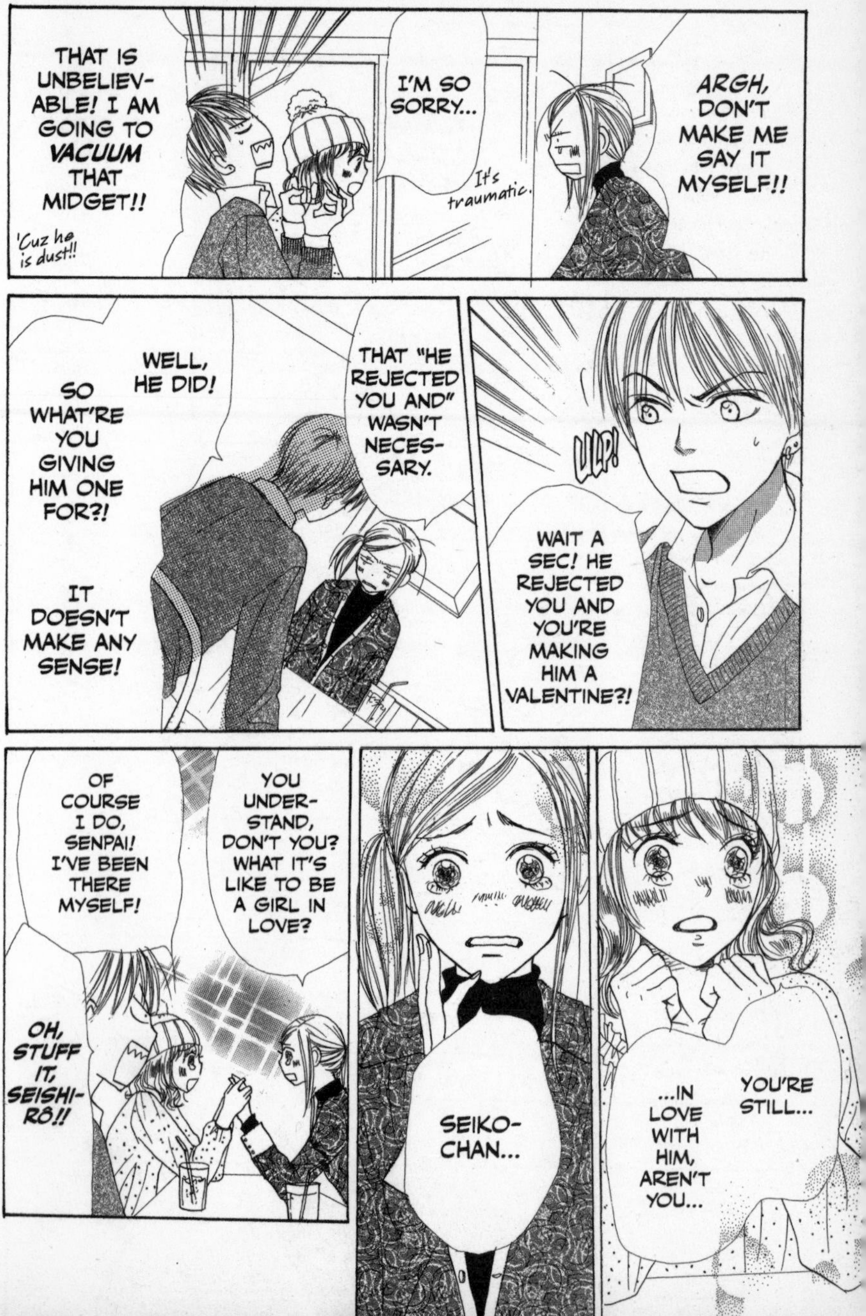
ARGH, DON'T MAKE ME SAY IT MYSELF!!
I'M SO SORRY...
It's traumatic.
THAT IS UNBELIEVABLE! I AM GOING TO VACUUM THAT MIDGET!!
'Cuz he is dust!!
ULP!
WAIT A SEC! HE REJECTED YOU AND YOU'RE MAKING HIM A VALENTINE?!
THAT "HE REJECTED YOU AND" WASN'T NECESSARY.
WELL, HE DID!
SO WHAT'RE YOU GIVING HIM ONE FOR?!
IT DOESN'T MAKE ANY SENSE!
YOU'RE STILL...
...IN LOVE WITH HIM, AREN'T YOU...
SEIKO-CHAN...
YOU UNDERSTAND, DON'T YOU? WHAT IT'S LIKE TO BE A GIRL IN LOVE?
OF COURSE I DO, SENPAI! I'VE BEEN THERE MYSELF!
OH, STUFF IT, SEISHIRÔ!!

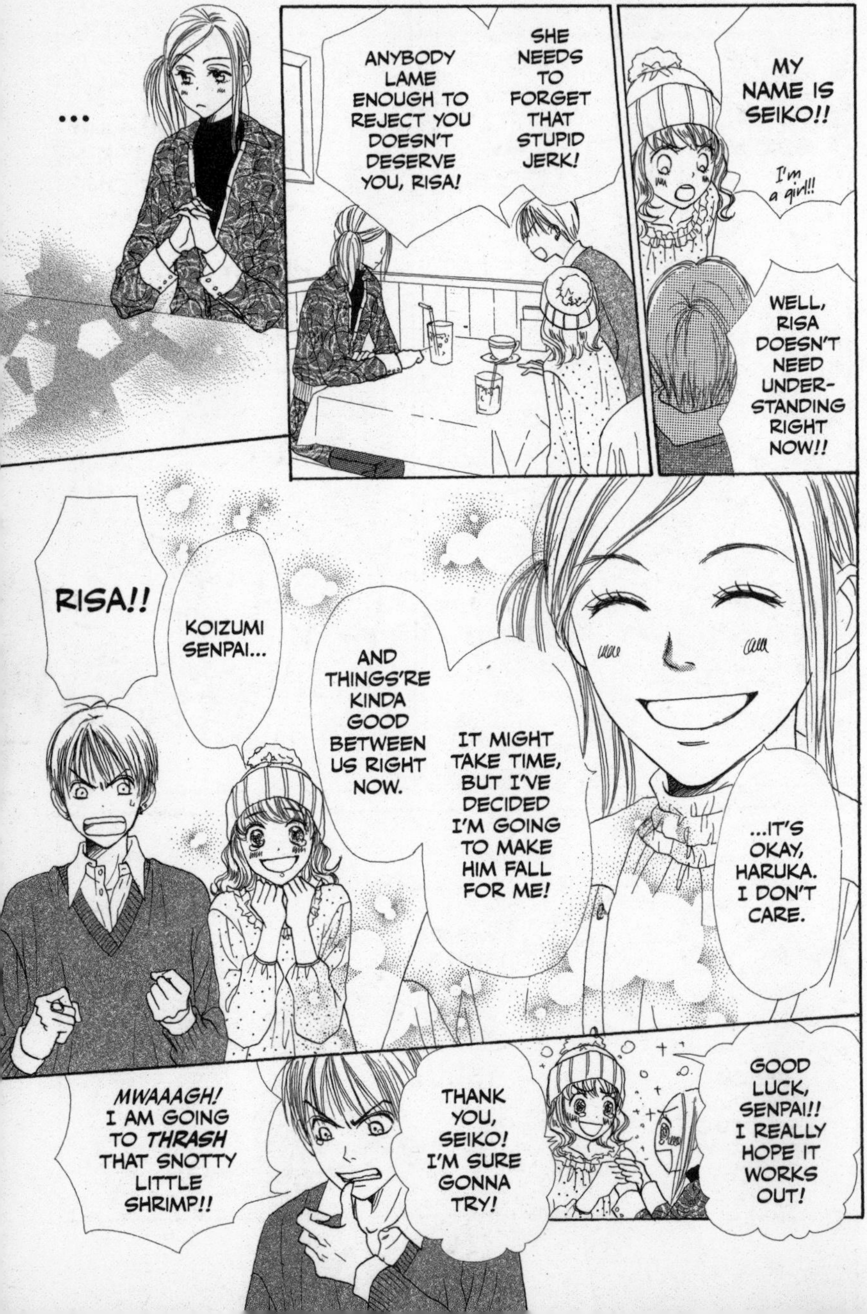
MY NAME IS SEIKO!!
I'm a girl!!
WELL, RISA DOESN'T NEED UNDER-STANDING RIGHT NOW!!
SHE NEEDS TO FORGET THAT STUPID JERK!
ANYBODY LAME ENOUGH TO REJECT YOU DOESN'T DESERVE YOU, RISA!
...
...IT'S OKAY, HARUKA. I DON'T CARE.
IT MIGHT TAKE TIME, BUT I'VE DECIDED I'M GOING TO MAKE HIM FALL FOR ME!
AND THINGS'RE KINDA GOOD BETWEEN US RIGHT NOW.
KOIZUMI SENPAI...
RISA!!
GOOD LUCK, SENPAI!! I REALLY HOPE IT WORKS OUT!
THANK YOU, SEIKO! I'M SURE GONNA TRY!
MWAAAGH! I AM GOING TO ***THRASH*** THAT SNOTTY LITTLE SHRIMP!!

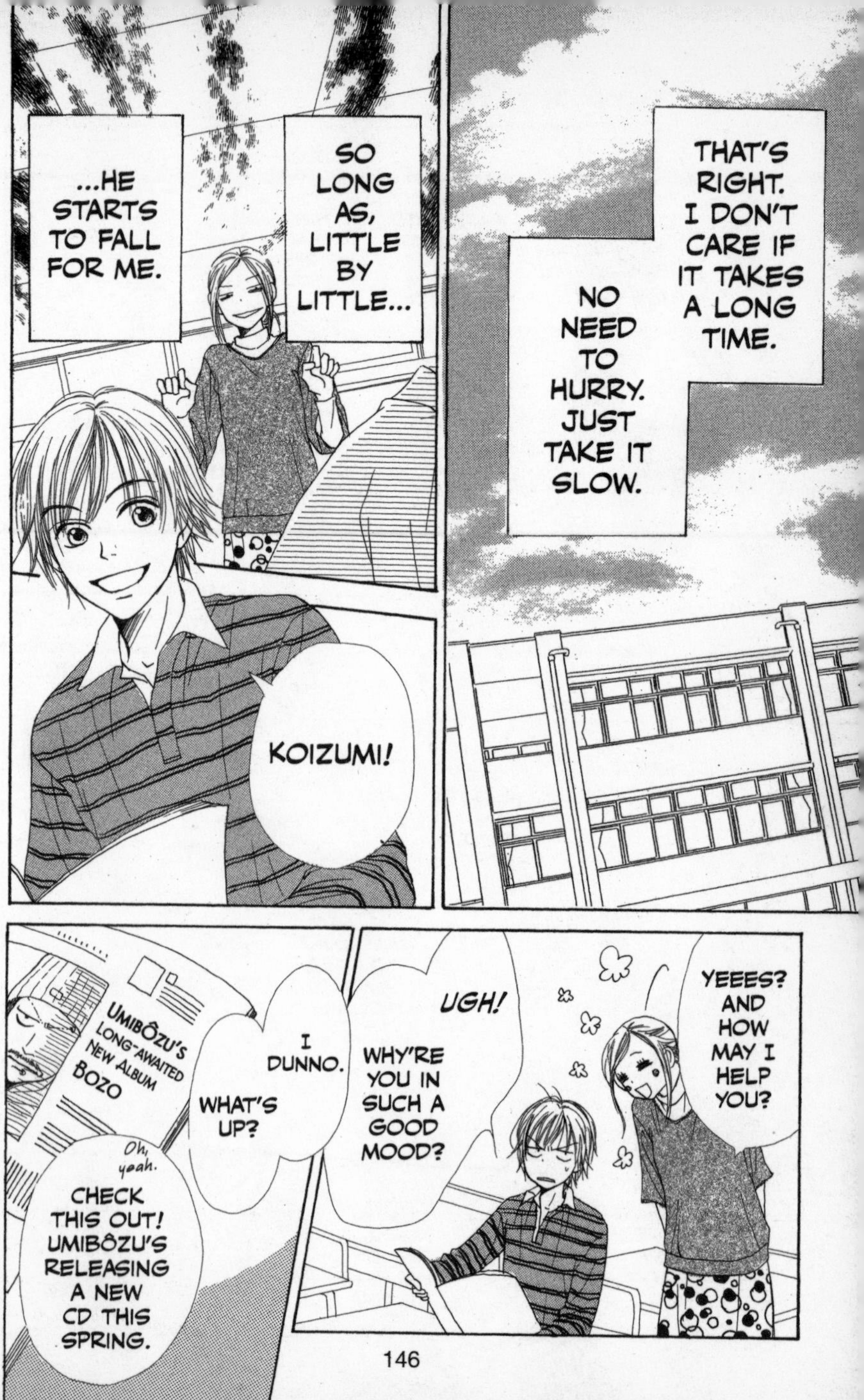
THAT'S RIGHT. I DON'T CARE IF IT TAKES A LONG TIME.
NO NEED TO HURRY. JUST TAKE IT SLOW.
SO LONG AS, LITTLE BY LITTLE...
...HE STARTS TO FALL FOR ME.
KOIZUMI!
YEEES? AND HOW MAY I HELP YOU?
UGH!
WHY'RE YOU IN SUCH A GOOD MOOD?
I DUNNO.
WHAT'S UP?
UMIBÔZU'S LONG-AWAITED NEW ALBUM BOZO
Oh, yeah.
CHECK THIS OUT! UMIBÔZU'S RELEASING A NEW CD THIS SPRING.

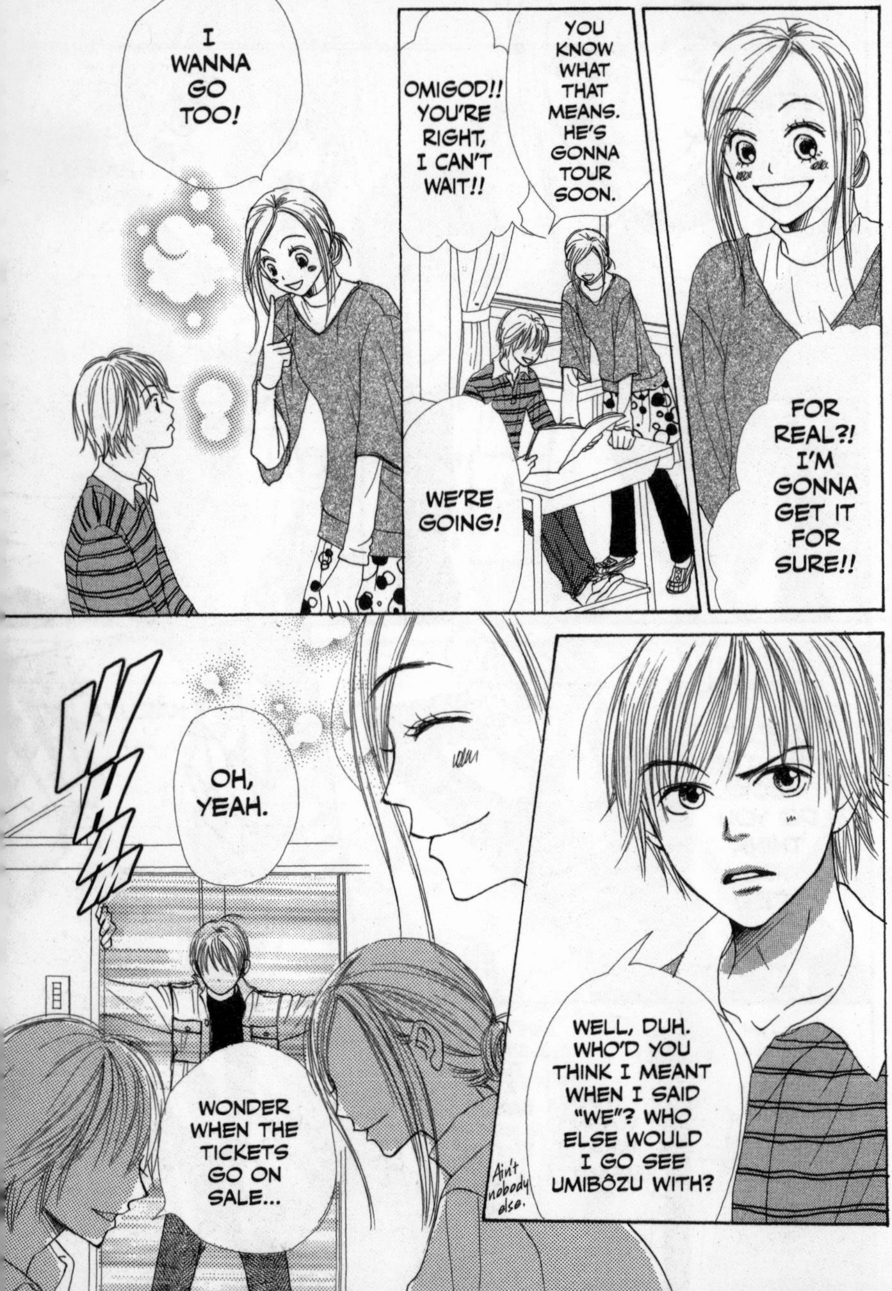
FOR REAL?! I'M GONNA GET IT FOR SURE!!
YOU KNOW WHAT THAT MEANS. HE'S GONNA TOUR SOON.
OMIGOD!! YOU'RE RIGHT, I CAN'T WAIT!!
WE'RE GOING!
I WANNA GO TOO!
WELL, DUH. WHO'D YOU THINK I MEANT WHEN I SAID "WE"? WHO ELSE WOULD I GO SEE UMIBÔZU WITH?
Ain't nobody else.
WHAM
OH, YEAH.
WONDER WHEN THE TICKETS GO ON SALE...

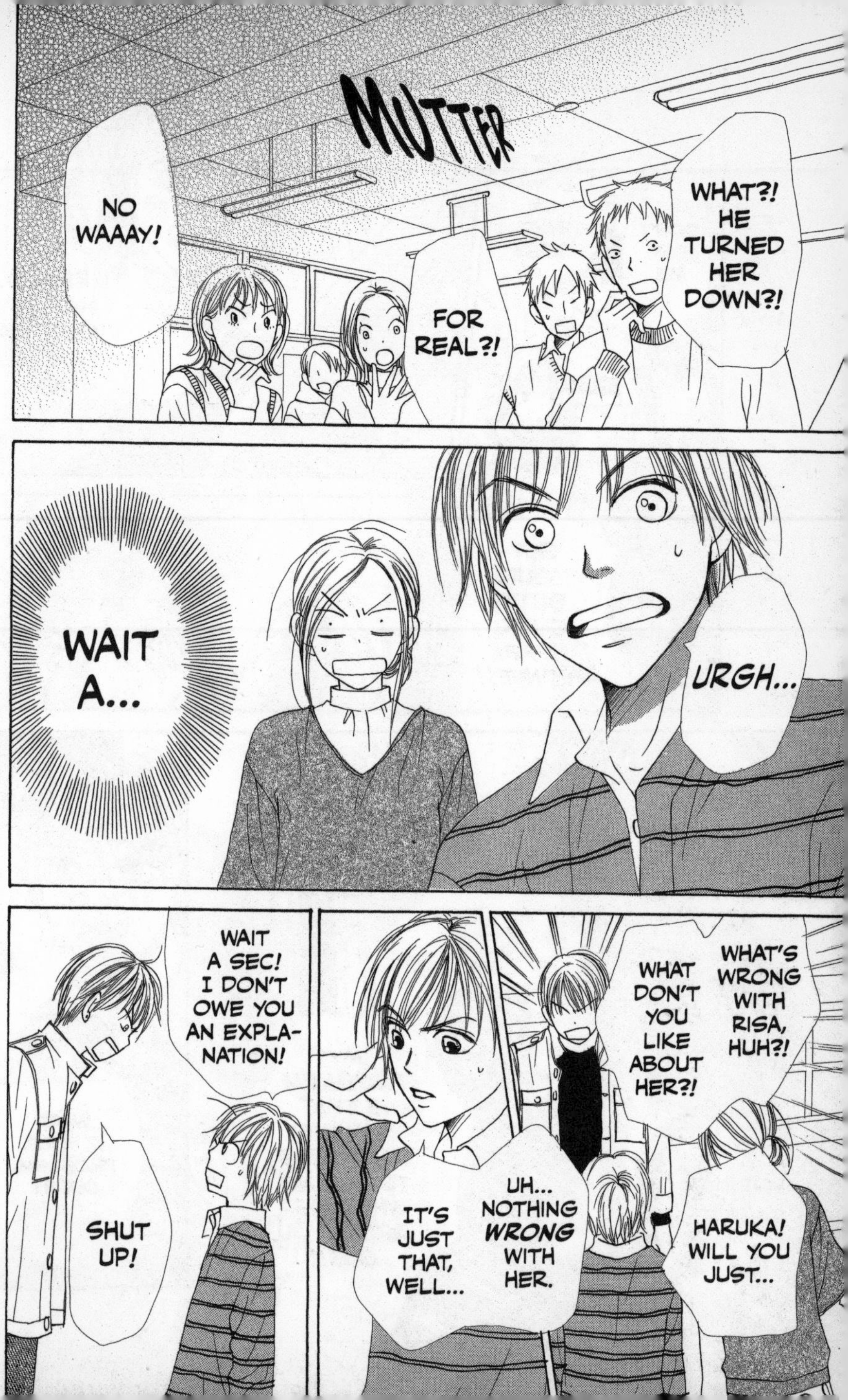
WHAT?! HE TURNED HER DOWN?!
MUTTER
FOR REAL?!
NO WAAAY!
URGH...
WAIT A...
WHAT'S WRONG WITH RISA, HUH?!
WHAT DON'T YOU LIKE ABOUT HER?!
HARUKA! WILL YOU JUST...
UH... NOTHING *WRONG* WITH HER.
IT'S JUST THAT, WELL...
WAIT A SEC! I DON'T OWE YOU AN EXPLA-NATION!
SHUT UP!

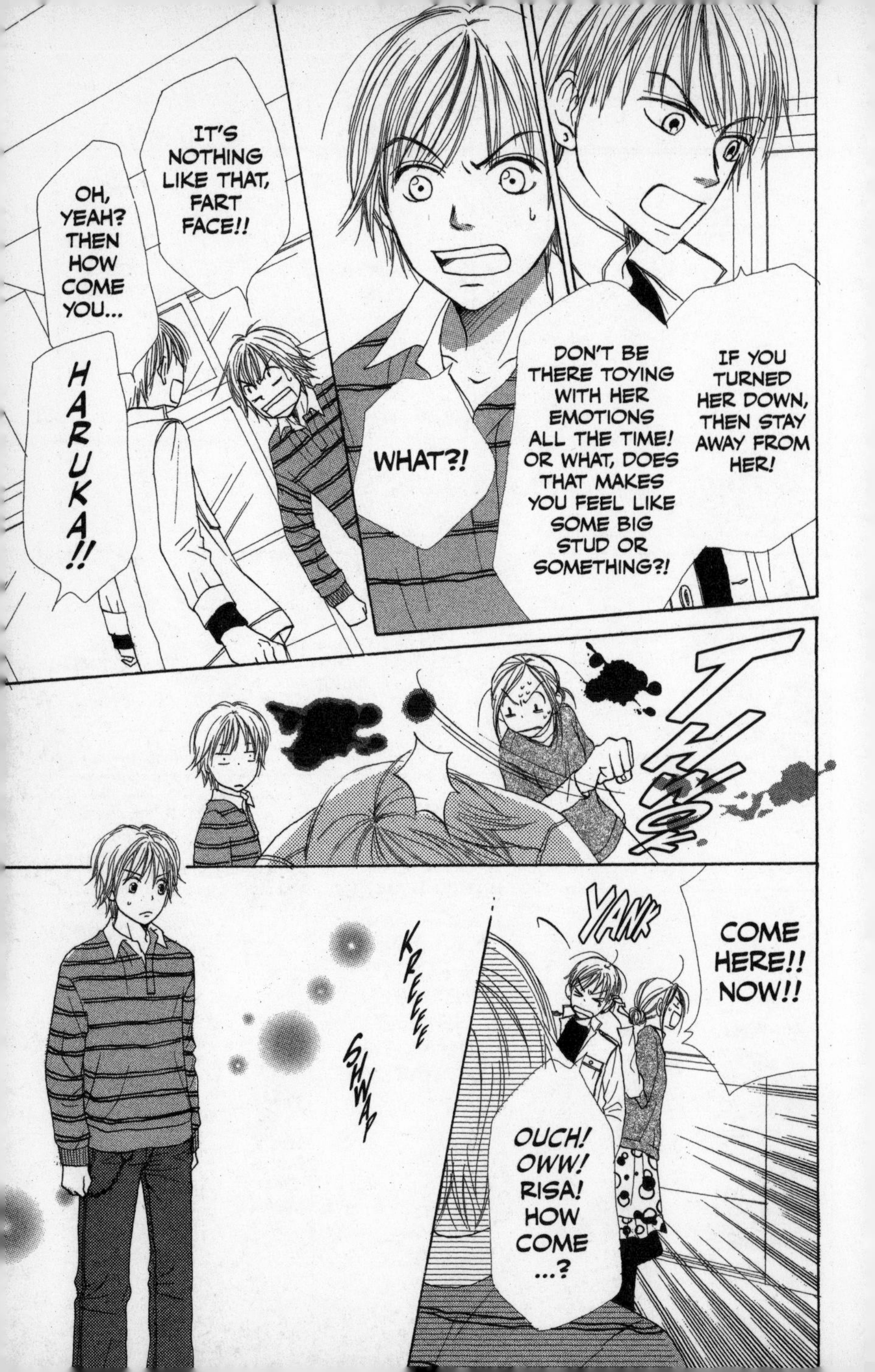
IF YOU TURNED HER DOWN, THEN STAY AWAY FROM HER!
DON'T BE THERE TOYING WITH HER EMOTIONS ALL THE TIME! OR WHAT, DOES THAT MAKES YOU FEEL LIKE SOME BIG STUD OR SOMETHING?!
WHAT?!
IT'S NOTHING LIKE THAT, FART FACE!!
OH, YEAH? THEN HOW COME YOU...
HARUKA!!
THWOK!
COME HERE!! NOW!!
YANK
OUCH! OWW! RISA! HOW COME ...?
SHWAM

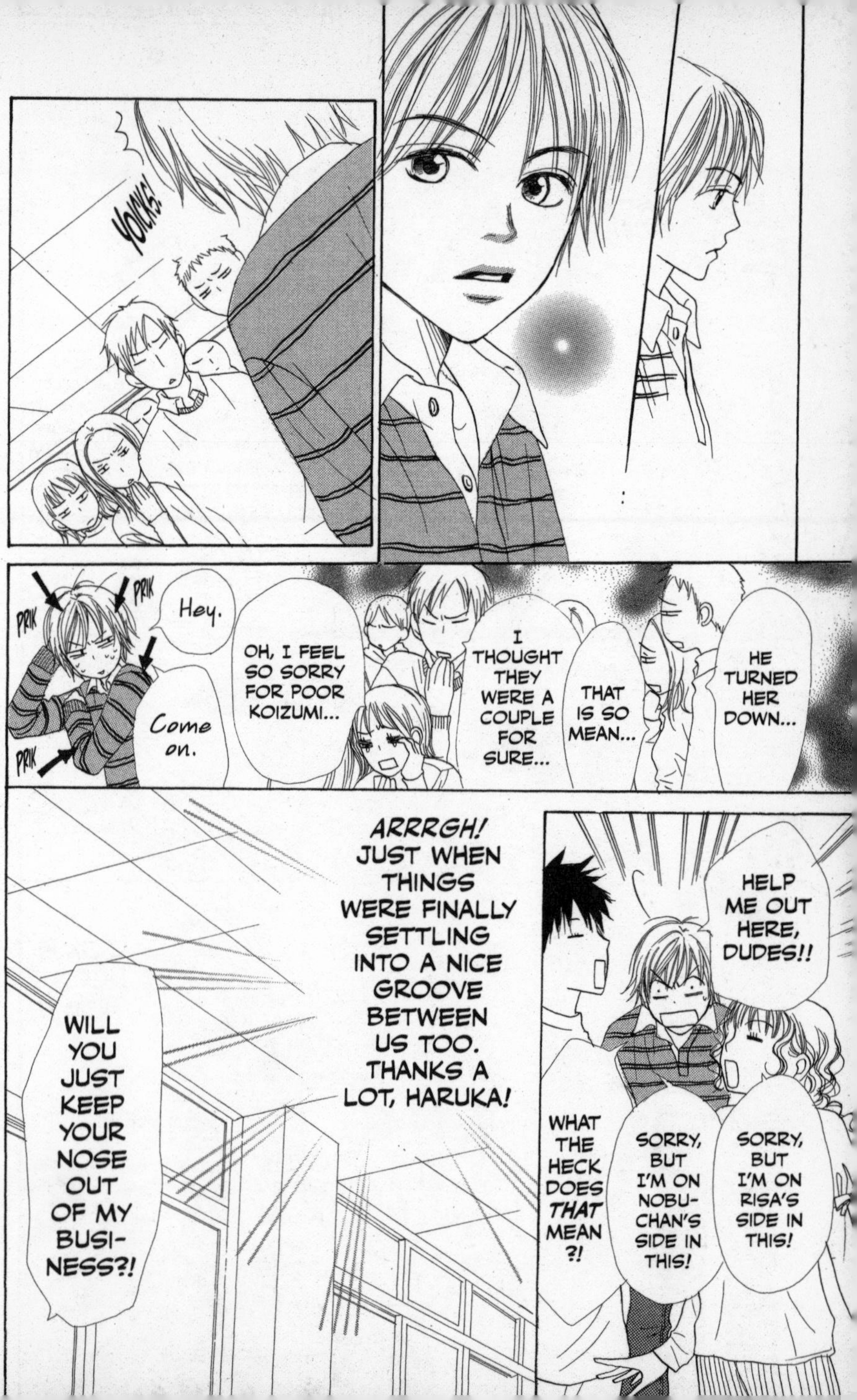
YOICKS!
HE TURNED HER DOWN...
THAT IS SO MEAN...
I THOUGHT THEY WERE A COUPLE FOR SURE...
OH, I FEEL SO SORRY FOR POOR KOIZUMI...
Hey.
Come on.
PRIK PRIK PRIK
HELP ME OUT HERE, DUDES!!
SORRY, BUT I'M ON RISA'S SIDE IN THIS!
SORRY, BUT I'M ON NOBU-CHAN'S SIDE IN THIS!
WHAT THE HECK DOES *THAT* MEAN?!
ARRRGH! JUST WHEN THINGS WERE FINALLY SETTLING INTO A NICE GROOVE BETWEEN US TOO. THANKS A LOT, HARUKA!
WILL YOU JUST KEEP YOUR NOSE OUT OF MY BUSI-NESS?!

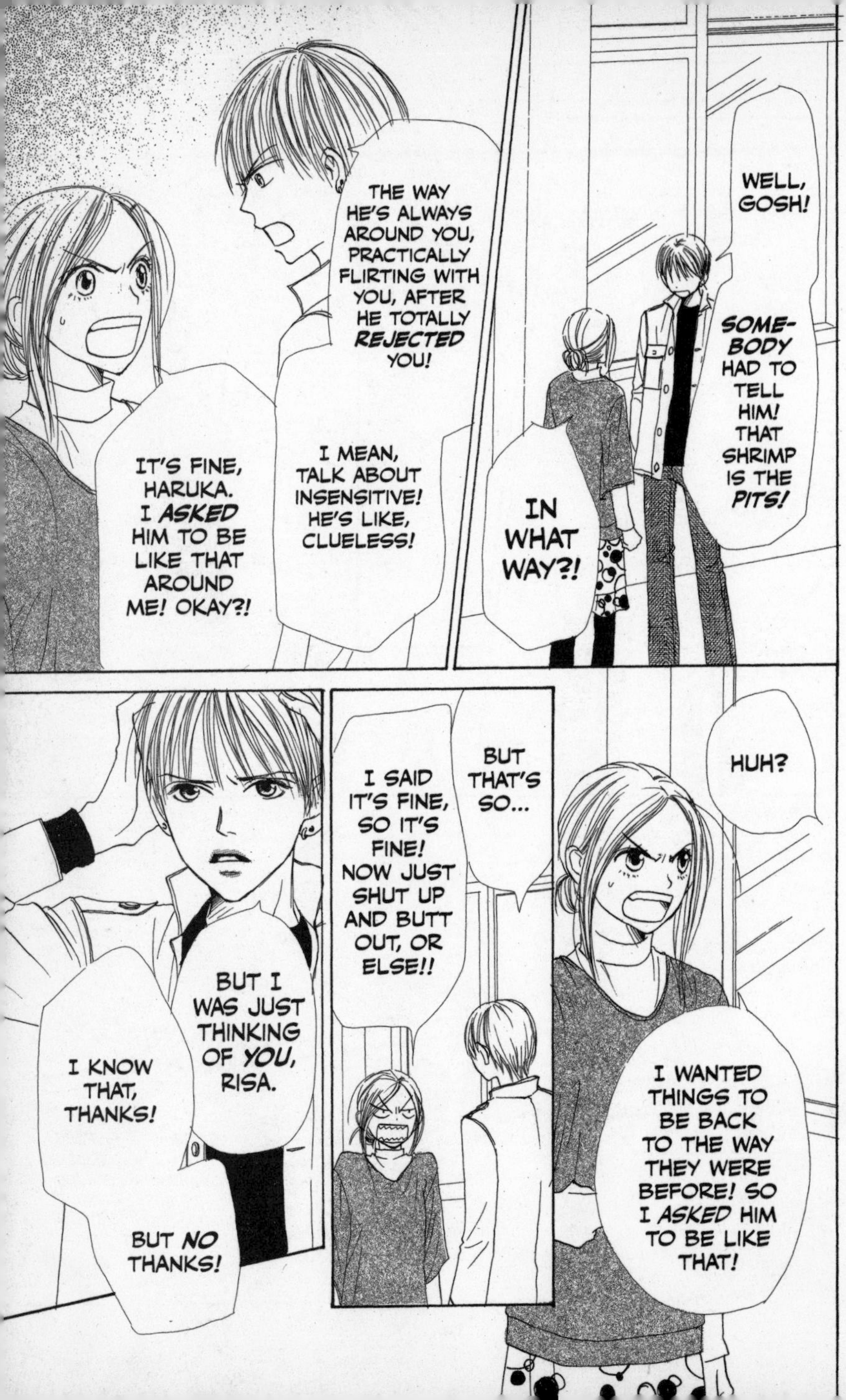

WELL, GOSH!
SOME-BODY HAD TO TELL HIM! THAT SHRIMP IS THE *PITS!*
IN WHAT WAY?!
THE WAY HE'S ALWAYS AROUND YOU, PRACTICALLY FLIRTING WITH YOU, AFTER HE TOTALLY *REJECTED* YOU!
I MEAN, TALK ABOUT INSENSITIVE! HE'S LIKE, CLUELESS!
IT'S FINE, HARUKA. I *ASKED* HIM TO BE LIKE THAT AROUND ME! OKAY?!
HUH?
I WANTED THINGS TO BE BACK TO THE WAY THEY WERE BEFORE! SO I *ASKED* HIM TO BE LIKE THAT!
BUT THAT'S SO...
I SAID IT'S FINE, SO IT'S FINE! NOW JUST SHUT UP AND BUTT OUT, OR ELSE!!
BUT I WAS JUST THINKING OF *YOU*, RISA.
I KNOW THAT, THANKS!
BUT *NO* THANKS!

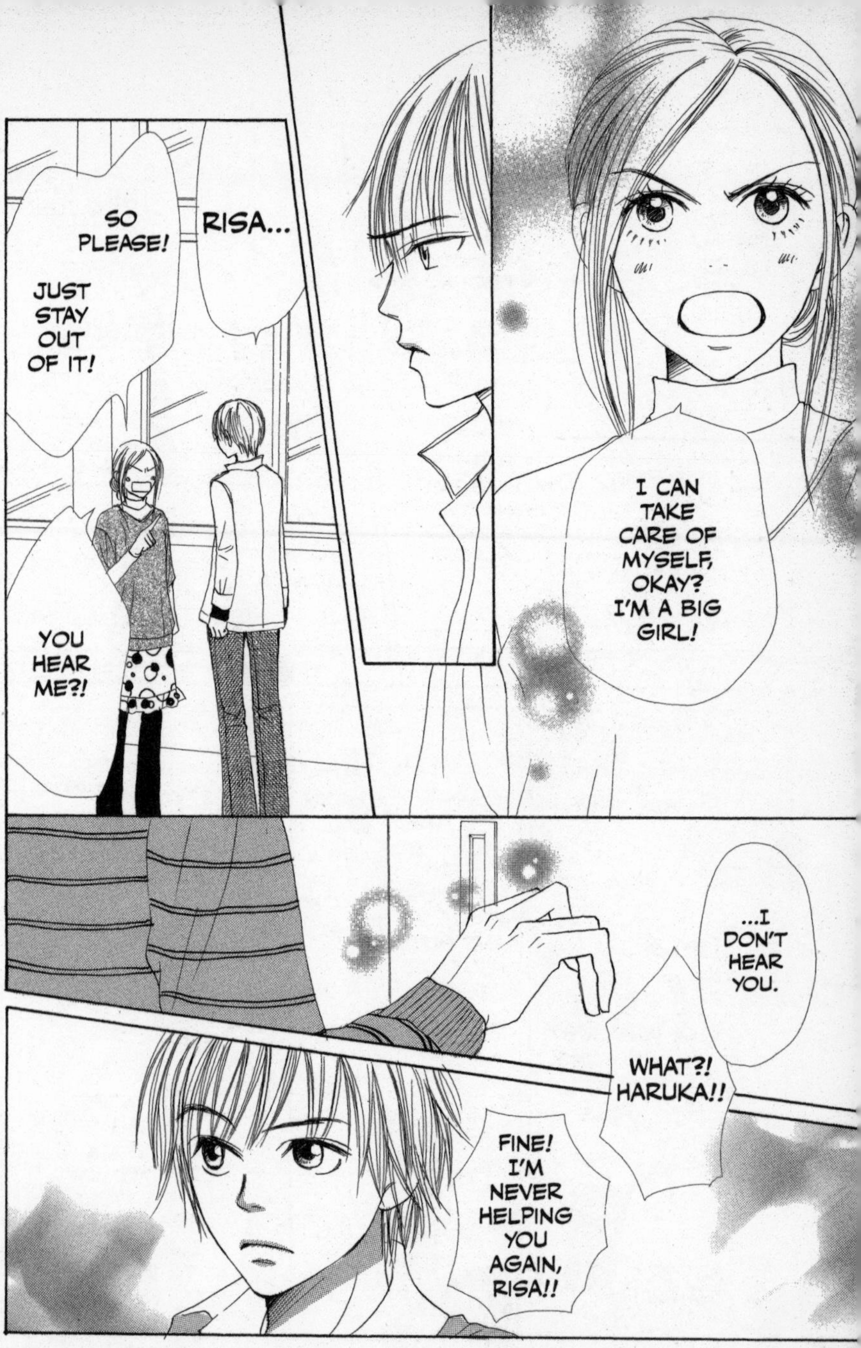
I CAN TAKE CARE OF MYSELF, OKAY? I'M A BIG GIRL!
RISA...
SO PLEASE!
JUST STAY OUT OF IT!
YOU HEAR ME?!
...I DON'T HEAR YOU.
WHAT?! HARUKA!!
FINE! I'M NEVER HELPING YOU AGAIN, RISA!!

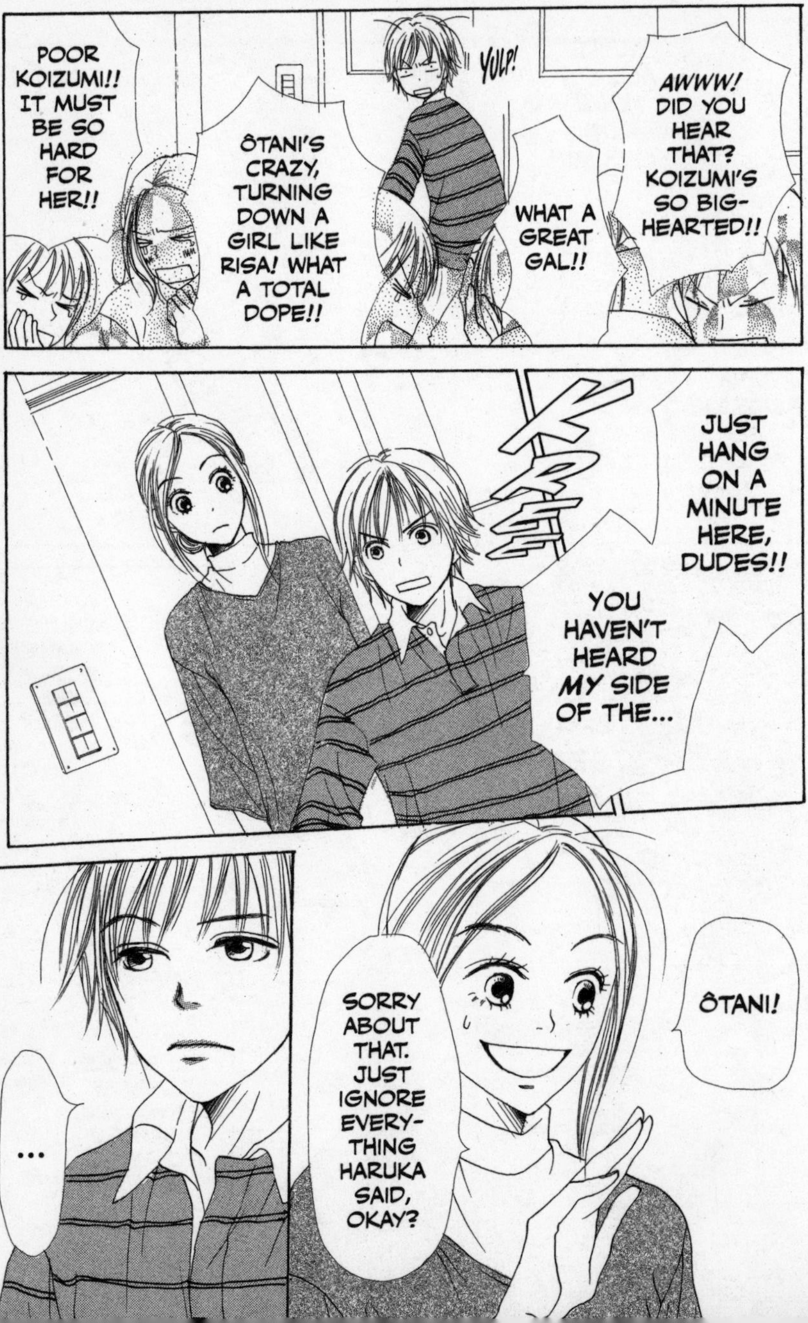
AWWW! DID YOU HEAR THAT? KOIZUMI'S SO BIG-HEARTED!!
YULP!
WHAT A GREAT GAL!!
ÔTANI'S CRAZY, TURNING DOWN A GIRL LIKE RISA! WHAT A TOTAL DOPE!!
POOR KOIZUMI!! IT MUST BE SO HARD FOR HER!!
JUST HANG ON A MINUTE HERE, DUDES!!
YOU HAVEN'T HEARD *MY* SIDE OF THE...
ÔTANI!
SORRY ABOUT THAT. JUST IGNORE EVERY-THING HARUKA SAID, OKAY?
...

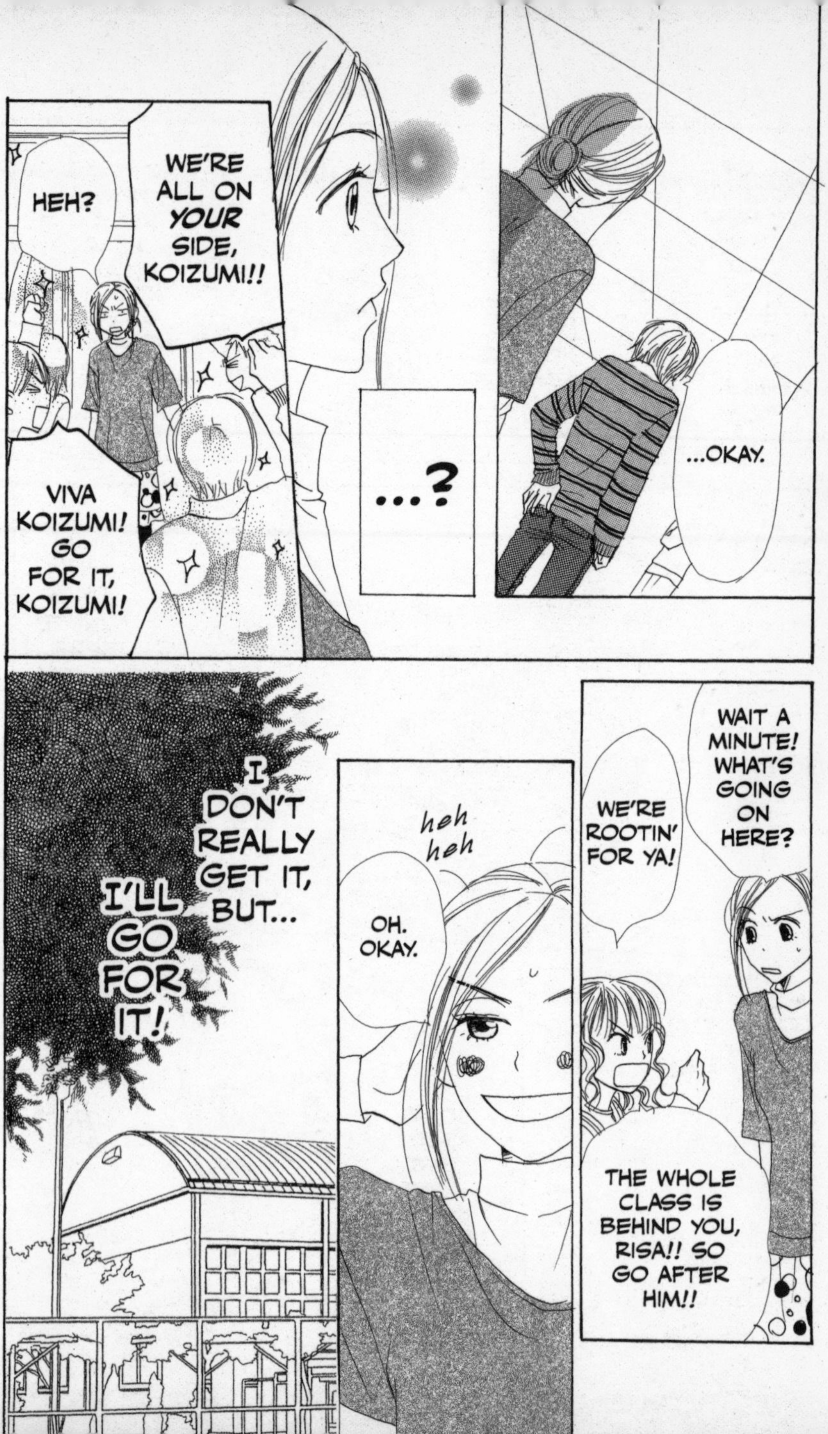
...OKAY.
...?
WE'RE ALL ON *YOUR* SIDE, KOIZUMI!!
HEH?
VIVA KOIZUMI! GO FOR IT, KOIZUMI!
WAIT A MINUTE! WHAT'S GOING ON HERE?
WE'RE ROOTIN' FOR YA!
THE WHOLE CLASS IS BEHIND YOU, RISA!! SO GO AFTER HIM!!
heh heh
OH. OKAY.
I DON'T REALLY GET IT, BUT...
I'LL GO FOR IT!

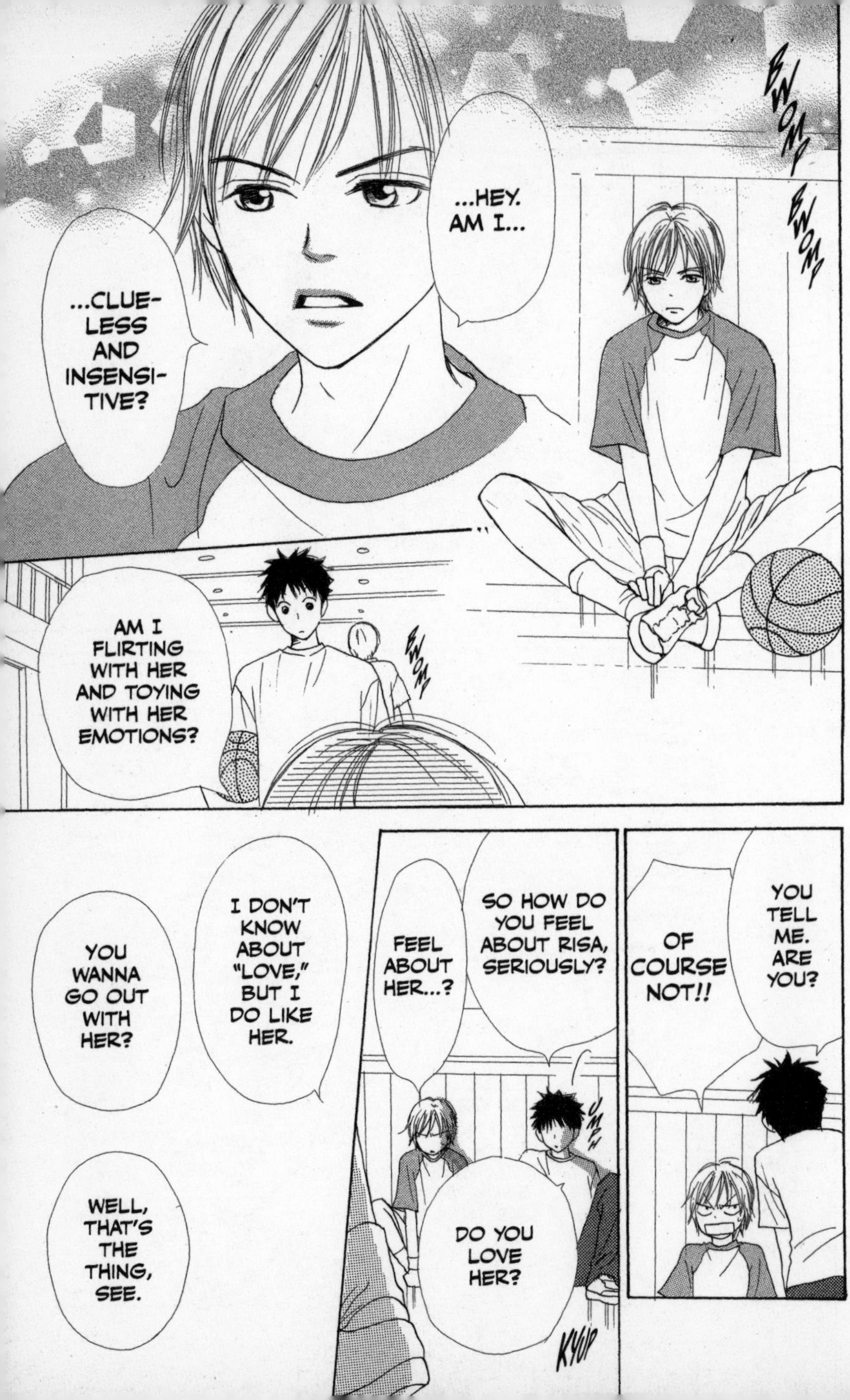
BWOM
BWOM
...HEY. AM I...
...CLUE-LESS AND INSENSI-TIVE?
BWOM
AM I FLIRTING WITH HER AND TOYING WITH HER EMOTIONS?
YOU TELL ME. ARE YOU?
OF COURSE NOT!!
SO HOW DO YOU FEEL ABOUT RISA, SERIOUSLY?
FEEL ABOUT HER...?
UMPH
DO YOU LOVE HER?
KYUP
I DON'T KNOW ABOUT "LOVE," BUT I DO LIKE HER.
YOU WANNA GO OUT WITH HER?
WELL, THAT'S THE THING, SEE.

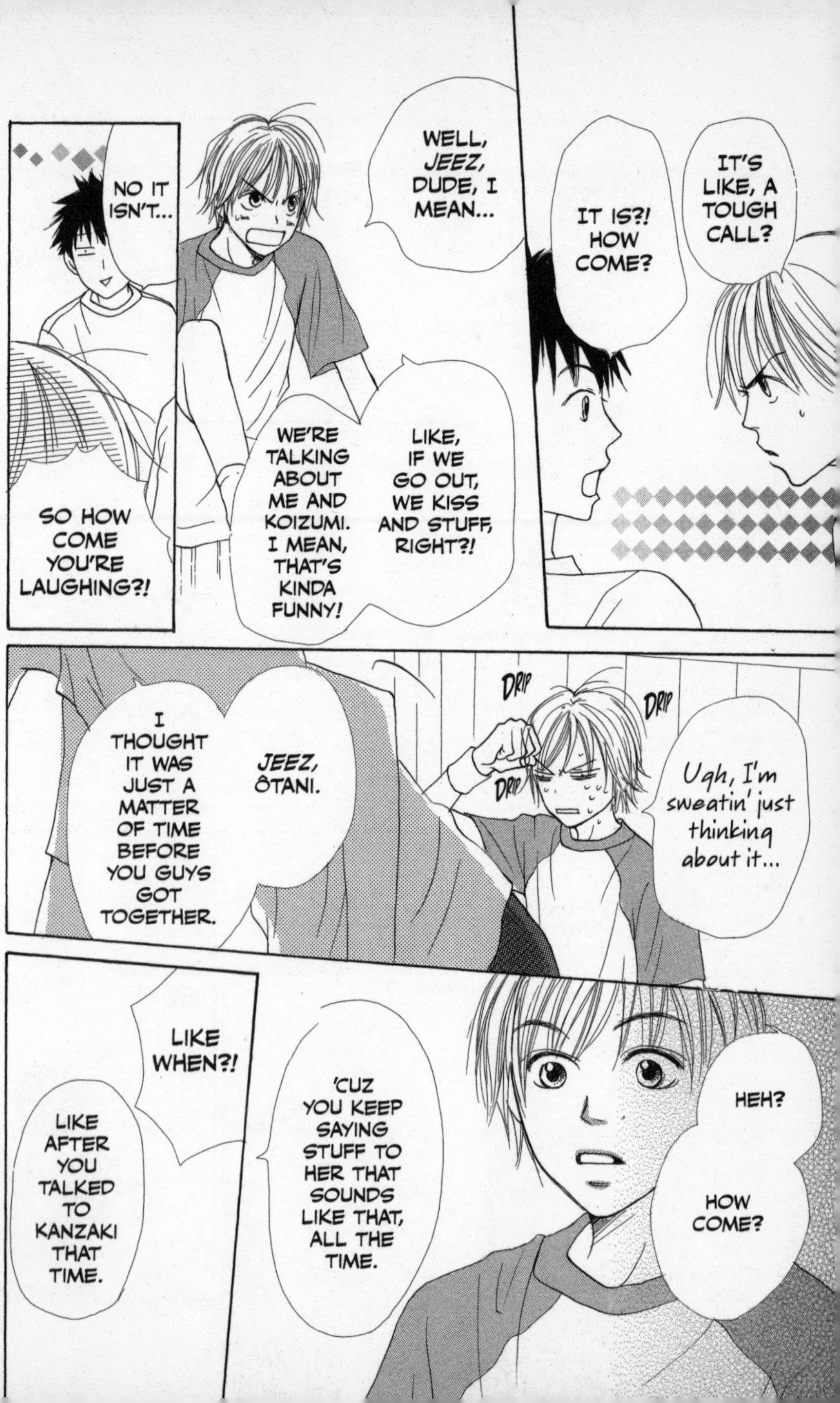
IT'S LIKE, A TOUGH CALL?
IT IS?! HOW COME?
WELL, JEEZ, DUDE, I MEAN...
LIKE, IF WE GO OUT, WE KISS AND STUFF, RIGHT?!
WE'RE TALKING ABOUT ME AND KOIZUMI. I MEAN, THAT'S KINDA FUNNY!
NO IT ISN'T...
SO HOW COME YOU'RE LAUGHING?!
DRIP
DRIP
DRIP
Ugh, I'm sweatin' just thinking about it...
JEEZ, ÔTANI.
I THOUGHT IT WAS JUST A MATTER OF TIME BEFORE YOU GUYS GOT TOGETHER.
HEH?
HOW COME?
'CUZ YOU KEEP SAYING STUFF TO HER THAT SOUNDS LIKE THAT, ALL THE TIME.
LIKE WHEN?!
LIKE AFTER YOU TALKED TO KANZAKI THAT TIME.

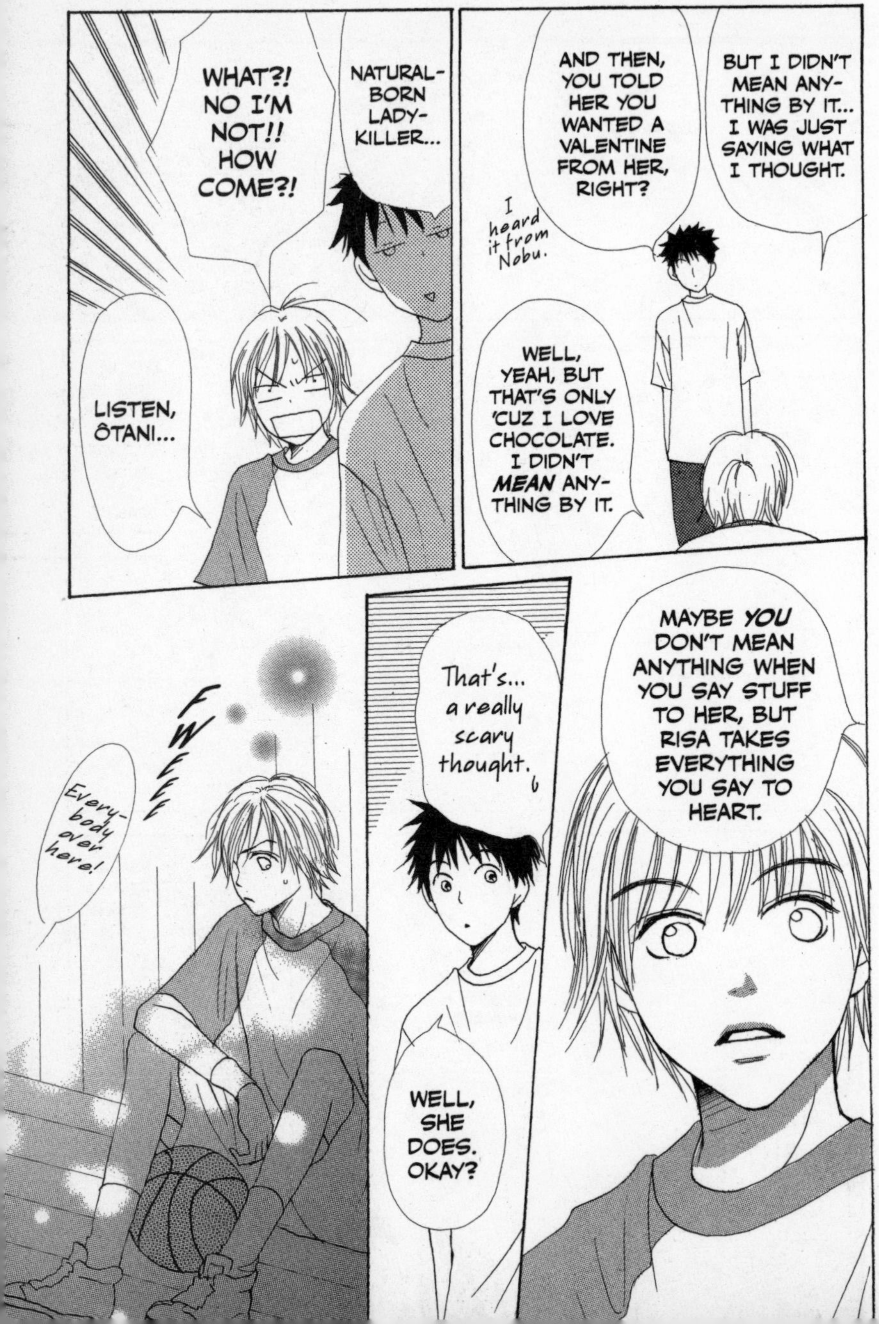
AND THEN, YOU TOLD HER YOU WANTED A VALENTINE FROM HER, RIGHT?
I heard it from Nobu.
WELL, YEAH, BUT THAT'S ONLY 'CUZ I LOVE CHOCOLATE. I DIDN'T *MEAN* ANYTHING BY IT.
BUT I DIDN'T MEAN ANYTHING BY IT... I WAS JUST SAYING WHAT I THOUGHT.
NATURAL-BORN LADY-KILLER...
WHAT?! NO I'M NOT!! HOW COME?!
LISTEN, ÔTANI...
MAYBE *YOU* DON'T MEAN ANYTHING WHEN YOU SAY STUFF TO HER, BUT RISA TAKES EVERYTHING YOU SAY TO HEART.
That's... a really scary thought.
WELL, SHE DOES. OKAY?
FWEEEE
Everybody over here!

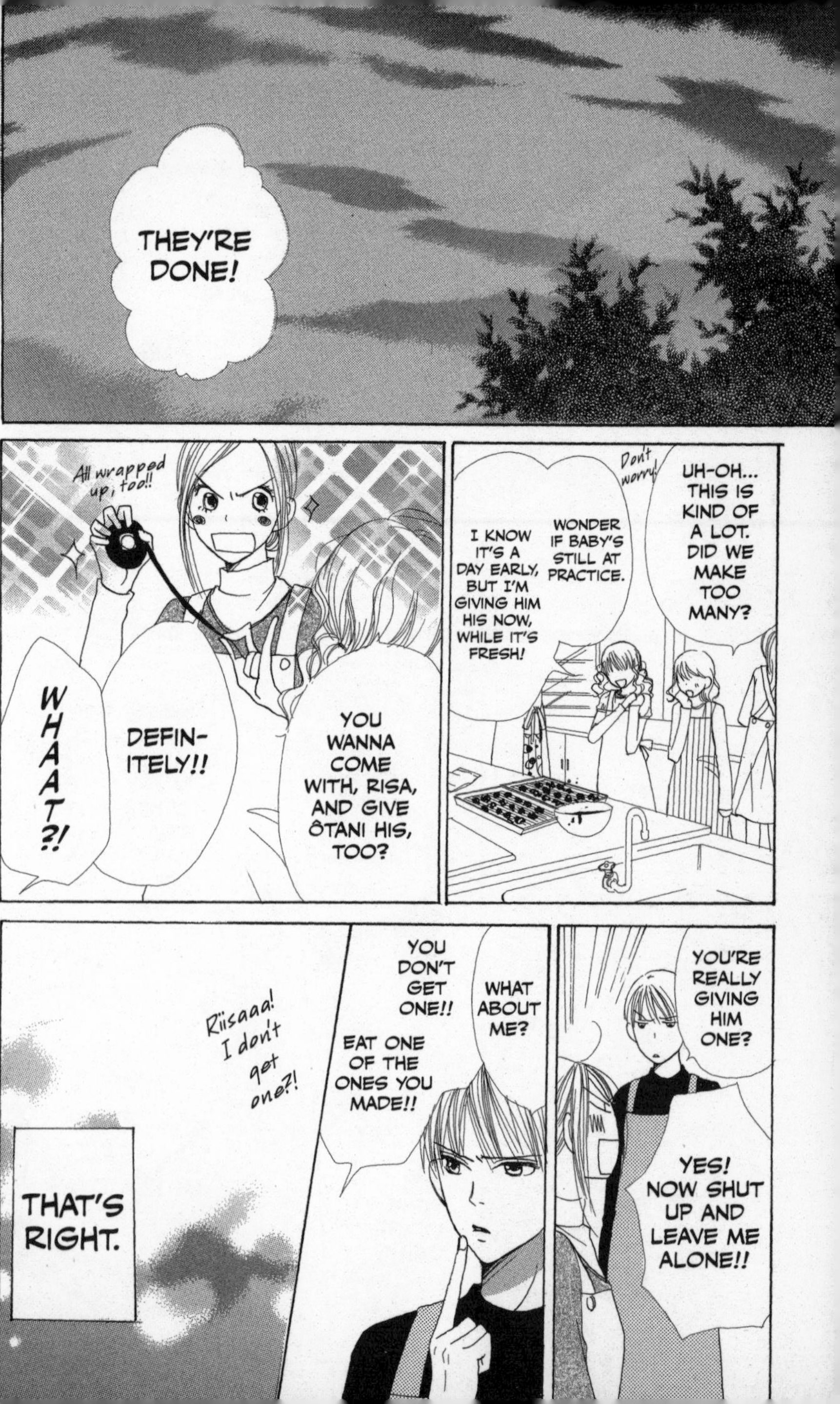
THEY'RE DONE!
UH-OH... THIS IS KIND OF A LOT. DID WE MAKE TOO MANY?
Don't worry!
WONDER IF BABY'S STILL AT PRACTICE.
I KNOW IT'S A DAY EARLY, BUT I'M GIVING HIM HIS NOW, WHILE IT'S FRESH!
All wrapped up, too!!
YOU WANNA COME WITH, RISA, AND GIVE ÔTANI HIS, TOO?
DEFIN-ITELY!!
WHAAAT?!
YOU'RE REALLY GIVING HIM ONE?
YES! NOW SHUT UP AND LEAVE ME ALONE!!
WHAT ABOUT ME?
YOU DON'T GET ONE!!
EAT ONE OF THE ONES YOU MADE!!
Riisaaa! I don't get one?!
THAT'S RIGHT.

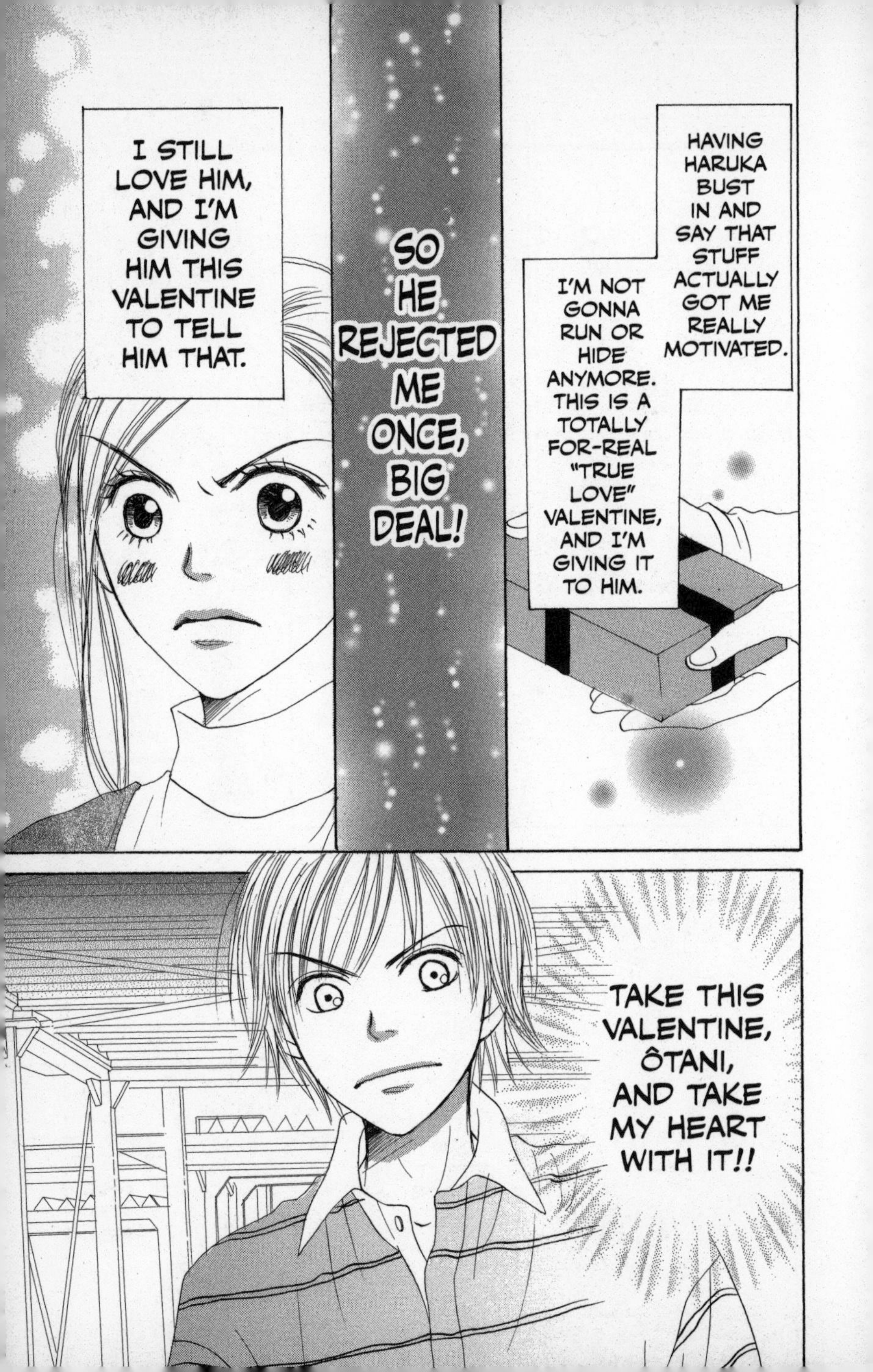
HAVING HARUKA BUST IN AND SAY THAT STUFF ACTUALLY GOT ME REALLY MOTIVATED.
I'M NOT GONNA RUN OR HIDE ANYMORE. THIS IS A TOTALLY FOR-REAL "TRUE LOVE" VALENTINE, AND I'M GIVING IT TO HIM.
SO HE REJECTED ME ONCE, BIG DEAL!
I STILL LOVE HIM, AND I'M GIVING HIM THIS VALENTINE TO TELL HIM THAT.
TAKE THIS VALENTINE, ÔTANI, AND TAKE MY HEART WITH IT!!

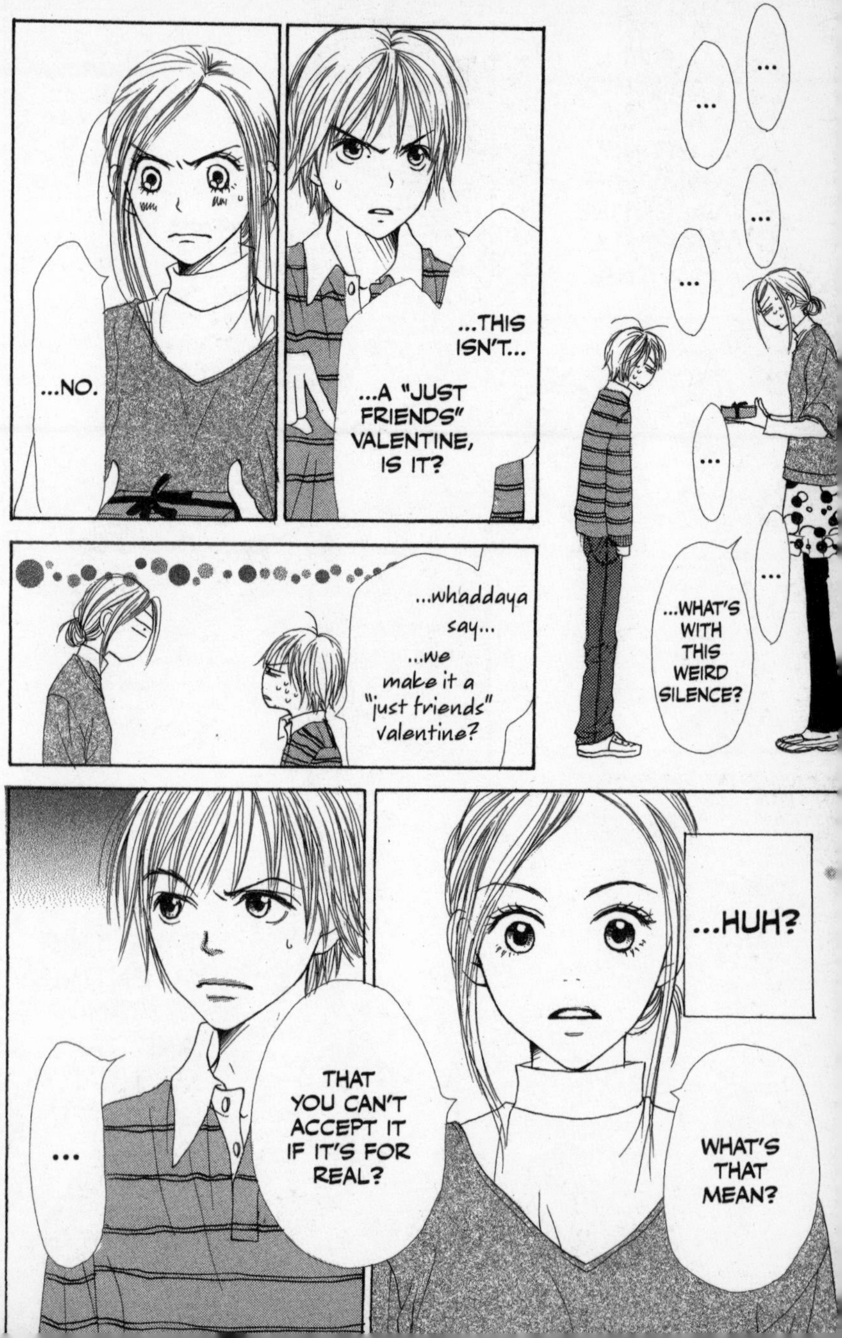
...
...
...
...
...
...
...WHAT'S WITH THIS WEIRD SILENCE?
...THIS ISN'T...
...A "JUST FRIENDS" VALENTINE, IS IT?
...NO.
...whaddaya say...
...we make it a "just friends" valentine?
...HUH?
WHAT'S THAT MEAN?
THAT YOU CAN'T ACCEPT IT IF IT'S FOR REAL?
...

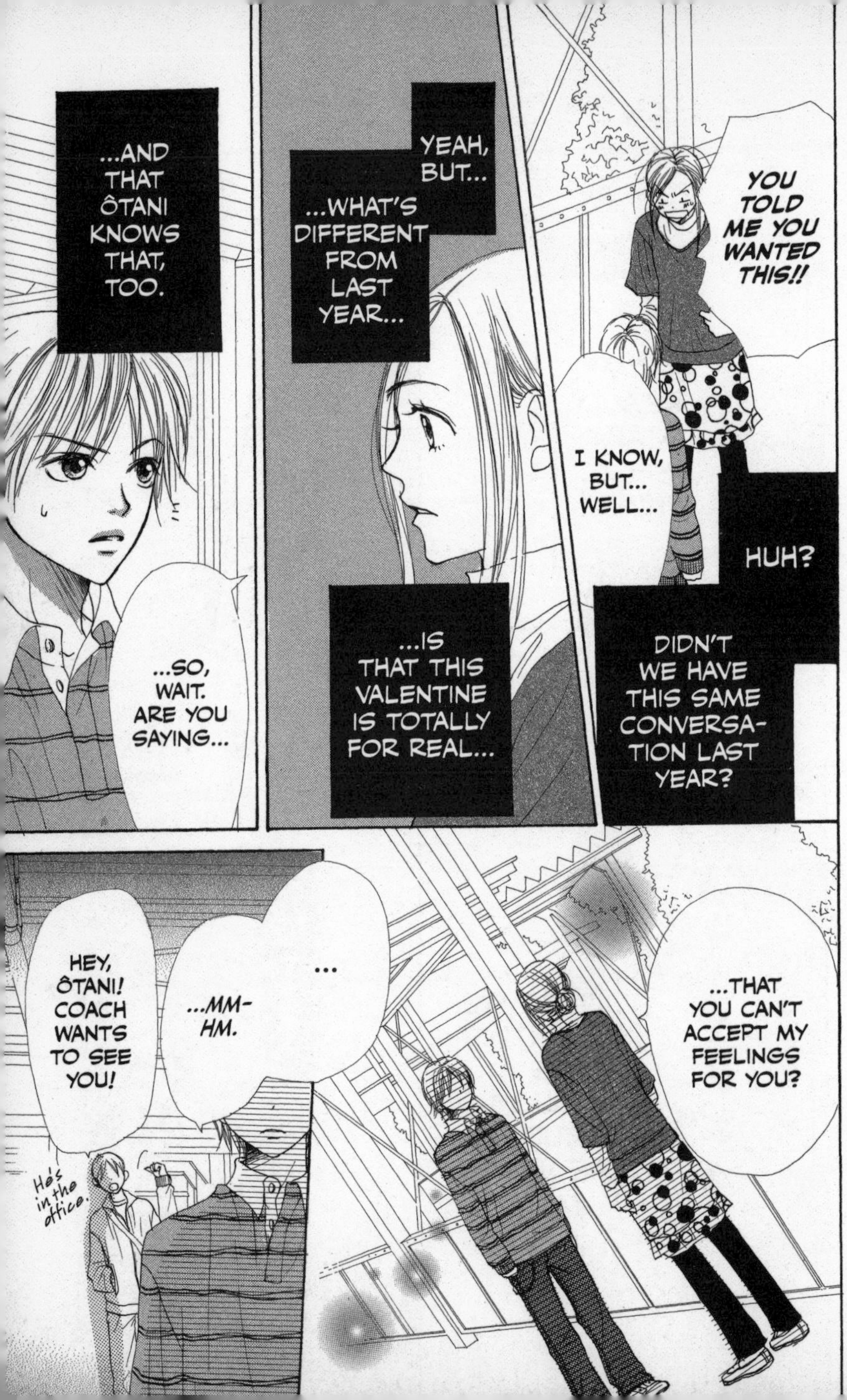
YOU TOLD ME YOU WANTED THIS!!
I KNOW, BUT... WELL...
HUH?
DIDN'T WE HAVE THIS SAME CONVERSA-TION LAST YEAR?
YEAH, BUT...
...WHAT'S DIFFERENT FROM LAST YEAR...
...IS THAT THIS VALENTINE IS TOTALLY FOR REAL...
...AND THAT ÔTANI KNOWS THAT, TOO.
...SO, WAIT. ARE YOU SAYING...
...THAT YOU CAN'T ACCEPT MY FEELINGS FOR YOU?
...
...MM-HM.
HEY, ÔTANI! COACH WANTS TO SEE YOU!
He's in the office.

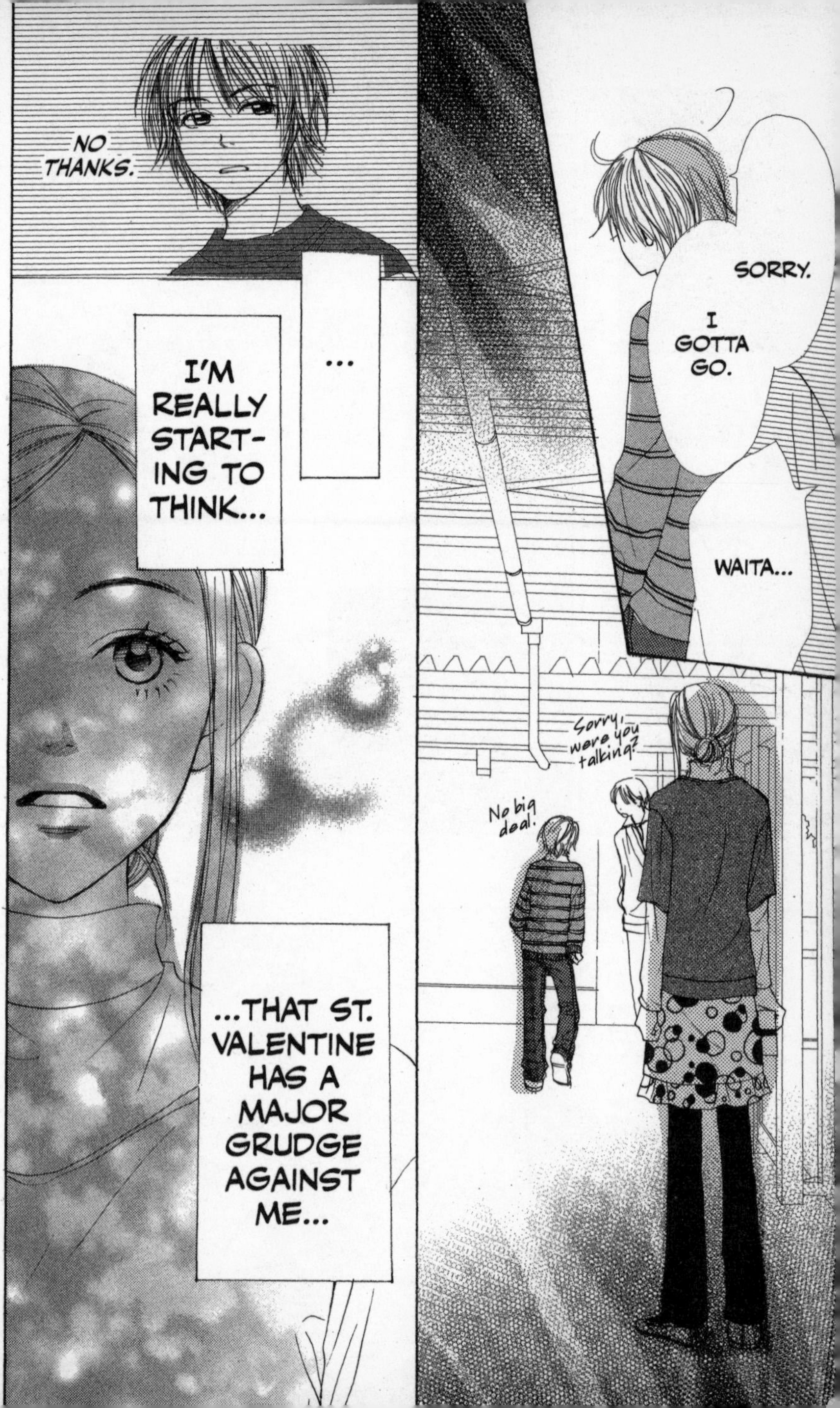
SORRY.
I GOTTA GO.
WAITA...
Sorry, were you talking?
No big deal.
NO THANKS.
...
I'M REALLY START-ING TO THINK...
...THAT ST. VALENTINE HAS A MAJOR GRUDGE AGAINST ME...

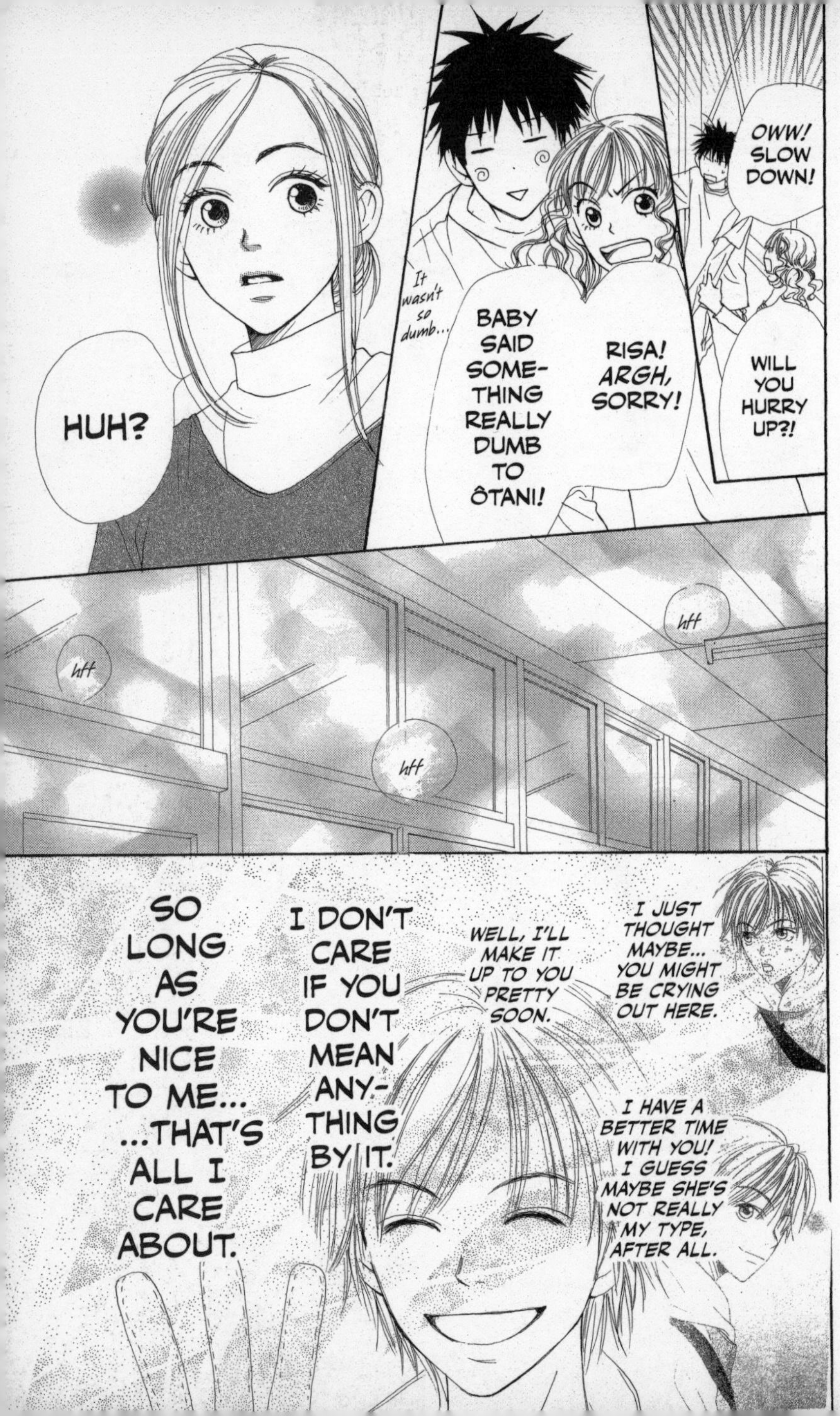
OWW! SLOW DOWN!
WILL YOU HURRY UP?!
RISA! ARGH, SORRY!
BABY SAID SOMETHING REALLY DUMB TO ÔTANI!
It wasn't so dumb...
HUH?
hff
hff
hff
I JUST THOUGHT MAYBE... YOU MIGHT BE CRYING OUT HERE.
I HAVE A BETTER TIME WITH YOU! I GUESS MAYBE SHE'S NOT REALLY MY TYPE, AFTER ALL.
WELL, I'LL MAKE IT UP TO YOU PRETTY SOON.
I DON'T CARE IF YOU DON'T MEAN ANYTHING BY IT.
SO LONG AS YOU'RE NICE TO ME... ...THAT'S ALL I CARE ABOUT.

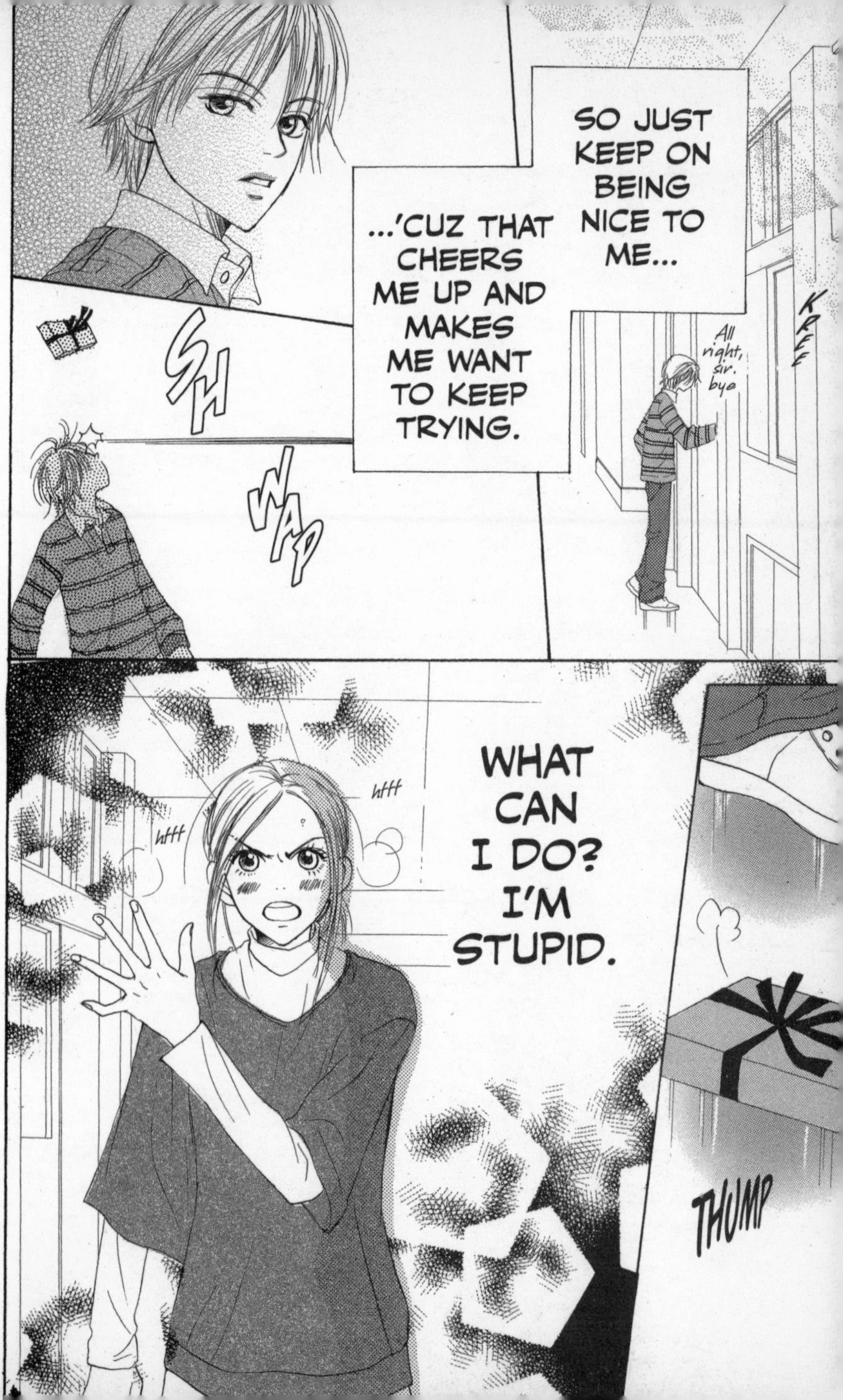
SO JUST KEEP ON BEING NICE TO ME...
...'CUZ THAT CHEERS ME UP AND MAKES ME WANT TO KEEP TRYING.
KREE
All right, sir. bye
SH
WAP
THUMP
WHAT CAN I DO? I'M STUPID.
hfff
hfff

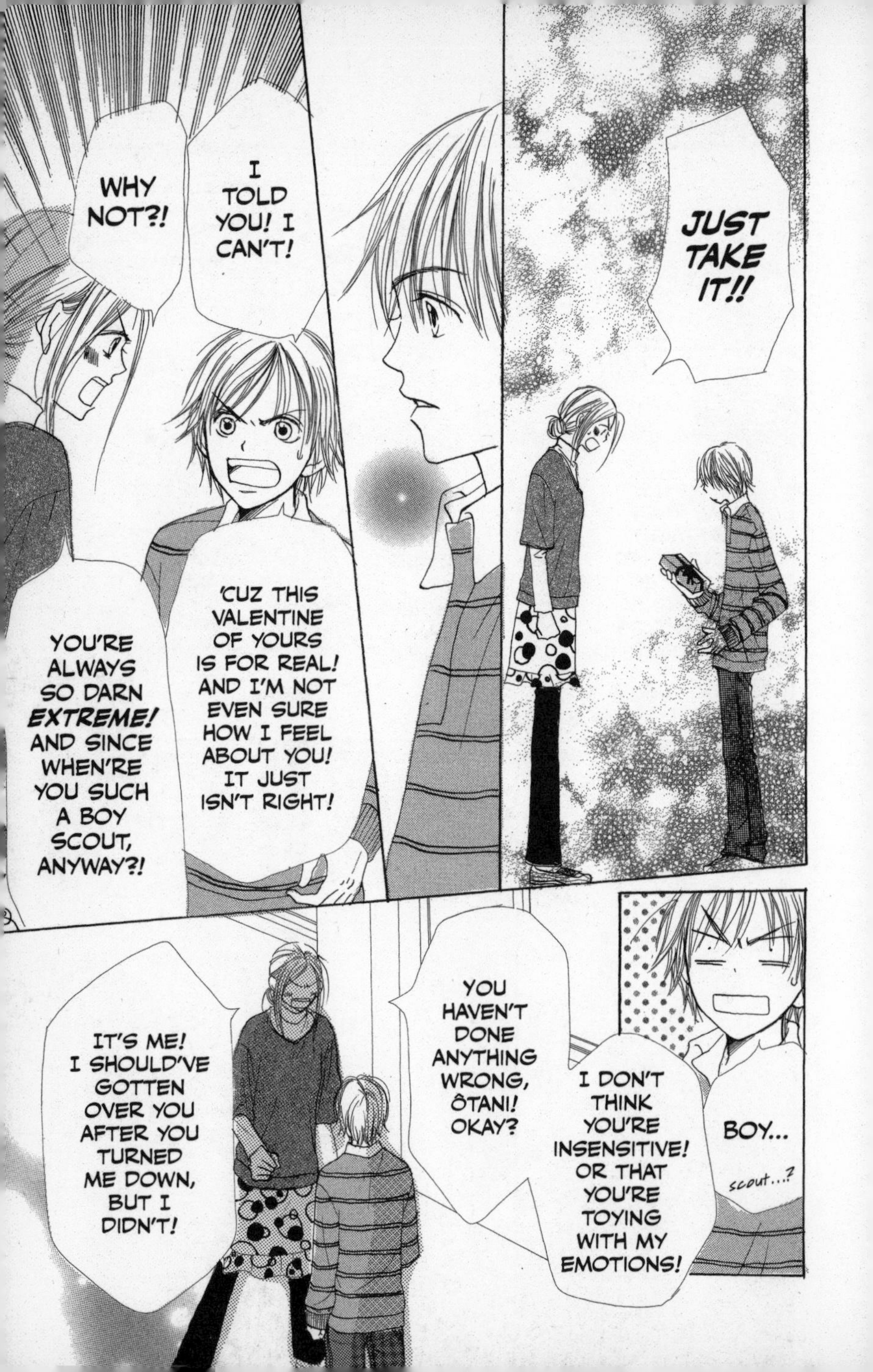
JUST TAKE IT!!
WHY NOT?!
I TOLD YOU! I CAN'T!
'CUZ THIS VALENTINE OF YOURS IS FOR REAL! AND I'M NOT EVEN SURE HOW I FEEL ABOUT YOU! IT JUST ISN'T RIGHT!
YOU'RE ALWAYS SO DARN *EXTREME!* AND SINCE WHEN'RE YOU SUCH A BOY SCOUT, ANYWAY?!
BOY...
scout...?
I DON'T THINK YOU'RE INSENSITIVE! OR THAT YOU'RE TOYING WITH MY EMOTIONS!
YOU HAVEN'T DONE ANYTHING WRONG, ÔTANI! OKAY?
IT'S ME! I SHOULD'VE GOTTEN OVER YOU AFTER YOU TURNED ME DOWN, BUT I DIDN'T!

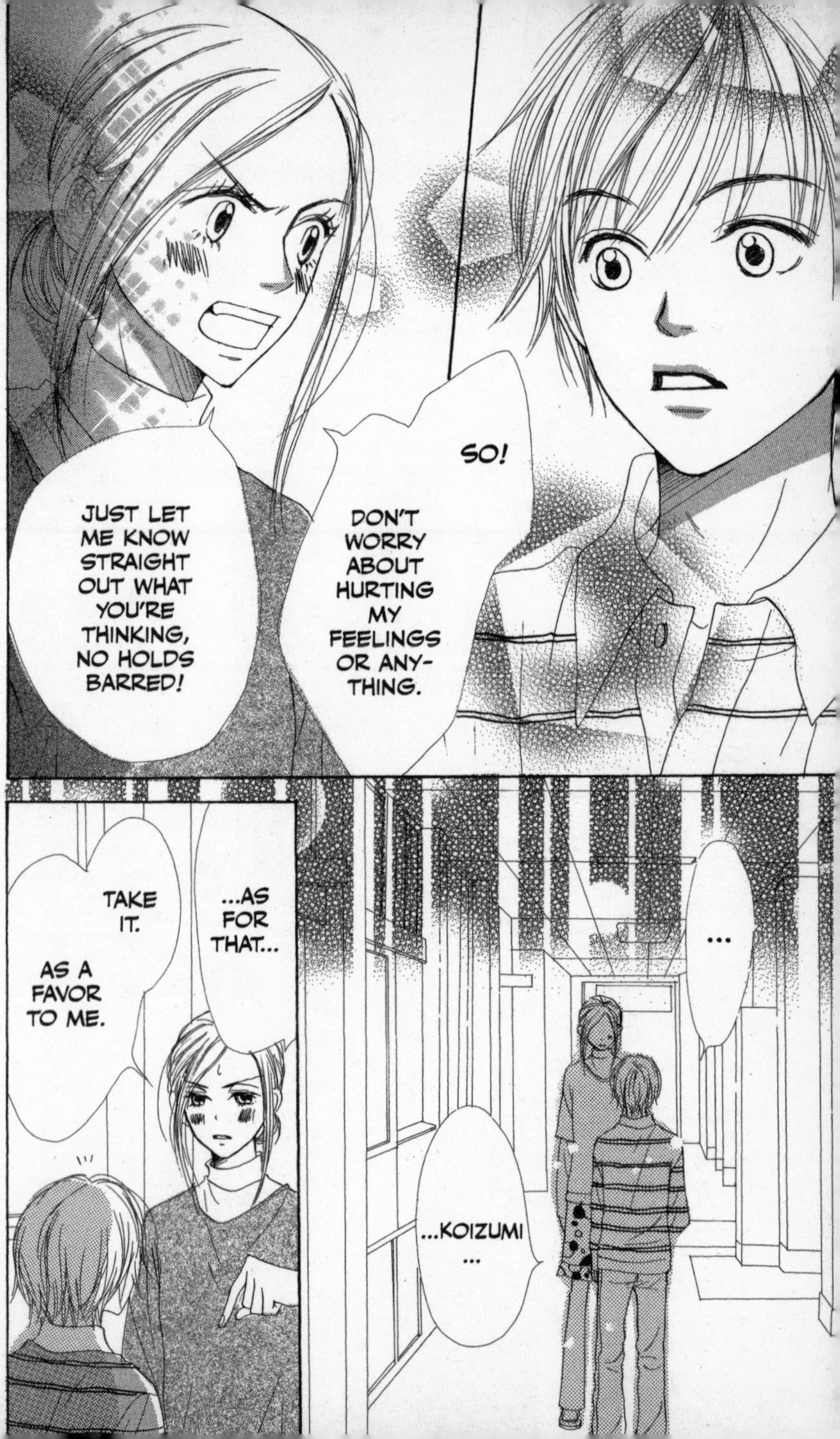
SO!
DON'T WORRY ABOUT HURTING MY FEELINGS OR ANY-THING.
JUST LET ME KNOW STRAIGHT OUT WHAT YOU'RE THINKING, NO HOLDS BARRED!
...
...KOIZUMI ...
...AS FOR THAT...
TAKE IT.
AS A FAVOR TO ME.

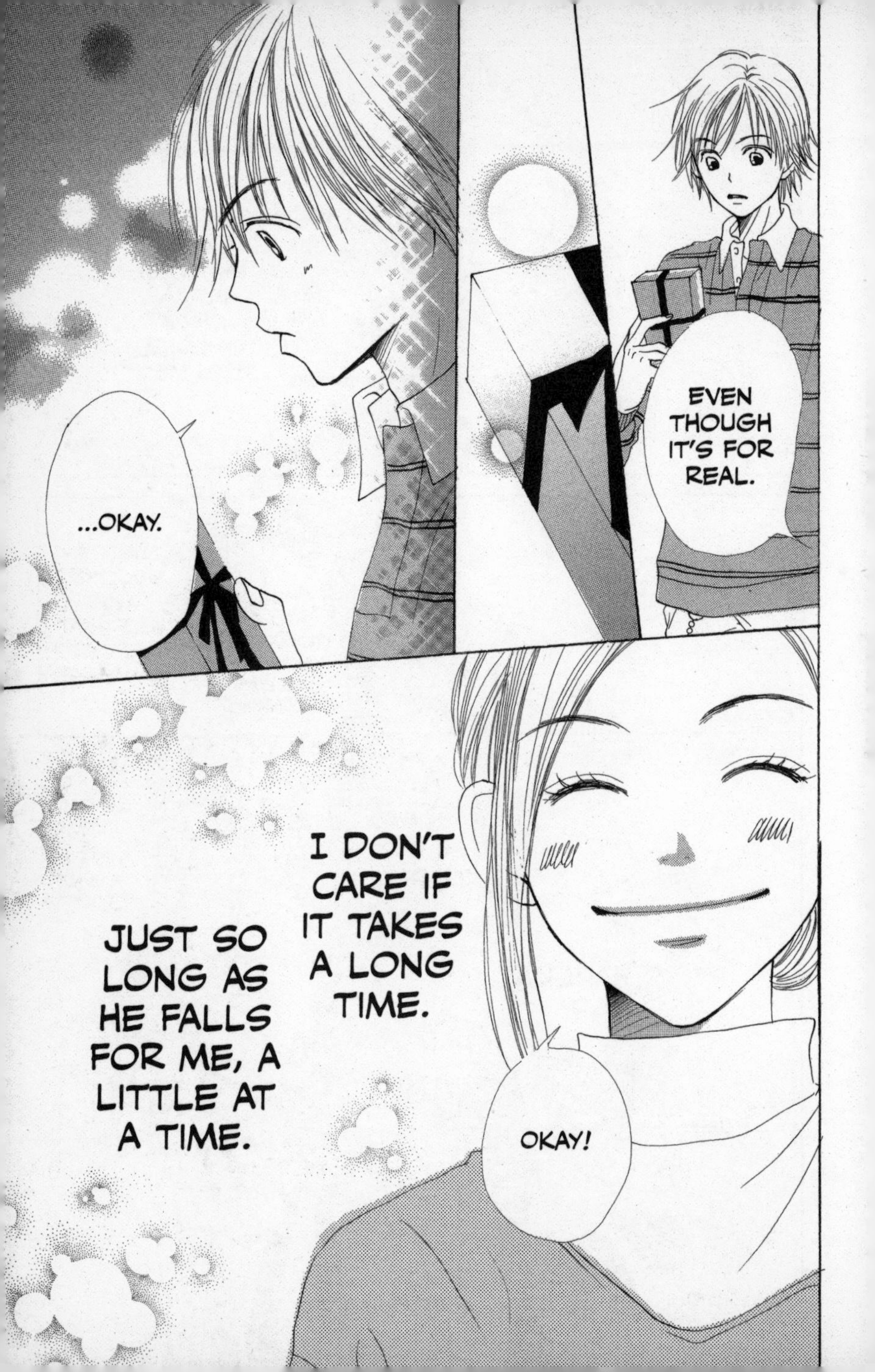
EVEN THOUGH IT'S FOR REAL.
...OKAY.
I DON'T CARE IF IT TAKES A LONG TIME.
JUST SO LONG AS HE FALLS FOR ME, A LITTLE AT A TIME.
OKAY!

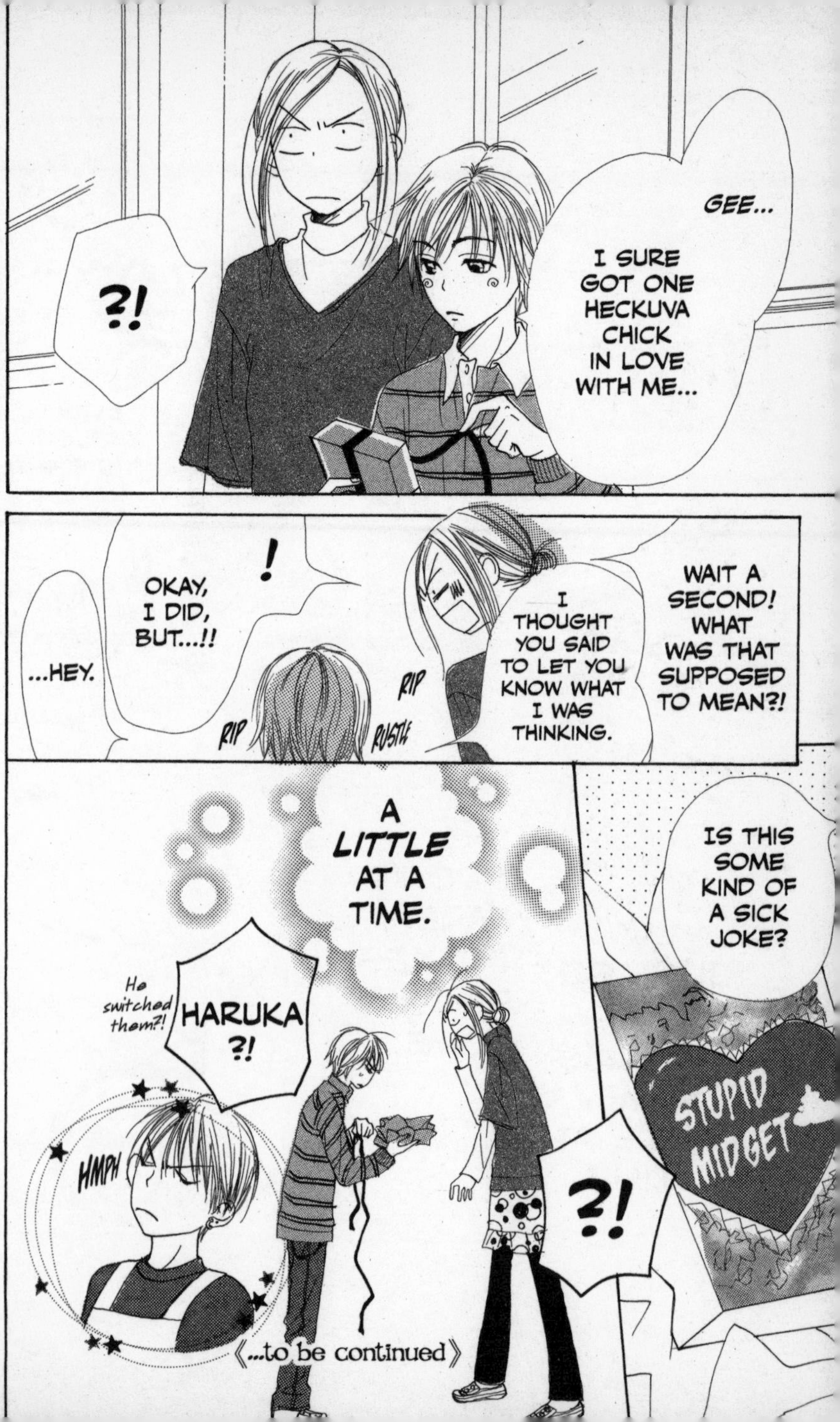
GEE...
I SURE GOT ONE HECKUVA CHICK IN LOVE WITH ME...
?!
WAIT A SECOND! WHAT WAS THAT SUPPOSED TO MEAN?!
I THOUGHT YOU SAID TO LET YOU KNOW WHAT I WAS THINKING.
RIP
RUSTLE
RIP
!
OKAY, I DID, BUT...!!
...HEY.
IS THIS SOME KIND OF A SICK JOKE?
STUPID MIDGET
?!
A *LITTLE* AT A TIME.
HARUKA ?!
He switched them?!
HMPH
《...to be continued》

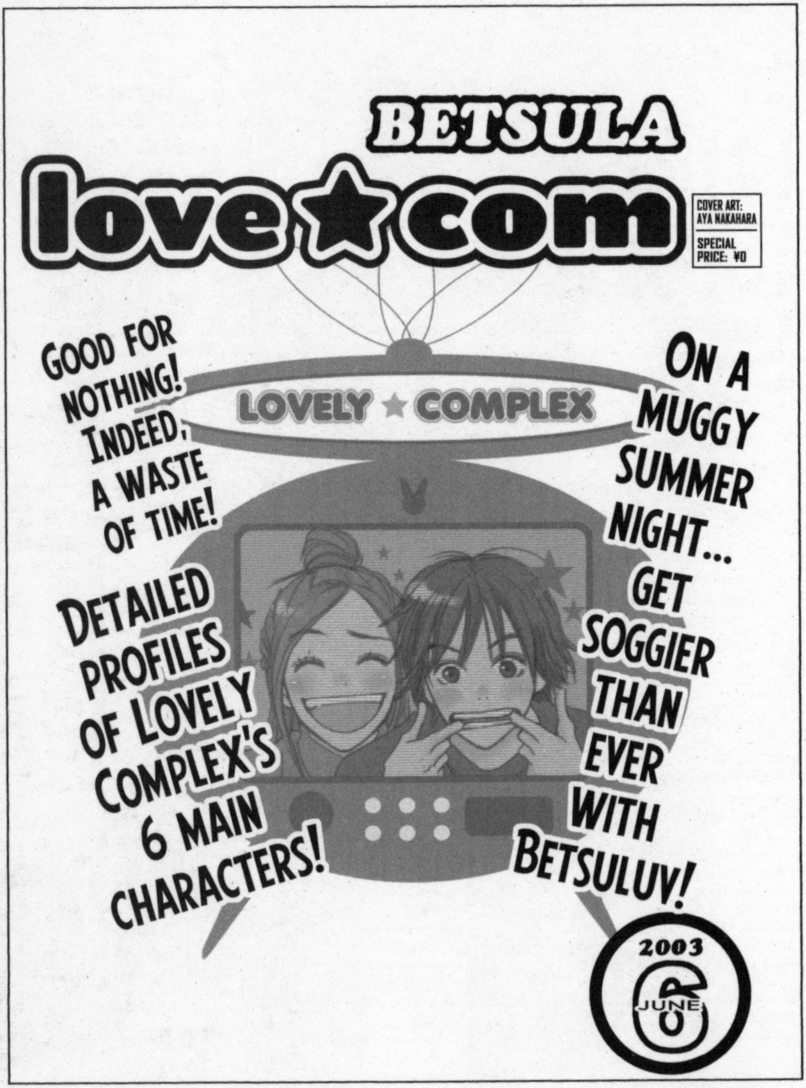
BETSULA
love★com
COVER ART: AYA NAKAHARA
SPECIAL PRICE: ¥0
LOVELY ★ COMPLEX
GOOD FOR NOTHING! INDEED, A WASTE OF TIME!
DETAILED PROFILES OF LOVELY COMPLEX'S 6 MAIN CHARACTERS!
ON A MUGGY SUMMER NIGHT... GET SOGGIER THAN EVER WITH BETSULUV!
2003
6
JUNE

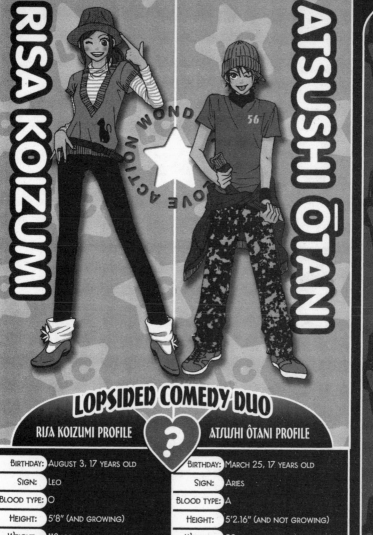

RISA KOIZUMI

ATSUSHI ŌTANI

LOPSIDED COMEDY DUO

RISA KOIZUMI PROFILE   ?   **ATSUSHI ŌTANI PROFILE**

	RISA KOIZUMI		ATSUSHI ŌTANI
BIRTHDAY:	AUGUST 3, 17 YEARS OLD	BIRTHDAY:	MARCH 25, 17 YEARS OLD
SIGN:	LEO	SIGN:	ARIES
BLOOD TYPE:	O	BLOOD TYPE:	A
HEIGHT:	5'8" (AND GROWING)	HEIGHT:	5'2.16" (AND NOT GROWING)
WEIGHT:	110 LBS	WEIGHT:	99 LBS
FAMILY:	MOM, DAD, YOUNGER BROTHER	FAMILY:	MOM, DAD, OLDER SISTER, DOG (HUGE)
HOBBIES:	GAMING, SLEEPING	HOBBIES:	BASKETBALL, WATCHING ACTION MOVIES
LIKES:	UMIBÔZU, FESTIVALS, NOSE PACKS	LIKES:	UMIBÔZU, DOGS, CHOCOLATE, K-1
DISLIKES:	NATTÔ (FERMENTED SOYBEANS), DENTISTS	DISLIKES:	OCCULT/PSYCHIC TV SHOWS, GHOST STORIES
DREAM:	TO NOT GROW ANY TALLER	DREAM:	TO GROW TALLER

★ **FASHION GUIDE** ★
FAVORITE COLORS ARE RED AND YELLOW.
WEARS COMFY CLOTHES AND CHEAP CLOTHES.

★ **FASHION GUIDE** ★
FAVORITE COLOR IS ORANGE.
LIKES USED CLOTHING.

LOVELY★COMPLEX CHARACTER DATA FILE

NOBUKO ISHIHARA

HEIKICHI NAKAO

HONEY BUNNIES

NOBUKO (NOBU) ISHIHARA PROFILE

BIRTHDAY:	MAY 28, 17 YEARS OLD
SIGN:	GEMINI
BLOOD TYPE:	B
HEIGHT:	5 FT.
WEIGHT:	92.5 LBS
FAMILY:	MOM, DAD, GRANDMOTHER
HOBBIES:	SHOPPING, FASHION
LIKES:	DARLING (NAKAO) ♥
DISLIKES:	HIGH PLACES, ALL BUGS
DREAM:	TO BE A BRIDE ♥

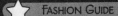

★ FASHION GUIDE ★

LOVES CUTE, EYE-CATCHING CLOTHES.
INSPIRATION: MASAMI HISAMOTO

HEIKICHI NAKAO PROFILE

BIRTHDAY:	JANUARY 15, 17 YEARS OLD
SIGN:	CAPRICORN
BLOOD TYPE:	B
HEIGHT:	5'11"
WEIGHT:	127.5 LBS
FAMILY:	MOM, DAD, YOUNGER BROTHER, YOUNGER SISTER, GRANDMOTHER, GRANDFATHER, DOG
HOBBIES:	BASKETBALL, COSPLAY
LIKES:	NOBU ♥
DISLIKES:	OYSTERS (GOT SICK ONCE)
DREAM:	TO BE A BRIDE (TEE HEE)

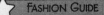

★ FASHION GUIDE ★

NO PARTICULAR POLICIES.
CLOTHES PICKED OUT BY NOBU.

LOVELY★COMPLEX CHARACTER DATA FILE

RYŌJI SUZUKI

CHIHARU TANAKA

THE AWKWARD COUPLE

CHIHARU TANAKA PROFILE

Birthday:	June 23, 17 years old
Sign:	Cancer
Blood type:	A
Height:	4'11"
Weight:	88 lbs
Family:	Mom, dad, two younger brothers
Hobbies:	Reading, sewing
Likes:	Tea, kombu pickle, children
Dislikes:	Revolving doors, jogging
Dream:	Preschool teacher

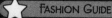

Fashion Guide

Likes simple clothes in pastel colors.

RYÔJI SUZUKI PROFILE

Birthday:	February 4, 17 years old
Sign:	Aquarius
Blood type:	AB
Height:	6 ft
Weight:	125 lbs
Family:	Mom, dad, older sister, two cats
Hobbies:	Spacing out, collecting figurines
Likes:	Spacing out
Dislikes:	Getting up early, cars (gets carsick)
Dream:	Civil servant

Fashion Guide

Favorite colors are black and blue. Likes sharp but casual clothing.

glossary

Page 10, panel 2: Daikon pickle

Daikons are white radishes, and the most common variety is the Japanese aokubi daikon, shaped like a fat carrot. *Daikon* literally means "big root" in Japanese. Daikons are traditionally picked in fall to preserve for the winter, most often by pickling. One popular daikon pickle is called *takuan*, the bright yellow variety you might find in sushi.

Page 25, panel 1: Hakodate

Hokkaido's third largest city, located on the island's southern tip, was one of the first cities opened to foreign trade after the Japanese era of isolation. It is known for the beautiful views from Mt. Hakodate, and the official city fish is the squid.

Page 25, panel 1: Sapporo

The capital of Hakkaido Prefecture and the fifth-largest city in Japan. The city was established on land traditionally occupied by the indigenous Ainu, and *sapporo* is derived from an Ainu word that some say means "large river running through a plain." It is home to the annual Sapporo Snow festival (*yuki matsuri)* and Sapporo Breweries, and the city hosted the 1974 Winter Olympics.

Page 69, panel 1: Senpai

A term of respect for someone with seniority in an organization, such as clubs, schools, and offices.

Page 150, panel 5: Bozo

This is a play on the Japanese word *mikkabōzu*, which means someone who never sticks to anything, and the English meaning "fool."

Our Doggie of the Day is the Nakahara family's Kozaru (male, mixed breed). He's getting quite advanced in years, but still going strong. Whenever we have female visitors to the house, he gives them a bored sniff and then ignores them, but male visitors get him very excited! He follows them everywhere. And his daily routine is to leer charmingly at passers-by. Today, as always, you can be sure he's there out front, his auburn fur waving in the breeze as he searches avidly for his favorite treat, a middle-aged man.

Aya Nakahara won the 2003 Shogakukan manga award for her breakthrough hit *Love★Com*, which was made into a major motion picture and a PS2 game in 2006. She debuted with *Haru to Kuuki Nichiyou-bi* in 1995, and her other works include *HANADA* and *Himitsu Kichi*.

LOVE★COM VOL 5
The Shojo Beat Manga Edition

STORY AND ART BY
AYA NAKAHARA

Translation & English Adaptation/Pookie Rolf
Touch-up Art & Lettering/Gia Cam Luc
Design/Yuki Ameda
Editor/Pancha Diaz

Editor in Chief, Books/Alvin Lu
Editor in Chief, Magazines/Marc Weidenbaum
VP of Publishing Licensing/Rika Inouye
VP of Sales/Gonzalo Ferreyra
Sr. VP of Marketing/Liza Coppola
Publisher/Hyoe Narita

LOVE★COM © 2001 by Aya Nakahara. All rights reserved.
First published in Japan in 2001 by SHUEISHA Inc., Tokyo. English
translation rights in the United States of America and Canada
arranged by SHUEISHA Inc. The stories, characters and incidents
mentioned in this publication are entirely fictional.

No portion of this book may be reproduced or transmitted in
any form or by any means without written permission from the
copyright holders.

Printed in Canada

Published by VIZ Media, LLC
P.O. Box 77010
San Francisco, CA 94107

Shojo Beat Manga Edition
10 9 8 7 6 5 4 3 2 1
First printing, March 2008

PARENTAL ADVISORY
LOVE★COM is rated T for Teen and is
recommended for ages 13 and up.
ratings.viz.com

store.viz.com

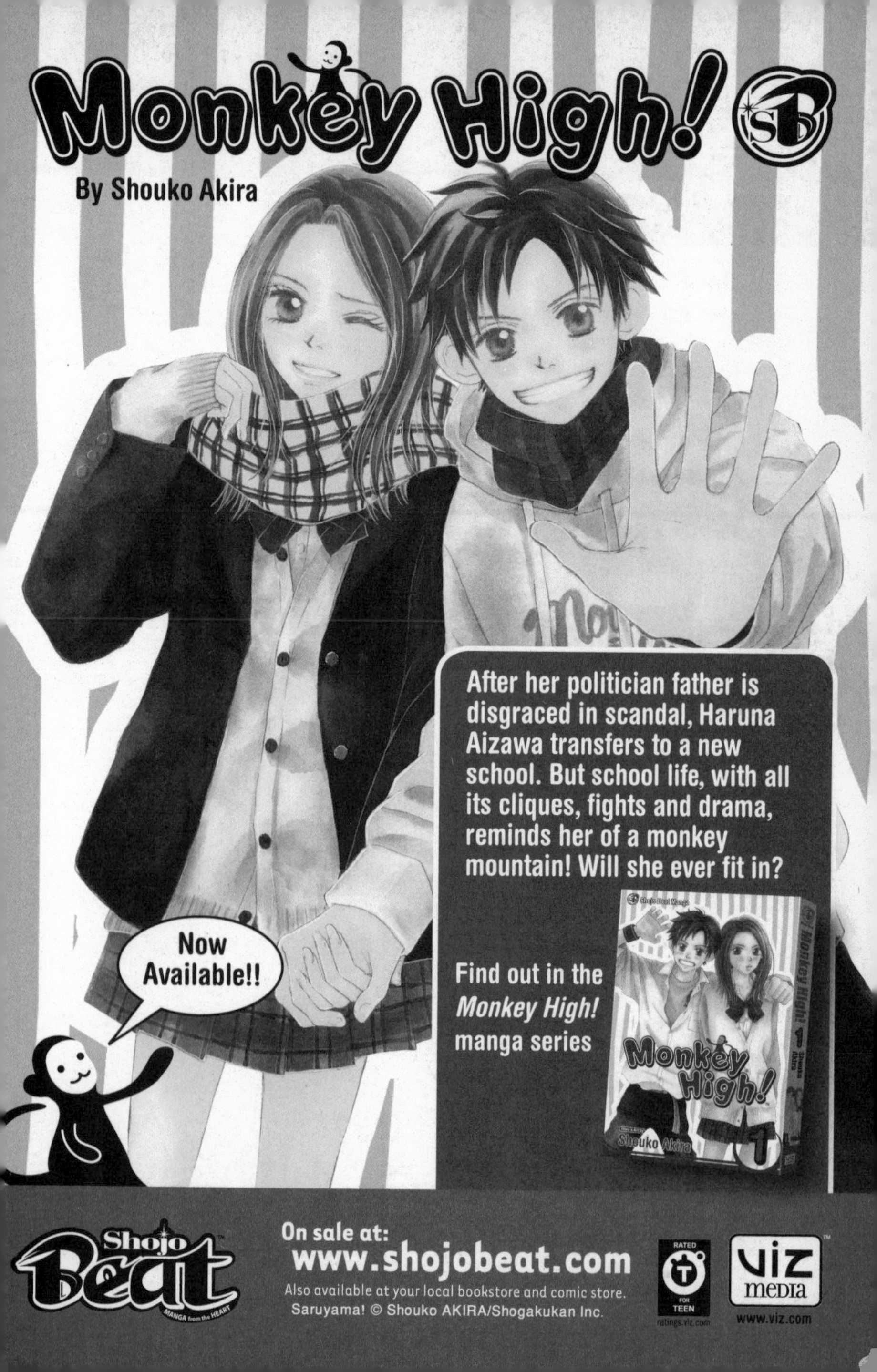
Monkey High!
By Shouko Akira
After her politician father is disgraced in scandal, Haruna Aizawa transfers to a new school. But school life, with all its cliques, fights and drama, reminds her of a monkey mountain! Will she ever fit in?
Now Available!!
Find out in the *Monkey High!* manga series
Shojo Beat Manga
Monkey High!
Shouko Akira
1
Shojo Beat
MANGA from the HEART
On sale at:
www.shojobeat.com
Also available at your local bookstore and comic store.
Saruyama! © Shouko AKIRA/Shogakukan Inc.
RATED
T
FOR TEEN
ratings.viz.com
VIZ media
www.viz.com

Beauty Pop

By Kiyoko Arai

Although a truly gifted hairstylist, Kiri Koshiba has no interest in using her talent to pursue fame and fortune, unlike the three popular boys in the "Scissors Project" at school. They give showy makeovers to handpicked girls, determined to become the best makeover team in Japan. As much as Kiri tries to shy away from the Scissors Project spotlight, she finds herself responding to beauty's call...

MANGA from the HEART

Only $8.99

On sale at:
www.shojobeat.com

Also available at your local bookstore and comic store.

Beauty Pop © 2004 Kiyoko ARAI/Shogakukan Inc.
Covers subject to change.

www.viz.com

High School DEBUT

By Kazune Kawahara

When Haruna Nagashima was in junior high, softball and comics were her life. Now that she's in high school, she's ready to find a boyfriend. But will hard work (and the right coach) be enough?

Find out in the *High School Debut* manga series—available now!

On sale at:
www.shojobeat.com
Also available at your local bookstore and comic store.

KOKO DEBUT © 2003 by Kazune Kawahara/SHUEISHA Inc.

Shojo Beat

S·A
Special A

by Maki Minami

Manga series on sale now

Only $8.99

Her whole life, Hikari Hanazono has been consumed with the desire to win against her school rival, Kei Takishima—at anything. He always comes out on top no matter what he does, and Hikari is determined to do whatever it takes to beat him!

Shojo Beat
MANGA from the HEART

On sale at:
www.shojobeat.com
Also available at your local bookstore and comic store.

S·A-Special A© Maki Minami 2003/HAKUSENSHA, Inc.

RATED T FOR TEEN
ratings.viz.com

VIZ MEDIA
www.viz.com

Tell us what you think about Shojo Beat Manga!

Our survey is now available online. Go to:

shojobeat.com/mangasurvey

Help us make our product offerings better!

THE REAL DRAMA BEGINS IN...

FULL MOON WO SAGASHITE © 2001 by Arina Tanemura/SHUEISHA Inc.
Fushigi Yûgi: Genbu Kaiden © 2004 Yuu WATASE/Shogakukan Inc.
Ouran Koko Host Club © Bisco Hatori 2002/HAKUSENSHA, Inc.